AMERICAN HOME AND FAMILY SERIES

WEBSTER DIVISION, McGRAW-HILL BOOK COMPANY

*New York St. Louis San Francisco Dallas Dusseldorf London
Sydney Toronto Mexico Panama*

THE HOME
its furnishings
and equipment

RUTH MORTON, Consultant, Home Furnishings

HILDA GEUTHER, Teacher of Housing and Interior Design, Homewood-Flossmoor High School Flossmoor, Illinois

VIRGINIA GUTHRIE, Asst. Professor Home Management, Dept. of Home Economics, University of Illinois

Drawings by Luanne Harff Burchinal and Mary Gibson

Acknowledgments for photographs appearing on the front and back cover:
Front Cover
Top: Olympic State Company
Left: Better Homes and Gardens
Right: Paul Morris Associates

Back Cover
Top: Mutschler Kitchens
Left: PPG Industries
Right: Mobile Homes Manufacturers Association

THE HOME — ITS FURNISHINGS AND EQUIPMENT

ISBN 07-043415-8

345678910 VHVH 987654321

ABOUT THE AUTHORS

Ruth Morton

Part II: Furniture and Furnishings was prepared by Ruth Morton who is a consultant and lecturer on home furnishings. Miss Morton is a graduate of the Layton School of Art and the University of Minnesota. She has had wide experience in the retail and wholesale furniture fields. She is a member of the American Institute of Decorators and has lectured to clubs, on radio and TV, and for the University of Wisconsin Extension Division. Miss Morton is author of the McGraw-Hill textbook *The Home and Its Furnishings*. In private life she is married to the painter Gerhard C. F. Miller.

Hilda Geuther

Part I: Housing was prepared by Hilda Geuther who is a teacher of Housing and Interior Design at Homewood-Flossmoor High School in Flossmoor, Illinois. Mrs. Geuther holds both the Bachelor's and Master's degrees from the University of Illinois. For many years she was a teacher, head of the home economics department, and supervisor of student teachers at Carl Sandburg High School, Orland Park, Illinois. Mrs. Geuther has been a visiting lecturer in the Home Economics Education Department at the University of Illinois where she taught a graduate workshop on "Teaching Housing and Interior Design."

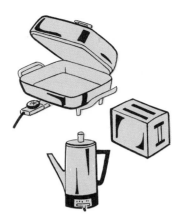

Virginia Guthrie

Part III: Household Equipment was prepared by Virginia Guthrie who is Assistant Professor of Home Management at the University of Illinois. Miss Guthrie began her college teaching career as a Graduate Assistant at the University of Illinois. She became an Instructor in Home Management at Michigan State University, then returned to the University of Illinois to teach home management courses. She conducted a Consumer Education Workshop at North Dakota State University and taught a summer school course on equipment at the University of Alberta, Edmonton, Canada. Miss Guthrie served a three-year term on the Consumer Interest Committee of the American Home Economics Association.

Preface

Current trends show the number of new households established continues to rise each year. Some of these consist of student apartments; some of young adults on the job; some of newly established families.

In view of the fact that each will soon be establishing some kind of separate living facilities, high school students will find it worthwhile to have knowledge and information about selecting, furnishing, financing, and maintaining a place to live.

THE HOME—ITS FURNISHINGS AND EQUIPMENT is presented to introduce the high school student to the concept that where he lives tends to influence how he lives; the quality of living facilities tends to influence his way of life.

PURPOSE

Part I: Housing is written to stimulate young adults to study the relationship of the social, psychological, and economic aspects of providing shelter for themselves and others; to encourage them to be open-minded about new designs, new materials, and new methods of construction in housing, home furnishings, and equipment; to make them aware of the moral and legal responsibilities inherent in establishing a home of one's own; to enable them to become informed, intelligent consumers in shelter-related areas; and to help them recognize the problems unique to the mobile under-25-years-of-age group.

Part II: Furniture and Furnishings is written from the basic premise that a functionally and attractively furnished home can play an important role in creating a sense of stability and solidarity for the entire family as well as stimulate intellectual and cultural growth. The subjects of historic and contemporary styles of furnishings deal with products on the market today and the way each can help to produce a functional background for today's living. The information on selection recognizes the mobility of society, which requires planning for changes in types of dwellings, communities, and climates as well as for the usual demands of a family. The material on the arrangement of furnishings is based on family-life patterns as they adjust to customary house plans. And finally the material of the entire section is planned not only for use in furnishing a home later on, but for the one in which students live now.

Part III: Household Equipment is written to help young people become better informed consumers of household equipment. This includes not only selection but use and care of equipment. The scope of this section is not limited to the needs of the immediate future of high school students but recognizes their longer range goals as well. Experience in correct use of equipment puts one in a better position to evaluate and select equipment when the need arises. Consumers' know-how in use has not kept pace with industry's know-how in production of equipment. When one has to make a selection among places to live, knowing how to identify quality in equipment could be an influencing factor in deciding which place to rent or buy.

CONTENT

THE HOME — ITS FURNISHINGS AND EQUIPMENT consists of twenty-two chapters divided into three parts:

The first part consists of eight chapters on housing: Housing Today and Tomorrow, Families on the Move, Choosing a Place to Live, Financial Aspects of Family Shelter, Evaluating the Ready-Built House, Use of Space for Storage, Maintenance and Remodeling, and Planning for Outdoor Areas.

The second part consists of nine chapters relating to furniture and furnishings: Importance of Home Furnishings, The Study and Use of Color, Backgrounds in the Home, Knowing Furniture, Selecting Furniture, Arranging Furniture, Fabrics, Accessories, and Tableware and Household Linens.

The third part of five chapters deals with household equipment: Equipment for the

Home, Small Electrical Appliances for the Kitchen, Major Kitchen Appliances, General Equipment, and Laundry Equipment.

PLAN OF USE

THE HOME – ITS FURNISHINGS AND EQUIPMENT is written to encourage students to look at their standard of living as an expression of the economic, technological, and cultural development of a nation, community, or neighborhood as well as the means for fulfilling the human physical and psychological needs of individuals and families.

The scope of the text, the organization of the three major parts, and the manner of presentation make the book adaptable for use by young people at the senior level in high school. The students need not have had previous home economics courses. The eight chapters of Part I combined with the five chapters of Part III could make a one-semester sequence. The nine chapters in Part II are adequate for a semester course. Teachers who include housing and interior design units in other courses, such as Home Economics 3 or 4 or Family Living courses, may select appropriate single chapters or combinations of chapters.

SUPPLEMENTARY MATERIAL

The Learning Experiences at the end of the chapters are intended to extend the scope and depth of the material presented in the chapters in several ways: (1) by involving students in life situations so that they can apply the knowledge presented in the book and thereby more likely understand and use the knowledge acquired; (2) by encouraging individual responsibility on the part of students to supplement the book material with relevant information secured from current literature or local specialists; and (3) to provide flexibility in study and use by students of different interests and abilities.

The illustrations, both photographs and drawings, have been chosen for their instructional qualities. Some will help students visualize a concept, some identify a particular product, and some will help students to understand a principle of operation, as in equipment.

A teachers manual is available for use with the text.

Ruth Morton
Hilda Geuther
Virginia Guthrie

Acknowledgments

The authors wish to express their thanks to the many people who helped in valuable and varied ways with the preparation of the manuscript or the obtaining of the illustrations for THE HOME – ITS FURNISHINGS AND EQUIPMENT.

To the following people for their help with Part I on Housing:

Dr. Louise Lemmon
Associate Professor
Home Economics Education
University of Maryland
College Park, Maryland

Miss Julia Herron
Director of Educational Services
Mobile Home Manufacturers Association
Chicago, Illinois

Mr. Roy Craik Kollenborn
Former Executive, Longbell Lumber Co.
Consulting editor to real estate and
    construction industry
New York, New York

Mrs. Iva Pidcock, Chairman
Home Economics Department
LaGrange Township High School
LaGrange, Illinois

Miss Catherine Carter
Supervisor, Home Economics Occupations
Division of Vocational-Technical Education
State Department of Education
Springfield, Illinois

Mrs. Maxine Schroth
Home Economics teacher
San Diego City Schools
San Diego, California

Donald E. Helper and Paul I. Wallach
for permission to use several drawings

from *Architecture Drafting and Design*
(McGraw-Hill Book Company, 1965).

Dr. Marjorie Savage
Professor of Home Economics
Western Michigan University
Kalamazoo, Michigan

Mrs. Isabel Reynolds
State Supervisor of Home Economics
Department of Public Instruction
Division of Vocational Education
Indianapolis, Indiana

Mrs. Ruth Evers who did such a conscientious job of typing the chapters

To the following people for their help with Part II on Furniture and Furnishings:

Miss K. Virginia Seidel
Extension Specialist in Home Furnishings
College of Agriculture
University of Illinois
Urbana, Illinois

The staff of the Sturgeon Bay (Wisconsin)

library who aided in locating reference material

Alice Sautebin who gave such careful attention to the typing of the chapters

To the following people for their help with Part III on Household Equipment:

Dr. Mary E. Mather
Associate Professor
Vocational-Technical Education
College of Education
University of Illinois

Mrs. Jacqueline Anderson, Instructor in

Home Equipment, University of Illinois, who served as consultant and assisted substantially in the preparation of the chapters

Mrs. Juanita Benson who performed typing service so competently

The authors also wish to express thanks to Mr. Kenneth McDougall of Better Homes and Gardens Magazine who helped greatly in supplying photographs and transparencies from their files.

Ruth Morton
Hilda Geuther
Virginia Guthrie

Contents

Pictorial Themes   **Part III**

CHARTS

PART I

By Hilda Geuther

Housing

1

Housing Today

and Tomorrow

THE MANY unique ways in which people the world over provide family shelter can be observed on television and in films, books, and magazines.

In the Arabian Desert, Bedouins build tents for protection from the sun and blowing sand. In mild weather Eskimos build skin tents or crude frame structures. In winter they build igloos. In Central Africa people build grass huts over frames of sticks and poles. In Southern Europe, Asia, Africa, and South America thousands of people live in caves. In the Philippines people build tree houses. In New Guinea natives build thatched houses on pilings.

In the United States many people dream of a penthouse high in the sky, while others live in houseboats. In China many people live and operate businesses in riverboat cities; in Holland thousands live on canalboats. For people on the move, there are gypsy caravans in Eastern Europe and mobile homes in the United States.

More permanent houses everywhere are built of mud, wood, stone, masonry, metal, glass, and plastic. The mountain chalets of Switzerland, the log houses of Norway, and many houses in this country are made of wood. In Ireland people build houses of sod. In many places of the world, such as Bolivia and the United States houses are built of easily found fieldstone.

Housing everywhere reflects the mastery of man over his environment. New construction in the more technically advanced nations is frequently made of materials developed by science and it makes use of technological methods developed by industry to provide better housing for more and more people.

WHAT IS HOUSING?

"Mansion," "castle," "building," "cabin," and "home" are some of the words used to describe a house. A house might also be described as a product of the building industry that is used for shelter. It provides living space for a family and serves as a home base for a wide variety of individual interests and group activities.

The term "housing" has a broader meaning than the word "house." It generally refers to the social and economic forces that affect people in their search for satisfactory places to live.

2

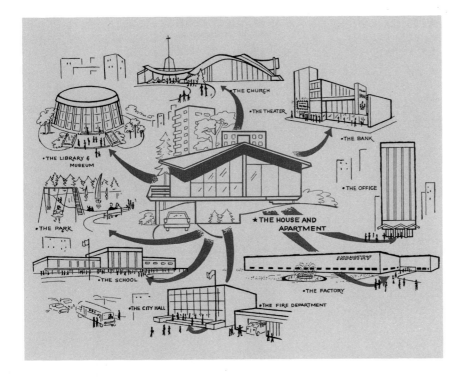

People, housing, jobs, schools, and recreation go together. Each factor depends on all the others.

Housing includes the problem of finding adequate space in a satisfactory location and within the budget of those with low incomes and those with high, those with large families and those with small, those who rent and those who buy, those who live in warm climates and those who live in cold climates.

To understand the problems of providing decent shelter for all, it is necessary to study the relationship between the people and the house, the house and the neighborhood, the neighborhood and the community, and the people of the individual family and the complex social, political, and financial interests that affect their way of life.

Economic and Social Implications

Population patterns in the United States indicate a steady increase in the number of new families established. This means a greater need for houses and apartments. Because the income of these new families determines the amount that can be spent for housing, the number and quality of new houses will depend on the wages and salaries paid by the industries and professions in given geographical areas.

The broad concept of housing today recognizes the role of the community in providing opportunities that supplement or reinforce those offered in the home. A family cannot live in an apartment or house and remain isolated from the influences of the schools, churches, and cultural groups in the area. Communities differ in such factors as the number and kinds of public services provided, the quality and range of educational opportunities, the presence of recreational facilities, and the extent of public transportation available and the number and kind of highways available.

HOUSING TODAY

The building industry, along with social action groups and government agencies working in the housing field, find themselves faced with an expanding population that is better educated, has a larger income, and is more mobile than any preceding generation. This population demands quality houses and apartments, expanded suburban developments, and the replacement of vast slum areas with modern housing units.

3

(A) Arab tents are made from thick cloth of camel's or goat's hair. A curtain wall divides the tent into two rooms: one for the men and one for the women. (B) Many people in China and India live on houseboats. (C) Grass houses are built in hot lands. The grass roof extends over the walls. (D) Improved caves are used as homes in many parts of the world today. (E) Gypsies have maintained a migratory way of life in Europe and the United States up to the present time. The colorful wagons are gradually being replaced with more modern equipment. (F) In New Guinea homes are built on pilings over the water.

(G) In rural areas many Filipinos live in thatched huts built in trees or on platforms supported by bamboo poles. (H) Many houses in Norway have birchbark roofs covered with earth in which grass and flowers grow. The sod protects against fire and acts as insulation. (I) In the summer, Eskimos live in tents called topeks. (J) In rural Switzerland the barn and house are a combination unit. (K) Rural people built houses from blocks of earth cut from the sod-covered prairies. On our western plains some sod houses are still in use. (L) Walls of native stone laid without mortar are common in Bolivia. There are no chimneys.

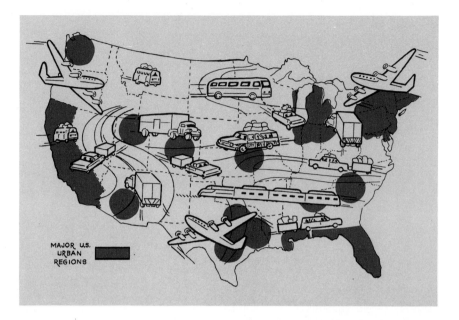

The United States has changed from a rural nation to one of urban character. This map shows the probable location of large metropolitan areas and supercities of the future.

MAJOR U.S. URBAN REGIONS

Population Patterns and Trends

The problems involved in housing a growing population become more overwhelming from day to day. It is estimated that there were about one billion people in the world in 1830. During the next one hundred years (by 1930) the population doubled. However, only thirty years later, in 1960, the world population increased to three billion. This means that about 200 million people were born into the world *every four years*. (The 1960 population of the United States was about 200 million.) During a thirty-minute period, there is a net gain in world population—births over deaths—of 2,700.

Because of the large number of post-World War II marriages and the high birthrate of the 1940s and 1950s, our population probably will continue to increase substantially during the next several decades. This implies a steady increase in the number of households. By "household" we mean all the persons who occupy a house or an apartment. In the postwar decades there has been an even more rapid increase in the number of individuals living alone—this group increased by 44 percent.

Mobility of the Population

The census of the United States in 1790 showed only 5 percent of the population living in urban areas. "Urban areas" are defined by the U.S.

Census Bureau as "those incorporated or unincorporated places of 2,500 or more inhabitants and the densely settled fringe areas around cities having a density of 1,500 persons per square mile."

By the time of the 1960 census, approximately 70 percent of the population lived in urban areas. It is estimated that by 1975, 60 percent of our population will be living in fourteen large urban units called "megalopolises." A megalopolis results from the merging of major population centers, as on the Eastern Seaboard.

Historically the people in the suburbs earned their living in the city, and the labor force moved in a steady one-way direction to and from its place of employment. Today many business groups and industrial concerns have moved to the suburbs. The labor force moves in a series of crosscurrents between suburb and suburb or between suburb and city.

In addition to the movement of people from one residence to another within a community or county, there is long-distance migration. A study of recent census statistics shows movements of population from one region of the United States to another; the pattern of movement is to the West from the North and South, to the North from the South, and from rural to urban areas. As each move means giving up

Cooperation between local, state, and federal government agencies, or between government and private builders, is replacing obsolete housing with modern, safe units to house the large number of low-income families now moving to urban areas.

Many upper-income houses are built in Contemporary style.

one place (of living) and finding another, this pattern of movement is an important factor in the study of ways and means to meet housing needs.

Housing in an Affluent Society

Through the cooperation of large-scale builders, the materials-and-supply industry, the financial institutions, and the government, it has become possible to give the public many advantages. They include better planning; quality materials; equipment for heating, lighting, cooling, and plumbing; and a variety of built-in conveniences never before available to so many with such favorable financing arrangements.

Before World War II many people saved for years to make a substantial down payment on a house and paid the rest of the cost as soon as possible. Such buyers expected to live in the house for a lifetime. Today's buyer is offered a wide range of choices with small or large down payments and monthly payments varied to fit his budget. The small down payment, minimum monthly payment plan has been described as paying for a "housing service," as distinguished from "home ownership" in the traditional sense.

Low-income housing. One-third of the population of the United States have incomes so low

that they cannot be expected to provide adequate housing for themselves. The Emergency Relief and Construction Act of 1932 gave a start to public housing programs in the United States. In 1933 Congress passed the National Industrial Recovery Act, which authorized the use of federal funds to finance low-cost housing, slum clearance, and subsistence homesteads. The United States Housing Act of 1937 was followed by the establishment of the Federal Public Housing Authority in 1942, the Public Housing Administration in 1947, and the Department of Housing and Urban Development in 1965.

This government interest has provided funds to public agencies set up under state legislation to build and operate low-rent housing. Local housing authorities establish their own policies for admission of tenants. At the end of 1961, the income limit imposed by the average public housing authority was $3,200 for a family consisting of father, mother, and two children. Some local authorities have added other limitations for admission, such as a minimum period of residence in the locality or a limitation on assets.

There has long been controversy over whether to provide subsidized housing for low-income families. After considering arguments against the construction of public housing to meet these needs, we face the fact that there is no alternative plan available. While the physical design and management of low-rent housing projects in large urban centers are frequently criticized, every city must handle the problem of finding shelter for thousands of low-income workers who are displaced when their housing is demolished for slum clearance, when land is taken for highway right-of-way, or when housing is destroyed by some disaster.

Middle-income housing. Approximately 40 percent of our population have incomes of $6,000 to $10,000 annually. Families in this group are moving to the suburbs in unprecedented numbers. Here they tend to find mass-produced houses that are designed, built, and financed by large-scale builders. Such houses often lack individuality. Such communities may not have been planned to provide adequate space and financial support for educational and social needs.

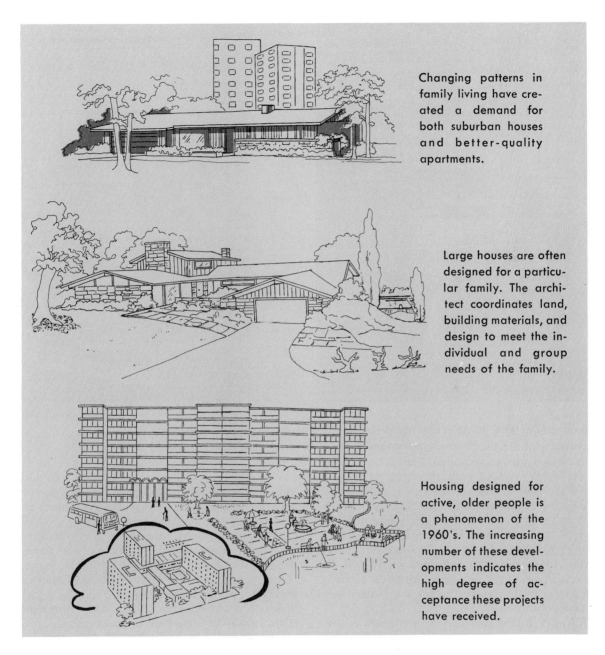

Changing patterns in family living have created a demand for both suburban houses and better-quality apartments.

Large houses are often designed for a particular family. The architect coordinates land, building materials, and design to meet the individual and group needs of the family.

Housing designed for active, older people is a phenomenon of the 1960's. The increasing number of these developments indicates the high degree of acceptance these projects have received.

Some forward-looking developers work from a master plan that includes schools, recreation areas, shopping facilities, and professional services in new communities. To produce better-quality, well-designed houses, some large-scale builders and producers of manufactured houses use the services of architects. By using several compatible designs and building a large number of identical units of each design, they spread the cost of architects' services and get better design results. Some developers, however, are interested solely in selling houses, not in producing quality construction that will ensure long-term usage.

Both houses and schools are being designed to make near-normal activity possible for the physically handicapped who want to be independent. Ranch houses are easily remodeled, if a specially designed house is not possible.

Favorable financing makes it possible for a family in the $6,000 to $10,000 income bracket to select from a fairly large range of house styles and locations. If the builder uses Federal Housing Administration—insured loans, the down payments may be small and the period of the loan may range up to thirty years. Conventional financing requires a larger down payment.

Upper-income housing. As a family's income rises beyond $10,000, it becomes possible to finance a more expensive house. Toward the upper end of the income scale are people with the financial capability and personal values to take advantage of the services of an architect who is trained to act as consultant and technical adviser. The architect can interpret the family's needs and wishes and incorporate them into the space design for their house. As he does this on a fee basis, usually related to the cost of the work, it is easy to see why such houses fall in the upper-price bracket

At the top of the socioeconomic scale there is a small group—about 1 percent of the population—who rarely consider building a house. These people tend to live in houses which were built by previous generations. The fact that a house is old enough to have some historical significance is important to these people.

Housing for the elderly. The number of persons sixty-five or older is increasing at the rate of about 1,000 a day. One out of every eleven persons in the United States is now over sixty-five. By 1970 there will be nearly twenty million people numbered among our nation's "elderly." The housing needs of this large and increasing number of older people are different from those of any other age group.

The city of the future may be underground, on the surface of the land, and in the air.

The architect R. Buckminster Fuller says it is technically possible today to enclose large areas of a city under a geodesic dome in which the climate could be controlled. When he compares the cost with that of snow removal, there seems to be an economic advantage.

Since most of them are retired, they depend for their income on social security payments, on pension plans, or on both. Their income is generally lower than the wages or salaries they earned when working. Many of these people continue to live in the houses they bought when their families were living at home but which now require more care and maintenance than retired people can afford or are physically able to provide.

Various ways to meet the social and emotional needs of older people have been studied. Space and facilities for meaningful activities are included in privately developed retirement villages and subsidized housing areas built by public housing authorities, churches, fraternal groups, labor unions, or other nonprofit institutions.

Housing the physically handicapped. In houses adapted to their special needs, many heart patients, blind persons, amputees, and paralytics can take on the duties of homemaking. Some houses are built with wide doors for wheelchairs and ramps instead of stairways. Other helpful aids are recessed-base cabinets, pullout work tables, grab bars, and electronically operated doors. In almost all communities there is a need for housing that is specially designed for the comfort and convenience of physically handicapped men and women.

A model of an under-water hotel shown by General Motors, Inc. at the New York World's Fair of 1964-1965 may hint at the use of the sea for meeting housing needs in the next century.

HOUSING TOMORROW

What will houses be like at the beginning of the 21st century? Speculation about innovations in house design includes cars equipped for family living, airborne saucer-shaped living units, houses spun from translucent fiber glass, and add-a-room modules or units. Car homes might be mounted on endless conveyers that would take the family to school, work, shopping, and recreation areas. The family would leave and return to the car home as it passed a particular service area on its cycle. The saucer-shaped houses, complete with furnishings and equipment, and moved by wing, might be set down on pads for single-family units or stacked to form apartment buildings. Spun-glass fiber houses might be produced in a variety of shapes and colors.

With the add-a-room-module plan you might start with one or two large units (perhaps a living room and bedroom) plus a smaller module that included a kitchen with space for eating, a bath, and a utility room. You would add rooms as needed when the family size or income became larger. When your children married or left home, you might give a child his room as a present to furnish him the bedroom space needed for his own home until his children come along.

Developing Trends in Housing

While some of these ideas are highly imaginative and extreme, there are exciting trends developing. With increasing urbanization, more and more middle-income people will be settling in the suburbs. Prefabricated parts will be used more widely in both houses and apartments. Some of these will be from newly developed products, while others will be from familiar materials used either in new forms or in parts of the house usually reserved for more traditional materials. There will be more mobile homes and manufactured houses in communities planned to satisfy the physical, social, and economic needs of a wide range of age and income groups.

Urbanization has caused planning officials to look for better ways to use land within easy reach of metropolitan centers. There is a growing belief that communities planned to include various types of living have advantages over developments geared to one socioeconomic group. It is also generally believed that high-rise apartments, garden apartments, duplex units, and single-family houses may be successfully combined in a community if they are designed to suit the character of the town and to differ enough to give variety to the total plan. Special attention needs to be given to

HOMES OF THE FUTURE

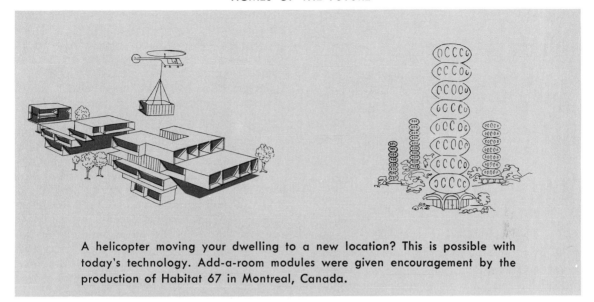

A helicopter moving your dwelling to a new location? This is possible with today's technology. Add-a-room modules were given encouragement by the production of Habitat 67 in Montreal, Canada.

COMMUNITY PLANNING

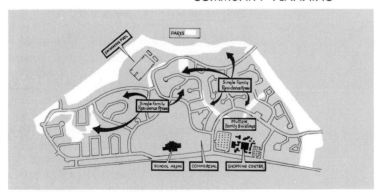

A master plan for a self-contained community with provision for nearly all family needs.

Many middle-income families choose to live where housing projects provide parking space, playgrounds, pools, and other services.

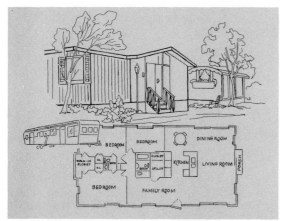

The manufactured house is produced in sections at a factory, moved to a site, and placed on a permanent foundation. Floor space can be compared with that in a small conventionally-built home.

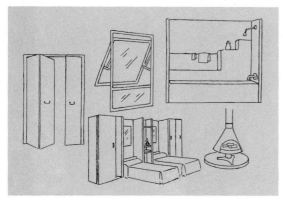

Prefabricated components may be used to speed up construction and to reduce costs. Units are being used in both new construction and remodeling.

transportation, schools, and ways to provide open space for recreation.

While many middle-income families are moving to the suburbs, urban renewal projects and public-housing-authority projects are reshaping slum areas in almost all cities. Phillip Hauser, of the University of Chicago, has predicted that there will be no slums left in 1984, "because there will be no profit in them under laws to be passed."

Middle-income housing in the city will be planned around centers that will include shopping facilities, churches, schools, medical and professional offices, and recreational areas. Open space will be provided for malls, golf courses, parks, and playgrounds. These open spaces are referred to as "greenbelts."

In many large cities a new pattern of urban living is developing in the skyscraper apartments located in the inner city area. Psychologists and sociologists point out that these high-rise apartments lack person-to-person contacts, children, a feeling of community, friendships, and civic sentiments; yet many middle-to-upper-income families are becoming tenants as fast as the apartments become available. In spite of the criticisms, more buildings of this type are on the drawing boards or in process of construction. These apartment complexes may be thought of as planned communities, since they provide many of the social, economic, and physical needs of the people who live in them, and they eliminate the time and traffic problems of commuting.

Industrial Methods Applied to Housing

The application of industrial methods in the production of houses is readily seen in manufactured houses (mobile homes) which are now being designed for residency rather than for movement on the highway. Less evident is the use of prefabricated components in houses assembled or constructed on a permanent foundation.

Manufactured houses. Manufactured homes have accounted for an increasing share of single-family houses produced in the past decade. It has been said that if all the mobile homes were assembled in one place, they would create the third largest city in the United States. The trend in mobile home design is toward units with walls that open up, pads which can be added so that beds can be in alcoves thus providing more space in the room, and modern styling that includes solar screens and vaulted ceilings.

Prefabricated components. The use of components produced in factories, with assembly-line methods, is making it possible for the builder to reduce labor costs in the construction of a house or an apartment. Fireplace

New construction techniques allow manufactured apartments to be lowered into position at the apartment site.

Courtesy "House and Home"

units, window and door assemblies, storage units, stairways, plumbing walls, and standard walls are produced in factories and delivered to the site where the house is being built. Complete bathrooms and kitchens are being produced as package units that can be delivered to the home site, to be placed in position on the subfloor. The walls are raised around them. These units require only connections to the gas and water supply lines, the sewage outlet, and the electrical system to complete the installation.

The extent to which a builder uses prefabricated components depends to some extent on the sale price of the house he is building. Builders who produce houses in the low to moderate price range are more likely to take advantage of the savings made possible by mass production of components.

The Use of New Materials and Designs in Houses

Architects, designers, producers of building products, government agencies, and research groups are working to develop new materials or new uses for standard materials that can improve the quality of buildings, both industrial and residential. Some industrial applications now in use will be adapted to residential construction. Aluminum, glass, plastics, concrete, asbestos cement, steel, and wood are among the basic construction materials that are being used in new and creative ways in houses and apartments. The problem of public acceptance of the new and different is the greatest single barrier to improvement of housing for the masses.

Aluminum. Aluminum has characteristics that make it suitable for use in residential construction. It permits more rapid construction because it can be produced for precision fitting of one part with another. Both its natural and applied finishes provide easy and economical maintenance. At least three major producers of aluminum products are planning mass production of an all-aluminum house.

Some developments that can be expected in the aluminum house of the future are walls that conduct heat, air conditioning, and illumination; shapes other than the cube; roofs that

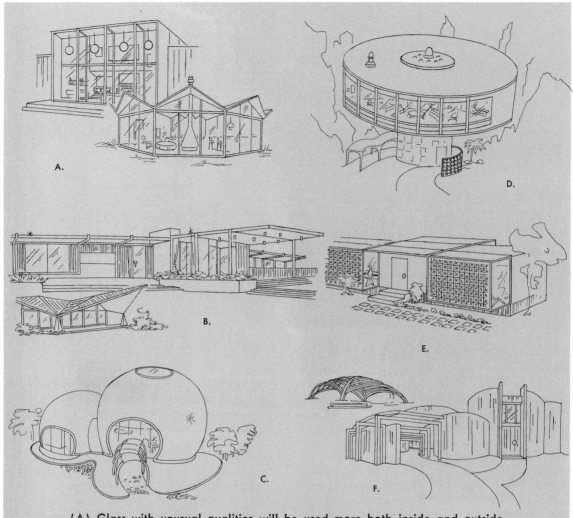

(A) Glass with unusual qualities will be used more both inside and outside houses. One of the possibilities is glass walls that become opaque at sundown. (B) Steel can be expected to appear more frequently in residential buildings. The design possibilities are unlimited if the public will accept the material in place of more conventional wood and masonry. (C) Plastics in many forms are being accepted in new construction. (D) The art of preforming concrete components for a building allows for great creativity in design. Surface textures can be designed into the structural walls. (E) A trend in the use of aluminum for varied home construction can be seen in the better mobile homes and manufactured houses now in production. (F) Laminated pressed woods in new shapes will be used in the design of wood houses. Wood pulp combined with other materials may be used to produce building materials for free-form designs.

can be push-button-controlled to advance outdoor living; houses that revolve to "follow the sun"; and domes to protect large areas from bad weather.

Glass. Glass has many possible uses in houses. Some designers believe we will have glass that will serve uses other than for visual effects. By blending the right combination of nearly fifty chemical elements and with special processing techniques, glass technicians can now create glass that will produce heat, resist fire, control light, reduce glare, enhance textiles, strengthen plastics, and perform many other functions.

The house of the future may have glass floors, walls, ceilings, and doors that change color, become transparent or opaque, or become hot or cold to condition the air in the room. Ceilings may be made of cellular glass that breathes and also acts as a light source. Buildings with glass walls may be surrounded by a sun-break wall of topaz-tinted glass to filter heat and light. In time we may even have completely glass-domed cities.

Plastics. Plastics may be molded, formed, extruded, or fabricated into complex and intricate shapes by relatively simple manufacturing processes. The advantages of the material and the relatively low cost of production make it a natural product for use in the construction of houses. We can anticipate acceptance of complete kitchens and bathrooms of plastic and fiber glass materials when used in combination with conventional building design. Acceptance of all-plastic houses is dependent on public acceptance of a new concept in house design. Some researchers in the plastics industry believe tomorrow's house may even be "shot in place." A balloon structure could be inflated on the site and sprayed with foamed plastic, after which the balloon would be removed. Others predict huge cast structures that will be transported by helicopter and "dropped in place."

Concrete. The basic ingredients of concrete are cement and water, and broken stone, slag, gravel, or sand. Almost any form designed by an architect or builder can be produced in concrete. As a result, in most parts of the country there are examples of soaring arches, curvilinear canopies, lacelike grills, and cantilevers. The use of concrete in house construction can

Art Sechrest Photo

This geodesic dome, 250 feet in diameter, was designed by R. Buckminster Fuller for Expo '67.

This geodesic dome, 39 feet in diameter, is the residence of the architect R. Buckminster Fuller at Carbondale, Illinois.

Exterior and floor plan of Century 21 Plywood Home of Living Light.

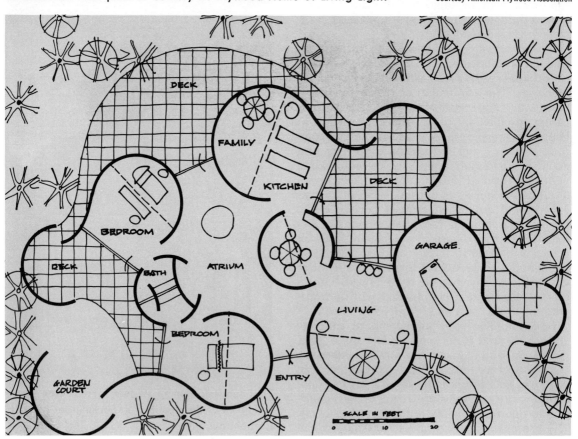

DECK

FAMILY

KITCHEN

DECK

BEDROOM

GARAGE

DECK

BATH

ATRIUM

LIVING

BEDROOM

GARDEN COURT

ENTRY

SCALE IN FEET

0   10   20

18

Contemporary design, new uses for familiar building products, and imaginative
landscaping combine to produce useful and attractive single-family homes.

Prefabricated rooms and complete dwellings are being produced and accepted by the public today.

Much of the land surrounding major cities is being developed into typical suburban living areas for upper- and middle-income groups.

The lake front near Chicago's central business district is lined with middle- and upper-income apartments.

Some mobile homes now provide living space equivalent to that found in small conventional houses or apartments. Attractively landscaped parks in convenient locations add to the desirable features of mobile-home living.

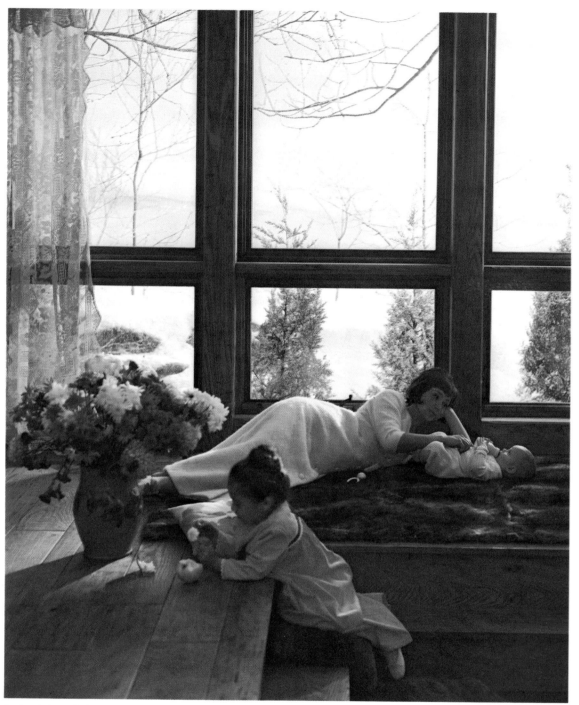

Window walls open the house to the view outside. Insulating glass makes window walls practical in climates with extreme weather changes.

Efficient kitchen cabinets furnish readily-accessible storage for everyday living as well as entertainment.

A fence provides privacy for the patio when houses are located close together.

A well-planned kitchen laundry area should contain all necessary laundry equipment in a convenient arrangement.

Courtesy Mutschler Kitchens, Nappanee, Indiana

A well-planned kitchen combines beauty with efficient work space.

A home may combine the kitchen and dining area for convenience of serving. For a kitchen without a view from the sink, indirect lighting gives the illusion of a window.

Courtesy Mutschler Kitchens, Nappanee, Indiana

Good kitchen planning is illustrated by the following features: the refrigerator opening next to the work counter; the dishwasher to the left of the sink; and counter space on both sides of the recessed cooking surface and the sink.

The large hood serves two types of cook tops which have below-counter storage space. The dishwasher is placed to the left of the sink, permitting a right-to-left work-flow.

Courtesy St. Charles Custom Kitchens

A well-planned kitchen saves energy in preparing and serving a meal. The compact stack-on-range with eye-level twin ovens and pull-out cooking platform provides equipment for most types of cooking without sacrificing kitchen storage space.

Pass-through room dividers can be used in small homes to give a spacious feeling while separating the kitchen and living areas.

This combination laundry and sewing area provides ample counter space for folding clothes from the dryer or for use when sewing. The sewing machine folds away for under-counter storage when not in use.

be expected to increase when color and texture are offered in greater variety. It is expected that lightweight concrete made with wood chips will be used for houses and farm buildings. The colors, patterns, textures, sizes, and shapes of structural blocks may include slump blocks resembling weathered stone, patterned blocks, vitreous glazed units, blocks with exposed aggregate texture, and units with custom-designed shapes.

The concrete house of the future may be any one of a variety of shapes. A sphere, an oval, a doughnut, or some other special shape may be produced to give unusual architectural effect.

Steel. The steel house of the future may be either a mass-produced, prefabricated modular assembly or an architect-designed custom house cantilevered from a hillside. The house built primarily of steel will have large open areas without interior supports, flexible designs, and room layouts. The structure will use steel in combination with other materials to make the house both economical to build and attractive. The house may include one or more of the construction developments which resulted from study of research buildings. The features to look for in the future include a steel roof-ceiling system, a combination concrete and steel-panel floor slab, a light-gauge roll-formed steel wall section, steel wall panels, and movable steel sunshade screens.

Wood. Wood is one natural resource that is renewable with intensive forest management, and it is expected that such management will produce enough wood to meet the demands of the future. The wood house of the immediate future may well be made of self-contained units arranged around an inner court. The curved walls of the plywood house of the future may accompany the development of floor plans based on the circle and oval instead of on the straight lines which have figured so prominently in traditional architecture.

LEARNING EXPERIENCES

1. Define the meaning of the following words: house, housing, implication, economic, social, cultural, and trend.
2. Individually, or in small groups, investigate and report to the class on the characteristics of housing in (*a*) a distant region of the United States or (*b*) a nation outside the continental United States.
3. Discuss the economic implications of housing, and prepare a bulletin board or mural to illustrate the relationship between housing and the business community.
4. Discuss the social implications of housing, and prepare a bulletin board or mural to illustrate the relationship between housing and the educational, recreational, and cultural resources in the community.
5. Discuss the effects of population patterns and trends on housing.
6. Interview a representative of the Department of Housing and Urban Development and report on the functions of governmental agencies in providing adequate housing for many people. This representative may be from the FHA, the PHA, or a local housing authority.
7. Draw a diagram to show how local, state, and federal governments cooperate in an effort to provide adequate housing for people in different situations.
8. Individually, or in small groups, collect or make drawings of houses of the future. Share your findings with the class.
9. Write a description of the most "far-out" house you can imagine. Doodles or drawings may be used to help express your idea.
10. Summarize your conclusions about "Housing Today and Tomorrow." Support your conclusions with related facts. Your papers may be supplemented with illustrations, charts, or drawings.

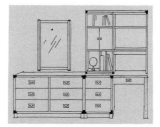

2 Families on the Move

THERE ARE families in the United States who hold family values or religious beliefs which influence them to put down roots and stay in one place. Perhaps they farm the same land, and transact business in the same way that generations of their ancestors did. But for most of the population, moving is a part of the American way of life.

Today every American, whether he is civilian, military, old, young, wealthy, or poor, is likely to become a part of a moving society. The United States census provides a great deal of information about this movement of people. For instance, we know that one-fifth of the population moves each year. Each new housing unit which becomes available makes it possible for as many as thirteen families to move, each to a better place. You will probably become a part of this process when you finish high school—whether you go into the armed services, take a post–high school vocational-technical training program, go to college, or go to work.

How Often Do People Move?

Every five years an equivalent of the entire United States population changes its address.

Perhaps you and your family have not moved recently. But check the names and addresses of your class when they were freshmen, and compare it with the current list. You will no doubt find additions and deletions, caused by people moving in and out of your community. It is estimated that 40 million people move from one address to another each year. When you finish school and take your first job, you will become a part of the most mobile group of all. We know from the census that 42 percent of the twenty- to twenty-four year age–group moves each year. This is your future.

Why Do People Move?

Families move for many reasons. Basically, people move because they are dissatisfied with their present situation or see an opportunity to improve on it. This dissatisfaction may be related to their job, the community, the neighborhood, or their private living quarters.

School. The first move for many teen-agers is from the family home to student housing associated with vocational-technical training or college. This is a relatively simple move, involving clothing, books, and room accessories which are frequently moved by car. It is esti-

The housing provided for personnel in the services is adequate. Generally regulations will not permit any expression of personal interests.

On many campuses, a room in a private home is rapidly being replaced by high-rise dormitories and apartment buildings. The private quarters for the student are usually separated from the study, lounge, and recreation space in the building.

mated that 40 percent of all moves are made by car with relatively little use of special cartons or packing materials.

Employment. A person's job and the related moves that result from promotions, or changes that promise greater opportunity for advance-

ment, explain some moves among families. Studies indicate that more than half of all moves result from employment changes.

Family changes. Young couples with expanding families and older couples with contracting families move to meet their changing

The increasing number of single-family households may be partially explained by the number of unmarried business people living in apartments. There are buildings in most cities in which the units and location are designed to appeal to the young single market.

Retired couples often move to a more convenient location or to a more favorable climate.

needs. These needs usually have to do with the size of an apartment or house and the desire for educational, social, and cultural activities.

Climate. Preference for one section of the United States over another because of unique climatic conditions exists for a variety of personal reasons. Dry climates are recommended for certain health conditions, and warm climates have attracted a substantial number of retired persons.

Where Do People Move?

People are moving to places all over the world. A breakdown of moves by a major interstate carrier of household goods gave these figures: 50 percent move within the city or suburbs; 25 percent move within a given state; 24 percent move to another state; 1 percent move to a foreign country.

Lure of the city. Victor Gruen in *The Heart of Our Cities* says, "the well-functioning city gives each inhabitant a free choice between sociability and privacy, according him the opportunity to express his human gregariousness in meeting with others, but also the chance to disappear, if that is his desire, in the anonymity of its huge organization." Whatever an individual's reasons, the cumulative effects of many individual decisions to live in the city

One's choice of a place to live is influenced by the composition of the family. The single-family dwellings in outlying areas of the city and suburbs have traditionally attracted the family with young children.

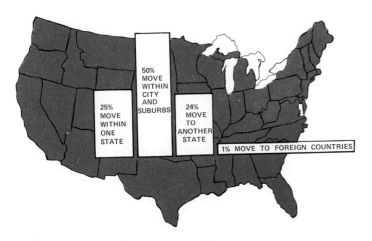

50% MOVE WITHIN CITY AND SUBURBS

25% MOVE WITHIN ONE STATE

24% MOVE TO ANOTHER STATE

1% MOVE TO FOREIGN COUNTRIES

Changes of location caused by moving fall into the categories and percentages shown.

When possessions include only clothing, books, records, and sports equipment, it is easy to move by car. Clothes rods and other accessories may be added to the car.

23

Trailers and trucks may be rented for moving either a very few pieces or an entire household.

Courtesy Arcoa, Inc.

are apparent in the urban growth pattern discussed in Chapter 1.

Lure of the suburbs. Most cities are surrounded by a series of suburbs, each initially catering to a particular group, differentiated by income and age. Mass media tend to equate success with a house in the suburbs. The desire of many people to achieve the appearance of success is sometimes used to explain the attraction of the suburbs. However, most people probably move to a suburb simply because they like the extra space or feel it is a good place to rear their children.

How Do People Move?

People move in a variety of ways: 45 percent move by van, 40 percent by car, 14 percent by truck, and the rest by rail freight and other means. Many companies transfer personnel and pay moving charges for them. The armed services pay moving charges for some personnel.

There are rental services and commercial carriers you can contact for specific information. When the prospect of moving becomes a real part of your life, investigate and compare the costs and the advantages and disadvantages of these different moving methods.

By car. If you are moving suitcases, shoebags, and books, the transfer may be made in a car. Even on such a simple move, it is wise to have insurance covering your personal property while it is in transit.

By rented equipment. Trailers varying in size and style may be rented at one point and left with another dealer at the destination point. For loads too large to be moved by a trailer, van trucks may be rented. Furniture pads and special packing containers and cartons are available from many rental companies. Hand trucks and dollies may be rented to aid in loading and unloading large pieces. The savings in labor costs is a major advantage when you use a rental service.

By commercial carriers. Large movers of household goods are regulated by the Interstate Commerce Commission of the federal government. These companies offer a variety of services, such as packing and unpacking, and furnishing wrappings and cartons needed for specific items. They will arrange for crating items that need this protection. It is plain to

Commercial vans are large enough to move the household goods for two or more average families at one time.

This view of the interior of an interstate van shows the large capacity of such vans.

see that the services offered by such companies contribute to the physical ease and peace of mind of families who can afford to move by commercial carrier.

PROBLEMS OF MOVING

Because moving is an experience that does not occur often enough to become a habit, the family may need help in organizing details. Nationally known van lines provide aids designed to take the confusion out of family moving. When you know you will be moving, it is of prime importance to locate a satisfactory home in the new location and dispose of your present home in a suitable manner. The housing divisions of many schools, personnel departments of business firms, and real estate companies are experienced in helping individuals and families locate housing that meets their needs and desires.

Moving Preparation

Many details can be taken care of during the several weeks preceding the actual moving day. This is the time when the children may be prepared for the changes the move will cause for them. The young children of the family need to know the advantages of moving to a new location and the new things there will be for them to see and do. Preplanning and scheduling of jobs related to the move will help lessen last-minute confusion. A month before moving day is not too soon to determine what to take and how to have it moved. Drawing a rough diagram on scored paper showing the size, location, and architectural details of each room in your new house will help you decide what to move.

What to move. When planning the move, take time to check the house, garage, patio, and storage areas. Decide what to take and what to dispose of. The floor-plan sketches of the new home may indicate that some furnishings should be disposed of before you move or that new pieces may be needed to fill a functional or decorative need.

Professional or do-it-yourself. You should compare the choices and decide whether you will be moved by a transport company or whether you will do it yourself with rented equipment. Before you make a decision, you

Deciding what to keep, pack, and move often becomes a family project with each person making decisions and helping with the work.

Moving offers an opportunity to give a critical look at items not being used. Many items no longer useful for your family may be of use to others.

will want to compare the costs or the alternatives in time, money, and energy.

General preparations. Timing is important if you want to ensure uninterrupted service from publishers of papers and periodicals, from banks, and from medical services. Enrolling children in school will be made easier if you have their records sent ahead. The earlier you can give the van line a definite contract, the more likely it will be that they move you on the date chosen.

A plan for handling the personal business of the family needs to be started as soon as the family knows the moving date. Including children in planning details and allowing those old enough to help with some of the jobs will help ease the tensions caused by the uprooting of the family.

Addresses. You should prepare lists of friends, relatives, and business firms that should be notified of your change in address. You can get special cards free at the post office. Change-of-address cards should be sent to magazines, book clubs, and other monthly publications to which you subscribe. Children of letter-writing age may help with this task by notifying their friends.

Charge accounts and credit cards. All charge accounts should be closed or transferred to the new address by using the free post-office cards or those provided by individual companies. Local credit cards should be de-

Special equipment is needed for safe, easy moving of large items.

stroyed and new ones secured. Utility and service companies should be advised of the tentative moving date.

Resignations and introductions. Now is the time to resign from local clubs and organizations and to get letters of introduction or transfer from your church, your organization or club presidents, and your business associates for those memberships you wish to continue at the new location.

School records. Have confidential student records sent to the school the children will attend, or pick up a transfer form from the school so that it can be taken along to present when enrolling the children at the new location.

This will aid in placing the student in the most suitable class or section available to him.

Medical and dental records. Arrange to have records transferred to the doctor or clinic of your choice. You may need to take prescriptions or recommendations along.

Moving contract. The companies that gave estimates on moving costs should be notified of your final decision. Then you will need to sign the necessary orders with the chosen company and set a definite date for packing and moving.

Moving Day

This is the day to leave young children with friends or a familiar baby-sitter so that you

Boxes protect mattress and box springs from damage in transit.

Some house furnishings need to be crated before being moved.

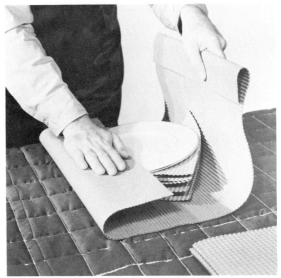

Special packages, such as the cell pack, and careful packing techniques protect fragile glassware and dishes.

can give your attention to questions from the van operator. It takes approximately five or six hours to load the furniture from a five- or six-room house and the same time to unload. A van travels an average of about 300 miles a day. Knowing these averages, you can pick the moving day and determine the time the furniture will reach its destination.

Reaching the Destination

The first people you will get to know will probably be those associated with the move— the mover's agent, the personnel at the school the children will attend, and representatives from service companies. The process of getting information needed to get settled will make opportunities to get acquainted.

When you arrive. You should make certain that your new house is ready for occupancy when the van operator arrives. Have the keys available so that no time is lost.

Mover's agent. You should contact the van company representative and give him a local telephone number where you may be reached. You should also make final arrangements to accept delivery when your household goods arrive.

A sketch showing where large pieces of furniture should be placed will help the mover follow your plans.

Plan the placement of furniture. When unloading, the van operator and his assistants will place each piece of furniture where directed. They will lay rugs and set up beds, but they are not permitted to install or attach appliances. Separate arrangements must be made for this service.

Utilities. You should telephone the utility companies and make arrangements for service. Details vary in different cities and states; it is best to contact the local companies for details.

Appliances. Make arrangements for the installation of appliances and for an operation checkup. The utility company may help you do this. Some companies will not let you use equipment until it has been checked.

Unpack. You may wish to unpack the cartons—many people prefer to do this as it allows exact placement of items as they are unpacked. However, if you paid for packing, you are entitled to unpacking service and the removal of the cartons by company employees.

LEARNING EXPERIENCES

1. Discuss the mobility trends and population patterns developing in the United States.
2. Conduct a survey to determine the number of families who have moved in or out of your school district within (*a*) the past year and (*b*) the past five years. Report your findings to the class and discuss the implications of the trend.
3. Imagine that you have been working two years and now want a place of your own. Describe yourself and your job situation and tell what kind of place you are looking for and why.
4. Inventory your personal belongings. Group them into categories, such as, (*a*) those to be placed in seasonal storage; (*b*) those to be discarded; (*c*) those to take with you on your move to your first home away from parents. Determine the packing materials you would need to safely move the items listed.
5. Divide into groups and demonstrate the correct methods for packing commonly moved articles, such as books, records, sporting equipment, clothing, bedding, and framed pictures.
6. Write and present a one-minute drama based on getting ready to move.
7. Talk over ways in which individual family members may contribute to a relatively trouble-free move.
8. Interview a representative for a nationwide mover, and report to the class about the services and rates offered by professional movers.
9. Interview a representative of a trailer or truck rental center and report to the class about the equipment available, the services offered, and the cost of do-it-yourself moving.
10. Organize a round-table discussion of the advantages and disadvantages of each type of moving service.

3

Choosing a

Place to Live

FEW FAMILIES live in a home or neighborhood which is completely satisfactory to all the members at all times. The choice of a place to live will be influenced by the stage of the family in the life cycle, their social and cultural needs, and the amount of money the budget allows for shelter. The decision on the amount to spend is almost always a compromise between the family's desires and the apartments or houses available for rent or for sale.

Since the standards and the living habits of people vary, there can be no single rule for all homes. The emphasis should be on what the home can do to enrich the lives of its occupants. Having decided on the area in which you prefer to live, the size of place wanted, and the price you can afford to pay, you are ready to shop for specific housing.

People will want space that serves a variety of purposes: places to meet and talk, study, entertain or be alone, and to keep possessions. A look at your family helps you to realize that each succeeding year the needs and interests of the various members change. If the location

of the apartment or house is convenient to work, recreation, and public services and if the overall plan provides adequate space, circulation between rooms, and space for equipment, the use of different areas may be adapted or modified as the family changes its pattern of living.

Attitudes and Values

A study by the research division of the *Chicago Tribune* revealed that those who already live in the suburbs tend to prefer to remain there, while those who live in the city look for their new dwellings in the city. Being close to the job, to recreational facilities, or to educational facilities is important to the urban-oriented person; his choice of a place to live will be influenced by such things. When rural people move to the city (particularly when they move to an apartment), they tend to look upon this as a temporary situation which will continue only until they can afford to move to the suburbs where there is more room for activities of the type they prefer.

31

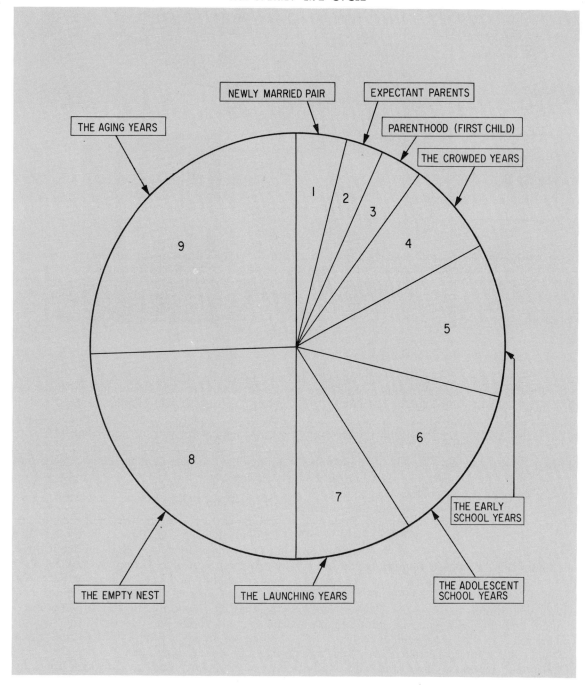

NEWLY MARRIED PAIR

EXPECTANT PARENTS

THE AGING YEARS

PARENTHOOD (FIRST CHILD)

THE CROWDED YEARS

THE EARLY SCHOOL YEARS

THE EMPTY NEST

THE LAUNCHING YEARS

THE ADOLESCENT SCHOOL YEARS

The family life-cycle consists of various stages. During each stage, family housing needs change.

The young couple expecting a child often look for a larger home than they had as a working couple.

Psychological Satisfactions

At each stage of your life cycle the choice of a place to live will be influenced by what you want to achieve at that particular time. In looking for your first home away from home, you may wish to look for an economically priced place where there are other active, young, gregarious individuals to share community-owned facilities, such as a swimming pool, skating rink, or barbecue pit. After you have worked a few years, you may develop a taste for more comfort and individuality. You would then look for a somewhat different place to live—perhaps one with more privacy.

If you are married and working, you may be looking forward to a larger apartment or to a house in the suburbs. Your present location may be serving as a transition home before you have children. A family with young children may get much satisfaction from living where there are playgrounds and nurseries. As the children grow, the quality of the schools may be the important factor in the choice of neighborhood.

CHOOSING A NEIGHBORHOOD

Choosing the right neighborhood for all members of the family may prove to be more of a challenge than locating a particular house that meets family needs. It is relatively easy to check the physical characteristics of an area. You can use one of the checklists in magazines or how-to-do-it house-hunting books to pinpoint the location of shopping facilities, churches, schools, buildings, playgrounds, and public transportation.

More time will be required to check the quality of the educational program in the schools and other intangible factors that affect the quality of family life. Zoning regulations, the direction of growth of the town or city, and similar factors that affect property values should also be checked, especially if the home is to be bought rather than rented.

Metropolitan Areas

There has been a continually expanding urban development in some 212 metropolitan areas. Metropolitan areas include cities, suburbs, and exurbs.

Some writers believe that by 1985 there will be about thirteen areas of the United States consisting of interdependent cities, suburbs, and exurbs so large that they will be referred to as "megalopolises." They foresee three super-cities, one on the West Coast, one occupying the state of Florida, and one spreading from

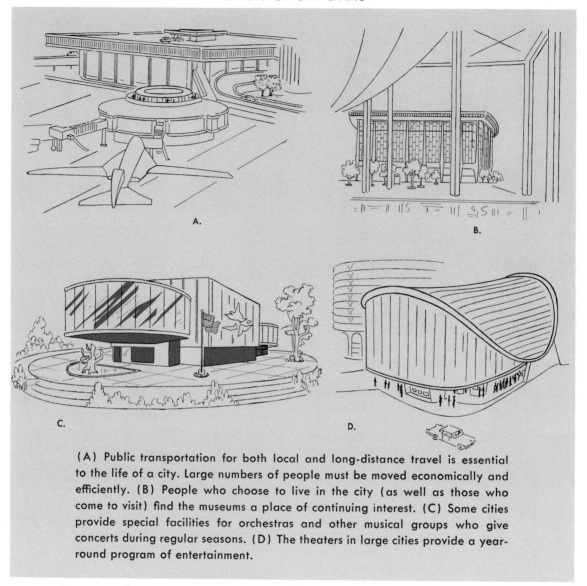

(A) Public transportation for both local and long-distance travel is essential to the life of a city. Large numbers of people must be moved economically and efficiently. (B) People who choose to live in the city (as well as those who come to visit) find the museums a place of continuing interest. (C) Some cities provide special facilities for orchestras and other musical groups who give concerts during regular seasons. (D) The theaters in large cities provide a year-round program of entertainment.

New York westward along the Great Lakes to the Chicago metropolitan area.

The city. There are many definitions of a "city." Some are based on population while others are based on other facts or characteristics. One writer defines a city as a place with a balance between the pleasures and comforts of private life and the cultural offerings which only the public can support. In all sections of the United States, the standards for private life are the highest in the world, but theaters, museums, and concert halls are generally concentrated in the cities. Traditionally, cities are "home" to many nationality groups; they hold a wide range of economic and social classes within a concentrated area.

Many people prefer the city as a way of life and a place of residence. People find the city a source of inspiration and income, since a large concentration of people can more easily

Middle-income families are buying houses in many suburban developments.

support the research centers, museums, theaters, parks, beaches, pools, concert halls, and public transportation systems that give the individual such a wide range of choices among social, cultural, and economic interests.

The suburbs. Towns and villages which make up the outlying parts of a city and are in direct physical contact with it make up the suburbs. These are a collection of houses which may or may not be incorporated as a municipality. "Incorporation" means that the village or town has the organization and power necessary for self-government.

Exurbia. Two distinct developments, known as "exurbia," are emerging outside the city and beyond the suburbs. On the one hand are the estates of well-to-do families who can afford the extra acreage and the cost of providing and maintaining private wells and sanitation systems and enough cars to get the family to scattered activities. The distance of some of these estates from the business centers where the members of the family are employed may be so great that the family also maintains an apartment in the city. On the other hand, "exurbia" also means the small clusters of houses built in areas lacking most of the services and conveniences offered by the suburbs.

Well-built, well-kept farm buildings make rural housing attractive to city dwellers wishing more space.

35

Many small towns are gradually changing from their original role as farm-support centers to a new role as dormitory towns for urban workers.

Rural Areas

"Rural" and "rural nonfarm" are terms used by the U.S. Census Bureau to differentiate between housing in the open country on farms and housing in small towns.

Rural. The house, or houses, and other farm buildings generally included in the rental or sale of farmland are known as rural housing. Besides the house occupied by the operator of a farm, there may also be a second house which is furnished to a farm tenant or to an employee of the owner in exchange for services. In areas where migrant farm workers are employed, the owner-operator generally furnishes housing for the workers.

Rural nonfarm. Small towns, whose population in the past provided the services to support the surrounding farm area, are now attracting commuters from urban areas. This trend may change the nature of the hamlet or small town because families with urban values and attitudes demand more in the way of schools and community services than has traditionally been available in rural areas.

Schools

Although a good school system may exist anywhere, suburban schools, with their newer buildings and spacious campuses, are attractive to many middle-class families who place emphasis on academic education. Parents who want the best possible education for children will look for a school with a stable faculty, a counseling service to help pupils identify their potentials, good library facilities, an administration which believes in a program to meet the needs of all ability groups and all interest groups, and school-district salaries which are high enough to meet area competition.

For the young person who is not college-bound, most schools, particularly those in inner city areas, are now trying to offer something in the way of vocational and technical training and cooperative work-study programs. Area vocational schools for any student in a given area are becoming popular in many parts of the United States, thus bringing vocational education to large numbers of young people everywhere. At the college and graduate level,

The modern facilities in new school buildings attract teachers and parents who place emphasis on education.

cities have always contributed to education and research. The quality of education provided by a prospective living area should be judged by each family in relation to its needs.

Recreation

Theaters, concerts, museums, and exhibits traditionally have been centered in the cities. These projects cost money, and as long as wealth remains concentrated in metropolitan areas, this is where you will find a concentration of high-level entertainment and culture. Commercial forms of recreation, such as bowling alleys, swimming pools, and golf courses, also require a certain concentration of population to support them. The more convenient these facilities are to the home, the more likely families will be to develop an interest in them.

Professional Services

Health centers, including a medical, dental, and mental health staff, along with hospital and convalescent care, are facilities that all people need at some time. Considering your family's present situation, you may feel that you could travel twenty or thirty miles to get the kind of medical service needed. However, if a chronic situation developed, the driving could become time-consuming and costly. If there are children, or plans for children, in the family, you will want to know the driving time to the nearest hospital where a doctor is always on duty in the emergency room.

Local Government

Before making a final decision about a community, find out what services are provided by the local government. Your family will want to know about the water supply, for example. In some areas water should be treated before it is used in the household; in others, the amount of water used may be restricted because of short supply. In still other areas, the cost of water is high enough to be an expense that needs special consideration. Similar information is needed about sewage disposal, garbage disposal, and other necessary services and utilities.

It may be easy to learn the present tax levied against the property being considered. It may be equally important but not so easy to learn the attitude of the local government toward

Swimming pools, tennis courts, and playing fields are being included in the overall plans to provide recreation in many communities where there is the leadership and financial support for such projects.

supplying and maintaining schools, streets, and hospitals which will affect the value of the property and future tax levies.

Special assessments may be voted for improvements to an area to cover such things as storm sewers, street lighting, sidewalks, and curbs.

Police and fire protection provided by the local government may add to the feeling of safety and also affect the cost of insurance premiums which must be paid to protect the property from damage or destruction.

DECIDING ON THE SIZE OF PLACE WANTED

There are many types of structure in which to make a home. They vary from one another as to the amount of interior space as well as the amount of outdoor living area provided. There are wide variations in the amount of space offered within each type of structure.

Some families prefer to live in a house. (Chapter 5 presents a detailed discussion of houses.) Others prefer to live in apartments, and still others prefer the mobile home.

APARTMENT LIVING

Apartments may be as small as a single room or as large as many single-family houses. What-

ever its size, an apartment is a living unit arranged and equipped for housekeeping and designed to meet the needs of either urban or suburban living. The rental apartment has certain advantages, particularly for the young and old, because there is no long-term financial commitment and no responsibility or burden for its upkeep. Also, the flexibility of apartment living offers good interim housing for the young and freedom for travel for the older occupants. In recent years there has been a tremendous increase in apartment living, which may be explained by the increasing number of young families, single-person households, and older people among our population, as well as the growing cost of land for house building in areas with good transportation.

Positive Aspects

For many people, there are advantages in apartment living: families are smaller and more mobile than those of the past; many wives work outside the home; more people eat out frequently; food comes to the consumer partially or fully prepared; laundromats replace or supplement the home laundry; and more and more nursery schools and day-care centers provide child care. Such services allow people to give priority to aesthetic, educational, and recrea-

When the family lives in a house, the mother can supervise children playing in the yard at the same time that she works around the house. The suburbs characteristically attract families with children.

tional activities by freeing them from the responsibility of maintaining a house.

Negative Aspects

The advantages of apartment living may become disadvantages if you are the kind of person who wants to be active doing things around the house. Generally, you live in an apartment as it is. You cannot add a patio, change the walls, or make other major alterations. Garden apartments provide some outdoor space, but not enough to satisfy the man who wants a riding mower or a vegetable garden. Storage space is usually limited; there is generally no attic or basement for keeping obsolete or infrequently used belongings. In this respect, most apartments are similar to a house without a basement.

The family with children may have difficulty finding good schools near an apartment which meets their needs. Many city apartments today have playgrounds either on the rooftop or in a courtyard, but mothers or sitters need to be with the children during play periods, while in the suburbs children can often play unsupervised by an adult.

Location of Apartment Buildings

Urban and suburban locations each have unique advantages and disadvantages. The

H. Armstrong Roberts

Apartments provide housing for many city families.

39

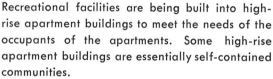

Recreational facilities are being built into high-rise apartment buildings to meet the needs of the occupants of the apartments. Some high-rise apartment buildings are essentially self-contained communities.

apartment near the central business district may offer the occupants quick access to work, shopping districts, and amusement centers, and also, in some cases, a fashionable address. The suburban location may offer more in the way of view, access to playgrounds and garden space, and usually lower rentals, with the frequent disadvantage of more time spent traveling to and from work. Suburban locations tend to meet the needs of retired people who want to be near friends and family.

What to Know about Apartments

Descriptive terms need to be defined so that you can understand what to expect after reading an advertisement for an apartment. More

Garden apartments provide many of the advantages of both a house and an apartment.

people seem to be familiar with descriptive terms applied to single-family houses than with those which apply to multifamily dwellings. To the individual who owns an apartment building, an apartment is an investment. The rent paid by the tenants is income from which the owner anticipates a profit. To the occupant of one of the units, an apartment is a home.

Apartment Buildings According to Structure

"High-rise," "garden," and "balcony-entrance" are terms used to describe multifamily buildings, each of which has certain characteristics that distinguish it from the others. In general, buildings are divided into categories according to the means used for access to the individual apartments.

High-rise apartments. Multistoried, corridor-type buildings are usually found in prime loca-

In colder climates, some balcony-entrance apartments have enclosed walkways.

tions, often within walking distance of work, amusement, and shopping areas. The high-rise apartment has certain advantages which the low structure seldom has—good light, magnificent views from upper floors, and a feeling of great space.

This type of building requires elevators to move people to and from their floor levels. The use of the word "corridor" implies that corridors of varying lengths give access to five or more apartments on each floor. High-rise apartment buildings contain mostly efficiency units and one- and two-bedroom units that appeal to unmarried working people, to young married couples both of whom are employed, to older retired couples, and to widowed older people. Roof decks and balconies are common features. Many new high-rise apartments include shops, restaurants, and garage space.

Garden apartments. In areas where relatively inexpensive land is available, apartment units, each of which has a private outside door opening on landscaped courts and yards, provide group living that is particularly suitable for families with young children. Usually garden apartments have parking and garages grouped nearby but separated from the living units—an arrangement that tends to reduce noise near the apartments.

Balcony-entrance apartments. These are two- or three-story buildings, with mostly efficiency and one- and two-bedroom apartments which the occupants enter from an open corridor, or balcony. This corridor is built on the outside of the building along one side of the units only. Since apartments of this type are limited to walk-ups, they are usually found in areas where the cost of land is less than in more central locations.

Apartments According to Size

Apartments vary in both number and size of rooms. However, in any one apartment building there will be a limited range of sizes. Each unit is designed to provide complete living facilities for the type of tenant for whom it is intended.

Motels. When a motel room includes a kitchenette, it is a one-room home. Motels may be occupied on a semipermanent basis. While motels may be found in any location, they are most often located on the fringes of the community.

Efficiency or studio apartments. These are one-room units with kitchenette, bathroom, dressing area, and storage space. They frequently are the choice of single persons who want to be close to work or school. Some studio apartments are large enough to accommodate two persons.

One- and two-bedroom apartments. These larger units are designed for a married couple or a small family. Groups of up to four single persons sometimes share an apartment of this

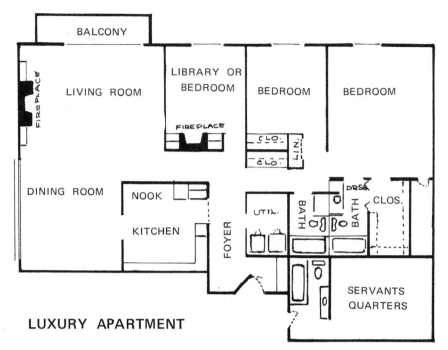

Luxury apartments provide space for a wide variety of family-centered activities.

LUXURY APARTMENT

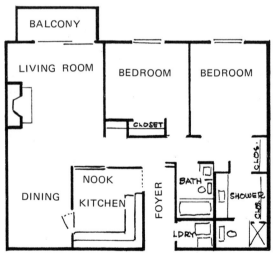

TWO BEDROOM APARTMENT

Most high-rise apartments are one- and two-bedroom units.

size. In some areas, apartment managers limit the number of persons who may share an apartment.

Luxury apartments. Buildings composed of luxury-type units are generally built only in prime locations, such as those with a view of a river, a lake, the mountains, or a park. Such buildings offer every possible service and facility. One element that may be found in luxury apartments that is not found in other units is space for servants. Room size and number of rooms do not necessarily make a luxury apartment, for luxury also depends on achieving an air of spaciousness and livability. This means space for entertaining, usually on a fairly large scale, and for privacy and relaxation for the family at all times. Bedrooms in luxury apartments are large to accommodate more pieces of furniture than are ordinarily used. They may even be large enough to include sitting and dressing areas.

Low-rent apartments. Apartments with relatively low rents are made possible by reducing the number and size of rooms per person and by building skyward to reduce the land cost in relation to the apartment unit. Costs are further reduced by eliminating closet doors, substituting open shelves for kitchen cabinets, and reducing the number of electric outlets. When there are separate heating units, the rent may be lower because the tenant is paying for a utility generally furnished by the landlord.

Community Areas & Play Areas

Many apartment complexes provide community rooms, buildings, and play areas for use by the people who live there.

Low-income housing can provide for the various interests of the apartment dweller.

Services for Apartment Dwellers

There are special service provisions which may be offered to apartment dwellers. These may be in separate buildings in the development or they may be special areas within the individual building and its grounds.

Community buildings. Community buildings are sometimes provided to supplement the facilities in apartment buildings. These may include assembly rooms, club rooms, and hobby workshops. There may also be gymnasiums, indoor pools, and indoor play space for children.

Play areas. Apartments which welcome children should include play apparatus interesting enough for children to want to play there. Larger projects sometimes provide space for court games. Large playgrounds with supervised facilities for general recreation and areas for baseball, outdoor basketball, etc., are generally found only in public housing projects. Private owners are usually unwilling to provide and supervise such facilities. Swimming pools, wading pools, and putting greens are fairly common adjucts to large apartment complexes.

Classification of Apartments

Apartments are classified according to the way they are owned and managed. In investment apartment buildings the tenant rents a unit and must accept the lease as written by the management. In cooperatives each tenant owns shares in a corporation which owns and manages the building. In condominiums occupants own their apartments.

Investment apartment buildings. To the individual who owns an apartment building, an apartment is an investment. The rent paid by the tenants is income from which the owner anticipates a profit. To the occupant of one of the units, an apartment is a home. The occupant of an investment apartment has the same privileges and obligations as any other home renter.

Cooperative apartments. In a cooperative apartment building, occupants are shareholders in a corporation that owns and manages the building. This idea originated in Scandinavia over a hundred years ago. It is popular in European countries and the United States. To be successful, a cooperative must be organized and operated on a sound financial basis.

Cooperative apartment living combines many of the conveniences of apartment living with the satisfaction of home ownership: for example, the freedom to travel without concern about the security of the premises during your absence; the fact that cooperative apartment owners, through a sifting committee, can select neighbors who they believe will be congenial and financially responsible; the fact that special facilities (such as swimming pools, lounges, sundecks, and parking areas) are usually available to occupants; and the fact that maintenance and operating costs are minimized because they are shared.

The savings under cooperative management are derived from the elimination of vacancies and saving of fees for rental commissions, since the profit that normally would go to the landlord goes to the tenant in the form of a saving in rent. In a cooperative apartment, assessments are made for maintaining and operating

Large investments are required to build apartment complexes and shopping centers.

Prairie Shores Apartments, Courtesy Draper & Kramer, Inc.

the building. The amount of money needed to meet the budget is divided by the number of shares involved, and each owner pays on the number of shares represented in the purchase of his apartment.

There are disadvantages in a cooperative: an owner must adhere to rules established by the majority; without committee approval an owner cannot sell his stock for more than he paid for it; if some tenants fail to pay, the others must make up for the liabilities; an owner can sell his stock in the cooperative or rent his apartment space only if he has the approval of the committee set up by the board of directors.

Condominium apartments. A condominium is a building whose occupants own (obtain the title to) their unit as well as a share of the common elements of a multiunit structure. "Con-do-min-i-um," a Latin word dating back to the sixth century, means "joint ownership." Although the term can be traced to the Romans, the concept of condominium living is relatively new in the United States. The advantages are much the same as for cooperatives.

Condominium owners can also prepay their mortgages or refinance if they need to. They also can sell their property and keep any profit they make.

In a condominium each owner pays a monthly maintenance fee, which pays for that part of the structure that is held in common—the roof, hallways, gardens, lobbies, elevators, and all other common areas. The monthly maintenance fee for the owner of a two-bedroom apartment will be less than that paid by the owner of a three-bedroom unit.

The occupant who buys into a condominium is the sole owner of his own apartment in a multifamily project, and he may make changes within his unit. The owners select a board of directors who manage the property.

LIVING IN A MOBILE HOME

A mobile home is a movable or portable dwelling constructed to be towed on its own chassis, connected to local utilities, and designed for year-round living. A distinguishing characteristic of the mobile home is that it is without

An ideal mobile-home park provides modern facilities equal to those provided in other communities.

a permanent foundation. It may consist of one or more units that can be folded, collapsed, or telescoped when towed and expanded later for additional cubic capacity. Some homes consist of two or more units, separately towable but designed to be joined into one integral unit, capable of being separated again into components for repeated towing. Mobile homes are sometimes referred to as manufactured homes or sectional homes.

Nearly five million people live in mobile homes. They represent all age groups and all walks of life: skilled workers, military personnel, professional people, retired persons, students, and semiskilled and unskilled workers. Nearly 50 percent are young married couples under thirty-four years of age; 25 percent are over fifty-five, nearing or living in retirement. The average family occupying a mobile home consists of fewer than three persons. Mobile homes are selected for economy, comfort, and convenience. A survey of mobile-home owners indicates that more than 90 percent consider them satisfactory.

According to recent surveys, the average American family moves once every five years. The survey of mobile-home owners showed that 54 percent had not moved in the past five years, and 23 percent had moved only once in that time. Although the movability of the home is a seeming advantage, apparently this is not the reason for the growing popularity of this type of dwelling. A mobile home does provide security for families in certain vocational groups. The family knows that the home and its furnishings can be quickly moved without separating the family for long intervals of time, as well might be the case if the family had to sell real estate before moving.

Selecting a Mobile-home Park

Mobile-home living is greatly influenced by the park facilities that meets one's specific needs, in much the same way that a neighborhood may supplement the facilities of a house. No two parks are alike. It is necessary to shop around until the best possible choice is found.

Mobile-home parks vary in size and quality and in the type of facilities offered. Those which are "housing-oriented" provide the immediate housing needs near attractive features outside the park boundaries. They serve residents who want to be near their employment and have shopping and recreation facilities nearby.

Parks that provide recreational and social facilities within their own boundaries are generally preferred by retired or semiretired families. Some parks have areas where playgrounds are provided for families with children.

There are more than 22,000 mobile-home parks in the United States. The average park has 75 spaces. Some are larger, but only a few parks exceed 500 spaces. Developing and operating a park is a full-fledged business venture; the estimated cost of building a park is $2,000 per space. At least 60 percent occupancy is necessary to meet operating expenses.

Traditionally, mobile-home parks have been on a single level and might be compared to horizontal apartments; but with the increase in the number of mobile-home owners and with the need to be conveniently located, there is a growing interest in multilevel mobile-home communities in urban areas. In several areas of the United States, architects have plans under way for luxury developments of this high-rise type.

Judging a Park

By driving through a mobile-home park and by talking with the manager, you will learn much about the physical layout and the park regulations. Features that will affect your choice are the size and monthly cost of a lot; services, such as clubhouse, recreational and laundry facilities; and extra charges. These extras may cover large items such as steps, awnings, and a particular type of cabana, or even such small items as waste containers and collection. The more desirable parks require the home to be "skirted" between the floor level and the ground to hide the wheels and underframe.

Roads. Width and surfacing of roads are important. In some parks there is offstreet parking for each four or six homes. Here the roads need not be as wide as those that must accommodate on street parking. Sidewalks and curbing are provided in better parks. Street Lighting should also be present in the park area. There is common agreement that well-

Part of the monthly rental payment at a mobile-home park may provide for the use of recreational facilities provided by the park management.

lighted, attractive entrances to a park give a good impression.

Storage facilities. There are advantages to having some space available for storing seasonal items, such as sports equipment, yard tools, and outdoor furniture. In some parks, space is provided in a central building. In others, each occupant provides his own storage building. The better parks have regulations covering the kind and location of storage buildings permitted on individual lots.

Gas, electric, and water utilities. In most parks, utilty connections are built under ground. Each home has its own meter and is billed by the utility company according to the services used.

Telephone service. Most parks provide telephone service for each home at the owner's expense. Some of the more highly developed parks have switchboards to handle calls. The operator can receive and give messages when occupants are not at home.

Recreation facilities. The larger and more progressive parks provide pools, recreation buildings, game courts, and putting greens. A few in the more expensive bracket are built around a golf course or marina.

Trends in Mobile-home Parks

Architects in all areas of the United States have proposed the use of mobile or manufactured

Factory-built units transported to the building site, lifted in place by crane, and attached to a center core that houses elevators and common utilities may be the answer to the housing needs of low-income families.

units in the systems concept of housing. These units could be installed on high-value land closer to the population and employment centers of a metropolitan area. The systems concept permits the manufactured or mobile unit to be used in urban areas for row houses, two-level town houses, and walk-up and garden apartments, as well as for bi-level or multilevel high-rise housing. In general, the plans for systems-concept high-rise developments include restaurants, shops, pools, and sundecks and a lower-level parking area for cars. Mobile homes can be transported to upper-floor levels by specially built elevators and positioned on the lots so that all homes face outward. They may be replaced if the owner wants a new home or, with the systems concept, portions of the home can be replaced if they become outmoded.

Size and Mobility of Homes

Mobile homes range from 50 to 70 feet in length and from 12 to 24 feet in width. They are towed to their sites by trucks regulated by state highway authorities. The maximum width that can be moved without permission from highway authorities is 12 feet. Twenty-four foot homes are made in two separate units, each 12 feet wide. They are towed separately and joined at the home site. Expandable mobile homes comply with the 12-foot highway regulation. One or two rooms are telescoped for transit and expanded at the new site. This expansion often adds 5 or 6 feet to the width of a living room or a bedroom. The professional towing service that moves mobile homes handles all arrangements, including towing fees, insurance, cost of permits, and other incidentals. Charges are usually estimated on a mileage basis, though there may be a minimum fee. Rates vary with the size of the unit. Besides the mileage charge, there are charges for packing, unpacking, and stabilizing the mobile home.

The size of a home a family selects will depend on the needs and interests of its members. Since there are costs involved in each move, the probable number of moves and the distances likely to be covered need to be considered when reaching a decision. Beyond this, a buyer can depend on the Mobile Homes

Manufacturers Association's Standards Seal as evidence that the home has been manufactured to comply with National Industry Standards.

Criteria for Judging Quality

Certain external and interior construction features may be checked when seeking a quality mobile home. Each may be judged in relation to cost and anticipated performance. Interiors of mobile homes vary widely and are a matter of personal choice.

Exterior walls. The exterior walls may have a surface of aluminum, sheet steel, or some other conventional siding material. They should contain adequate insulation, such as fiber glass wool or plastic foam. Highly-polished sheet-metal exteriors reflect the sun's heat away from the home in summer and trap and reflect radiant heat from interior sources back into the home in winter.

Ventilation. There should be a ventilating fan near the kitchen range and one in the bathroom wall or ceiling.

Circulation of heat and air conditioning. Because the mobile home is generally long and narrow, adequate circulation of hot or cold air can best be accomplished by a system equipped with a blower. For greater satisfaction and trouble-free service, the system should be thermostatically controlled and have a minimum number of gadgets. For quiet operation, the air-duct sizes should be large enough to keep air velocities low. The unit should be readily accessible for cleaning and servicing.

Plumbing. The plumbing should be checked to determine that all fixtures function correctly. One clue to an adequate supply of water is the existence of a 3/4-inch IPS (iron pipe size) water connection, which will provide adequate pressure at the fixture even if three outlets are used at the same time.

Electrical wiring. The ability of an electrical conductor to carry electric current is proportional to the size of the wire. Branch lighting circuits should be no smaller than 14 gauge. There should be a minimum of six branch circuits. All electrical materials, appliances, and equipment should bear the UL label.

Since parts and service are generally more readily available for nationally advertised

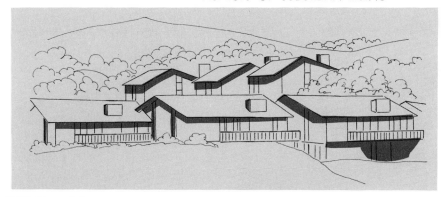

The suburbs provide housing for many modern families.

Suburban shopping centers are designed to provide the shops and services needed by the surrounding community.

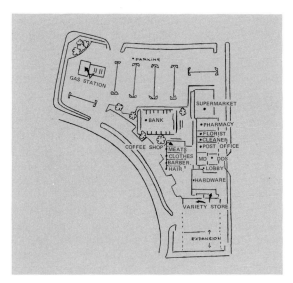

Many shopping centers include places for people to meet and visit. Some of them sponsor seasonal art and special interest shows for the neighborhood.

49

brands, there may be advantages in having such brands in homes that are moved from one section of the country to another.

DECIDING TO RENT OR TO BUY

The question of renting or buying is academic unless both types of units are available in an area. Arguments can be presented in favor of either decision. In the final analysis, it becomes a matter of attitude, or "feeling," about home ownership. Patterns of living have changed so much that home ownership does not command the importance it had for previous generations.

Renting

People may prefer to rent for many reasons. Families who expect to be transferred to another city in a short time may find that renting makes it easier for them to move. Some people prefer to leave the major maintenance problems to a landlord. Still others decide to rent for economic reasons; they may feel that renting is cheaper than buying or they may feel that renting gives them more value for the same cost.

Not all writers agree that a house is an investment. One writer has gone so far as to call a house a "sinkhole for money." Real estate depreciates and becomes obsolete unless the owner makes periodic replacements of equipment and does major remodeling. On the other hand, the renter can move when his needs change or when more desirable rental units are built.

Real estate does not always appreciate in value, and the home owner cannot be sure this will happen. If, however, home ownership gives you a feeling of security, it may be worth giving up the advantages of renting which include greater mobility, freedom to move where and when you want to, and the additional leisure you have because a tenant is not responsible for major repairs to either house or ground.

Tenant and Landlord Obligations

A tenant must pay rent. In return, he can use the leased premises in a manner similar to an owner while he is in possession. The landlord must turn over the property to the tenant.

Repairs. The landlord usually assumes the responsibility for structural repairs, while upkeep repairs are the tenant's job. It is up to the tenant to notify the landlord when repairs are needed. If the landlord fails to make them in a reasonable length of time, some states permit the tenant to make the repairs and deduct the cost from his rent. Tenant repairs are supposed to keep the property as it was when it was rented.

Improvements. Additions or changes should not be made on rented property without the consent of the landlord. A general rule is that anything attached to the building or ground must be left when the tenant moves.

Buying

There is no research to show conclusively that home ownership is more or less costly than renting a house or apartment. However, renting can be less costly if you can adapt to its psychological limitations. In some cases, buying with a small down payment makes it possible for large families to have better housing than they could have by renting for the same amount of money. Large apartments which welcome children are not readily available to low- or middle-income families. Single persons, families without children, and older couples whose children no longer live at home have the widest range of choices in types of shelter.

Except in times of material shortage, or of inflation, the disadvantages of low-down-payment buying may outweigh the advantages. These houses are often in developments where the next buyer can get a new-built house with a smaller down payment than you can afford to take in selling your place. And the additions and changes you may have made to adapt the house to your particular needs may not be worth the extra money to another purchaser. Unless you are reasonably sure that you will be located in an area for some time or that you can afford to become a landlord when you need to move, home ownership may not be a wise financial decision.

The American Council to Improve Our Neighborhoods has reported that housing has been strongly affected by the changing spending habits of Americans. Most house buyers want more space in their houses for less money at the same time that they increase expenditures for cars, television, and recreation. Some sociological studies indicate that the house as a status symbol is losing importance. Indications are that lower-income groups derive status from automobiles, middle-income groups from culture and travel, and the rich from public and community service. On the other hand, there are many people who feel that a man's house is his castle, and they are willing to forego many other things in order to buy and maintain a house. Such decisions are now recognized as expressing personal preferences.

As you consider what you will want to do, the important thing is to identify your needs and long-range goals; buy if you are owner-oriented and have the financial means to meet the responsibilities that go with ownership. You will be expected to maintain your place at the same standard as others in the block, the neighborhood, and the community. For some families, keeping up with the Joneses creates financial and emotional problems.

How you feel about where you live and how much you can afford to pay will influence your final decision.

LEARNING EXPERIENCES

1. Form buzz groups to recall and analyze television programs that center around a family theme. Discuss the obvious personal values affected by where each family lives.
2. Identify the thirteen developing megalopolises and the three supercities projected by population experts. Locate and illustrate these on a map of the United States.
3. On a map of your geographic area use a color code to show city, suburbs, exurbs, and rural areas. Discuss the characteristics of each.
4. Read and evaluate the advertising for land, houses, and apartments in your local and nearby metropolitan papers to learn how much information is supplied to the reader looking for a place to live.
5. Identify the types of housing available in the area served by your school. On a map of the district show the location of single-family houses, duplex houses, apartments for rent, cooperative apartments, condominium apartments, town houses, mobile-home parks, and estates.
6. Add the location of schools, churches, libraries, parks, theaters, shopping centers, hospitals, clinics, and other public facilities to the map.
7. Read relevant materials and select students to participate in a symposium to present the pros and cons of renting, buying with a long-term mortgage, paying cash, buying into a cooperative, and buying into a condominium.
8. Interview someone familiar with zoning regulations, and if possible secure copies of local zoning ordinances, to learn the purpose and need for zoning. Organize a panel to report to the class on local, county, state, and federal zoning regulations.
9. Collect news articles relating to land use, community planning, building design, new construction methods, and new materials. Analyze the articles and discuss developing trends in housing.
10. Investigate the growth of the manufactured-house industry, and discuss the role of the mobile home and manufactured house in meeting housing needs.

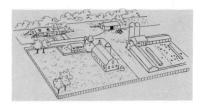

4

Financial Aspects

of Family Shelter

Determining the size and quality of living accomodations calls for a careful study of your income and spending patterns. For most people housing is the largest single item in the budget. Some general rules about the proportion of income that can be safely spent for a place to live have come to be generally accepted. If you rent, the monthly rent should not exceed one week's take-home pay; if you buy, the cost of the house should not exceed 2½ times your annual income. The Income Apportionment Index on page 67 shows the multiple needs and wants that must be paid for.

There is a vocabulary unique to financing the rental or purchase of real estate. While it is wise to depend on legal advisers when finalizing a lease or the purchase of property, it is important for everyone to have sufficient knowledge of commonly used terms to understand the general principles involved in renting or buying.

WHEN YOU RENT

A tenant must pay rent. In return he can use the leased premises in a manner similar to the way an owner would so long as he is in pos-

session. The landlord is expected to turn over the property to the tenant.

Rent. Rent is a fixed periodic payment made by an individual or family for the use of an apartment or house. Utilities and services, such as heat and water, may be included as a part of the rent. Many people do not understand the many factors involved in determining the rent for a piece of property. For an apartment, the first element is capital cost, meaning the cost of the land, the erection of the building, and other expenses related to construction. In addition, there are operation and maintenance expenses, insurance costs, taxes, renting and administration costs, and allowances for vacancies. Also, there are financial expenses, such as interest on money invested in the building and ground, depreciation and maintenance reserves, and last but not least, profit for the individual or corporation whose money is invested in the rental property.

Security deposits. Some landlords require a payment of the first and last month's rent before a tenant moves in. The rent for the last month is held by the landlord as security for the tenant's guarantee to leave the apartment in good condition when he moves out.

52

ROOMING HOUSE AGREEMENT
FOR USE IN APPROVED STUDENT HOMES

Read this entire contract carefully before signing. Use of this form is optional, but if executed, it will be enforced by the Housing Division. Familiarize yourself, also, with the Housing Regulations, a copy of which may be obtained at the Housing Division office, 420 Student Services Building, 610 East John Street, Champaign, Illinois 61820.

ONE SEMESTER AGREEMENT FOR RESIDENCE IN AN APPROVED STUDENT HOME WITH OPTION TO RENEW
Offered for use by the Housing Division of the University of Illinois

A. I,..., the undersigned student, agree to rent space in the room (as described in Part B) in the approved student home located at.., ...Champaign ....Urbana.

(Street Address)

DESCRIPTION AND LOCATION OF ROOM
Room is Numbered............

B.

Floor Location	Type of Accommodation	Room is Occupied by
............First Floor	............Study Room with Dormitory Sleeping	............One Student
............Second Floor	............Combined Study and Sleeping Room	............Two Students
............Third Floor	............Other (Explain............................	............Three Students
............Fourth Floor	....)	............Four Students

C. I, the undersigned student, further agree to pay the sum of...dollars ($................), this sum to be the full and complete charge for my use of the room for the semester commencing...19.......... (the day before the first official day of registration), and ending upon and including...19.......... (last day of scheduled examinations). This sum is payable as follows: $10.00 upon execution and delivery of this agreement as security, $................payable in installments as shown on the back hereof and according to Plan I. If, for any reason I fail to enroll in the University, it is agreed that the $10.00 security shall be forfeited to the house director unless I shall have served a notice in writing with the house director of my intention not to enroll at least twenty days before the first day of official registration.

D. I,..., the undersigned house director, agree to rent the room described above to the undersigned student for the semester herein designated upon the terms herein stated. I further agree to operate and maintain this student home in full compliance with all University Standards for Approved Student Homes and the Housing Regulations for student homes. I further agree to refund the $10.00 security upon receipt of the notice given in accordance with the conditions set forth in Paragraph C above.

E. The undersigned student and house director mutually agree to comply with the following conditions and rules:

1. Upon the termination of this agreement, this room will be available for rental to others unless the parties hereto execute a renewal of this agreement upon the form provided herein not less than two weeks nor more than six weeks before the termination of this agreement. It is further agreed that the renewal agreement shall be upon the same terms and conditions as this agreement except as to the date of the agreement, the semester rental charges, installment payment plan, and renewal.

2. Graduating seniors are permitted to retain the use of housing accommodations until five p.m. on Commencement Day without payment of additional rental.

3. Except in emergencies, in which case the Housing Division may be consulted directly, the student agrees to discuss his/her complaints concerning operation or maintenance of the student residence with the house director. In those instances in which a satisfactory settlement is not reached within a period of time agreed upon by both parties, the student shall then submit to the Housing Division and to the house director a written report concerning details of the complaint.

4. The measures to be taken to protect the student's personal property from loss or damage from any cause shall be a matter of agreemeht between the student and the house director.

5. Disputed claims by either party for loss or damage shall be referred promptly to the Housing Division whose determination of the amount of damage involved shall be final.

6. The use of heating units is prohibited. Electrical equipment, such as radios, electric clocks, record players, and electric fans, may be installed and operated upon the following terms and conditions:

....

....

7. The house director agrees to furnish all bedding except as follows:...

8. This approved student home is closed to students during the official Christmas vacation period. During such period, the student may leave his/her belongings in the room, but the student must vacate the premises unless there is a special agreement between the house director whereby the student may use the room during this period. If the space covered by contract is occupied by another during the Christmas vacation period (conditions of such occupancy outlined in Parts a, b, and c) the student is entitled to a deduction from or a refund of a proportionate part of rent.
   In order for the house director to permit some one person other than the student renter to occupy the room during the Christmas vacation period, the house director must:—
   Part a. Obtain permission in writing in advance from the student.
   Part b. Make adequate adjustment with the student with respect to rent for such period.
   Part c. Assume full responsibility for loss or damage of student's personal belongings in the room when the cause of such loss or damage is related in any way to the occupancy of such room by another.

9. This agreement may be terminated under any one of the following conditions:
   a. By mutual agreement between student renter and the house director, with notice in writing to the Housing Division.
   b. By providing another occupant acceptable to the house director together with the permission in writing of the Housing Division.
   c. By official withdrawal from the University after registration, regardless of the reason for such withdrawal.
   d. By incorporation in this agreement of any additional provision not included in the standard form, the Housing Division to be the sole judge of the validity of such alteration in or addition to the agreement.
   e. By material breach of any of the terms of this agreement, the Housing Division to be the judge of such materiality.
   f. By withdrawal of approval of the student home by the Housing Division of the University.
   g. By marriage of the student or by his/her public announcement of marriage for the first time after signing this agreement, termination of the agreement becoming effective when:
      (1) The student pays rent due to date of termination plus one-half of the rent remaining due for the balance of the semester, or
      (2) Another student occupant acceptable to the house director is provided and permission in writing is secured from the Housing Division.
   h. By the student's failure to register in the University.

10. If termination of this agreement is not obtainable by mutual consent of the parties hereto, termination may be sought in accordance with the following procedure:
   a. The party desiring to terminate shall file with the other party, with a copy thereof to the Housing Division, a notice in writing stating his intention to terminate.
   b. The Housing Division may then investigate the circumstances and determine whether reasonable grounds exist for terminating this agreement.
   c. If the decision of the Housing Division is unsatisfactory to either party, he or she may appeal to an Appeal Board appointed for the purpose of reviewing the decision. The Appeal Board shall consist of three persons, one selected by each of the parties to the Agreement. The third person shall be appointed by the Director of the Housing Division and shall be the Chairman of the Board.
   d. The decision of the Appeal Board shall be final.

11. This agreement may not be assigned without the written consent of the other parties thereto endorsed hereon.

12. This agreement shall become binding upon the parties hereto and in full force and effect only when signed by all the parties hereto, i.e., the student (if a minor, the parent's signature must also be affixed), and the house director.

13. The House Director is under no obligation to hold the specific room reservation beyond 12:00 noon of the last day of scheduled registration unless the student renter notifies the House Director by 12:00 noon of the last day of scheduled registration of his/her intention to occupy the space later.

SIGNED...

(Student Renter)

SIGNED...

(House Director)

* I hereby guarantee payment of this contract..

(Parent's Signature)

Agreement Dated:.....................................19..........   ....

(Address of Parent)

* If student renter is a minor, this agreement must have signature of parent.   **(OVER)**   O-1309

Courtesy Housing Division, University of Illinois

Room contract in use at a midwestern university.

Application for Lease

NOTICE OF TERMINATION OF TENANCY

If there is damage to be repaired, the cost comes from this deposit; if not, the money is refunded.

Lease. A lease is a legal document, or a contract, which generally is written. While a lease is a simple document as legal papers go, it should be dated, and it should identify the leased property. It is important that the landlord and the tenant each retain a copy of the lease which both have signed. There is no prescribed form for a lease. The word "lease" need not be used to create one. In many states, leases for one year or less need not be written.

Whether verbal or written, a lease sets forth the tenant's basic responsibilities and enumerates what may be expected from the landlord. Forms for leases may be bought at many stationery stores. The customary forms usually contain blank spaces for stating the rent to be paid, when it is payable, and the date the lease expires. Further provisions may be included which obligate the tenant to abide by

This Indenture, made this_____day of_____, A. D. Nineteen hundred_____

between _____party of the first part, lessor, and

_____party of the second part, lessee.

Witnesseth, that the said lessor, for and in consideration of the covenants and agreements hereinafter mentioned, and to be kept and performed by the said lessee, does hereby demise and lease to the lessee the premises, in the City of Chicago, County of Cook, and State of Illinois, known and described as follows, to-wit: Apartment _____on the_____floor of building known as_____

in said City of Chicago, to be occupied solely as a private dwelling and not otherwise.

To Have and to Hold, the above described premises, with the appurtenances, unto the said lessee from the _____day of_____A. D. 19____, until the_____day of_____A. D. 19____,

And the said party of the second part, in consideration of said demise, does covenant and agree with said party of the first part as follows:

FIRST.—To pay as rent for said demised premises the sum of_____DOLLARS per month, payable on date of commencement of said term and monthly thereafter in advance, until termination of this lease, as above provided, at the office of

Second.—That said lessee has examined and knows the condition of said premises and has received the same in good order and repair, except as herein otherwise specified, and that no representations as to the condition or repair thereof have been made by the party of the first part, or the agent of said party prior to or at the execution of this lease, that are not herein expressed or endorsed hereon; and upon the termination of this lease, in any way; will yield up said premises to said party of the first part in as good condition as when same were entered upon by said party of the second part, ordinary wear and tear and loss by fire only excepted.

any door, window or wall of the building, nor by advertising the same directly or indirectly, in any newspaper, or otherwise; that there shall be no lounging, sitting upon, or unnecessary tarrying in or upon the front steps, the sidewalk, railing, stairways, halls, landing or other public places of the said building by the said lessee, members of the family, or other persons connected with the occupancy of the demised premises; that no provisions, milk, ice, marketing, groceries or like merchandise, shall be taken into the demised premises through the front door of said building, except where there is no rear entrance; that said lessee and those occupying under said lessee, shall not interfere with the heating apparatus, or with the gas or other lights of said building which are not within the apartment hereby demised, nor with the control of any of the public portions of said building.

Sixth.—To allow the party of the first part free access at all reasonable hours to the premises hereby leased for the purpose of examining or exhibiting

the same, or to make any needful repairs on said premises which said first party may see fit to make; also to allow to have placed upon said premises, at all times, notice of "For Sale," and "To Rent," and will not interfere with the same. The lessee agrees to abide by all reasonable general rules of the building which shall be adopted by the lessor for cleanliness, good order and management in other respects than is herein provided; and all such rules and all amendments thereof shall be taken as of full force and effect from and after delivery of a copy thereof to the lessee.

Eleventh.—Said party of the first part agrees to pay all water rates assessed against said property and supply hot water for use of said tenant at all hot water faucets in said apartment, and the heat for the heating apparatus in said building. The heat is to be furnished at all reasonable hours, day or evening, when necessary, from the first day of October until the thirtieth of April of the succeeding year, but it is hereby understood and agreed that said lessor shall not be liable in damages for unavoidable delay or any other reasons whatsoever in not furnishing hot or cold water or heat for the heating apparatus; also in the event that there is not sufficient heat supplied, the party of the second part hereby waives any and all right to claim an eviction.

Twelfth.—The lessor shall not be liable for any loss or damage of or to any property placed in any store room or storage place in the building, such store room or storage place being furnished gratuitously and no part of the obligation of this lease.

SPECIAL CLAUSE.—Lessee hereby acknowledges receipt of the complete furnishings of the above described premises, as listed on the reverse side hereof, and agrees to deliver possession of same to lessor in good condition (ordinary wear excepted). Lessee further agrees to pay lessor in cash for any articles broken or missing at the expiration of this lease by lapse of time or otherwise.

Thirteenth.—IT IS EXPRESSLY AGREED, between the parties hereto, that if default be made in the payment above reserved or any part thereof, or in any of the covenants or agreements herein contained, to be kept by the party of the second part, it shall be lawful for and the party of the second part requests the party of the first part, or his legal representatives, at his or their election, to declare said term ended, to re-enter said demised premises or any part thereof and the said party of the second part or any other person or persons occupying the same to expel, remove and put out, using such force as he may deem necessary in so doing, and the said premises again to repossess and enjoy as in his first estate; and in order to enforce a forfeiture of this lease for default in any of its conditions it shall not be necessary to make demand or to serve notice on the party of the second part and said party of the second part hereby expressly waives all right to any demand or notice from said party of the first part of his election to declare this lease at an end or declaring is so to be; but the fact of the non-performance of any of the covenants of this lease, shall in itself, at the election of the party of the first part, without notice or demand constitute a forfeiture of said lease, and at any and all times, after such default, the said party of the second part shall be deemed guilty of a forcible detainer of said premises.

Fourteenth.—That in case said premises shall be rendered untenantable by fire or other casualty, the lessor may at his option terminate this lease, or repair said premises within thirty days, and failing so to do, or upon the destruction of said premises by fire, the term hereby created shall cease and determine.

Fifteenth.—The party of the second part hereby irrevocably constitutes any attorney of any Court of Record of this State, attorney for said lessee in lessee's name on default by lessee of any of the covenants herein, and upon complaint made by said first party, his agent or assigns, and filed in any such Court, to enter lessee's appearance in any such Court of Record, waive process and service thereof, and trial by jury, and confess judgment against lessee in favor of said party of the first part, or lessor's assigns for forcible detainer of said premises with cost of said suit; and also to enter lessee's appearance in such Court, waive process and service thereof, and confess judgment from time to time. for any rent which may be due to said party of the first part, or the assignees of the said party, by the terms of this lease, with costs, and reasonable attorney's fees, and to waive all errors and all right of appeal from said judgment and judgments and to file a consent in writing that a writ of restitution or other proper writ of execution may be issued immediately, said party of the second part hereby expressly waiving all right to any notice or demand under any statute of this State, relating to forcible entry and detainer.

Sixteenth.—IT IS FURTHER AGREED, by the parties hereto, that after the service of notice, or the commencement of a suit or after final judgment for possession of said premises, the first party may receive and collect any rent due, and the payment of said rent shall not waive or effect said notice, said suit, or said judgment.

The party of the second part further covenants and agrees to pay and discharge all reasonable costs, attorney's fees and expenses that shall be made and incurred by the party of the first part in enforcing the covenants and agreements of this lease.

Seventeenth.—IT IS HEREBY FURTHER EXPRESSLY STIPULATED AND AGREED, by and between the parties hereto, that the words "Lessor" and "Lessee" wherever herein occurring and used, shall be construed to mean "Lessors" and "Lessees" in case more than one person constitutes either party to this lease; and that all the covenants and agreements herein contained shall be binding upon, and inure to, their respective successors, heirs, executors, administrators and assigns and be exercised by his or their attorney or agent.

Witness the hands and seals of the parties hereto the day and year first above written.

In the presence of

_____ [SEAL]

_____ [SEAL]

_____ [SEAL]

An example of a lease for a furnished apartment.

the rules outlined by the landlord, to refrain from illegal or objectionable acts and from assigning the lease or subletting the apartment, and to turn in the keys when he moves.

"Subletting" means rerenting. Under a sublet, the original renter remains the landlord's tenant at the same time that he becomes the landlord to the person renting from him. If the landlord allows a sublet clause in the lease, he sometimes requires a percentage increase in the rent.

Renewal of a lease. A tenant does not automatically renew his lease by staying on in the apartment. The landlord's agreement is necessary. His consent does not have to be formal, and it can be implied by his accepting the rent. How long the implied renewal is good depends on the terms of the original lease. If the lease is for a year, the implied renewal is for a year, even though the yearly rental was paid in monthly installments. But if the specified lease is monthly, the renewed occupancy will be month-to-month. Some forms include a provision that the lease will be renewed for another full term unless the management is notified, in writing, thirty or sixty days before the lease expires, that renewal is not wanted. Some leases automatically renew unless this written notice is given.

Terminating a lease. When the landlord chooses not to permit renewal, he can notify the tenant to vacate. The notice required varies from state to state. If the tenant refuses to move, the landlord can collect double rent in some states and triple rent in at least one state. A landlord can also evict a tenant, but this involves legal action.

WHEN YOU BUY

The vocabulary used for ownership of real estate is different from that used for renting. The terms that follow are explained in nontechnical language.

Mortgage. A mortgage is a written agreement showing that the real estate described in the document is given as security for the repayment of a loan. The borrower is the mortgagor; the lender the mortgagee. When a piece of real property is mortgaged to secure a loan, the borrower generally gives the lender a mortgage, and a note or a bond. The effect of the

mortgage on the title to the property depends on the laws of the state where the real estate is located.

The mortgage need not be in any particular form nor contain any particular words. However, to be valid, it should include the following essential items:

1. The names of the borrower and the lender, along with an indication of the borrower's marital status.

2. A statement of the debt, including the amount, interest rate, date payable, maturity date, and documentary evidence of the debt

3. The legal description of the real estate used to secure the debt

4. The signature of the borrower and his spouse, plus the seal and signature of witnesses in states where these are required by law

There are other provisions that are not essential to the legal validity of the mortgage but which should be included. These items are (1) the date the papers were signed, (2) a statement of money paid to bind the deal, (3) an agreement that the borrower will pay taxes and assessments upon the property and carry insurance on it, and (4) a warranty of title. Such a title is issued to the borrower by an insurance company to protect him against loss resulting from an invalid title. In addition, it is possible to write in special provisions regarding foreclosure procedures, building restrictions, and many other details. A mortgage should always be recorded in the county clerk's office.

FHA-insured loan. In an FHA-insured loan, the United States government, through the Federal Housing Administration, insures the lender against loss in case the borrower fails to pay. Because of this guarantee, lending institutions tend to accept smaller down payments. The percentage of a mortgage guaranteed by the Federal Housing Administration varies with the amount of the mortgage. Rulings on this change from time to time, depending on the money market. An FHA loan may be insured up to 93 percent of the appraised value. For this reason, FHA loans tend to require a smaller down payment than conventional loans.

Veterans Administration guaranteed loan. A veteran must obtain a certificate of eligibility

CHICAGO TITLE AND TRUST COMPANY

for valuable consideration, does hereby guarantee the owner, from time to time, of the indebtedness described in the trust deed noted in item 2 of Schedule A against all loss or damage which such owner shall sustain by reason of defects in the title of the mortgagor (or mortgagors), which title is set forth in item 1 of Schedule A, to the real estate described in item 3 of Schedule A, or by reason of liens or incumbrances affecting the title, at the date of this policy, excepting only such defects, liens, incumbrances and other matters as are set forth in Schedule B.

This Company also guarantees that the signatures to the trust deed described in item 2 of Schedule A are the genuine signatures of the grantors therein, and that the trust deed was properly acknowledged by the grantors, and that, in case the grantor is a corporation, the officers who signed the trust deed on behalf of the corporation were authorized so to do by its board of directors.

This Company agrees to defend, at its own cost and expense, the title, estate or interest hereby guaranteed in all actions or other proceedings which are founded upon, or in which is asserted by way of defense, a defect, claim, lien or incumbrance against which this policy guarantees.

The total liability of this Company under this policy is limited to the amount of policy shown in Schedule A, exclusive of costs and expenses of defending the title, estate or interest guaranteed.

This policy is subject to the conditions set forth on the last page hereof, which conditions, together with Schedules A and B, are made a part of this policy.

In Witness Whereof, CHICAGO TITLE AND TRUST COMPANY has caused its corporate seal to be hereto affixed and these presents to be signed by its President and attested by its Assistant Secretary, on the date of policy shown in Schedule A.

Paul W. Goodrich President.

ATTEST:

Assistant Secretary.

A mortgage title guarantee policy.

CHART 1. MONTHLY PAYMENTS REQUIRED TO AMORTIZE A LOAN

Interest	Amount	10 Years	15 Years	20 Years	25 Years
6%	$ 5,000	$ 55.52	$ 42.20	$ 35.83	$ 32.22
	10,000	111.03	84.39	71.65	64.44
	15,000	116.54	126.58	107.47	96.65
	20,000	222.05	168.78	143.29	128.87
7%	$ 5,000	$ 58.06	$ 44.95	$ 38.77	$ 35.34
	10,000	116.11	89.89	77.53	70.68
	15,000	174.17	134.83	116.30	106.02
	20,000	232.22	179.77	155.06	141.36
7½%	$ 5,000	$ 59.36	$ 46.36	$ 40.28	$ 36.95
	10,000	118.71	92.71	80.56	73.90
	15,000	178.06	139.06	120.84	110.85
	20,000	237.41	185.41	161.12	147.80
8%	$ 5,000	$ 60.67	$ 47.79	$ 41.83	$ 38.60
	10,000	121.33	95.57	83.65	77.19
	15,000	182.00	143.35	125.47	115.78
	20,000	242.66	191.14	167.29	154.37
8½%	$ 5,000	$ 62.00	$ 49.24	$ 43.40	$ 40.27
	10,000	123.99	98.48	86.79	80.53
	15,000	185.98	147.72	130.18	120.79
	20,000	247.98	196.95	173.57	161.05

from the Veterans Administration as a first step toward getting a guaranteed loan. The property must have VA appraisal, after which a Certificate of Reasonable Value (CRV) is issued. Government guarantees make it possible for a veteran to get a loan with little or no down payment and a low interest rate. The inspection and paper work necessary for a VA loan take at least five weeks to complete.

Conventional mortgages. This term refers to a two-party loan between lender and borrower which is not backed by any government insurance or guarantee. Conventional loans may be straight loans or amortized loans. The re-

payment schedule is usually worked out between the borrower and the lender on an individual basis. Conventional loans require a down payment ranging from 10 to 35%. This may vary with the availability of mortgage money, the competition in the area, and the financial position of the borrower.

Amortization. Mortgages are commonly reduced, or amortized, by paying the interest and a part of the principal at regular intervals in equal payments. When these payments are made on a monthly basis, the transaction is called the "direct reduction monthly payment plan." Generally the mortgage payment in-

THIS MEMORANDUM WITNESSETH, THAT seller,_____

_____,

hereby agrees to SELL, and purchaser,_____,

agrees to PURCHASE, at the price of_____

_____Dollars,

the following described real estate, situated in_____County, Illinois:

Subject to: (1) existing leases, expiring_____
the purchaser to be entitled to the rents, if any, from the time of delivery of Deed; (2) all taxes and assessments levied after the year 19_____; (3) any unpaid special taxes or assessments, levied for improvements not yet made; also subject to:

Purchaser has paid_____Dollars,
as earnest money, to be applied on said purchase when consummated, and agrees to pay, within five days after the title has been examined and found good, the further sum of_____
_____Dollars,
at the office of_____, provided a good and
sufficient_____Warranty Deed, conveying to purchaser a good title to said premises with waiver and conveyance of any and all estates of homestead therein and all rights of dower, inchoate or otherwise, (subject as aforesaid), shall then be ready for delivery. The balance to be paid as follows:

with interest_____at the rate of_____per cent per annum, payable semi-annually, to be secured by notes and mortgage, or trust deed, of even date herewith, on said premises, in the form _____. Seller shall furnish within a reasonable time a certificate of title issued by the Registrar of Titles of_____County or a complete merchantable abstract of title, or a merchantable copy, brought down to date, or a merchantable title insurance policy (or commitment) of _____ brought down to date. In case the title upon examination, is found materially defective, within ten days after said abstract, certificate of title or title insurance policy (or commitment) is furnished, then, unless the material defects be cured within sixty days after written notice thereof, the said earnest money shall be refunded and this contract is to become inoperative.

Seller warrants to purchaser that no notice from any city, village or other governmental authority of any dwelling code violation has heretofore been issued and received by the owner or his agent with respect to any dwelling structure on said real estate.

Should purchaser fail to perform this contract promptly on his part, at the time and in the manner herein specified, the earnest money paid as above shall, at the option of seller, be forfeited as liquidated damages, and this contract shall be and become null and void. Time is of the essence of this contract, and of all the conditions thereof.

This contract and the said earnest money shall be held by_____
_____for the mutual benefit of the parties hereto.

In testimony whereof, said parties hereto set their hands, this_____day of_____, 19_____.

_____(SEAL)   _____(SEAL)

_____(SEAL)   _____(SEAL)

A real estate sales contract.

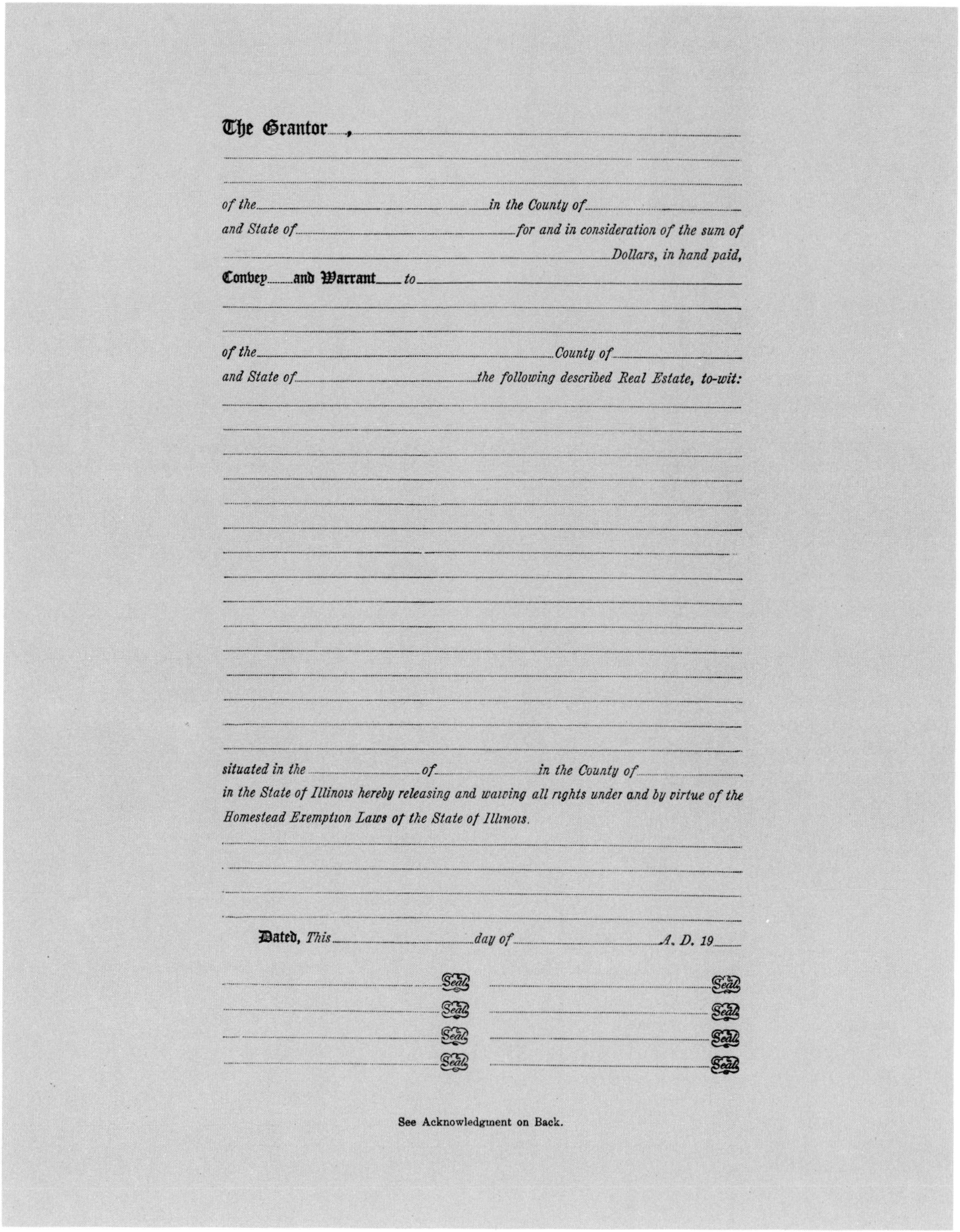

𝕿𝖍𝖊 𝕲𝖗𝖆𝖓𝖙𝖔𝖗___, _____

_____

of the_____in the County of_____

and State of_____for and in consideration of the sum of

_____Dollars, in hand paid,

𝕮𝖔𝖓𝖛𝖊𝖞___𝖆𝖓𝖉 𝖂𝖆𝖗𝖗𝖆𝖓𝖙___ to_____

_____

of the_____County of_____

and State of_____the following described Real Estate, to-wit:

_____

_____

_____

_____

_____

_____

_____

_____

_____

_____

_____

situated in the_____of_____in the County of_____,

in the State of Illinois hereby releasing and waiving all rights under and by virtue of the

Homestead Exemption Laws of the State of Illinois.

_____

_____

_____

𝕯𝖆𝖙𝖊𝖉, This_____day of_____A. D. 19_____

_____ Seal   _____ Seal

_____ Seal   _____ Seal

_____ Seal   _____ Seal

_____ Seal   _____ Seal

See Acknowledgment on Back.

A warranty deed.

cludes the mortgage insurance charge, taxes, special assesments, and hazard insurance.

Federal Housing Administration and Veterans Administration loans and many conventional loans are of the level payment plan. In this plan the borrower pays a fixed amount each month for the entire period of the loan. Part of this payment is applied to the interest and part to the principal. In this way the amount applied to principal increases with each payment, while the amount applied to interest decreases. This is a common example of amortization.

Straight loan. Some loans on real estate are made for a definite number of years at a specified interest rate with no payment made to the principal until the due date, when the loan is payable in full. This type of loan is usually made for short periods of time, from three to five years, and may be renewable. However, straight loan is seldom used in family situations because of the hardship imposed by the lump sum payment of principal at the end of the loan period.

Open-end mortgage. Any mortgage which contains a clause providing that the mortgage is to secure not only the original debt, but also any additional advances that may be made by the lender, is called an open-end mortgage. This type of financing makes it possible for the home buyer to use long-term financing for improvements after he has paid off part of the original debt without a great deal of additional paper work or expense. The maximum amount to which an open-end mortgage may be raised is usually stated in the original contract.

Second mortgage. When financing real estate by means of a junior mortgage that is secondary to the first mortgage, the junior mortgage is a second mortgage. A second mortgage was not uncommon when loans were limited to 50% of the value of the property, but since first mortgages have become larger (up to 93 percent of the loan with some FHA-insured mortgages), the second mortgage has almost disappeared. However, if a second mortgage is used, the first mortgage takes priority in the event the buyer defaults.

Principal. The amount of money loaned or invested is the principal. In relation to housing, this is the amount of money invested in land and building which may be rented or sold.

Interest. Money that is paid by the borrower for the use of capital is interest. The amount of interest is based on (1) the principal, or the amount of debt on which the interest is to be paid, (2) the time, or the duration of the loan, and (3) the rate of interest which is the percentage of principal that is to be paid each period. The maximum rate of interest that can be charged is governed by law. A mortgage should include a statement fixing the rate of interest and a schedule of payments.

Sale of property. Installment contracts, contracts for deed, sales contracts, and other names may be applied in situations where the buyer makes a small down payment and follows with regular payments of a fixed amount at regular intervals. This agreement between the buyer and seller usually provides a clause which states that when a certain percentage of the purchase price has been paid, title will be delivered, subject to a mortgage for the balance due.

Contracts make it possible for people to buy with a down payment that would be too small to qualify for a mortgage. Many people are excellent risks but lack the down payment required under the purchase-money-mortgage plan of financing. In some states the seller remains the owner of the property until the buyer is entitled to a deed. In states where this is true, failure to make a payment gives the owner the right to repossess the property through a relatively simple, short legal procedure. In this case the payments made by the buyer are kept by the seller as liquidated damages, or as rent. In other states the unpaid balance is considered a security interest similar to a mortgage, and the seller is limited to the same legal actions that he would have had in the case of a mortgage.

Deed. Ownership of a piece of property is transferred from the seller to the purchaser by means of a legal paper known as a deed. When the deed is turned over to the buyer, the seller gives up the use of the property along with responsibility for its condition. Not all deeds are the same. The contract of sale usually specifies the kind of deed that will be required to transfer title to the property. War-

CHECK-LIST FOR CLOSING REAL ESTATE DEALS

PROPERTY: BROKER:

SELLER: ATTORNEY FOR SELLER:

BUYER: ATTORNEY FOR BUYER:

DATE OF CLOSING:

CHECK ✓		REMARKS
	CONTRACT EXAMINED	
	LETTER OF OPINION, ABSTRACT OR TORRENS CTF.	
	AFFIDAVIT OF TITLE	
	1ST MORTGAGE AND NOTE; 2ND MTG. & NOTE	
	LEASES AND ASSIGNMENTS. NOTICES	
	INSTRUMENT OF CONVEYANCE (DEED)	
	REVENUE STAMPS	
	BILL OF SALE FOR PERSONAL PROPERTY	
	REFRIGERATOR AND ROOF GUARANTEES	
	INSURANCE POLICIES	
	ASSIGNMENTS OF INSURANCE	
	RENT REGISTRATION CERTIFICATES	
	LETTERS TO TENANTS	
	POSSESSION—DELIVERY OF KEYS	

ITEMS PRO-RATED

CHECK ✓		
	PURCHASE PRICE	
	EARNEST MONEY	
	TAXES AND SPECIAL ASSESSMENTS	
	1st MORTGAGE; 2nd MORTGAGE	
	INTEREST	
	RENTS	
	FUEL	
	JANITOR (INCL. VACATION PERIOD)	
	SALARIES	
	WATER BILLS	
	ELECTRIC AND GAS	
	EXTERMINATOR	
	SCAVENGER SERVICE	

FINAL SETTLEMENT

CHECK ✓		
	PAYMENT OF BALANCE OF PURCHASE PRICE	
	RECEIPT FOR PAYMENT	
	ESCROW AGREEMENT	
	COMMISSION	
	RECORDING	
	TITLE CHARGES	
	CLOSING STATEMENT	

ADDITIONAL ITEMS

Cross out items not applicable.
Insert additional items when required.

Check ✓ each item as completed.
Retain check-list in your file.

ranty deeds, covenants of title, and quitclaim deeds each have certain characteristics. The first two give the greatest protection to the purchaser, while the quitclaim places the least responsibility on the seller. The type of deed should be a matter of negotiation between the buyer and the seller.

When all stipulations have been met, the deed is delivered to the purchaser. In some cases the deed is delivered to a disinterested third person to take effect when some condition is met by one of the parties. This is known as a delivery in escrow. Printed forms of deeds may be obtained from stationers or title companies for study. However, it is usually advisable to consult an attorney before actually using such a document.

Escrow. The interests of both the buyer and seller can be protected by making use of an escrow. The escrow holder, usually a bank, records the deed and mortgage and pays the seller. Escrow agreements are actually conditional deliveries of property to a third person to be held until specific agreements have been completed.

Taxes. Governing bodies, public schools, libraries, forest preserves, and parks are supported by a *general property tax.* This tax differs from an *assessment* in that it is payable every year, while an assessment generally is levied only once. The amount of tax depends upon the services provided by the various levels of government. The borrower is obligated to pay the taxes and assessments on mortgaged property. If the taxes are not paid, the taxing agency may sell the property as a tax sale.

Closing costs. Besides the down payment on the house, the buyer must pay certain charges that are referred to as "closing costs." Some of the items normally included in the closing costs are the fee charged by the buyer's attorney, the mortgage recording fee, the mortgage tax, an advance payment on hazard insurance, and an appraisal fee.

Appraisal. Many banks and building and loan associations include on their staffs men who are experts at estimating the value of real estate. Training and experience qualify these people to evaluate and establish a fair market price for renting or selling a particular piece of property; to establish a basis for a mortgage loan; to establish the tax base for real estate; and to determine the amount of insurance needed. In the process of making an appraisal, it is a general practice to take into consideration general data about the city, such as population trends, employment trends, transportation facilities, social and cultural institutions, zoning and building controls, and housing conditions in general.

The appraiser collects specific data on the property, including the site, the building, comparable property, photographs of the exterior, and blueprints showing the floor plan. He analyzes the data and considers all the factors affecting the value of the property to arrive at an estimate, and he prepares an appraisal report. Appraisal reports may be made in a variety of forms. It is important that the report form be acceptable to the agency for which it is being prepared.

Basis for Credit

Character, current credit rating, present financial position, and capacity to earn are important assets when shopping for housing credit, whether it is a lease or a mortgage. When you start to earn money, you should make a plan for spending that will include both short-term and long-range goals; for instance, an apartment next year and a house in the suburbs in ten years. Then estimate how much you will need to set aside regularly to achieve these goals.

Philosophy about Debt

Financial planning is essentially the practice of looking ahead and making plans to get what is wanted with the money you have to spend. Generally speaking, only the income of the head of the family is used as the basis for determining how much you can borrow to finance a place to live. It may be advisable at this point to review the fixed and flexible expenses that must be covered by the disposable income left after taxes and business-related deductions. This may also be the time when the family sits down together to identify and determine the relative importance of individual and collective goals, both immediate and long range. Personal values will influence whether you look for a short-term or a long-term mort-

CLOSING STATEMENT

PROPERTY   BROKER

SELLER   ADDRESS

PURCHASER   ADDRESS

DATE OF CONTRACT   DATE OF CLOSING

	CREDIT PURCHASER	CREDIT SELLER
Purchase Price		
Earnest Money		
First Mortgage		
Interest		
Second Mortgage		
Interest		
General Taxes 19		
General Taxes 19 pro rated from to		
Special Assessments		
Special Assessments		
Insurance premiums, Unearned (see statement on reverse side)		
Rents from to		
Coal tons @ $		
Janitor from to		
Water Taxes from to		
Gas & Light from to		
Check or cash to Balance		
TOTAL		

SETTLEMENT	DEBIT	CREDIT
Balance as above		
Earnest Money		
Abstract or Guaranty Policy		
Recording fees		
Commission		
Balance		
Total		

Accepted   Accepted

_____   _____

gage. There are arguments favoring each. The final decision must rest with the purchaser.

Short-term mortgage. Accepting the fact that a mortgage is a debt, and recognizing that interest is money paid for the use of money, tends to make some people look for a relatively short-term loan that will build an investment fast and get them out of debt quickly. Reference books include charts that make the arithmetic of borrowing costs clear. Short-term mortgages cost less than long-term ones because the debt is paid off faster by making larger monthly payments than is a long-term mortgage for the same amount. For the person who expects to buy the house he mortgages and ultimately enjoy the advantages of debt-free ownership, the short-term mortgage will build an investment fast and save thousands of dollars in interest payments.

Long-term mortgage. In contrast to those who want to reduce a mortgage as fast as possible, there is another group who prefer a long-term mortgage with the smallest possible monthly payment. The attitude of this type of buyer may be similar to that of a renter. It is often possible to provide more adequate housing for the family by using a long-term mortgage than is available on the rental market. Some buyers consider the fact that interest paid on the mortgage is tax deductible. While this is true, it must also be kept in mind that the interest is an added expense.

Private Sources for Money

There is no one best place to borrow money to pay for your house. Banks, savings and loan associations, and private lenders are in the business of making money by lending money. The prudent borrower will shop for the best deal that suits his financial situation.

Commercial banks. Commercial banks are business corporations operated by and for stockholders. There are two types of commercial banks: national banks that are chartered by the Comptroller of the Currency and state banks that operate under charters issued by the state. A national bank may be restricted in its lending program. For example, at a certain time a national bank might grant straight loans for no more than 50 percent of the appraised value and for a period of no more than five years. Amortized loans might be for 75 percent of the appraised value for up to thirty years. State laws vary greatly, ranging from no restrictions to restrictions similar to those for national banks.

Savings and loan associations. Savings and loan associations are the largest single source of financing for single-family houses. In some areas the name used for basically the same organization may be building and loan association, homestead association, or cooperative bank. All are forms of cooperative lending institutions or mutuals. As semipublic financial institutions, they are subject to supervision by

CHART 2. LONG-TERM MORTGAGES COST MORE

The longer-term loan costs less per month but more by the time the loan is paid in full. The excess over $12,000 mortgage is interest.

Amount of Mortgage	Term of Loan	Monthly Payment	Total Payment	Total Interest	Percent of Principal
$12,000	15 years	$98.16	$17,649	$ 5,694	47%
$12,000	20 years	$82.56	$19,811	$ 7,811	65%
$12,000	25 years	$73.80	$22,107	$10,107	84%
$12,000	30 years	$64.56	$24,528	$12,528	104%

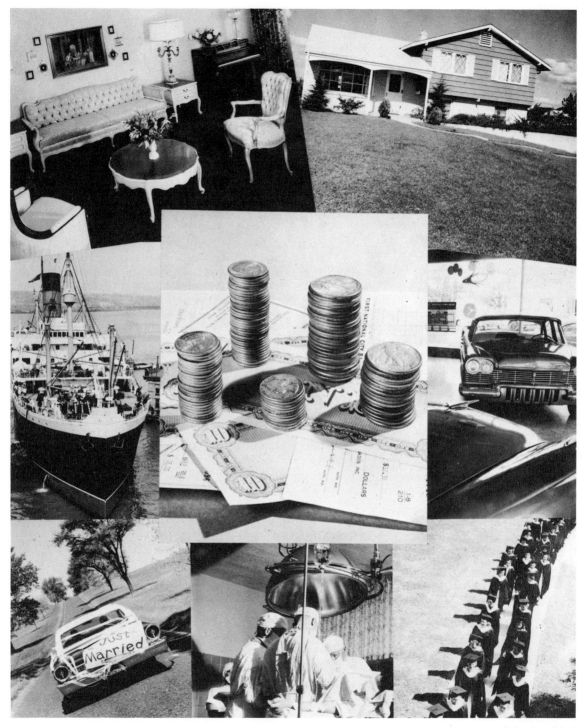

Income must be budgeted to cover many expenses.

INCOME APPORTIONMENT INDEX

The following list suggests some of the common demands on personal or family income. It may help in money management planning.

Housing
Rent
Mortgages
Taxes
Equipment
Maintenance
Improvement

Savings
Bank
Savings and loan association
Credit union
U.S. government securities
Growth investment
  Stocks
  Bonds

Operating Expenses
Income taxes
Retirement payments
Supplies
Water
Fuel
Gas
Electricity
Telephone
Transportation
Laundry
Services
Postage
Banking charges

Allowances
Head of the family
Homemaker
Children and other dependents

Food
Meat, fish, and poultry
Milk, cheese, and other dairy foods
Fruits and vegetables
Breads and cereals
Delicacies
Eating out

Insurance
Life
Health
Income protection
Accident
Liability
Home
Possessions

Health and Personal Care
Accessories
Toilet and grooming aids
Professional services
Illness and disability
Remedies
Birth expenses
Baby care needs
Death and burial

Indebtedness
Principle
Interest
Carrying charges
Finance charges
  Fees
  Credit investigation
  Appraisal

Furnishings
Purchases
Maintenance

Wearing Apparel
Purchases
Maintenance

Automobile
Purchase
Insurance
License
Operation
Repairs
Equipment
Garage and parking fees

Recreation, Advancement, and Community Improvement
Entertainment
Sports
Hobbies
Plants and garden supplies
Pets
Entertaining
Liquor
Tobacco
Vacation
Radio, television, and phonograph equipment
Periodicals
Books
Dues
Instruction
Church
Civic contributions
Gifts

both state and federal agencies. In 1934, Congress established the Federal Savings and Loan Insurance Corporation which currently protects all depositors in federal associations for individual accounts of up to $15,000. This amount may vary with the national prosperity.

Individuals. The rise of the long-term amortized mortgage has reduced the importance of the individual in real estate financing. However, in many areas real estate brokers will help buyers contact those interested in buying mortgages. In areas where mortgage capital is limited, the individual investor has a more important role than he has in areas where more choices are available.

Government Sources of Money

Several federal organizations provide services which assist private citizens and local governments in the financing of housing. Operating under these organizations are secondary financing agencies.

The Department of Housing and Urban Development embraces numerous activities in community housing situations and, through its agency the Federal Housing Administration, makes loans available for public and private residential construction.

The Veterans Administration, under the GI Bill of Rights and subsequent legislation, has a broad home construction and modernization loan program.

The Department of Agriculture, through its agency the Farmers Home Administration has a comprehensive loan program for homes and farms.

Department of Housing and Urban Development. The U.S. Department of Housing and Urban Development was established November 9, 1965, to administer a wide range of federal programs relating to housing and urban areas.

Among these programs are urban renewal, urban beautification, housing for the elderly and handicapped, urban mass transportation, neighborhood facilities, model cities, loans and grants for low-rent housing, and mortgage insurance for private home and multifamily construction and modernization.

Family home financing. To help families undertake home ownership on a sound basis, the Federal Housing Administration, which is part of the Department of Housing and Urban Development, insures mortgages to finance the purchase of one- to four-family homes.

In general, any person with a good credit record, the cash needed to initiate the transaction, and enough regular income to make monthly mortgage payments may apply to an approved lending institution for an FHA insured mortgage.

Full information on FHA insurance for small homes may be obtained from the many insuring offices of FHA in principal cities as well as at local banks and building and loan associations.

Several other FHA programs offer financing for rental and cooperative housing for families with low and moderate incomes. Full information on these and other programs may be obtained from the U.S. Department of Housing and Urban Development, Washington, D.C.

Veterans Administration. Under the G.I. Bill of Rights, the Veterans Administration insures loans made by public or private lenders and,

In many cities large high-rise apartments are replacing slum housing for low-income families.

H. Armstrong Roberts

68

under certain conditions, makes direct loans to qualified veterans.

World War II veterans who served in the Armed Forces between September 16, 1940, and July 25, 1947, and were honorably discharged, and any person who served in the Armed Forces anywhere in the world after June 26, 1950, and before February 1, 1955, including Korea, may be able to secure a G.I. loan as late as January 31, 1975.

Two major laws have provided benefits to veterans of service since January 31, 1955: the Veterans' Readjustment Benefits Act of 1966 and the Veterans' Pension and Readjustment Assistance Act of 1967. The latter provides additional benefits to veterans of the Vietnam era, defined as the period beginning August 5, 1964. The Vietnam era is considered a period of wartime, providing benefits to eligible veterans like those granted to veterans of Korea. Since there is sometimes overlapping between the various laws, it is always advisable to check with your local VA office to see which benefits you might be entitled to.

G.I. loans may be made to purchase, build, alter, or repair a home to be occupied by a veteran; to buy a farm or farm equipment; or to purchase a business. What will be done for veterans in the future will depend on congressional action and will be reported in the press.

Farmers Home Administration. The Farmers Home Administration, an agency of the U.S. Department of Agriculture, makes and insures rural housing loans. These loans are made to farmers and other residents of rural areas and small rural communities of not more than 5,500 population. Funds may be used to finance dwellings, building sites, and essential farm service buildings. Loans are made only to applicants unable to obtain credit from private lenders. Applications from veterans are given preference.

The agency also makes loans for farm and home operating expenses, for buying and developing family farms, for water development and soil conservation, for rural water and waste disposal systems, for developing small watershed projects, and for emergency credit needs.

An applicant inquires at the county Farmers Home Administration office serving the area in which he expects to buy or improve a farm or nonfarm tract.

Secondary markets for mortgages. The Federal National Mortgage Association, an agency of the Department of Housing and Urban Development, provides a national secondary market for FHA-insured and VA-guaranteed mortgages by buying, servicing, and selling such mortgages. Rural housing loans insured by the Farmers Home Administration of the Department of Agriculture (FHDA loans) are also bought and sold.

FNMA also provides funds, under its special assistance functions, for a number of special-purpose programs. The effect of FNMA's operations is to increase the amount of housing money available.

Lists of mortgages and FHDA loans available for sale are obtainable from FNMA offices.

Federal Home Loan Bank System. Operating under the executive branch of the government, the Federal Home Loan Bank System provides local thrift and home-financing institutions with a dependable source of credit when supplementary funds are needed for mortgage loans. By so strengthening the structure of the home-financing industry, the system reaches into every area and locality. Its benefits extend to millions of savers and homeowners. Members of the system are savings and loan associations, savings banks, and insurance companies.

Supervising the system is the Federal Home Loan Bank Board, which operates through eleven regional Federal Home Loan Banks. These banks supply local member institutions with credit to smooth their operations and enhance their service to the public.

SUBSIDIZED HOUSING

Public money is used to assist private investors to build housing when it is determined that doing so would be advantageous to the public. Among the groups benefiting from public housing are low-income families, those living on pensions or limited savings, and personnel of the armed services who are eligible for housing allotments.

Private sources often provide housing which may be considered to be subsidized. For example, some colleges and universities furnish housing for their faculties and staffs. Private

Interior views of apartments designed for low-income elderly families.

businesses located where private housing is not available often furnish housing for their employees.

The Ninetieth Congress passed legislation that brought decent housing within the reach of thousands of families whose incomes range from $3,000 to $7,300 annually. This is done by means of supplements that cut the monthly mortgage payments to a level the family can afford. The act also brings rental housing within the range of low-income families by providing a rent supplement. The act also provides for expanded insurance programs under FHA. Still another phase of the act provides the means for middle-income families to acquire vacation homes. There are also provisions for making grants to families displaced by slum-clearance projects. The law will affect many families as its vast and complicated provisions are put into operation.

BUYING THE MOBILE HOME

The price of a mobile home is based on the quality, the number of appliances, and the elaborateness of the furnishings. The market provides a wide range of models within reach of most income levels, from a modest home at $4,000 to more elaborate models at $10,000 to $12,000. The cost of a mobile home is about $8 per square foot for one with major appliances and furniture. An unfurnished site-built house costs approximately $14 per square foot.

For people who move frequently, the cost of transporting furniture and household goods can be a large expense. In a mobile home the furnishings are moved with the unit; however, the cost of moving a mobile home is an expense which the mobile family should also consider.

Financing. Most mobile-home purchases are financed like the purchase of a car. Most dealers require a down payment of one-third or one-fourth of the retail price. The balance is payable monthly over a period of up to 120 months. A single purchase provides a dwelling, insurance, furniture, and appliances. This may be the most economical way for the very mobile and for those with a limited income to meet their housing needs.

LEARNING EXPERIENCES

1. Define the following words in relation to housing: amortize, appraisal, collateral, contract, credit, debt, deed, escrow, guarantee, insure, interest, lease, mortgage, planned spending.

2. Examine sample budgets and discuss the use of income to meet the needs of the family in general and housing in particular.

3. Identify the expenses that need to be paid from the money budgeted for housing. Discuss the factors that cause these expenses to vary between families in the same age group.

4. Identify and discuss the housing costs included in a rent payment.

5. Identify and discuss expenses related to home ownership.

6. Discuss the situations under which renting may have advantages over home ownership.

7. Discuss the situations where buying a house or an apartment has advantages over renting. Can you make a firm recommendation that it is always best to rent or buy?

8. Collect and study applications for a lease, contracts to buy a house, and mortgage forms being used in your community. Discuss the features common to all and the specific features unique to each type of document.

9. Individually, or in groups, prepare a bulletin board that shows the unique services of banks, savings and loan associations, and private lenders in financing home loans.

10. Prepare an interview form concerning housing costs, interview renters and home-owners, and report your findings to the class.

5

Evaluating the
Ready-built House

MANY WRITERS believe it is impossible to find a house which exactly meets a family's needs because needs are changing constantly. Robert W. Murray, Jr., Deputy Director of the Division of Public Affairs of the Department of Housing and Urban Development, has written that everyone goes through ten stages of housing:

1. The first eighteen years living at home with parents
2. The second shorter period living away from home at school or with the military service
3. The third interval of the unmarried worker living in his apartment
4. The fourth phase of young marrieds with both working
5. The fifth stage involving the family with preschool children who need fairly constant supervision
6. The sixth stage involving parents who are glad to have their preteen children close by but not under foot
7. The seventh period when teen-agers need a place for active living and parents want a quiet place, away from the action, to relax

8. The eighth stage when the children are married and parents look for less responsibility with house and yard and greater convenience to work and recreation
9. The ninth phase when the parents seek the associations and comforts of retirement
10. The tenth, statistically probable phase, when the widow moves to an apartment close to her children and grandchildren

THE CHOICE OF A LOT

The buyer may or may not have a choice in selecting the lot on which his house is built. In some developments buyers have a choice between the same model house on a corner or on a center block lot. A lot that allows a view of a public playground, golf course, or park may have an advantage over a lot that does not have a view.

A lot on a cul-de-sac, or dead-end street, has the advantage of having no intersection of streets carrying through traffic. The front yard, facing a cul-de-sac, may be reduced to a minimum. This smaller front yard may also reduce assessments based on the front footage of prop-

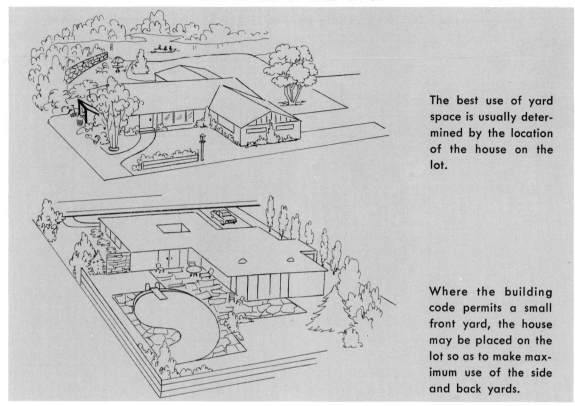

The best use of yard space is usually determined by the location of the house on the lot.

Where the building code permits a small front yard, the house may be placed on the lot so as to make maximum use of the side and back yards.

erty. While the front yard is smaller, the yard to the back of the house may be larger and more adaptable to outdoor living.

It is desirable to have the service area of the yard located to one side of the house, preferably in an inconspicuous spot or where plantings or fences can be used to form a screen for the work area. If cost is not a factor, a wide lot is usually preferable to a long narrow lot because it is easier to landscape and more useful for outdoor living.

The position of the house on the lot will affect how much the outdoor living space can be used. If there is a choice, it is desirable to have the house placed so that there is a minimum yard on the approach, or street side, a minimum side yard on one side of the house, and a wider side yard on the other side connecting with an ample rear yard for use in outdoor living. While it is more difficult to make good use of narrow

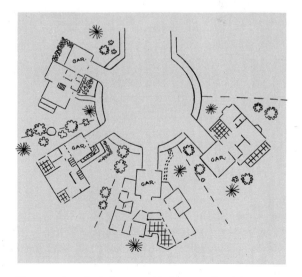

Houses located in a cul-de-sac furnish many safety advantages which are especially attractive to families with young children.

Most children spend the years between infancy and adulthood in the home of their parents. The first experience of living away from their parents may come when young people undertake further training at school or in the service. The increasing number of single-family households may be explained by the number of unmarried workers who have their own apartments. When husband and wife both work, they may want housing close to their jobs. The arrival of a child creates a need for more space. Preteen children need space and equipment for active games.

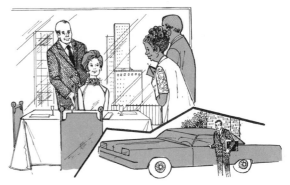

Teen-agers enjoy a place for entertaining friends without conspicuous chaperoning by parents. The parents enjoy being separated from the activity but present if needed. When the children are on their own, parents have time to enjoy recreation and luxuries not always possible during their child-rearing years. There is much interest in providing companionship and recreation for couples who have retired from business careers. Special housing for the elderly is being built in many sections of the United States to meet the needs of healthy people, advanced in years, who wish to live alone but near relatives or friends.

The desires of home buyers may or may not change after their experiences in a home. This is true no matter what the price range of the housing.

lots, most gardening books include examples of plot plans as narrow as 25 feet.

THE EXTERIOR OF THE HOUSE

The essential thing to keep in mind when looking for a house is how the time will be spent at home.

The Style of House

The exterior design of the house your family chooses will be influenced by personal tastes, size of the family, geographic area, the models available, and the amount of money to be spent for housing. Some styles are more expensive to build and maintain than others. There are times when a larger initial investment may save money in maintenance costs over a period of time.

The one-story house. The one-story house is commonly referred to as a ranch house. It offers convenient one-floor living, with flexibility in arranging areas for rest, relaxation, and work. It has easy entrance, access to the outdoor area, and gives fewer problems when you decorate or make repairs. It also allows greater freedom to add rooms, porches, or covered outdoor living space.

The initial cost of a one-story house tends to be higher than some other types because of the larger foundation, roof, and exterior walls required to enclose the space. Besides the original construction cost, heating and cooling expenses will be higher because of the exposure and the distance that heat or cold must be circulated. The larger lot required by some ranch-style houses may increase the original cost and may also add to the taxable value of the property. Special assessments for water, sewers, and lighting are usually based on front footage. This would raise the taxes for houses on larger lots. On the whole, the one-story house is very flexible; it can be used with both conventional designs and experimental contemporary models.

The one-and-one-half-story house. This type often is designed along the lines of the Cape Cod, Northern Colonial, Dutch Colonial, or Salt Box traditional styles. There is some question about the economy of the expansion attic, which is a feature of many one-and-one-half-story houses. Some builders finish the first floor, and rough in plumbing and heating for rooms

Hip roofs are especially attractive on one-story ranch-style houses.

Courtesy Sanford Truss Company

The regularity of the placement of the studs within the framework of a house affects the strength of the structure.

H. Armstrong Roberts

to be finished on the second floor at a later date. The cost of finishing the second-floor space is uncertain and sometimes proves to be more than the buyer had anticipated.

The one-and-one-half-story house may be accommodated on a smaller lot, since it puts twice the floor area under one roof. In addition, it allows for economical installation of plumbing assemblies, one over the other; concentrates heating and air-conditioning equipment; and provides space under the sloping roof for storage. The height of the house makes it difficult to paint and repair without special equipment. Some critics feel that too much space is used by stairway and halls. In some smaller models, the hall may be eliminated and the stairway may rise at one end of the living room. The story-and-a-half house tends to be more satis-

One-story ranch homes are most acceptable in areas where the cost of land and of heating are not major considerations.

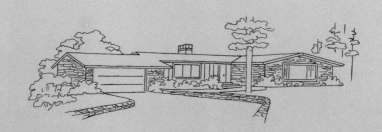

One-and-one-half-story houses are built in many styles, both traditional and modern.

The split-level house has had such wide acceptance that the style has been adapted for use in all types of areas.

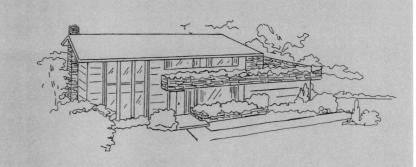

Modern duplex houses are increasingly popular as income property. Many are designed to agree with the style of the surrounding housing.

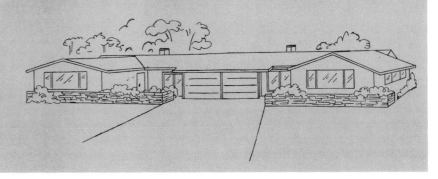

Split-level house designs fit well on lots which are too steep or hilly for traditional housing designs.

H. Armstrong Roberts

factory when the plan includes a bedroom and bath on the first floor.

The two-story house. This familiar type makes it possible to double the floor area within a given enclosure, resulting in savings in land, foundation, and roof costs. Where land costs are high, this is a particularly desirable style. Floor plans vary greatly in two-story houses. A garage may be added on either side. Outdoor living areas may be developed on any side. The two-story house lends itself to both traditional and contemporary designs. The traditional styles are represented in Southern Colonial, Regency, and Georgian styles of architecture.

The height of the house makes maintenance and repair more expensive. Windows should be examined for ease of cleaning and screen and storm windows for ease of installation. The two-story house has a definite disadvantage in areas where outdoor living space adjacent to the bedrooms is desirable because such space can be obtained only by building an outdoor deck.

The split-level house. As the name suggests, the split-level house features rooms on two or more levels. It generally provides more living space with privacy and a variety of views than is possible in a one-story house under the same amount of roof. It has the advantages of taking up less space on the lot and adapting well to rolling land. It is relatively less expensive to build than a one-story house with the same

floor area because it requires less excavation, foundation, and roof.

It is often an advantage to have bedrooms on a separate quiet level and to have the living room and family room widely separated, as is common in this type house. The utility level of the split-level house is usually higher than the conventional basement and has more natural light. Floor plans provide good traffic patterns by eliminating most cross traffic. Some families find the stairs between levels a disadvantage.

While split-level houses are being built in many locations, they fit best on rolling land. The savings in construction could easily be used up in the cost of grading the land and building retaining walls. Careful consideration should be given to the heating system in a split-level house; each level should have its own thermostat to distribute the heat evenly.

The duplex house. The name indicates that there are two separate housing units under a single roof, sharing a common dividing wall. Each has its own front and back yard. The general effect is that of a single-family house. Savings result from the elimination of the side yard and the openings that would be put in that wall. The common wall separating the two units should be soundproofed. This is a form of income property which appeals to many people. When reasonable restrictions are written into the lease, it is possible to maintain an at-

Town houses are a part of many planned urban developments.

tractive exterior. Any style of architecture, with the exception of the split level, may be adapted to duplex usage.

The row house. The popular town house, appearing in urban areas where the cost of land is high, is today's version of the row house. Each house has its own front and back walls, but shares sidewalls with its neighbors. Rows commonly include from four to ten houses, two or three stories high, with small front yards

H. Armstrong Roberts

Row houses have their own front and back walls but share side walls.

and enclosed backyard gardens. The cost is generally less than for separate houses, since sidewalls are shared and there are no windows or doors in the sidewalls. The greatest saving comes in land cost because there are no side yards. Good locations are characteristic of town-house developments.

The Structure of a House

When you shop for a house, it is helpful to know the names and functions of the various parts of the structure to understand what the salesman is telling you about the house. Besides knowing the parts of a house, it is helpful to know the advantages and disadvantages of construction materials commonly used. Some materials and construction methods will give better service than others. However, when you cannot afford the best of everything, it is important to know when and where to compromise.

While houses are built in many styles and sizes, they have common construction features such as the foundation, floors, exterior and interior walls, the roof and windows. Heating, air conditioning, lighting, and plumbing are common conveniences now included in most housing construction. These construction features can be selected from a variety of materials and models to suit individual tastes.

The foundation for the house. Every house has a foundation. It may be built with either poured concrete or masonry block. In a house with a basement the foundation also serves as the basement walls. Houses with poured concrete basement walls tend to be more satisfactory than masonry block because they are more

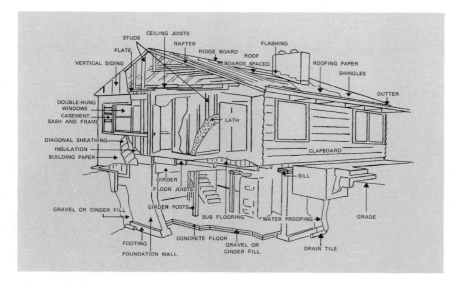

The diagram is labeled with the following structural elements:

CEILING JOISTS, STUDS, RAFTER, PLATE, RIDGE BOARD, FLASHING, ROOF, VERTICAL SIDING, BOARDS SPACED, ROOFING PAPER, SHINGLES, GUTTER, DOUBLE-HUNG WINDOWS, CASEMENT SASH AND FRAME, LATH, DIAGONAL SHEATHING, INSULATION, BUILDING PAPER, CLAPBOARD, GIRDER, FLOOR JOISTS, SILL, GIRDER POSTS, GRAVEL OR CINDER FILL, SUB FLOORING, WATER PROOFING, GRADE, FOOTING, CONCRETE FLOOR, GRAVEL OR CINDER FILL, FOUNDATION WALL, DRAIN TILE

The ability to recognize structural elements within the design of the house helps the potential home buyer evaluate the soundness of the house.

often watertight. When houses do not have basements, they are built either with crawl spaces or slab floors. The kind of foundation used depends on the type of soil and on the climate and type of house that is built on the foundation. When buying a house inspect the basement walls for signs of moisture. Avoid buying a house that does not have a dry basement.

The floors of the house. Floors may be either wood or masonry. The most common form of masonry is the reinforced concrete slab poured over a gravel base that has been covered with a vinyl sheet to prevent moisture from rising to the surface. Brick and slate floors are less common but more architecturally and decoratively interesting. Since the concrete slab is poured on the prepared ground surface, it does not have the assortment of structural parts characteristic of floors built over a crawl space or a basement.

Houses with basements or crawl spaces have wood beams which support the flooring. These beams, known as joists, are supported by the foundation walls. The joists are given additional support at the midpoint by a girder, which in turn rests on a post. Additional strength may be built in by the addition of bridging, or cross bracing, between the joists. The joists are covered with subflooring, usually plywood, and then covered with a flooring material.

The walls of the house. Most houses are built on a wood-frame skeleton. Sills are bolted to the foundation walls; floor joists are laid on the sills; studs are raised to a vertical position and nailed to the sill at the bottom and to the plate at the top. (The plate is a horizontal piece of lumber.) In better-quality construction, a termite shield of copper sheeting is placed between the sills and the foundation. Sheathing is applied to the studding to make the walls airtight and watertight. Plywood, gypsum board, and various forms of insulating board are more commonly used for sheathing than rough lumber. The kind of sheathing used will be determined by the exterior finish that will be put on the walls.

The siding that covers the sheathing is fastened directly to it. Siding is the final layer on the outside of the house. It is added to give the house a weatherproof covering and to create the exterior effect that the architect planned. Wood, masonry, metal, stone, and fiber glass are available in a variety of forms for use on the exterior of a house. Wood siding is available in the form of shingles, bevel siding, plywood, or board and batten. Masonry siding includes stucco, brick veneer, stone, concrete block, and cinder block. Metal sidings are usually aluminum in a variety of forms, most of which have a prefinished exterior and an insulation backing.

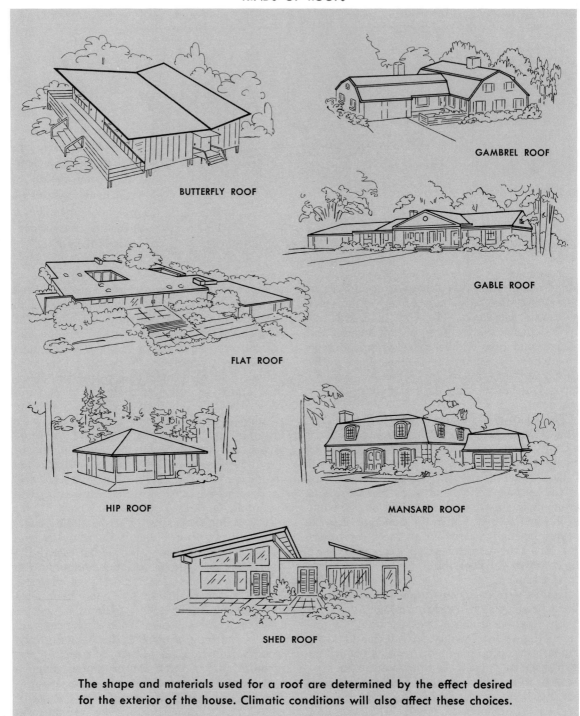

BUTTERFLY ROOF

GAMBREL ROOF

GABLE ROOF

FLAT ROOF

HIP ROOF

MANSARD ROOF

SHED ROOF

The shape and materials used for a roof are determined by the effect desired for the exterior of the house. Climatic conditions will also affect these choices.

Courtesy Sanford Truss Company

Prefabricated roof trusses assembled away from the building site can be transported to the site by truck and lifted into position.

In sections of the country where there is little cold weather, solid masonry walls are used. The walls are usually cement or cinder block, which provides support for the roof and protection from the weather. Where this solid-masonry-wall construction is used, the exterior may be coated with cement plaster to create the desired appearance.

The interior walls may be plastered, or furring strips of wood may be fastened to the inside to provide a nailing base for the interior-wall-finish material. Furring also creates an air space between the exterior and interior walls and keeps condensation from showing on the surface. There is no way to avoid condensation in areas where there is a wide variation in temperatures. When basements are finished off for living space, there should always be furring strips between the foundation wall and the interior finish.

The roof of the house. The type of roof covering the house depends primarily on the architectural style of the house. Roof styles are gambrel, gable, hip, mansard, shed, butterfly,

and flat. Gambrel, gable, hip, and mansard roofs allow space on the upper floor for attic storage or for additional rooms. Shed roofs allow for the greatest freedom in room layout. The use of roof trusses when building a gable roof allows flexible room layout but eliminates the attic space for storage. The more complex the roof shape, the more expensive it is to build. In evaluating a house, it is important to know that the roof is appropriate for the style of house, that the roof provides good drainage of water, and that the material will give long-lasting protection.

Good water drainage can be assured when metal or plastic is used for flashing, which spans the joint where two different roof sections come together and form what is known as a "valley." This also occurs where the chimney, vent pipes, or dormers come through the roof. To be effective, the flashing must extend at least 4 inches up the chimney and under the nearest shingles. Flashing materials may be tin, galvanized iron, aluminum, copper, or plastic. Asphalt shingles are used in less expensive types of construction and are not as satisfactory as the metal.

Some provision must be made for directing the runoff water from the roof away from the foundation. This may be done by building wide overhangs, by landscaping the house so that gravel may be placed out from the foundation to deliver the water to a storm-sewer connection, or by the use of gutters. Gutters are open channels of wood or metal around the eaves of a house which funnel water into leaders, called downspouts, connected with the storm sewer. Where there are no storm sewers, the downspouts should be connected to dry wells or field tiles that lead away from the foundation.

Roofs may be surfaced with a variety of materials. Galvanized steel sheets, flat or corrugated, may be used on roofs having a minimum 3-inch pitch. When painted white, these roofs reflect the sun's heat. While galvanized steel has exceptional strength and wind resistance, it is also noisy and difficult to repair. It is used on houses only when cost is a major consideration.

Asphalt shingles are most commonly used, appearing on two out of three new houses. These are made from a cellulose-fiber felt saturated with asphalt and covered with mineral granules. The life expectancy of asphalt shingles varies with the grade. The minimum grade allowed for FHA-insured loans is the 210- to 215 pound weight which can be expected to give fifteen to twenty years of service; the medium grade weighs 250 pounds per square and can be expected to last twenty to twenty-five years; the best grade weighs 300 pounds per square and lasts indefinitely. The type of roofing material together with the age of the house will give some idea as to when the shingles will need to be replaced.

Wood shingles are becoming increasingly popular because of their design properties. They may be cut from cedar, redwood, or cypress. The quality is determined by the thickness; ⅜-inch shingles are expected to give fifteen to twenty years of service. Thick shingles, called shakes, range up to 1¼ inches in thickness and have a life expectancy of fifty years. Wood shingles have the disadvantages of being combustible, of cracking, of attracting fungus, and of having the butts curl. Shingles are sometimes used to cover the exterior walls as well as the roof of a house. They may be painted or stained to create unusual effects.

Flat or almost flat roofs are usually covered with what is called a built-up roof. This is made from alternate layers of building felt or fiber glass and an asphaltic material covered with gravel, slag, or mineral particles. Built-up roofs are continuous from eave to ridge and from rake to rake in a smooth expanse of surface. Five-ply is considered good quality and can be expected to last twenty years. If white chips have been used on the roof, it will reflect heat.

There are shingles in the moderate-cost bracket made of asbestos cement, a combination of asbestos fiber and portland cement. These may be in any of several widths and thicknesses. On the roof they look like wood shingles. This fire-resistant shingle will last indefinitely. Another fireproof, wind-resistant, and long-lasting roofing material is clay tile. Clay tile is made from shale and clay, baked into a hard material which may be flat, rectangular, or barrel-shaped. Clay-tile roofs are commonly used on houses where the Mediterranean influence is reflected in the architecture.

Some of the contemporary roof shapes and roofing materials will need to be evaluated in terms of the new developments in materials and methods of construction. Plastic skins are being sprayed on base coatings to produce new textures and colors in roofing materials.

The windows. Windows are a part of the structure of the house. The kind of window used and its placement affect the furniture arrangement in the room, the amount of natural ventilation, the amount of light, and the amount of heat loss. The most common window type is the double-hung, or guillotine, type with a wood frame, factory weather-stripped, rotproofed, and supplied with full-length screens and storm windows. The double-hung window has two sashes, one or both of which slide up and down. It is more desirable to have double-hung sashes that come out of the frame for ease of cleaning. Windows should be checked to see that the sash may be raised and lowered easily.

In some architectural styles a casement window that opens to the inside or the outside may be more appropriate. Casement windows which open with a crank tend to be more

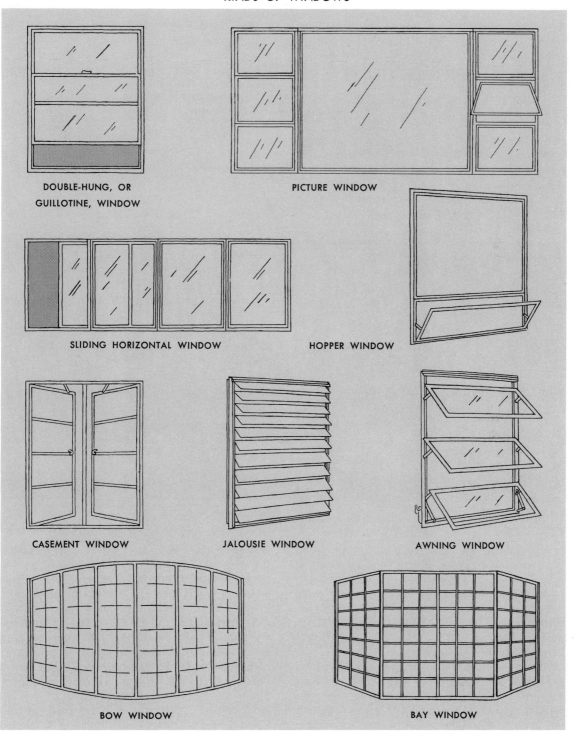

DOUBLE-HUNG, OR GUILLOTINE, WINDOW

PICTURE WINDOW

SLIDING HORIZONTAL WINDOW

HOPPER WINDOW

CASEMENT WINDOW

JALOUSIE WINDOW

AWNING WINDOW

BOW WINDOW

BAY WINDOW

Casement windows can swing either to the inside or the outside.

Courtesy Anderson Window Corporation

An awning window below a fixed sash opens outward for air control.

Courtesy Anderson Window Corporation

satisfactory than those that are opened or closed by a push bar on the frame. Windows which open inward limit the variety of window treatments. Outward-swinging windows allow more freedom in selecting curtains and draperies. This type of window should be checked for ease in opening and closing and for tightness of seal around the edges.

Awning windows and hopper-type windows are used in combination with fixed windows to allow for ventilation. The awning types are hinged at the top; when open, the sash projects out at an angle. Like other types of projecting windows, this may be a safety hazard unless the windows are positioned to avoid danger to persons walking near the houses. The hopper-type window is hinged at the bottom and opens inward. It has the same disadvantages for window treatment as the inward-swinging casement window. The jalousie window consists of a series of small horizontal glass slats, 3 to 8 inches wide, held by an end frame of metal, opening outward, similar to venetian blinds. Since the panels may be adjusted to the desired angle by a crank operation, these are considered desirable for ventilation and protection

Double-hung windows are common in all areas of the country.

from rain damage. They should be checked for ease of operation and tightness of seal when closed.

To preserve valuable wall space and also to provide both ventilation and privacy, sliding horizontal windows are frequently used in small ranch houses. This horizontal, sliding window, set high off the floor, is most satisfactory when the sections lift out for cleaning. It would be advisable to check to see that there are tracks for screens or storm windows included.

Picture windows are designed to frame an outside view. If there is not presently a view from a picture window, one should be created when landscaping the grounds. A picture window may consist of one large pane of glass or a combination of one large fixed pane of glass with movable sections at either side, top, or bottom. The movable sections are necessary for ventilation. Bow windows and bay windows are also designed to frame a view. The bow window is sometimes referred to as a circular bay. A bay window is a combination of three or more

Muntins that fit over a single pane of glass to give the effect of small panes are removable for easy cleaning or painting.

windows set at angles to each other to create a recessed area. A bow does not have any parts that may be opened, while the bay may be made up of a combination of fixed and movable units. If ventilation in the room is important, the windows should be checked to be sure that they open.

When the house being considered does **not** have the style of window the buyer wants, it may be possible to change the appearance by using muntins. Muntins are panels of metal or wood that may be slipped over a single panel of glass to give the effect of a multipaned sash. Muntin panels minimize the nuisance of paint on glass when painting, besides being removable for easy cleaning of a single glass pane.

In some rooms sliding glass doors are used in place of windows. They are the modern counterpart of French doors, incorporating two sliding sections in one large frame. A room will appear larger when a large portion of the wall is opened to a broad view of the landscape or garden. Except in mild climates, sliding glass doors should have insulating glass to control heat loss. Wood frames, while more expensive,

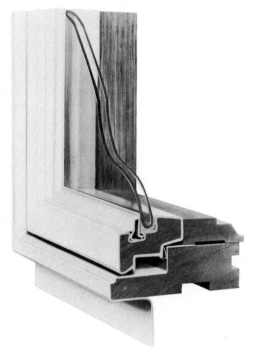

Insulating glass is a double-thickness glass which reduces the tendency for sweating and heat loss.

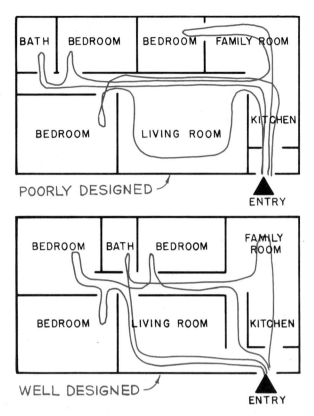

POORLY DESIGNED
ENTRY

WELL DESIGNED
ENTRY

A study of traffic patterns shows the differences in poorly designed interiors and well-designed interiors.

tend to control heat loss better than metal frames.

Windows may be both functional and decorative as they let in light or ventilation or both. The amount of light depends on the size of the glass area and the type of glass used; the amount of ventilation depends on the type of window and its position in the wall. It is advisable to evaluate the windows in a house on the basis of the service expected from them, the ease with which they can be cleaned, and their looks both inside and outside the house.

THE INTERIOR OF THE HOUSE

The interior of the house is of particular interest to the family because it is where each member may express his interests in the furnishing and decoration of his room, provided the space, interior finishes, and architectural features are compatible with his needs and wants. Some materials are more adaptable to certain inter-

pretations than others. The floors, ceiling and wall surfaces, trim and woodwork, windows, doors, and stairways need to be considered in determining how a particular house will suit the family.

The Floor Plan

Most writers agree that the rooms in a house should be grouped according to the activities commonly performed in them. The rest or relaxation area usually includes the bedrooms and baths. The work area includes the kitchen, laundry, and utility space. The recreation, or group-activity, area includes the living room, the dining room, and the family room. Not all the bedrooms need be grouped together, but each bedroom should be located where quiet may be achieved with soundproofed walls, halls, or other sound barriers.

In addition to grouping rooms in zones, they should be arranged so that there is easy movement between the areas. This is best accomplished by using hallways. Many builders of new houses will give prospective buyers either a single line drawing or an abbreviated floor plan, such as the one shown on page 90, along with a sketch of the exterior and a plot plan to study. While these simplified plans do not give as much detail as the fully dimensional floor plan used by a contractor in building a house, they do give the overall building dimensions, the room sizes, the location of doors, windows, stairwells, fireplace, and other architectural features.

With this information, a family can study the size and arrangement of rooms and, to a certain degree, determine how well a particular house will meet their needs. These fundamental requirements should be looked for:

1. Enough rooms large enough to meet the needs for eating, sleeping, and group activity

2. Storage space for clothing, cleaning equipment, linens, sports equipment, and hobby supplies

3. Windows placed to give good ventilation and allow for convenient furniture arrangement

4. Doors placed convenient to the approach and service areas of the yard

5. Traffic patterns that do not interfere with furniture arrangement or activities

6. Sufficient electric outlets with adequate capacity

7. Heating outlets that do not interfere with furniture arrangement

8. Access to the outdoor living area from the living room or family room

A knowledge of floor plan symbols is essential.

The Floor Surfaces in a House

Most houses today have a variety of floor-covering materials depending upon the function of the room. There is a wide range of materials in four basic groups: hardwood, softwood, masonry, and composition. You can expect good service from masonry floors in an entry hall, bathrooms, indoor-outdoor living areas, finished basements, and some kitchen areas. Ceramic tile, terrazzo, slate, and brick are long-wearing,

water-resistant, and grease-resistant, and they are relatively easy to care for. Masonry floors are more costly and are not usually found in less expensive houses.

The hardwood surface boards are laid over the subfloor. The finish used on the flooring will affect its wearing qualities. Shellac is less durable than other finishes. Varnish makes a durable finish if it is applied over a sealer on such open-grained woods as oak. For floors that will be subjected to hard wear, it is desirable to have a floor finished with a penetrating sealer that sinks into the wood rather than one that creates a surface finish. Plastic floor finishes can be expected to give as good service as the sealers.

If the subflooring in some rooms is covered with such resilient material as linoleum, rubber tile, cork tile, or vinyl, a check should be made to see that this surface material has been applied over a double thickness of wood subfloor, unless the house has been built with the extra-thick plywood designed for subfloors. The most satisfactory results are achieved when there is a layer of hardboard or plywood over the subfloor to serve as a base for the resilient flooring. This double floor will add to both the life span and appearance of the resilient covering. Of the resilient floorings, vinyl can be expected to give the best service. Solid vinyl is durable, resists grease, acids, water, and alcohol, and is hard to dent. Cork and rubber tile can be expected to give the next best service. Cork is a good sound absorber and creates an interesting background. However, cork has the disadvantage of denting easily and showing surface scuffs.

Rubber tile is grease-resistant and water-resistant and does not dent easily. Rubber tile will not give satisfactory service if applied to a concrete slab floor. Vinyl asbestos floors can be expected to resist water, grease, and chemicals and will give reasonably good service in any area. Asphalt tile, which is frequently used on slab floors, is brittle, dents easily, stains, and is not grease-resistant. Asphalt tile is frequently used on basement floors because it can be used on a slab-floor base. Inlaid linoleum is still used where cost is a factor. It can be expected to give moderately good service if the surface is protected with wax or a plastic finish.

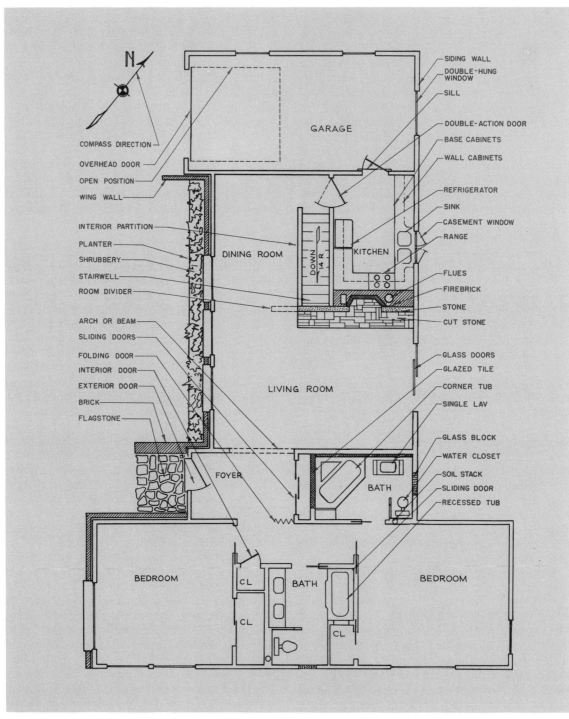

A knowledge of commonly used floor-plan symbols is necessary in order to read a blueprint.

Interior Walls

Plaster and dry-wall materials are the traditional construction materials for interior walls. New materials made from wood pulp, fiber glass, and vinyl are being used in creative ways, and materials once considered mainly for exterior use, such as brick and stone, are being used indoors.

A variety of panels are manufactured for surfacing ceilings and walls. These products tend to be easier and less expensive to install than plaster. Some come prefinished, while others may be treated with conventional painting or wallpaper for decorative effects. There is no conclusive evidence that plaster is better than dry wall from a construction standpoint.

Plaster. Plaster is a masonry surface applied to a base material. The final finish may be smooth or textured. The framework of the wall is covered with rough lumber, gypsum board, or metal lath and coated with plaster. This finish may be painted. If the surface is smooth, wallpaper may be applied. Plaster walls have a tendency to crack as the building settles. If the plaster shows many cracks, you may need to anticipate the expense of building new walls, applying new plaster, or covering the walls and ceilings with some form of wallboard. Small cracks can be repaired with Spackle paste before repainting the walls.

Gypsum wallboard. This paneling is made with a core of gypsum plaster covered with heavy paper. When properly installed, the surface is as smooth as a plastered wall and may be painted or papered. This is more fire-resistant than wood paneling.

Plywood paneling. Most plywood paneling has a core of inexpensive fir plywood that is covered with an outside veneer cut from attractive hardwoods. The cost is determined by the thickness of the base and the kind of hardwood used for the veneer. This gives an excellent interior finish if the paneling produces the desired background for the furnishings.

Board paneling. Sawed lumber is processed into paneling patterns with tongue-and-groove or shiplap joints. These may be made from many available woods. The choice of wood and the finish applied to it can produce a background color and surface that complement the furnishings. While paneling may be painted, it is more commonly used with the wood color and grain showing. Wood walls generally require less maintenance than walls finished with plaster or wallboard.

Ceramic interior walls. Ceramic tile is used frequently in bathrooms for both wall and floor surfacing. You may judge the quality of installation by checking the evenness of the surface, the uniform width of mortar between tiles, and the freedom from cracks and discoloration.

Plastic and metal wall tile. These tiles are applied with an adhesive, and the space between them is filled with caulking compound. Either form of tile makes a serviceable and attractive finish in areas where moisture is present. The tile market is served by importers, which brings the cost into a range whereby moderately priced houses may often have tile in the baths and in at least part of the kitchen.

Interior Trim

Trim is the finish material used in a house as molding around doors and windows, as floor baseboards, and for ceiling cornice. Traditionally, interior trim has been wood. Pressed steel is being used in many contemporary houses. The quality of the wood and the design of the molding will affect the character of the room and the cost. Better quality is required when the wood is to be finished in its natural color. Paint may be used with less expensive trim or when the design of the room calls for woodwork that matches the walls in color.

THE HEATING SYSTEM

The heating system is one area in which it is important to get the opinion of a specialist. Ask a reputable heating dealer to check (1) the quality of the equipment installed in the house, (2) the capacity of the heater in relation to the demands for heat and the estimated heat loss, (3) the adequacy of insulation and weather stripping, and (4) the adaptability of the heating system, including the number, quality, and location of thermostats and other accessory items.

Types of Heating Systems

All heating systems depend upon the circulation of heated air. Heating systems differ as to the

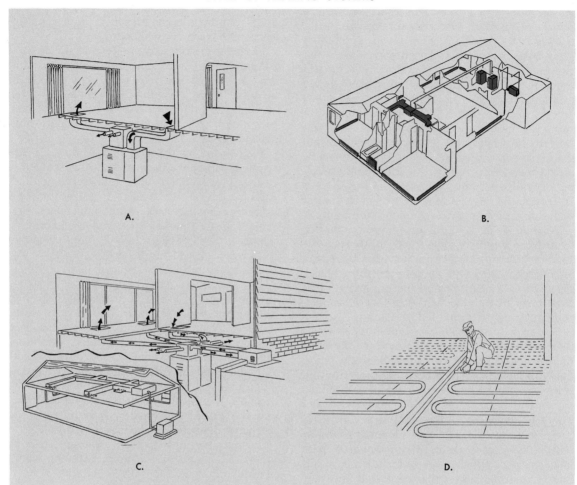

A.

B.

C.

D.

(A) In a forced warm-air heating system, air from the central furnace is forced by a blower into a system of ducts that deliver warmed air to the registers in each room. The duct system also returns cool air to the furnace to be filtered and recirculated through the heating system. (B) In a forced hot-water heating system, water is heated in a boiler, then pumped to radiators in each room. Modern hot-water radiators come in slim shapes that can be recessed in the wall or set around the perimeter of the room in a style that resembles a baseboard. (C) The central-heat pump is used for both heating and cooling. It operates on the same principle as the compressor of a refrigerator. In the winter the operation warms the air, in the summer the direction is reversed to cool the air. (D) In some radiant heating systems, copper tubing laid under the flooring carries hot water to heat the room. The same principle is used when electric coils are embedded in the ceiling or walls to give off heat.

method by which the air is heated and the source of the heat. Each system has advantages and limitations that may influence final selection of a house.

Forced warm-air heat. A furnace warms the air from the house. A blower attached to the furnace may then force the warmed air through a system of ducts to registers in the rooms. (In some older small-home construction, the warmed air circulates by convection only.) The placement of the warm-air outlets and cold-air returns affects the efficiency of a warm-air heating system. The preferred location for warm-air outlets is around the perimeter of the house, preferably near the windows.

An advantage of a forced warm-air heating system over other types is that air-conditioning can easily be combined with it. The warm-air ducts and the blower may be used for both heating and cooling. The presence of a humidifier allows the addition of moisture to the air during the heating season. Furniture should not interfere with the circulation from conditioned-air outlets or returns. This is sometimes considered a disadvantage. If the outlets are in the floor there may be an added disadvantage, since floor outlets may require holes to be cut in the carpeting.

Forced hot-water heat. A circulator pump forces heated water through pipes from the boiler to radiators in each room of the house. Forced hot-water heat tends to be more even than warm-air heat. One of the frequently heard criticisms of this type of heat is that it is slow to respond to changes in outdoor temperatures. This may cause overheating or underheating at times when the outdoor temperature fluctuates rapidly.

Steam heat (a variation of forced hot-water heating) is rarely used in new houses. Such heating systems are probably so old as to require a complete overhaul and perhaps replacement of the entire heating system.

Radiant heat. Newer homes may have the source of heat (hot water pipes or electric heating elements) embedded in the structure of the home. These radiant elements may be wall units, baseboards, ceiling elements, or radiant floors. The efficiency of such heating systems is frequently harder to judge than that of other types because the efficiency is affected by many complex factors, such as the provisions for ventilation and the structural insulation of the house, as well as the amount of carpeting or the style and fabric of the draperies in use, the climate in which the house is built, and the availability of the heating elements for maintenance work.

Central heat pump. The central heat pump uses refrigeration equipment to heat the air in winter and cool it in summer. Heat pumps may use air or water, singly or in combination, as heat sources. The choice of heat source depends upon the location of the home. In the winter heat is extracted from the heat source and pumped into the house where it is circulated through ducts. During the summer the same compressor acts as an air conditioner to cool and dehumidify the air. A central heat pump costs more to install than any other heating system.

Heat Sources

The three traditional fuels—gas, oil, and coal—are still the most common heat sources. Any of these fuels may be burned in a furnace to heat the air or water for warm-air or hot-water heating systems. Electricity is becoming more popular as a heat source.

In most areas, the gas furnace costs less to install and to service than other furnaces. The gas is piped directly to the burner with no need to check fuel supplies.

Oil burners operate automatically as long as the oil supply is sufficient. Most suppliers will keep the supply tank refilled during the heating season. There are high-efficiency oil burners on the market which operate with remarkable cleanliness. Some are said to be so efficient that they do not require a chimney.

Coal furnaces are less frequently used in new housing. Automatic feeding systems are available. Although some forms of coal are more efficient than others, coal furnaces are not as clean as other furnaces.

The cleanest heat source is electricity. Installation of electric heating units is low-cost and there are only minimal maintenance and service costs. At the present time, heating bills tend to be highest with electric heat, unless the electric rate is low enough to be competitive. For economical heat costs, the electric rate must be no more than 1 to 1½ cents per kilowatt-hour.

THE ELECTRICAL SYSTEM

Electrical requirements for cooking, laundry equipment, food storage, specialized small appliances, and outdoor living equipment are steadily increasing. It is advisable to evaluate the electrical system in terms of how adequate the installation is for both present and anticipated needs. The National Electrical Code sets capacity and safety regulations for all types of wiring installations; the existing systems should be checked against these standards.

Electrical Terms

A knowledge of some electrical terms is essential for understanding and judging the electrical system of a house.

Lighting outlet. This refers to the wired box in ceiling or wall to which various types of lighting fixtures may be attached.

Receptacle. A receptacle, or convenience outlet, is a contact device installed at an outlet for the connection of an attachment plug and flexible cord of an electrical appliance. Most convenience outlets are a duplex type which accommodates two plugs. In bedrooms and some other locations in the house, a receptacle which accommodates three or four plugs may be a convenience.

Some outlets designed for accepting a three-prong plug are called grounding receptacles. The third prong on such plugs is connected through its three-wire cord to the housing or frame of the appliance to which it is attached. The third opening in the receptacle is in turn connected to the grounding terminal of the service entrance switch of the house. The 1962 National Electrical Code requires that a grounding receptacle be used on 15- and 20-ampere circuits.

Receptacles with watertight covers are provided for outdoor locations. Locking receptacles are desirable for preventing disconnection of such equipment as motors or food freezers.

Service equipment. This term refers to the conductors and equipment used to bring electrical service into a house. The "feeder" connects the pole meter to the house.

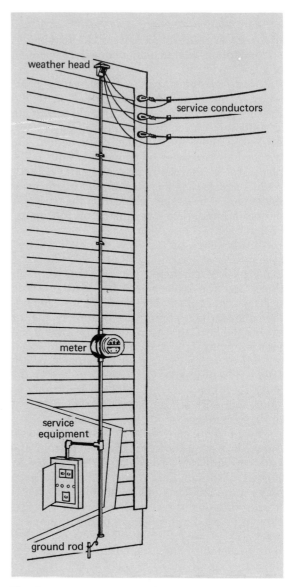

The home wiring system begins where the electric power reaches the house.

Ampere. This is a unit of measure of the rate of flow of electricity through a wire.

Volt. This is a unit of measure of electrical pressure. A given number of volts of electrical pressure causes a certain number of amperes of electricity to flow through a wire. The usual pressure is 115 volts for lighting and small electrical appliances and 230 volts for heating units.

94

Watts. This term denotes a unit of electrical power. It is a measure of the rate of electrical work which is the product of volts times amperes. A kilowatt equals 1,000 watts, and the kilowatt-hour is the unit that measures work done. Electrical energy is measured and sold by the kilowatt-hour.

Branch circuit. This is the portion of the wiring system extending from the final fuse or circuit breaker to the general-use outlets and those portions of the wiring system installed to supply current for a single appliance. You need to check both general and individual circuits with the appliances to be used to determine if the wiring is adequate.

Fuses, time-delay fuses, and circuit breakers. These safety devices are important parts of the electrical system. A fuse will carry the amount of current for which it was designed indefinitely but will melt and break when the current is excessive. A time-delay fuse is capable of carrying an overload of current for a short time without melting. Circuit breakers trip to open the circuit whenever an overload occurs. It is advisable to check the electrical system for one or more of these protective devices.

Electrical Service Entrance for a House

The capacity of wires serving the main central switch and the number of electrical circuits serving the house should be adequate for the electrical load to be placed on the electrical system. The minimum capacity service entrance should be at least 100 amperes. If the house is heated electrically, the service entrance should be at least 200 amperes. To determine the adequacy of the electrical system, calculate (1) the lighting load, (2) the small appliance load, (3) the special circuits needed for major electrical equipment, and (4) the heating or electric motor loads. An electrical contractor will evaluate the installation in relation to specific needs.

THE PLUMBING SYSTEM

Most plumbing installations are regulated by the building codes designed to insure the health of the community. This is an advantage to the house buyer who needs to know that there is an adequate source for fresh water to supply the fixtures in the house and that there is a sewer system that will carry the waste from the house to the street sewer or the septic tank.

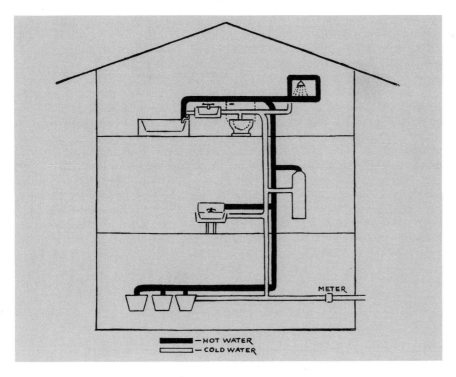

METER

■ —HOT WATER
▭ — COLD WATER

The installation cost and operating cost of the plumbing system in the house depend upon the relation of the locations of the plumbing outlets to each other.

Basically, plumbing is a system of unseen pipes and frequently used valves. Plumbing may depreciate over the years, depending on quality of materials, workmanship, and amount of daily use.

Plumbing Terms

A knowledge of some plumbing terms is essential for understanding and judging the plumbing system of a house.

Pipe. Pipe is available in materials selected for usage and cost. Water pipe may be galvanized iron, brass, copper, or plastic. Sewer pipe is generally cast iron. Pipe size is based on use. Water-supply pipes from the street main are ¾-inch diameter or larger.

Insulaton of cold-water pipes prevents drip from condensation of moisture in the air. Insulation of hot-water pipes stabilizes temperature and saves fuel.

Materials and size of gas and fuel-oil pipes vary with local requirements.

Air chambers are extensions of vertical pipes. Their tops are capped. Air, trapped in these extensions, acts as a cushion and eliminates the hammering of water or steam that sometimes occurs in pipes or radiators due to variances in pressure.

Shutoff valves. These valves permit shutting off water in one line without interrupting the water supply in other lines. This permits the repair of such fixtures as faucets and toilet tanks.

Hose outlets. These connections (and other connections that supply water outside the house) should have stop and drain valves inside the house to prevent freezing.

Grease traps. These catch the grease that flows through the waste pipe from the kitchen sink. Such traps are particularly important in systems connected to septic tanks.

Hot water system. The water heater should have sufficient capacity to supply the maximum demand in the heavy-duty hours when the bathrooms are in constant use.

Hot-water pipes should be installed in a loop. This provides a system in which hot water can circulate, so that it flows immediately from the tap when the faucet is opened. The loop system eliminates the nuisance of letting cold water run out before hot water comes up. Insulation of the pipes helps to keep the water hot and conserves fuel.

Water heaters, independent of the house-heating equipment, may require a different type of fuel.

The Water Supply

Water may be supplied by the city, by a private utility, or from individually owned wells. Whatever system is used, the home buyer should become familiar with the rates charged for water and any restrictions that the governing body may place on its use.

Hard water. The water in some localities contains minerals that make the water "hard." Where this condition exists, the homeowner may need a water softener to condition the water for household and laundry use. A water softener removes the minerals before the water enters the pipes leading to the water heater or plumbing fixtures. If the local water is hard, the home buyer should expect to find the house equipped with a softener.

Red water. Some ground water contains iron salts that cause it to have a red color that damages household items and discolors laundry. Some red water can be cleaned as it passes through a water softener. However, in some areas the iron content is so high that an iron filter must be used ahead of the softener to remove the mineral. A simple check for red water is to fill a jar from the tap and observe its color. In older houses, the red color may come from rust in pipes and tanks. In such a case the pipes should be replaced with copper or plastic pipes.

LEARNING EXPERIENCES

1. Write and present skits that dramatize housing needs at different stages in the life cycle. Summarize and discuss the needs that are identified in the skits.
2. Organize into buzz groups to identify the design fundamentals by which you can evaluate floor plans. Report to class and form committees to prepare checklists for judging floor plans.
3. Collect blueprints and bring to class to use in learning the meaning of common architectural symbols and analyzing floor plans.
4. Collect illustrations of doorways, roof lines, windows, chimney styles, and other architectural features. Compare the use of similar styles on one-story, one-and-a-half-story, and two-story houses.
5. Organize a panel to discuss the advantages and disadvantages of commonly used windows for natural lighting, appearance, view, heat loss, privacy, ventilation, and decorating.
6. Survey the class to determine the types of heating systems used in students' homes.

Discuss the advantages and disadvantages of each system from the standpoint of climate, fuels available, cost of operation, adaptability to type and size of house, etc.
7. Prepare a checklist for determining the number, type, and location of electrical outlets needed in homes under 1,200 square feet, homes with 1,200 to 2,000 square feet, and homes over 2,000 square feet. Analyze blueprints to determine that adequate wiring is planned.
8. Study trade magazines and advertising to learn about interior wall finishes. Discuss available materials and trends in relation to design and performance. How would children in the family affect your choices?
9. Study trade magazines and advertising for new developments in exterior construction materials. Discuss the merits of each in relation to design and anticipated maintenance costs.
10. Select a plan for a house or apartment that appeals to you. Write a critical analysis of its design and structural features.

6

Use of Space for Storage

There is a great deal written about the storage requirements of American families in general and the detailed requirements for storing various personal and household articles in particular.

As it seems to be human nature to accumulate enough possessions to fill whatever storage space is available, it is important to evaluate the amount of space built into the home and to analyze how the space may be adapted to family needs at a particular stage in the family cycle. Many homes are short of storage space, and many homes have storage space that is not used to best advantage.

Principles of Storage

Storage space should be judged on its location and arrangement. Consider location in relation to the items to be stored and the place where they are most frequently used. Judge arrangement to see how well the space will accept the items to be stored in this area.

Location of storage space. Small equipment and supplies should be stored near the place where they are to be used according to the sequence of operations. More frequently used articles should be easily seen and reached. Supplies and equipment for one activity should be stored together.

Arrangement of storage space. Efficiency depends on how well the internal arrangement accommodates the articles stored. Flexible shelving allows greater freedom in adjusting shelf space to particular needs. Special fittings, such as hat stands, take care of specific items and increase efficiency.

Storage in the Living Area

The living area includes rooms used for group and personal activities. Group activities require space for guests, for family-centered activities, for family hobbies, and for recreation. Personal activities require space for reading, studying, and writing; sleeping, grooming, and dressing; sick care; and personal hobbies. Storage for each area and activity has unique features.

The guest closet. It is desirable to have a closet where outer wraps, hats, and purses may be left while guests are in the home for short visits. This guest closet should be in or near

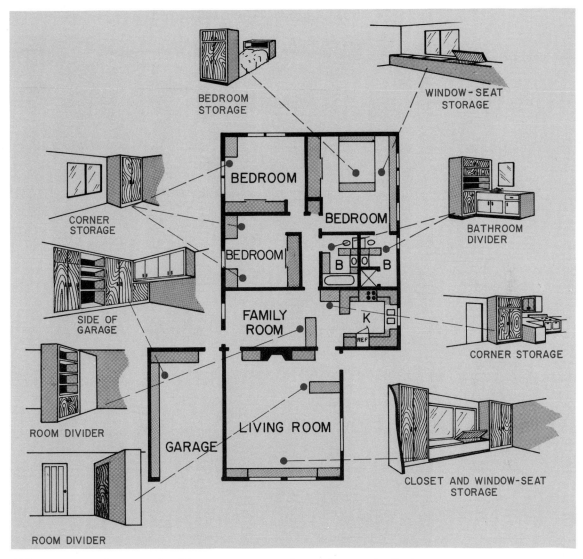

Different types of storage facilities are necessary for each room in the house.

the front entry. A mirror on the inside of the closet door is convenient for checking personal appearance when entering or leaving the house.

Storage for family-centered activities. Many families like to be together when they have free time. Some members may be reading, working on crafts, or writing at the same time that other family members are playing games or listening to music. Whatever room is most frequently used—a family room or the living room—it needs storage space arranged to keep records, tapes, games, writing supplies, projection

equipment, and a host of other items that help make being together a pleasure.

Where the room is not large enough for a permanent game table, it is desirable to have storage space for a folding table and chairs. It may be more convenient and space-saving to store writing supplies in cupboards and use a folding table as a desk. Paper, pens, pencils, paper clips, etc., can be stored in shallow trays arranged in slots between the shelves. Valuable papers may be kept in box files on the shelves. The important thing is to plan the storage for

Built-in storage space may be adapted to meet changing needs.

Courtesy Better Homes and Gardens, © Meredith Corporation, 1964

Components to store the supplies and equipment for a variety of activities may be placed along one wall.

Pass-through storage units which separate living and dining areas can be used for storage of equipment needed in either room.

this room to fit family needs. Some rooms have a storage wall, with closets, cabinets and shelving built against a room wall, while others may have a divider wall with closed storage below and open shelves above.

Clothes storage. There are obvious advantages to putting all the articles used for dressing in a single well-organized area in the room occupied by a particular family member. Most people want a rod in the closet for hanging garments, closet shelves for hats and boxes, and a place for shoes and boots, purses, and/or belts and ties. The closets in ready-built houses may be equipped with shelves and accessories to meet these needs.

Research indicates that 3½ feet of rod space is considered the minimum for each person in the family. However, the clothing budget and buying habits of the family need to be considered in evaluating or planning rod space for a clothing closet. When closets are inadequate, it may be necessary to use space in corners, beside doors, windows, or chimney, or at ends of rooms or halls to make closets, or it may be necessary to use movable cabinets as closets. Out-of-season clothing might be stored in a hall closet or in the attic. Sometimes people store out-of-season clothing with a cleaner in order to have more space for this season's garments.

Families with young children can adjust the rods and shelves to a height the children can reach.

Bathroom storage. Many modern bathrooms lack adequate storage space for articles used in dressing, undressing, bathing, shaving, or applying makeup. It is convenient to store towels, soap, toilet tissue, and cleaning supplies in the bathroom. When no space has been provided for these items, cupboards may be added in or near the bath. Provision should be made for storing medicines and potentially dangerous cleaning products used in the bathroom. The size of the family and the number of bathrooms in the house will affect the amount of storage space needed in each bathroom. Adjustable shelves help adapt spacing to particular needs.

Bedding storage. A hall closet near the bedrooms is convenient for storing bedding. If the shelves are adjustable, they may be spaced to hold bulky blankets and extra pillows. Some women prefer drawers for bedding, while others prefer pullout shelves. It is necessary to have a place for sheets, pillowcases, blankets, spreads, and pillows.

Storage in the Service Area

Storage space must be especially well planned in parts of the house where most of the work

101

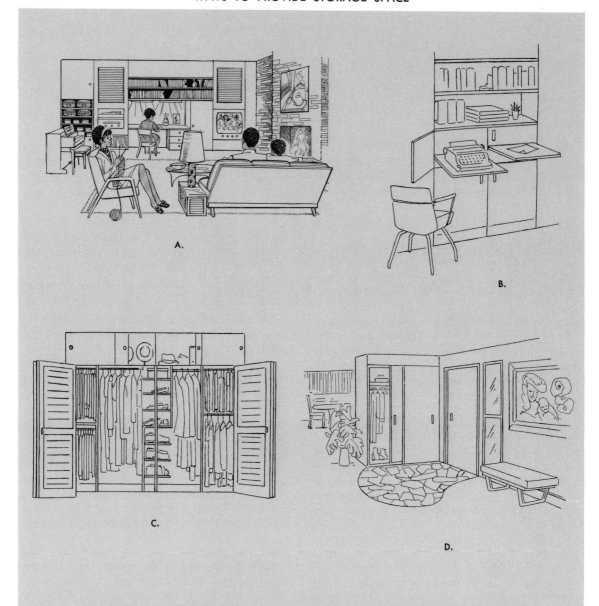

(A) Storage space for family activities should be both versatile and plentiful. (B) The supplies and equipment needed for keeping family accounts as well as those for social correspondence can be conveniently housed in a cabinet or closet adapted for this purpose. (C) Convenient clothing storage may be obtained by adding adjustable rods and shelves. (D) When no closet has been provided near the entry, it may be possible to add a unit that will provide storage space and also serve as a room divider.

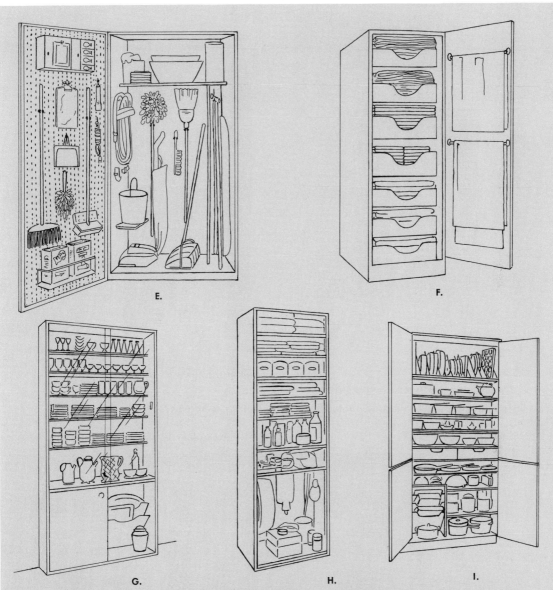

E.

F.

G.

H.

I.

(E) Cleaning equipment and supplies may be arranged in an existing closet. Pegboard makes it possible to hang small pieces. (F) Sliding trays provide storage for bed linens, blankets, and spreads. When the drawers are recessed, rods may be used on the inside of the door for storing frequently used bulky items. (G) Better dinnerware can be stored in a fairly small cabinet if the shelves are properly spaced. (H) Adjustable shelves make it possible to store a wide variety and a large quantity of household supplies in one closet. (I) A variety of kitchen equipment may be stored in specially arranged cabinets.

Courtesy Better Homes and Gardens, © Meredith Corporation, 1968

Space for storing folding chairs and tables may be built into a hallway.

Courtesy Pella Co. Architect: Charles Vincent George & Associates

Modern homes provide storage walls which make all types of clothing easily accessible.

Architect: George Fred Keck and William Keck

Wash basin and storage spaces may be built into the hallway leading to the bathroom. The added dressing area increases the efficiency of the existing bathroom unit.

Another good use of a storage wall is to provide space for blankets and other bulky bedding equipment.

is done. The kitchen and eating area need to be planned for storage of many items used in the preparation and serving of food—everything from measuring spoons to place mats, in addition to perishable foods and staple groceries. The laundry area must be equipped to store soiled clothing and laundry supplies. There must be a place for the tools and equipment needed to keep a house in good repair.

Basement Storage

New construction methods and equipment that eliminate problems caused by moisture in the basement have made this area usable for a variety of activities. The plan of the house and the habits of a particular family will influence their use of the space. Recreation rooms, play space for young children, and laundry rooms are commonly located in the basement. The activities will determine the kind and amount of storage needed.

In the basement recreation room. When the basement is finished to serve as a recreation room, it will probably be necessary to provide storage for card tables and folding chairs, radio, television, record player and records, musical instruments, toys, projector and screen, magazines, books, and a variety of small games and miscellaneous items. Some interior designers have created storage walls to house various combinations of these items without creating a cluttered look.

In the basement laundry. For safety reasons, laundry equipment in the basement should be separated from areas used by children for playing. Besides the washer and dryer, it is helpful

Shelves and storage units may be arranged for the convenience of any age group. The toy shelves used by small children can become bookshelves and hobby shelves when the children are older.

Shelves and a music file may be added to an ordinary closet to provide storage for all kinds of musical equipment.

Laundry equipment may be arranged to occupy a small space without sacrificing the safety and convenience features provided by larger laundry areas.

The garage or basement is most frequently used for tool storage. This use of hinged storage boxes provides storage that can be raised to keep the wall space free when the tools are not being used.

to have a sorting table; cupboards to store soaps, detergents, and other supplies; and a place to store clean, unironed clothes, and soiled clothing and linens.

When the basement has good natural light and family members use it for other activities, the homemaker may enjoy doing the ironing in the basement. This activity in turn creates a demand for a place to put the ironing board, pressing aids, and the iron.

Out-of-season storage in the basement. Sports equipment, electric fans, and luggage should be stored in dry, dust-free cabinets. Wheel toys that can be taken in and out of the basement easily may be stored here during winter months. Out-of-season clothing may be stored in plastic bags in cabinets built to accommodate different lengths of garments. Many apartment houses have lockers for use by the tenants in storing out-of-season items.

Storage for carpentry tools. The normal maintenance and repair jobs that are needed to keep a house in good condition require a few basic tools and supplies that may be stored in a workbench, combined with a pegboard, or panel of wood arranged for hanging tools not suited for drawer or shelf storage.

Some families store small garden tools, shovels, rakes, and hose in the basement during the winter season.

KITCHEN STORAGE

The family living in an apartment or ready-built house has little choice in the amount or location of storage units provided in the base price. It is sometimes possible to have more cabinets added at additional cost. It is frequently possible to increase the capacity of the storage space by adding shelves or accessories.

Shapes and sizes of kitchens vary. Most specialists agree that 20 linear feet of wall space is needed to provide for liberal base cabinets and appliances. Kitchens from 9 to 12 feet wide and from 10 to 20 feet long are usually designed in a U shape, which is considered the most convenient and step-saving arrangement. Rooms that tend to have a square shape are more often arranged with the cabinets and equipment in an L shape. When the

A lazy susan (revolving shelves) provides for storage of a large amount of goods in an otherwise inaccessible area.

room is narrow, a one-wall or two-wall arrangement is used. Many families want eating space in the kitchen area. Whatever arrangement is used, there should be a comfortable sequence of work flow perhaps from right to left for the right-handed person or from left to right for the left-handed person. For example, you may place the food-storage-and-preparation center (or mixing center) at the right, the sink at the midpoint, and the cooking center at the left.

The Efficient Kitchen

The work triangle connecting cooking, mixing, and sink centers should not exceed 22 feet in an efficient work arrangement. Doors should

A St. Charles Kitchen

Kitchen planning specialists can suggest ideal ways to store items such as linens and serving equipment.

be located so that traffic lanes do not cross the work triangle. It is generally accepted that distances between appliances should be from 4 to 7 feet between refrigerator and sink, 4 to 6 feet between sink and range, and 4 to 9 feet between range and refrigerator. Efficiency will be improved if there is not more than 4 feet between cabinets and appliances on opposite walls, 3 feet between cabinets placed at right angles, 4 feet between appliances placed at right angles, 3 feet in front of an oven door, and 16 inches between the counter top and the cabinets above it. When there are cabinets over the range, there should be 24 inches of clearance between range top and cabinets.

EXAMPLES OF KITCHEN ARRANGEMENTS

An L-shaped kitchen
with snack bar

Courtesy National Homes

U-shaped kitchen with
island range

A St. Charles Kitchen

A corridor kitchen

Courtesy United States Gypsum

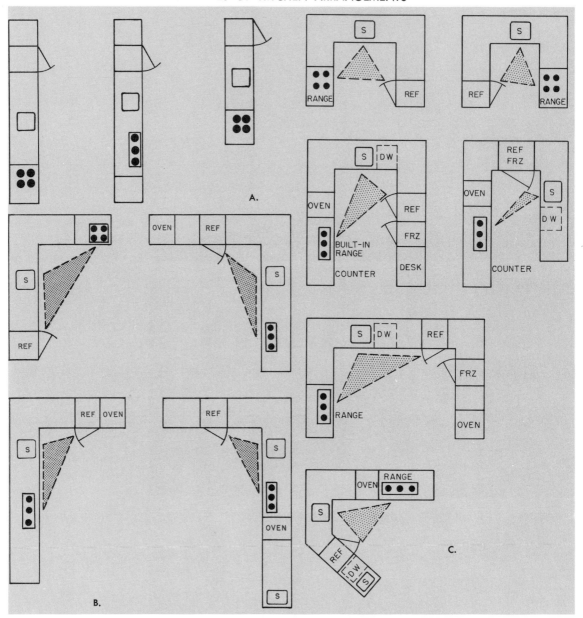

(A) The one-wall kitchen is common in apartments and smaller houses. The length of the area housing the stove, refrigerator, and sink should not exceed 10 feet. (B) The L-shaped kitchen usually has no traffic through the working area (represented by the triangle). The recommended standards for the amount of base-cabinet frontage range from a minimum 6 feet to a liberal 10 feet. (C) Because of the step saving arrangement of the work centers, the U-shaped kitchen is one of the most popular of the basic kitchen plans.

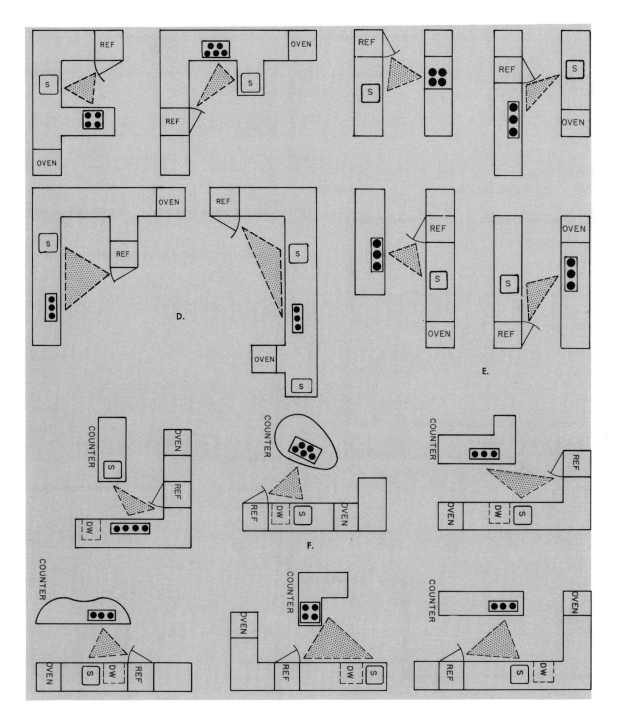

(D) Storage space can be added and efficiency increased by adding a peninsula to an existing kitchen plan. (E) The corridor kitchen frequently has traffic passing through the work area. (F) An island arrangement within the kitchen plan adds to the efficiency of the kitchen.

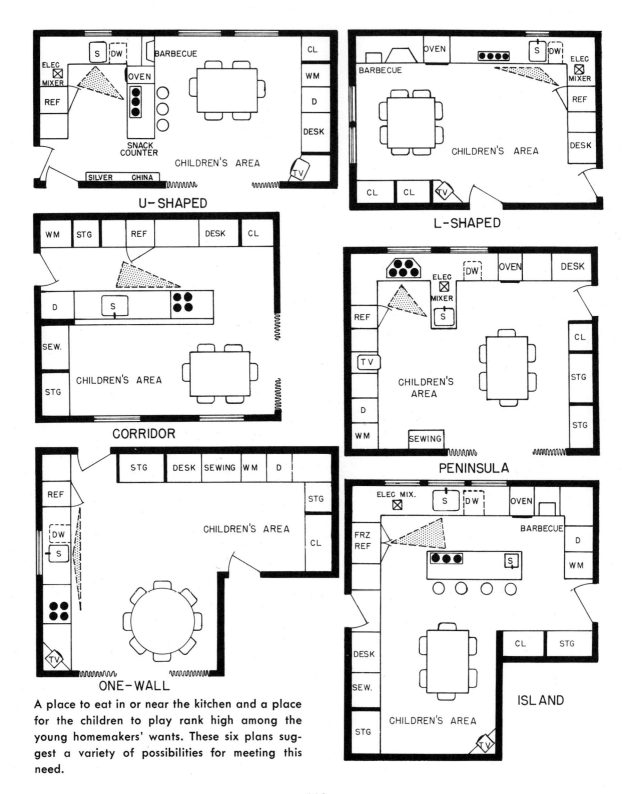

U-SHAPED

L-SHAPED

CORRIDOR

PENINSULA

ONE-WALL

ISLAND

A place to eat in or near the kitchen and a place for the children to play rank high among the young homemakers' wants. These six plans suggest a variety of possibilities for meeting this need.

Kitchen Patterns

The arrangement of counters and appliances tends to be more satisfactory when certain work sequences are used as the basis for positioning. Regardless of which arrangement is used, the measurement of the work triangle indicates the efficiency of the kitchen. It is desirable to have less than 23 feet in the perimeter of the triangle, measured from the center of the range, the refrigerator, and the sink.

One-wall kitchen. This arrangement is most frequently found in the minimum kitchen. When counter space is extended, the distances between working centers become less efficient.

L-shaped kitchen. The L-shaped kitchen has the advantage of freeing the opposite corner of the room for eating space. It is usually possible to eliminate traffic through the work triangle with the L-shaped pattern.

U-shaped kitchen. Since the counters and appliances are arranged on three sides of a room, there is no traffic through the work triangle of this kitchen pattern. The deep cabinets in the corner should be adapted to your storage needs so as to reduce the amount of dead space deep in the corners.

Occasionally a door will break the continuity of counters in a U-shaped kitchen. This is called a broken U. It has the disadvantage of causing traffic to pass through the work triangle.

The corridor kitchen. Arranging counters and appliances on opposite sides of the work area has the advantage of eliminating problem storage areas in corners. On the other hand, it may create a situation where traffic must pass through the work triangle. Some plans use an island arrangement to eliminate the traffic and to bring the work centers close together.

Working Centers in the Kitchen

Kitchen work may be easier if you organize the supplies and equipment around work centers which are basically (1) the food-storage-and-preparation center, (2) the sink center, and (3) the cooking-and-serving center. It is an advantage to have additional space for eating and for planning or record-keeping in the kitchen area.

The food-storage-and-preparation center. The refrigerator and the cabinets for storing staple foods make up the food storage-and-preparation center. This may be equally satisfactorily located between the sink and range, or the storage cabinets may be placed between the refrigerator and the range. When the kitchen plan has an L- or U-shaped arrangement, revolving shelves (sometimes called lazy susans) may be installed in the corner cabinets to increase the efficiency of the storage space. Some of these are portable; others are built-in.

The sink center. The sink center is the most frequently used kitchen center. It is generally located between the food-preparation center and the cooking-serving center. When equipment is arranged on either the L or U plan, it is important to have standing room at the side of the sink.

The cooking-and-serving center. This grouping of equipment and storage space should be located near the place where the family eats its meals. The range should not be under a curtained window, because of the fire hazard. If there are cabinets over the range, there must be about 24 inches clearance between the counter top and the bottom of wall cupboards.

Evaluating Kitchen Plans

Kitchen plans may be judged by the amount and quality of storage and counter space and by the arrangement of the storage cabinets, counters, appliances, and eating space.

Evaluating storage and counter space. There is a relationship between the amount of storage and counter space needed in a house and the overall size of the house. Counters should include drawers and shelves. Details are available from the Small Homes Council of the University of Illinois.

Evaluating the arrangement. Certain features are more desirable than others and should be given preference when there is a choice. Generally speaking, base cabinets are more efficient when equipped with drawers, pullout trays, or vertical pan dividers. Corner cabinets are more efficient when equipped with revolving shelves.

1. Read relevant materials on household storage and prepare a master list of items most commonly stored in each area of the house.

2. Select a stock floor plan and identify the storage spaces. Compare with recommended standards for each type of storage.

3. Develop a form to use for making an inventory of your personal belongings. Make the inventory.

4. Measure and make a scale drawing of the storage space you now use. Make another sketch showing how you could make this space more efficient. Share the before-and-after sketches with the class, explaining why you made the changes.

5. Make a scale drawing of one of the bedroom closets from your stock floor plan. Design the closet to meet the needs of a preschool child.

6. Collect illustrations of four room-storage arrangements. Discuss the desirable features of each with the class.

7. Working in small groups, survey the literature and develop a checklist for evaluating kitchen storage space. Compare the checklists and refine them to develop one usable form.

8. Evaluate the kitchen storage in your home. Suggest reasonable changes to improve the efficiency of the space.

9. Identify the basic kitchen type in your home. Compare the actual measurements with the desirable standards established by research.

10. Divide into buzz groups and discuss the storage problems related to seasonal items found in most households. Choose one of your group to serve on a panel to report findings to the class.

7

Maintenance

and Remodeling

THE TERMS "maintenance" and "remodeling" must be understood by both the renter and the owner of housing units. The day-to-day care necessary to keep an apartment or house in the same condition it was when completed is generally classified as maintenance. Keeping the apartment and hallways, or the house and yard, clean and making minor repairs as needed are a part of maintenance. The renter must also report any need for more extensive repairs to the rental agent or the landlord.

Remodeling, on the other hand, is an expense and obligation that occurs periodically. Most apartments and houses need to be rebuilt in some way every ten or fifteen years to keep them from becoming obsolete. The addition or extension of plumbing and lighting facilities are common examples of remodeling expenses which are needed to keep a house in good condition.

An understanding of both maintenance and remodeling must be included in the long-range plans of all property owners so that plans for both the actual work and the costs can be included in the family financial plans.

WHAT IS MAINTENANCE?

Maintenance is the technique of avoiding depreciation. Most maintenance jobs fall into two general groups: (1) chores to keep a place clean and orderly and to prevent excessive wear and depreciation; and (2) regular checks of all operating equipment to help prevent the expensive replacements often needed if minor repairs are neglected. Many maintenance jobs can be successfully handled by the do-it-yourself handyman or woman using a reference book that gives step-by-step directions for completing common repairs. A glance at a list of maintenance jobs indicates that they fall into a seasonal pattern closely related to climatic changes.

Typical Spring Maintenance Work.

Spring tends to inspire the paint-up, fix-up type of maintenance. The lengthened day, the bright sunlight, and the stimulation of nature coming into bloom seem to encourage both interior and exterior painting. Paint companies provide a wealth of material to help the consumer select the right paint. They also give directions for application to achieve a satisfying result. This is also the time when outdoor furniture may be

The wise home-owner plans for routine painting and cleaning that will help avoid depreciation of his property. In many areas of the United States it is routine to put up screens in the spring and to change these for storm windows for winter use. Freezing and thawing can cause seals to break at these especially vulnerable points: (1) Where an antenna is fastened to the roof. (2) Chimney flashings. (3) Gutters. (4) Vents for plumbing or heating systems. Failure to remove leaves from gutters could allow water to back up under the shingles and damage the roof. Water can also seep inside causing water damage to ceilings or walls. The home owner can do many simple maintenance jobs such as caulking cracks around the windows.

Lawn and garden equipment may be stored for the winter in the garage or basement storage area.

repaired, painted, and placed where it will be used for outdoor living.

Spring maintenance also includes such jobs as taking down the storm windows and putting up the screens unless combination storm windows and screens make this unnecessary. Winter dirt must be washed from all windows.

In areas where there are extreme temperature changes, another group of maintenance jobs needs to be routine. Alternate freezing and thawing of moisture in the valleys of roof joints may break the seals and allow water from spring rains to leak through and cause damage to the ceilings and walls. This damage usually occurs in the area where the chimney, skylight, or ventilating louvers join the roof of the house. The same weather conditions occasionally weaken the outside telephone and electrical connections. After a severe winter it may be advisable to have these points checked by a service representative.

The yard is a real challenge in the spring when so much needs to be done in such a short time. Mulch—used as winter protection—must be removed from plants; deadwood must be trimmed from trees and shrubs; and bare spots in the lawn must be seeded. Gutters on the house must be cleaned of leaves and other litter. The initial phase of yard work is getting the tools into operating condition. You may also

It is advisable to call in a qualified serviceman to service mechanical equipment.

need to move these tools to a storage area near places where they will be used.

Typical Fall Maintenance Work.

In many instances fall maintenance jobs are the opposite of the spring work. Screens come down and storm windows go up; yard and garden tools are stored, while snow-removal tools are put in a convenient place; tender plants are

117

shrouded in mulch; plantings may be added or changed.

The heating system must be thoroughly checked by a competent service man to assure satisfactory service. Consistent attention to reasonable maintenance practices such as this can slow down the depreciation process in any house or apartment.

WHAT IS REMODELING?

Remodeling differs from maintenance in the nature of the work and the frequency with which the needs occur. Generally, remodeling will change the appearance of some part of the house or even its overall appearance. It may also change the use made of certain parts of the house. Remodeling brings the house up-to-date through installation of new materials and equipment, rearrangement of space inside the house, or addition of new rooms.

Why Remodel a House?

Remodeling may be an economical solution to the problem of meeting changing needs. It may be the means by which a family can stay in the neighborhood they know and like even when they have outgrown the house in its present state. One big advantage of remodeling is that it can be done in stages.

Families may buy a used house with the idea of remodeling it to meet their needs. Such families should carefully check all the financial aspects involved. Zoning regulations and the development plans for the area need to be checked to determine that the area will remain residential for the foreseeable future. Plans for the development of the area that will influence property values must also be checked. For example, the addition of a new school would tend to increase both property values and taxes.

The neighborhood, personal associations, and family ties to community organizations may influence a family to remodel rather than to move when housing needs change. There are situations, particularly in housing developments, where the sale price of comparable new houses has risen enough over a period of time to make it economically sound for a family who bought at a lower price to make changes, even additions, and still stay within the resale price range of houses in that particular area. They may be able to have more space for less money, in a neighborhood they know they like, than in a new house.

Trees and shrubs add to the beauty, function, and value of a house. If a family has lived several years in one house, they have, no doubt, arranged the outdoor living area to suit their needs. The cost of planting trees and shrubs, as well as the time needed to develop mature plants, may influence them to remodel rather than start over with a new house and the development of a new outdoor area.

Many magazines feature remodeling ideas which help families meet changing needs while allowing them to remain in their present neighborhood.

When a run-down house in a good neighborhood can be bought at a favorable price, a complete restoration may be justified. This is especially true when you can do some of the remodeling work yourself.

The character of a house may be altered by changing architectural details, as an existing space is remodeled for year-round use.

Architect: J. W. Hoge

The addition of a screened porch on the ground level and a deck opening from the second floor supply areas for outdoor living.

Financing Remodeling

If you are established in your neighborhood and have acquired a substantial equity in your house, there will be little trouble getting a loan to make improvements. Among the possible ways to obtain financing are:

1. Adding remodeling costs to the present open-end mortgage

2. Having the contractor arrange for financing

3. Securing a Federal Housing Administration-insured Alteration, Repair and Improvement Loan

4. Buying the materials on credit and paying the labor charges as work is completed

Loans generally are made for making structural changes in a house, for reconstruction (such as new roofs), for eliminating obsolete equipment (replacing heating or plumbing that is out-of-date), for modernizing the kitchen or laundry space, for adding rooms or baths, for building garage space, and so on.

The Scope of Remodeling

Remodeling projects may range from changing the location of equipment in one of the work areas of the house to a complete overhaul of both the exterior and the interior of the house. As noted above, an advantage of remodeling is that it can be done in stages. Once you have decided what needs to be done, and what else you would like to have done, you are ready to have plans drawn, to arrange financing, and to let contracts for various phases of the work.

Most remodeling jobs fall into one of three groups: (1) converting space in the house and under the roof to new uses; (2) adding on rooms for more livable space; and (3) modernizing the kitchen, bath, and utility room area with new equipment. Occasionally a whole house is remodeled or restored. This is not often done, however, because of the inconvenience of living in a house while it is being remodeled, plus the uncertainty of the total cost of complete remodeling.

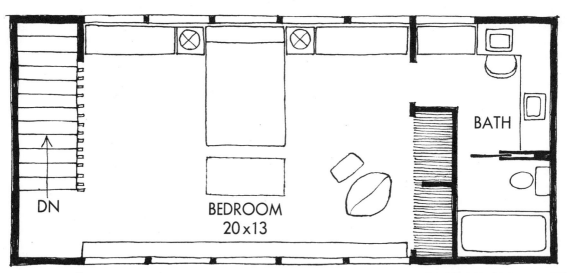

BEDROOM
20x13

DN

BATH

A rear wing which blends well with the original architectural style furnishes
an additional room and attached bath.

Courtesy Better Homes and Gardens, © Meredith Corporation, 1968

Combined outdoor-indoor living areas provide for a wide range of family-centered activities regardless of weather conditions.

Ten Steps to Successful Remodeling

In *Sunset Ideas for Remodeling Your Home* the editorial staff of Lane Publishing Company lists ten steps to successful remodeling:

1. Consult an architect or contractor.
2. Check building ordinances.
3. Draw up preliminary sketches.
4. Arrange for professionally drafted plans.
5. Draw up cost estimate.
6. Prepare specification sheet.
7. Have plans blueprinted.
8. Apply for a loan.
9. Buy a building permit.
10. Engage a contractor.

The remodeler will need plans to present when applying for either a loan or a building permit. Regardless of how small the job, you should have detailed plans in the form of scale drawings. The cost of getting scale drawings converted to a set of professional plans drawn by a draftsman is usually nominal and the cost of blueprints is small.

The role of an architect. Contrary to some beliefs, architects are not necessarily expensive. Once you have decided what to do in the way of remodeling, it may be wise to ask an architect to look at the proposal and tell you whether an architect is needed to accomplish your goals. He may suggest that your needs could be met by a well-qualified contractor.

It may be that you are planning an extensive remodeling job for which the services of an architect would be advisable. You may expect an architect to:

1. Interview you in his office to discuss the requirements and the size and makeup of the family, and how much you plan to spend on the job
2. Measure and photograph your house. From these measurements he will reconstruct a plan and elevation of the house as it is
3. Prepare rough sketches of changes he is suggesting for you to consider
4. Make up preliminary drawings showing materials to be used, equipment to be included, and fixtures needed
5. Make working drawings to be prepared as blueprints
6. Seek bids from contractors and help in the final selection of a contractor

7. Supervise the construction and make sure that all legal obligations are fulfilled

The charge for architectural service varies and should be discussed before the agreement with the architect is signed. Once an architect is hired, he should be left in charge.

The role of a contractor. There are contractors who specialize in remodeling work. In some areas contractors have architects on their staffs to help plan the changes to be made. It is a definite advantage to have drawings prepared by a draftsman. If several contractors are bidding on the job, each should be supplied with identical information on which to base his bid. Many contractors work on a cost-plus basis because of the uncertainty connected with work on older houses. The general contractor is responsible for scheduling the work of the subcontractors: the carpenter, the electrician, the plumber, the mason, and the painter.

The role of the handyman. For the most part, the jobs undertaken by the handyman consist of minor improvements in the existing house, for which no permit is needed. They include such jobs as installing bookshelves, paneling walls, finishing attic space, or arranging living space in the basement.

Remodeling Ideas

A portfolio of remodeling ideas can be a big help when you are making specific plans for changes in a house. While no solution will fit a new situation exactly, you can try out the ideas used by others for adding living space, for converting existing space into more usable form, and for modernizing by replacing or relocating equipment in the work areas. Whatever you propose to do, you must consider the changes in relation to the circulation pattern for traffic within the house, the appearance of the house, and the relationship to the outdoor living areas.

Additions to the house. Before starting to plan an addition to a house, you should check to see whether the zoning regulations will permit an extension of the house size. It is common for regulations to state what percentage of a lot may be covered by a house. Setback regulations—the distances one must stay from the lot lines—may also limit what can be added to

an existing house. The more common type of additions include such features as these:

1. An extension of the present living room or the addition of a new living-room wing to permit conversion of the former living room into a bedroom, family room, or dining room

2. The addition of a family room somewhere near the kitchen and outdoor living area

3. An in-law room—or room and bath—located in the quiet area of the house

4. A screened outdoor house, in geographic areas where this would be useful during the warm seasons

5. A terrace or porch to expand the living area to the outdoors

6. A second story to gain more room where it is not possible to add onto the first floor

7. A deck opening from the second-floor level to add space for living in a two-story house

New uses for existing space. A carport, breezeway, attached garage, or covered porch is relatively easy to convert to living space at moderate expense. The cost is less because the space is already covered by a roof and based on a foundation. The supports for the roof form the skeleton framework for the walls. The problem of finding a place for the family car, or cars, must be considered when a garage is converted to living space. If there are no restrictions, it may be possible to build a carport in front of the present garage, thus utilizing the same driveway. Magazines frequently show garages converted to quarters for in-laws.

There is difference-of opinion as to how successfully the basement can be used for living space. One of the more serious problems to be solved is that of moisture. However, there are products on the market that will seal the walls against penetration of moisture. The location of the stairway to the basement is an important factor in creating a feeling that the basement is a part of the living area of the house. Some families have found the need for space so great that they have installed additional windows or enlarged the existing window wells to increase the light in the basement area. Basements have been converted to playrooms, recreation rooms, bedrooms, and occasionally into separate quarters for live-in relatives. When bedrooms are built in the basement, it is advisable to add a

The extensive remodeling involved in the addition of a second floor is especially useful when the size of the lot or the design of the original house will not lend itself to a large ground-floor addition. A wood and concrete patio at the back of the house provides another living area.

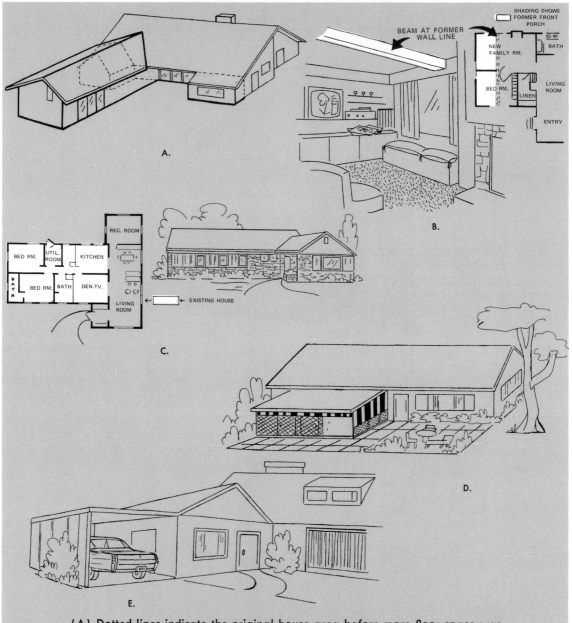

(A) Dotted lines indicate the original house area before more floor space was added to meet increased family needs. (B) A covered porch built on a good foundation can be converted into added living space. (C) A new wing can provide desired extra space. (D) The addition of areas which do not require heating and plumbing is less costly than conventional additions. (E) It may be desirable to add a carport, when the garage is converted into living space.

Attic space may be finished to add sleeping space for children or to provide a quiet place for adults.

bathroom on the same level. In some localities fire protection laws may require an outside exit from lower-level living quarters.

Modernizing the kitchen. The kitchen is usually the first room in the house to be modernized. This is probably because the kitchen is the center for more activities involving equipment than any other room. Besides being the center of activity, the kitchen needs to be closely related to as many other areas as possible. The kitchen should be accessible to the dining area for family and company meals. It is desirable to have the kitchen near the service area for bringing in supplies and disposing of garbage, near the living room for convenient serving of snacks, near the playroom so the children can be supervised while food is prepared, and convenient to the outdoor eating area as well. In remodeling the kitchen, keep this desirable location in mind. Changing the position of a door, or making a door where there is now a window, can add to the efficiency of the kitchen.

127

Courtesy American Plywood Association

In modernizing an older home, sometimes it is better to tear back to the walls and build in a new kitchen.

Manufacturers of kitchen equipment, home service representatives from utility companies, and home economists with the extension service are prepared to supply current information on new equipment. Modern equipment is often so flexible that kitchens are no longer so closely tied to the work-triangle theory that determined the location of the single-unit stove, refrigerator, and sink. Today some refrigerators come in separate sections so they may be built in wherever wanted. Ovens and broilers come in units that are separate from the surface cooking units, and can be placed in the most convenient spots. Dishwashers and multiple basin sinks also provide greater freedom of usage. Since you will probably have had some experience using a kitchen before remodeling it, you can remodel to suit your way of cooking.

When considering changes, you must recognize that replacing equipment or adding new appliances may require changes in the wiring.

Most houses need additional electrical circuits to ensure efficient operation of equipment.

Modernizing the kitchen may also mean creating a new atmosphere as well as improving the work areas. There is a growing trend toward making the kitchen not only a place for preparing food, but also a place for eating, for doing the laundry, and for relaxing.

Counter tops, wall and cabinet finishes, hardware, and floor coverings may be chosen from a wide variety of satisfactory materials to create the effect wanted and the service needed.

Modernizing the bathroom. Remodeling the bathroom is a complicated undertaking because of the complex plumbing installations, the need for safe wiring, and the many different materials used to finish the walls, counter tops, and floors. Many older bathrooms are so small and so situated that remodeling must be limited to replacing obsolete fixtures with their modern counterparts and using new materials on the

(A) A terrace added near the living area provides a place to relax or entertain. (B) Adding a second floor to a one-story house is one of the more extensive possibilities. (C) In some localities a deck may be added to the second floor to increase living space. (D) Basement recreation areas or living space become more desirable if grading allows the use of full-size windows at the lower level.

129

Plywood-styrofoam underlayment placed over the concrete to insure a warm, resilient base for plastic tile surface flooring

Decorative plywood panels used for walls

walls and floors. When there is space available to enlarge the bath, remodeling may include the addition of built-in vanities, linen storage cabinets, and compartments to separate the fixtures so that more people can use the facilities at the same time. A contractor will be able to tell you whether it would be better to remodel or to add a complete new bathroom by pushing out the walls for an addition.

Planning bathrooms for convenience with economy. A bathroom is one of the most expensive parts of a house. Its cost is seldom less than $1,000 and may be more. The cost may be roughly divided into one-third each for the basic fixtures, for plumbing labor and materials, and for the labor and materials for finishing walls, floor, and electrical work.

The bathroom location should be considered in relation to the total house plan and traffic

pattern. An only bath should open on a hall. Wall and floor finishes should be safe and easy to clean. There must be adequate lighting. Electrical outlets must be safely located. Storage cabinets should be ample for all bath accessories and supplies. The bathroom should be well ventilated and comfortably heated. In some climates supplementary heaters should be available. The door and the walls should retain sound.

Vertical and horizontal concentration of residential plumbing is a principle that has proved economical and useful in many home plans.

Complete vertical concentration in a two-story and basement house would align the basement laundry and utility room under the first-floor kitchen, and the second-floor bathrooms directly over the kitchen. All water and waste connections would be in one line of pipes.

130

A BASEMENT LIVING AREA

New focal point — a
fireplace with a raised
hearth

Snack bar and hobby
corner

Complete horizontal concentration on a single-floor house would have one common plumbing wall serve one or two bathrooms, the kitchen sink, the laundry and the water heater.

To centralize plumbing, it might be necessary to build an inside bathroom, which can be finished with a skylight and equipped with an automatic exhaust fan. A small, fully equipped bath can fit in a 5- by 5-foot space. A half bath (basin and toilet) needs a 3- by 5-foot area.

Varying floor layouts and cost estimates can be considered in relation to family preferences and budgets.

Modernizing the heating system. Mechanical units need replacement after fifteen or twenty years of service. Figuring the needs for heating should be left to a heating engineer who will study the present system and recommend changes. Many people believe that any system installed today should include the duct work or piping for cooling as well as heating.

Remodeling for convenience. Up to this point only remodeling that involved structural changes has been discussed. There are some changes that can be made with a minimum expenditure of money that will add to the livability of a house. Where the rooms are large enough, one wall, or a portion of one wall, may be used for closets and storage space. In smaller rooms, shelves for books and curios may be built on the walls above furniture arrangements. In the kitchen, storage space may be increased by adding more shelves to the cupboards. There are situations where removing the gingerbread (excessive decoration) will improve the appearance of a house.

In all remodeling it is essential to recognize the needs of the family, to plan in detail the changes in the present arrangement to meet these needs, and then to determine whether the cost is reasonable in terms of the satisfaction the family will derive from the changes.

LEARNING EXPERIENCES

1. Read and collect newspaper and magazine articles relating to home maintenance and repair work. Analyze the articles and prepare a guide for routine jobs.
2. Compare the rates of the family handyman and the professional serviceman in relation to house and yard work.
3. Divide into groups and prepare a skit dramatizing a family discussing whether to move or remodel. Present the skit to the class for evaluation.
4. Individually, or in small groups, interview one or more architects or builders who specialize in remodeling to learn their opinions about when it pays to remodel. Report to the class.
5. Discuss the role of the architect in a remodeling project.
6. Select members of the class to hold a mock interview with someone playing the role of an architect or a builder.
7. Assemble and share remodeling ideas with the class. Classify according to type.
8. Study trade publications and advertising for new developments in home equipment. Share your findings with the class.
9. Make a line drawing of your home to $\frac{1}{8}$-inch scale. On a tracing paper overlay, sketch changes you would like to make if you could remodel.
10. Read and report to the class on a restoration project.

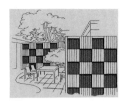

8

Planning for

Outdoor Areas

WHETHER THE outdoor area around your home is an apartment balcony, a patio, or the lot surrounding a single-family dwelling, you would like a landscape plan that will be ornamental and will serve as an extension of your home. The indoor-outdoor areas are more satisfactory when the details are planned to meet the work, play, and relaxation needs of the people who live there. While no two outdoor areas will be exactly alike, it will be helpful to know what others have done. Certain requirements and situations are common to all landscape plans, regardless of geography or location—whether urban, suburban, or small-town. The principles used by professional landscape gardeners may be applied.

INDOOR—OUTDOOR LIVING

The outdoor area of any dwelling may be divided into three parts according to use: (1) an approach area (usually on the street side of the property), (2) a living area for rest, relaxation, and entertaining, usually adjacent to the living area of the house), and (3) a work area (usually next to the kitchen-utility room or to the garage). A garden should be beautiful to look at and pleasurable to live in. What you consider beautiful will influence how your grounds are separated into activity areas and will determine the choice of plants to supply color, shade, and privacy. Creation of a yard for outdoor living requires careful attention to existing buildings, local zoning ordinances, climate, the grade of the land and the condition of the soil.

In devising an overall plan for your house and grounds consider the house in relation to the street, the lot lines, and the trees growing on the lot. Generally, a view from the living-room windows is desired, and some kind of accent planting will make a more interesting landscape for large lots. No matter how large or small the area you have to work in, you should strive for attractive views from the windows and activity areas of the house—views that are conveniently located and easy to maintain.

Permanent plant materials, including trees and shrubs, are relatively expensive and hard to move; therefore, it is important to have a landscape plan before buying even one planting. Many people believe the most beautiful

Some lots are designed so that the driveway provides the front entrance approach to the house for both pedestrian and automobile use.

home grounds blend naturally into the surroundings. Since plants change in size and shape as they mature, it may be necessary to prune plants to maintain the desired effect.

Approaching the House

Most outdoor areas provide a walk from the street to the main entrance of the house and a driveway to the service area and garage. These allow easy access to the buildings and grounds. More and more houses are being placed so as to allow for a small, but adequate, front yard with more space at the side or back of the yard for living and work areas large enough and private enough to be useful. Some housing developments have restrictions on what the individual property owner may do with the front yard. Community planners believe that simple lawns, with limited plantings that continue from one property to the next, contribute most to the overall beauty of the street and the neighborhood.

The sidewalk. The walk leading to the entrance of the house may have a concrete, flagstone, brick, or cinder surface. Some type of masonry or metal edging is probably needed to keep plants from growing on the walk area. If the walk is made of cinders or gravel, it is

necessary to use a solid edging material to keep the soil from mixing with the walk. The gardener must consider the surface material and the edging when planning accent plantings.

Stone and brick make good walks. They allow plantings that spill informally over the edge of the walk, adding color and texture interest. Curved walks tend to be less monotonous than long, straight walks, but they should be used only when there is an obvious reason for the curve. When planning a curved walk, you should keep in mind the limitations of the paving materials. Bricks with rectangular shapes do not blend well in curved lines. Flagstone with its irregular shapes is more flexible in the layout of curves.

The driveway. The driveway should be as straight as possible, and it should run directly from the street or alley to the service area. While a 14-foot width is considered adequate for a one-car driveway and 20 feet for a two-car driveway, an additional 18 inches or 2 feet of width make it easier to get in and out of the car without stepping on the grass or flower beds adjacent to the drive. In some layouts a circular drive may be necessary to allow access to both sides of the house. Concrete, asphalt, or gravel are commonly used for driveways. The plant-

The attractive arrangement of concrete slabs often adds to the landscaping possibilities of the approach area.

Texture variations coupled with random shapes provide interesting approaches to an elevated entrance.

The driveway may be enlarged to provide off-street parking plus a play area for children.

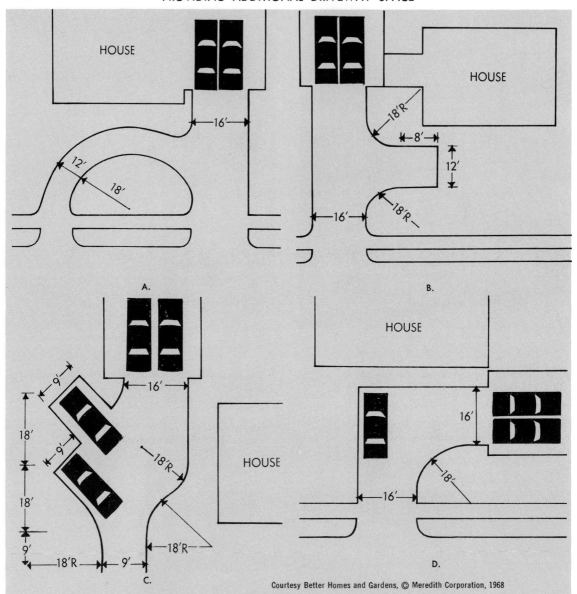

Courtesy Better Homes and Gardens, © Meredith Corporation, 1968

(A) A circular drive may be added to the straight drive which leads to the garage, in order to provide a turnaround. This arrangement is particularly desirable where the driveway leads into a busy street. (B) A stub added to a straight driveway provides additional parking space or space for turning around in order to head into street traffic. (C) Where the garage is located behind the house with some side yard space available, an angled system will provide more off-street parking. (D) An extra parking space to one side of the garage area can be provided by squaring off a curved driveway.

Paving all or part of the outdoor living area may add to the usefulness of the space.

ings along the edge of the drive should add to the beauty of the yard without interfering with the function of the drive.

The Outdoor Living Area

To be used to best advantage, the outdoors should be developed as an extension of the indoors. Space that is designed for rest, relaxation, or entertaining, in reasonable privacy, may include one or more of the following features: patios, terraces, lawns, and pools. To create privacy for your outdoor living area, it may be necessary to screen out all or part of the adjacent properties. A variety of architectural materials and plant life may be used for such screening. Wood, stone, plastics, brick, and concrete are suitable for fences, walls, or enclosures. Plants may be used as hedges to create masses of foliage. Many people feel that more pleasing effects are achieved by a combination of fences or walls and plantings.

If an outdoor living area is regularly used, it probably should be paved because grass will not grow where there is heavy foot traffic. Brick, flagstone, concrete patio squares, treated log cuttings, cedar shavings, or fine gravel all make satisfactory paving in areas used to accommodate outdoor furniture. Convenient access to the

kitchen or living room will add to the livability of outdoor space. If there is no shade tree, use a canopy or a large umbrella to provide shelter from the sun.

Porches. Perhaps the most familiar form of outdoor living space is the porch. Usually outside the main walls of a building but structurally attached to it, a porch is always covered by a roof, often one that is separate from the house roof. (In some localities the word "porch" is used to refer to similar structures which are not covered by a roof.) The traditional front and back porch served mostly as protection for the entrance and as a place to sit. Today porches are more thoughtfully integrated into the overall house plan and are made large enough to accommodate a variety of activities. When a porch is enclosed with glass or screen, it may be furnished for eating, resting, or games. The uses to be made of the porch will influence its size and location in relation to the rest of the house and the yard. In some climates supplementary heat extends the period of use into the fall and early spring seasons.

Patios. Strictly speaking, a patio is an open court enclosed by at least three sides of a building. Current writers frequently use the terms "terrace", "breezeway", and "loggia" as syno-

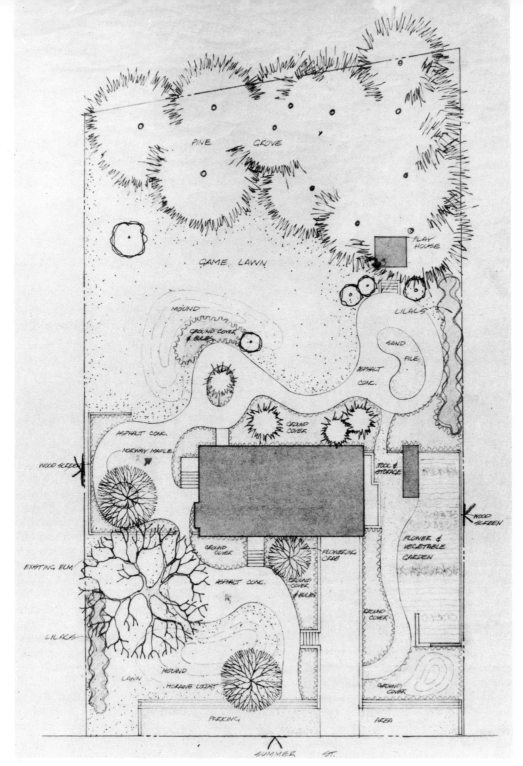

Within the plan the following labels appear:

PINE GROVE

GAME LAWN

PLAY HOUSE

MOUND

GROUND COVER & BULBS

LILACS

SAND PILE

ASPHALT CONC.

ASPHALT CONC.

NORWAY MAPLE

WOOD SCREEN

GROUND COVER

TOOL & STORAGE

WOOD SCREEN

FLOWER & VEGETABLE GARDEN

EXISTING ELM

GROUND COVER

FLOWERING CRAB

GROUND COVER & BULBS

ASPHALT CONC.

GROUND COVER

LILACS

LAWN

MOUND

MORAINE LOCUST

GROUND COVER

PARKING

AREA

SUMMER ST.

Courtesy Lawrence W. Zuelke, Landscape Architect, Lincoln, Mass.

A landscape architect can develop a beautiful plan which makes optimum use of the grounds, providing for a variety of activities for both children and adults.

nyms for patio when referring to outdoor space used for functions otherwise carried on in the recreation and kitchen areas of the home. Hepler and Wallach in *Housing Today* discuss the patio in connection with the part of the house to which it relates. They suggest living patios convenient to the kitchen and living room; play patios for use by children; and quiet patios, adjacent to the bedrooms, for relaxation. To obtain full advantage of a patio, it should be designed for both daytime and nighttime use.

Lanais. The Hawaiian veranda or terrace has been adapted to contemporary house design. "Lanai" generally refers to a covered exterior passageway which may function as a porch. If the lanai is wide enough, it may serve as a patio. When there is a pool, a lanai may provide poolside shelter. Like the patio and porch, a lanai is most satisfactory if it functions as a transition from the house to the yard.

Pools. If your family likes swimming and if you can afford the cost of building and maintaining a pool, you may provide convenient recreation for the family and add beauty to your grounds by building a pool. Pools are available in a variety of sizes and shapes that can be blended into the design of the patio or terrace adjoining the house. Many communities have codes that specify where and how pools must be built and maintained. It is safe to assume that no matter where your pool is, you will need a filtering system for the water and a fence or wall enclosure to meet health and safety requirements.

Outdoor eating. If food is generally prepared in the kitchen and carried outside to be eaten, it is especially important to locate the picnic table in a spot convenient to the kitchen. Some families who are enthusiastic about outdoor eating have adapted a kitchen or breakfast-room window as a pass-through to simplify the transfer of food and dishes from inside to outside. Those who prefer cooking outdoors can choose from among a wide range of portable outdoor grills and masonry grills. There are plans in gardening books and magazines for a variety of small buildings to house outdoor cooking equipment. In some sections of the country it is an advantage to have a screened porch or garden house as protection from insects.

Play space for children. There are obvious advantages in providing a paved area for the physically active games of growing children which is separate from the outdoor living area to be used by adults. Children will be able to play outside when the ground is wet. The paving will stand up under daily use. Wheel toys work better on paving. With proper planning, any building or shelter for children's use may be adapted to adult interests when the children are grown. When the play space is next to the garage or carport, the garage may be used to store toys and equipment and to provide shelter for active games when the weather is bad.

The Work Area

More people are doing more work around their houses. They need adequate, well-designed, easy-to-maintain space for their activities. The work area usually includes a drying yard, space for general service requirements such as trash cans, and perhaps a vegetable garden, a gardening shed, or a forcing frame. It may be a relatively small area, but it should be close to the kitchen and garage.

The paved play area may also serve as the drying yard, used to dry or air clothing and household linens. The work area should include a convenient place for delivery and storage of household needs. A small vegetable garden may be included in the work-area plan to provide fresh vegetables for the table. Gardening books sometimes give suggestions for forcing frames or miniature green houses which the serious gardener may wish to include in the work area.

THE LANDSCAPE PLAN

As the furnishings and accessories in the house reflect the special interests of its occupants, so the arrangement of space and plants in a garden reflects their personalities. Whether you hire a landscape architect to interpret your ideas, work with the consultant at a nursery, or strike out on your own, you can be sure that the pleasure you get from the use of the land will be greater if your individual tastes have been satisfied.

To do this, you may first need to learn the names of plants, their characteristics, and the

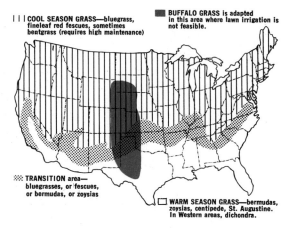

Local soil, temperature, and rainfall conditions will influence the choice of a grass for any geographic area.

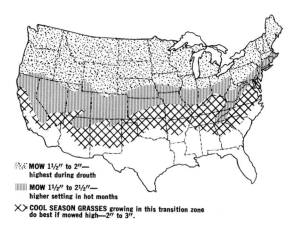

The cutting height for mowing grasses varies with the climate.

conditions under which they will grow. Catalogs from large nurseries, garden books, or periodicals from the library will give you a start. After getting basic information, you can supplement your knowledge by visiting parks and arboretums where growing plants are marked for identification, or by visiting a nursery to see particular plants that you have selected. When you know the names and characteristics of the plants you want, you will be ready to make a scale plan showing the exact name, size, and location of the plants you have chosen.

Most landscape plans will be threefold: (1) a background planting to soften the silhouette of the house against the sky, (2) plantings to frame and separate the house and grounds from their surroundings, and (3) accent plantings to draw attention to important features of the house or the grounds.

Maintenance of the Lawn

Grass is the basic planting of the lawn area in most sections of the United States, but there are some situations where ground covers are used in place of grass. For instance, a ground cover might replace grass when the ground slope is so steep as to prevent mowing. In the Southwest rock may be used for ground cover. Research by the U.S. Department of Argiculture has determined which grass varieties are best suited to different geographic areas. This information is available from the county agent. It is advisable to follow his recommendations. In the cooler parts of the country it is best to build, or fix up, lawns in the fall, while in the South and the Southwest spring is the better time for lawn work.

To get a good lawn, you need a perennial grass adapted to the soil and the climate. The United States is divided into six regions for which general recommendations may be made. However, it is a good idea to check locally about varieties that have proved successful in the area.

Keeping your lawn in good condition requires a knowledge of plant needs and much work. Lawns must be fertilized, watered, mowed, and weeded.

Fertilizers for the lawn. To produce a thick green turf, grass must be kept growing continuously. This requires both plant food and water. For the most part, lawn foods supply nitrogen in two forms—fast-acting and slow-acting. The fast-acting types release nitrogen more quickly but may cause burning of the plants, with brown spots appearing in the lawn. These fertilizers will be leached away when used in sandy soils. The more expensive slow-acting fertilizers last longer. They release nitrogen at a slow, even rate, and there is little danger of burning.

Planter blocks may be used for terracing a slope where grass would not be a desirable ground cover.

Watering the lawn. A new lawn must be watered every day if it doesn't rain. This means soaking the ground enough to permit moisture to get to the roots. Shallow watering of established lawns tends to draw grass roots to the surface and therefore is not a good practice. A thorough weekly watering is helpful during dry spells.

Mowing the lawn. Bluegrass and zoysia lawns are usually mowed to a height of 1½ to 3 inches, while bent grass lawns are mowed to 1 inch. Generally, the higher the grass is cut, the deeper the roots will be, and as a result the grass can obtain moisture from the soil for a longer period. Bent grass sometimes develops a maintenance problem by matting and thatching. This is best overcome by using a vertical cutting mower. Vertical cutting mowers do a better job than spikers, which were formerly used to cut into the thatch, to make normal penetration of water, fertilizer, and air possible.

Weed control in the lawn. In lawns where weeds have secured a foothold, it is best to start a control program early in the season. There are preemergence weed killers on the market for this purpose, which are effective when used according to the manufacturer's directions. Dandelion, plantain, and other broad leaf weeds may be eliminated with the 2, 4-D weed killers. A well-established lawn that is fertilized as needed, carefully watered, and mowed reasonably high will not have a serious weed problem.

Ground Covers

In places where grass is not suitable or will not grow because of soil or climatic conditions, there are plants that will produce a green mat. Ground-cover plants may be used effectively in moist, dry, or shady locations, on embankments and rocky slopes, and in crevices between stepping-stones. Ground covers may be evergreen or deciduous. There are annual ground covers to choose from as well as the perennial types.

Evergreen ground covers. These include Baltic and Bulgarian ivy, wintercreeper, creeping juniper, pachysandra, thyme, and myrtle. Each has characteristics that make it specially suitable for some problem spots and each must be considered in relation to the particular conditions under which it is to be planted.

Deciduous ground covers. These vines will spread on the ground if they are not trained to a trellis or other support. They are best suited to large areas such as embankments. Honeysuckle, grape, porcelain berry, rambler rose, and sweet woodruff may be used to cover areas for aesthetic reasons or to hold moisture in the soil.

141

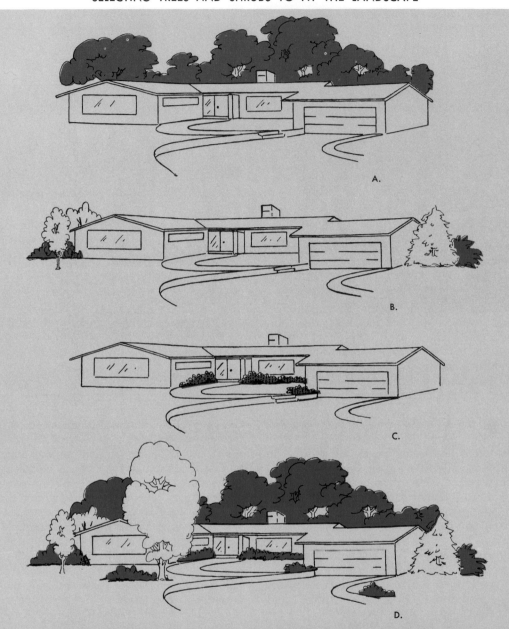

Trees and shrubs must be selected for the function they are to serve in the landscape plan. The shape of the crown and the height of the tree may serve to soften the roof line against the sky (A). Both the color and the shapes of the trees and shrubs used near the house may frame the house (B) or accent certain architectural features (C). The house and mature plantings should blend into a unified design (D).

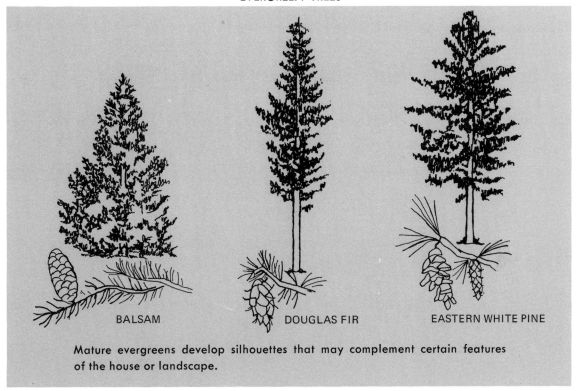

BALSAM DOUGLAS FIR EASTERN WHITE PINE

Mature evergreens develop silhouettes that may complement certain features of the house or landscape.

Perennial ground covers. A number of perennial plants that grow to less than 1 foot are available for use as ground covers. Among the most generally successful varieties are bugleweed and lily of the valley. Goutweed spreads rapidly in poor soil. Prostrate cotoneaster is good for planting among rocks, while St. Johnswort does particularly well in the shade. In southern California ivy and ice plant may be used.

Trees

Because trees take a long time to grow, they should be given priority over other plantings. Usually trees are selected to serve as shade in the summer or a windbreak in the winter, and to enhance the appearance of the property. Trees may be classified according to characteristics which the home gardener may wish to use to fit particular situations. Some trees grow so large that they are suitable only for spacious home grounds. Special strains of some trees are developed to keep them small to complement contemporary houses on small lots. There are trees for moist locations, trees for semidry locations, and trees to withstand city conditions. Still other trees are planted for their bloom or their fruit. Besides being visually attractive, such trees may attract birds to the yard.

Generally a tree will grow in reasonably good soil if there is plenty of aeration in the soil for the root system and adequate water. There are hundreds of tree varieties cultivated in the United States. They fall into two broad classifications: (1) deciduous trees which drop their leaves each fall; and (2) evergreens which stay green the year round.

Selecting deciduous trees. Arborists refer to trees as good and poor or as more desirable and less desirable. Some trees may be good if planted in one geographic area and not so good when used in another area. The shape of the head of the tree and the density of the foliage may also influence its choice.

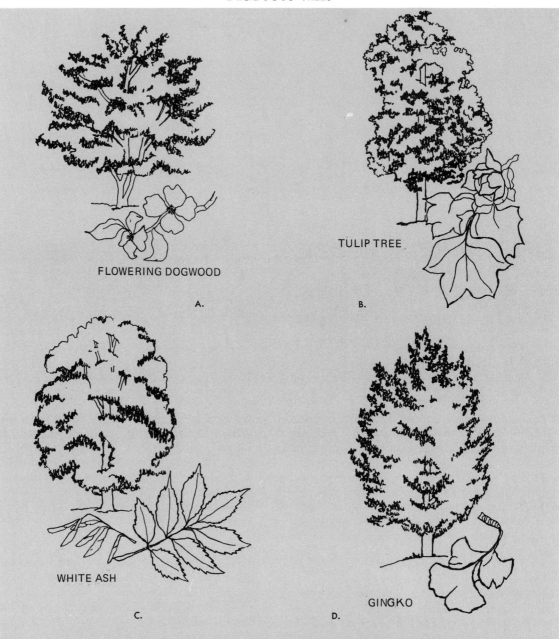

FLOWERING DOGWOOD

A.

TULIP TREE

B.

WHITE ASH

C.

GINGKO

D.

Deciduous trees grow to varying heights. They develop characteristic crowns that make each type desirable for creating particular landscape effects. Accent trees usually have special features such as blossoms (A and B) or ornamental berries (C). The unique shape of the crown and leaf may also provide a suitable accent (D).

Trees for street planting. Shade trees selected for street planting will be more satisfactory if they are selected from varieties that develop a symmetrical outline, are long-lived and resistant to disease and storm damage, and do not produce litter. Some trees are hardy under almost all conditions in both city and suburban areas. This group includes the sugar maple, red oak, and European linden. Trees such as the horse chestnut, box elder, black locust, willow, birch, and poplar should seldom be used for street planting. If the street is very wide, tall pyramidal trees, such as the pin oak and the maidenhair, may be good selections, provided the soil and climate are right. In smoky, congested areas the tree of heaven produces a vigorous growth and shade where other trees would not thrive because of the atmospheric conditions. It is important to know both the characteristics of a particular tree and its growth needs, as well as the soil and climatic conditions where it is to be planted.

Accent, or specimen, trees. Trees that are planted singly, or in groups of from one to three specimens to set them apart from other parts of the landscaping, are usually varieties that are desirable because of their flowers, foliage, fruit, color of bark, or interesting outline which shows off best when the plant is set apart. The same qualities may be used to provide accents in border plantings when the trees are used singly or in groups in combination with other plants. Among the many varieties suitable for specimen planting are the Japanese maple, birch, redbud, flowering dogwood, thorn, magnolia, crabapple, ginkgo, and mountain ash. To determine the variety that will thrive in your particular area, check with local or regional nurseries.

Selecting Evergreen Trees. Evergreen trees remain green the year round because they lose a few leaves at a time and grow new ones throughout the year so that at no time are the branches bare. The term "evergreen" is usually restricted to conifers—trees that bear cones and have needlelike leaves. Evergreens are particularly well suited to enclosing an area for outdoor living or serving as a screen.

While most of them stand cold well, evergreens sometimes react unfavorably to summer heat, deficient rainfall, and drying winds. Four factors are generally considered unfavorable to the normal growth of evergreens: (1) sudden changes in temperature, (2) unfavorable soil conditions, (3) exposure to winds, and (4) air pollution.

On the whole, evergreens are desirable because they provide year-round landscape effects. Evergreens may be selected from varieties that mature into columnar, pyramidal, round, spreading, or creeping forms. By using a variety of forms, you can create interesting landscape effects. The more commonly used varieties include the fir, hemlock, pine, and spruce.

Broad-leaved evergreens have large leaves rather than needles. Soil requirements are more specific for this group of plants, and they also have more limited geographic distribution than most evergreens.

Shrubs

Plants that have several woody stems and are relatively low-growing are called shrubs. In the garden, shrubs are used for screening and foundation plantings and to provide color and sometimes fragrance. Choices are limited only by local weather conditions, soil type, exposure, and prevailing winds. By combining several different plants, you may achieve interesting contrasts of foliage, flowers, and plant shape. Shrubs, like trees, develop into different forms: rounded, upright, spreading, or fountainlike. Generally speaking, you get the most from shrubs when they flower one season and produce berries the following season or have a colorful bark when the leaves have fallen. Some plants have these desirable qualities in addition to the foliage for which they were primarily chosen.

Evergreen shrubs, like evergreen trees, are covered with leaves throughout the year. They vary in the size, shape, and color of their leaves and in the form of the mature plant.

Selecting deciduous shrubs. The plants selected for the garden can, if carefully chosen, provide a succession of bloom from late winter to early fall. In addition, some plants produce colorful berries, while others add the color of their bark to the winter scene. If your catalogs do not specify the blooming period for your particular geographic area, the listed blooming period is assumed to be the 40th parallel. From

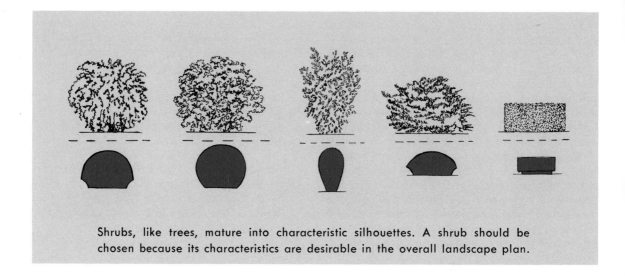

Shrubs, like trees, mature into characteristic silhouettes. A shrub should be chosen because its characteristics are desirable in the overall landscape plan.

this you may relate the blooming period to your area by considering your location in relation to a line that would run roughly through New York, Philadelphia, Pittsburgh, Columbus, Indianapolis, St. Joseph (Missouri), and Denver. Plants listed with no specific reference to blooming time can be expected to flower between April and June in areas close to this line, while plants that bloom in the late summer and fall will add color from July into the fall months.

The mature size of the shrub should be considered when selecting the plants for a particular location. Foundation plantings are necessary only when the foundation of the house is high or unattractive. Modern houses are often built with low or inconspicuous foundations so that a foundation planting is not needed. Instead plants can be placed to accent attractive features of the house, such as the entrance or a chimney.

Selecting evergreen shrubs. Evergreens vary in the way they adjust to soil and climatic conditions. Most evergreens stand cold well but react unfavorably to summer heat, drought, and drying winds. Given the care they need to thrive in a particular area, evergreens are good for accenting such features as the main entrance to the house. Many gardeners feel that a more interesting landscape plan results from combining evergreen and deciduous shrubs. Round, spreading, or creeping varieties of evergreens

are available to complement the forms of the deciduous plants.

OTHER ELEMENTS FOR OUTDOOR LIVING

Fences, storage sheds, and similar structural features should be considered in terms of the overall landscape plan. Special features such as outdoor lighting can be used to add beauty and utility to the grounds.

Fences

Landscape plans frequently make use of decorative or functional fences. A fence may be used as a background for plantings, to assure privacy, to serve as a snowbreak for the driveway, or, if high enough, as a windbreak. Before seriously considering a fence, check the zoning regulations for your neighborhood and also explore the attitudes of the neighbors toward fences. There are some areas where people feel strongly that the property between and around houses should be kept open and public. In some locations a look-through fence is used as a compromise, particularly where building codes prohibit a solid fence.

Materials for a fence. Fencing material is a matter of individual taste. The effect created tends to be more pleasing when the material is compatible with the exterior of the house. Molded concrete blocks, tile in decorative

Inexpensive wood fences may be designed to furnish privacy and add interest to the total landscape plan.

forms, wood, metal, and translucent fiber glass may be used in building a fence. Material used for the fence will be more satisfactory if it is designed to let in light and to allow circulation of air. There are many variations of open-work fences designed for this purpose. Wire fences permit circulation of air and confine pets, but they do not provide much privacy unless plantings are added.

Why fence? Fences may be used to screen in or to screen out a view. Where lots are not large, the view is often another house or garage. In this case a 4- to 5-foot fence will give privacy and screen out the nearby details, so that someone sitting in your yard will see only the tree tops, the sky, or perhaps the hilltops in the distance. In the great open spaces a fence may be desirable to limit the view. Here it serves as an accent to break up the vast expanse of land and sky, and it focuses the interest on a limited garden area.

Outdoor Lighting

When the yard is used as an extension of the living area in the house with facilities for eating, games, or relaxation, it is desirable to have lighting so as to extend the use of the area after sundown. Outdoor lighting can increase the hours for play, add time for yard work, and expand the comfort of sitting areas, as well as serve the more utilitarian purpose of lighting the entrances and walkways.

Portable, underground, or overhead wiring used in various combinations with suitable lamps will put light in places where it is needed for after-dark activities. Lighting may be used

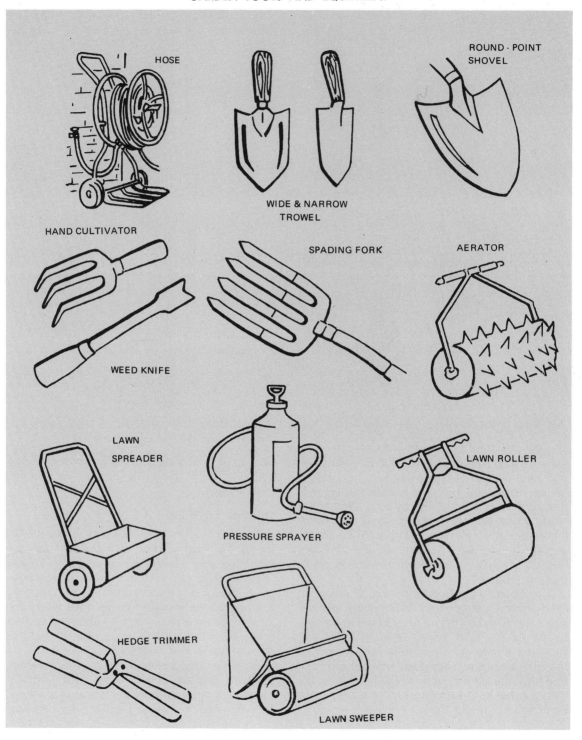

HOSE

WIDE & NARROW TROWEL

ROUND - POINT SHOVEL

HAND CULTIVATOR

SPADING FORK

AERATOR

WEED KNIFE

LAWN SPREADER

PRESSURE SPRAYER

LAWN ROLLER

HEDGE TRIMMER

LAWN SWEEPER

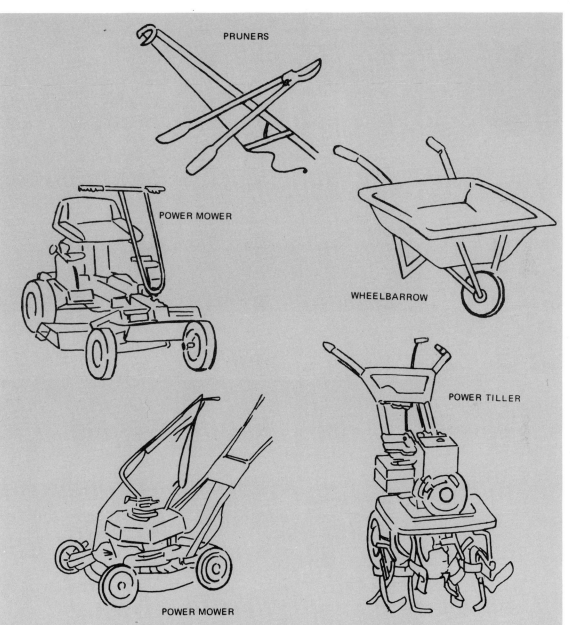

PRUNERS

POWER MOWER

WHEELBARROW

POWER TILLER

POWER MOWER

Personally owned basic garden tools allow you to match the tools to the user. The lawn roller, aerator, and spreader might be rented since these are used only occasionally. Wise selection is important in the choice of power equipment for use on the home grounds: A riding mower would be desirable only if you have lots of lawn to mow. A power tiller would be useful to the ardent gardener.

A decorative fence of masonry blocks may be used to define a lot line and provide a limited amount of privacy.

Outdoor lighting extends the usefulness of outdoor living areas. Such lighting may be planned to create interesting highlights and shadows.

to create aesthetic effects by silhouetting the trunk of a tree, creating shadows, or highlighting textures of walls or fences.

TOOLS FOR THE YARD AND GARDEN

A basic assortment of tools is needed for lawn and garden care. Each tool should have a weight and balance that suit the person using it, to make work easier and prevent undue strain. It is not unusual for each member of the family who actively gardens to have some personal tools. Certain garden tools are so frequently and regularly used that it is best to own them. Others, which are used only once a season, may be rented. Tools that are frequently used and relatively inexpensive belong in each gardener's workshop. They should be of good quality so that cutting edges stay sharp and handles are kept secure.

It is desirable to have a small building or an area in the garage set aside for the storage of garden tools. The space should have a few shelves, some hooks, some bins for fertilizer, and a work space. Electricity and water will add to the usefulness of the unit.

LEARNING EXPERIENCES

1. Interview local government officials to learn about restrictions applying to landscaping, fencing, and pools in your community.
2. Collect and share with the class pictures of porches, decks, patios, lanais, terraces, etc. Analyze how each meets the needs of a particular family that you have described.
3. Using the above pictures, identify the methods and materials used to create privacy for each of the outdoor living areas.
4. Make a plot plan of your yard, using a ⅛-inch scale. If you live in an apartment, sketch the nearest outdoor area.
5. Divide the class into groups and set up standards for evaluating outdoor living areas.
6. Collect and share with the class pictures that show the street side of the house, the outdoor living area, and the outdoor work-utility space.
7. Collect and share ideas for equipping and landscaping the work and utility areas of the yard.
8. Read relevant materials and discuss desirable characteristics for the children's play area.
9. Plan a walking tour on which you can identify desirable trees, shrubs, and ground covers in established plantings.
10. Study advertising and bulletins on garden tools. Prepare a shopper's guide for the basic garden tools.

PART

II

By Ruth Morton

Furniture and Furnishings

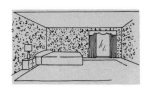

Importance of

Home Furnishings

How NATURAL it is to long for the time when you can select what you like for a home of your own. But to step from longing to doing requires knowledge. Begin now to accumulate knowledge so you will be ready to make wise selections when the time comes.

The foregoing chapters pointed to the tremendous changes in the lives of people in recent years. The next chapters analyze how these changes will affect the furnishings you will use, the skills you will need to handle them, and the importance of those furnishings in your personal and family life.

Obviously, there is no change in your basic need for beds, tables, and chairs. But there are definite changes in the ways you choose these essential pieces and other furnishings because you are living in an affluent, mobile society.

Begin all your choices of furnishings with the questions "Will it travel?" and "Will it adjust?" because, unless your life is most unusual, your furnishings will be moved fifteen or twenty times in the course of your lifetime. These moves may take you into different communities, different climates, perhaps even into foreign countries.

USES FOR HOME FURNISHINGS

Home furnishings have always been important, but they become more important in a mobile society. They are one of the few means by which you can create a sense of security and continuity in your life. Both government and industry recognize this, and often pay the tremendous costs of transporting home furnishings from one place to another for their employees.

To Provide Security

We all need material things to create a sense of familiarity in strange places. A small child, determinedly clutching a blanket as he walks on unsteady legs around a station or airport waiting room, is the visual expression of this need. The home furnishings which you stow into the moving van can, in part, satisfy that need for you.

Home furnishings can help establish a sense of continuity in personal and family life. A simple grouping of a card table and chairs,

Simple curtains can be adjusted to many situations. They may be individualized at little cost.

The importance of familiar furnishings is never so apparent as in those first hours in a new house before everything is unpacked.

when well lighted and used for a game the entire family enjoys playing, can be a tremendous help in creating a sense of "family life as usual." An extension dining table that has been the accustomed center of family celebrations is another piece of furniture that will help establish a sense of continuity in family life. Such a table set with familiar china, decorated with familiar objects to celebrate a familiar occasion, will help make a new community seem homelike. No matter where your furnishings are set down, if you plan ahead and arrange them skillfully, they will help provide a glowing sense of family security and solidarity.

To Provide Comfort

One glance around the average contractor-built home or apartment will show many structural lacks which make efficient housekeeping diffi-

cult and interfere with day-to-day comfort. If you move frequently, remodeling is not practical. Instead, it may be far more economical to supplement such structural lacks with home furnishings that you can take with you to successive homes.

Storage furniture. A common architectural fault is inadequate storage space. Built-in drawers, cupboards, and closets are expensive and so are often reduced to a minimum. Without adequate storage it is almost impossible to be orderly and this disorder makes it very difficult to do the cleaning. Family tensions and frictions are an inevitable result when one has no time to hunt for equipment that has no established storage place. In consequence, you will find that furniture with good storage features is important to your living comfort and your family happiness.

Adjustable high cabinets can be placed against walls or used as room dividers. Bunk beds conserve space in a small sleeping area.

Space dividers. Personal privacy becomes difficult to attain as contemporary architecture wins the economy-minded builder's approval. Open-style construction will often make it necessary for the entire family to share in the use of the living areas for many varied functions. Screens, bookcases, and high cabinets will help solve such problems. For example, screens can be hinged together and anchored to the floor to divide a single large bedroom into two small ones. They can be attached to a bookcase, hutch, or breakfront to divide the dining area from the living area or to divide a living area from a study area so that both can be used simultaneously, yet with privacy.

Personalized furnishings. Built-in light fixtures are frequently inadequate or poorly placed, yet well-placed light is essential. Extra lamps for halls and stairways will add safety and beauty. To many people, reading in bed is one of the important comforts of life. A portable wall lamp that can be installed at the head of a bed will mean solid, homelike comfort in each successive bedroom. Built-in bookcases may be hard to find. Wall shelves that can be hung over a desk or portable bookshelves placed within arm's reach will provide convenient book storage. Many people who

Inexpensive metal shelves may be used to provide order in a closet or an apartment storage locker.

Shelving and pegboard may be arranged for display of personal interest items.

A creative activity such as sewing requires working space while a project is underway.

love the outdoors find they must live in an apartment. Window boxes may be planted so that even a high-rise apartment can be near the world of nature.

To Encourage Personal Growth

Home furnishings are important for encouraging personal growth. They provide convenient activity centers and storage spaces for the tools and materials needed for such personal growth.

Stimulate study. Each year seems to demand higher standards of scholarship in school, of job training at work, and of general education everywhere. This tends to emphasize home study for everyone all through life. In consequence, every member of the family should have his own desk where he can work effectively and without interruption.

Encourage creativity. Shelves and files to hold reference materials and readily available equipment such as your easel, loom, or portable sewing machine will help you to continue an interest or to develop new ones.

Perpetuate cultural interests. As community cultural activities awaken your interests in

Many families who enjoy music need room for storage of musical instruments and equipment.

music, art, the theater, great-book clubs or church study groups, the furnishings in your home will reflect these interests. You will need furnishings that will help you store and display the materials you acquire such as books, records, music, musical instruments, crafts, and good pictures.

CURRENT NEED FOR
HOME FURNISHING SKILLS

A knowledge of interior design and of home furnishing skills helps people adjust to changing living patterns.

Recurring Need to Select Furnishings

Young people will continue to select home furnishings throughout their lifetime. They do not buy "once and for all," so the handling of the home furnishings budget is a constantly needed skill. How the money is spent and how questions are answered involving quality versus quantity, ready-made versus homemade, rental versus outright purchase, and temporary versus long-term buying are of prime importance, and they recur with each change of address.

Wise management of the furnishings budget is almost as important as the size of the budget in determining the beauty of a home. A knowledge of the furnishings field, what is available on the market, what fits your needs best, and how you can use it best becomes imperative.

For long-term use. When buying for a permanent need, select only furnishings that have timeless beauty, quality, and usefulness. As you move or travel, take full advantage of any local area specialties, such as Navajo rugs in Arizona; pottery, tin trays, and mirror frames in Mexico; or clocks in Switzerland. They will add long-term beauty, individuality, and comfort to your home.

For short-term use. Furnishings for short-term use can be rented or can be bought inexpensively. Such furnishings should be eval-

Small scaled furniture moves easily. Such furniture is a wise choice for people who move frequently.

Courtesy Masonite Corporation

uated differently from those for long-term use. Durability need only meet the strain of short-time use. Flexibility becomes unimportant, since these furnishings are not to be moved to another house. Utility may outweigh beauty if the piece is inconspicuously used. Temporary furnishings can represent quite a loss over a period of time. Consequently, take care to build up the amount of long-term furnishings you own and lessen the need for temporary buying.

Continuous Need for Home Furnishing Skills

In an affluent, mobile society, skills of rearranging and remodeling furniture and readjusting fabrics are called into continuous use.

Rearrangement of furniture. You will need to rethink the placement of your furniture in each new environment. Many pieces of furniture may have to serve in a different type of room or for a different purpose than in the preceding situation. A chest may hold china at one time, clothes at another, and radio and record player at a third. A studio couch may be a sofa in one house and a pair of narrow beds in a small double bedroom in another. How

skillfully you handle your furniture in each house will determine the comfort and beauty of your home. Your skill will also determine how well you can avoid buying supplementary furniture to meet temporary situations.

Remodeling of furniture. Older pieces of furniture and furniture from the secondhand market often require remodeling; even slight changes may completely change its function. If you develop skills in woodworking and refinishing, they can help you add both comfort and beauty to your home.

Readjustment of fabrics. It is seldom that any fabric is used in the same way in two successive houses. You may need to combine the curtains originally bought for several rooms in order to meet the demands of one big room, if the windows are large or numerous. You may use a pair of sheets for curtains in one house, curtains for bedspreads in another, and bedspreads for upholstery or a slipcover in still another.

The extent to which you are able to make these adjustments look professional rather than makeshift will determine the beauty that the

Multipurpose cabinets, chests, and shelving units can be rearranged to fit each new environment.

Many beautiful accessories such as this Indian screen reflect special interests or special travel opportunities.

Courtesy Better Homes and Gardens, © Meredith Corporation, 1963

Adjusting existing curtains to a new home situation gives you a chance to economically change your room decoration.

fabrics will add to your home. Sewing and upholstering skill will consequently be of untold value to you.

Readjustment of accessories. The ability to readjust accessories in a new home is one of the most satisfying home furnishing skills. The warmth and joy that can be added to a room by hanging up, effectively, a few well-loved pictures or by arranging groupings of familiar objects of art is almost startling. To place accessories well calls for a trained sense of balance, space divisions, and color harmony. Cultivate this skill carefully both now as you study the next few chapters and throughout the rest of your life as you read magazines, wander through shops, or study the homes of others.

CURRENT NEED FOR SIMPLIFIED HOUSEKEEPING

In these days of increased outside jobs and community responsibilities, the average homemaker compresses most of her housekeeping into early morning, late afternoon, or evening hours. This has had an amazingly far-reaching effect on home furnishings.

Reduced Housekeeping Time

The employed wife is an accepted part of our pattern of married life. The unemployed homemaker frequently works outside the home in volunteer jobs. This living pattern has changed our entire concept of how to furnish and run a house. In consequence, the time spent on housekeeping chores such as dusting fussy furniture or accessories, polishing silver, or ironing ruffled curtains, is reduced to a minimum. Time-conscious women adopt buying plans that are basically time-saving. Items such as drip-dry curtains, stainless steel, stain-repellent upholstery, and individual place mats have become customary for everyday use. Kitchen or household appliances that can further shorten the housekeeping process become valuable aids.

Rising Standards of Housekeeping

Nowadays, even the most dedicated housekeeper does not expect to polish from morn till night; every magazine published for women is full of suggestions on how to do the job of housekeeping in limited time. Yet our increasingly high standards of housekeeping, fostered by home economists and encouraged by manu-

161

Adjustable shelves on tension poles safely display family treasures. Such shelves can be installed without injury to the wall surface.

Courtesy Grant Pulley and Hardware Corporation

Courtesy Ebony Magazine

Wall shelving units can be used to store and display books and records so that they are well organized and readily accessible.

facturers, are made flagrantly obvious in every article and cannot be ignored.

Greater cleanliness. In a world of increasing urban grime and soot, manufacturers are realizing that one of the most attractive qualities they can build into their products is easy cleanability. For example, there are lamp shades that can be rinsed out or wiped off, bedspreads that are stain-repellent and wrinkle-resistant, wallpaper that can be scrubbed, and curtains that can be washed and rehung without ironing. All furnishings are expected to be maintained in pristine cleanliness, regardless of wear, sooty urban grime, and lack of housekeeping interest or time.

Greater orderliness. Many women are used to the orderly storage of supplies, the easy-to-find filing of reference materials, and the easy-to-use organization of cupboards and closets to be found in business offices. These storage techniques are being applied to the efficient running of homes.

CURRENT CONCEPT OF STABILITY IN HOMES

Years ago Kipling wrote his famous lines, "God gave all men all earth to love, but since our hearts are small, ordained for each one spot should be—beloved over all." At that time most people interpreted those words in terms of the permanent family homestead. They mistook the superficial meaning—the physically stable home—for the essence of Kipling's meaning.

Nowadays, with the full force of a mobile society, those lines become a challenge as you try to find the way to make the constantly changing "one spot" that will be your home, provide the sense of stability we all need. The way to do this will vary with each individual. In the succeeding chapters on home furnishings, you will find material that can help you provide the background that will encourage a sense of stability in home life for yourself and for your family.

LEARNING EXPERIENCES

1. Define the meaning of the following words and phrases as used in this chapter: mobile society, furnishings, personal creativity, cultural interests.
2. Interview an exchange student and tell the class how she used personal possessions to help her feel at home in a strange land.
3. Interview a newly returned wife of a serviceman or a businessman and tell the class how she used home furnishings to encourage family life as usual in a foreign country.
4. What piece of furniture or equipment, such as a loom, easel, typewriter, or sewing machine, would you like to add to your room or home so you could follow a talent or interest that attracts you? Explain where you would place it.
5. If you had a wish, which of these would you choose to increase your family's pleasure as a group, and its sense of solidarity: a game table, a TV, a hi-fi, or a

piano? Where could it be placed and how would you make it function importantly?
6. Using the phone book, find a small home workshop in your community that makes, repairs, refinishes, or reupholsters furniture. Visit it and report how using some of its skills might help you adjust furniture you have to a new home or new needs.
7. Make a list of interests or hobbies which can be pursued effectively as a result of the special geographical situation of your area. (Collecting shells, wild flowers, etc.)
8. What celebrations draw you closer as a family and so would make you feel at home in a new community?
9. What project could you work at as a family that would strengthen family solidarity?
10. Check your home for frayed electric cords, long extension wires, overloaded outlets, frayed carpeting, or inadequate lighting that might produce accidents.

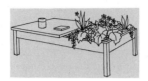

10

The Study and

Use of Color

IF YOU WERE ASKED right now "What is the first thing you see in a dress, a room, or a fabric?" your answer would probably be "color." Almost all of us see the world and everything in it in terms of light and color first, and we continue to enjoy and want both qualities in our lives. When the sky is leaden and a driving rain makes the world look dull and gray, our spirits droop. On dark winter mornings we think with envy of the people in warm, sunny climates, and we dig a little deeper under the covers. When spring appears with its sunshine and color, our whole mood changes. Like a young child who reaches for a colored toy, we revel in the colors of nature. We laugh easily and our friends and our future seem fresh and exciting.

THE IMPACT OF COLOR
ON DAILY LIFE

Since we enjoy color so much, it is natural to want to put it into our lives the year round—in our clothes, our homes, our food, and our cars. Certain choices, based on color, are so

standard as to be predictable. For example, an apple salad with a red cherry on it, market analysts tell us, will disappear from the cafeteria counter much faster than the same salad minus that touch of red, but a line of dazzling red-topped card tables which tired the eyes nearly broke one manufacturer a few years ago.

Color choices in clothes and upholstery, however, are completely personal and unpredictable. For subtle reasons, each of us automatically turns to a certain range of color. Subconsciously, certain colors seem to satisfy us, and those certain colors determine what we buy far more than any other one factor.

BASIC FACTS ABOUT COLOR

Understanding color is basic to using and enjoying it in our homes. However, since the study of color is too extensive to be given in its entirety, we will concern ourselves only with color as we use it in paint, in fabrics, in ceramics, in wallpaper, and in other applications to the home.

The warm brick tones of a background wall can be used to tie the colors of furniture and plantings into a unified effect.

Basic Colors

At first glance, the range of color in the home seems so great that it is difficult to believe that it can be reduced to a few basic colors. But all colors in the home or the world can be reduced to just three primary, three secondary, and six intermediate colors.

Primary colors. The three primary, or basic, colors from which the other colors can be developed are red, yellow, and blue. These cannot be created by the mixing of any other colors, but every other color (including all neutrals except white) can be developed from the primary colors.

The color wheel is a valuable tool which helps show the development of other colors from these three primary colors. On it, red, yellow, and blue are arranged in the same relationship as on the rainbow, except that on the color wheel they are spaced evenly, thus dividing the color wheel into three even parts.

Secondary colors. When pairs of primary colors are combined in equal amounts, secondary colors are produced. Equal amounts of red

165

and yellow produce orange; equal amounts of yellow and blue produce green; and equal amounts of blue and red produce violet. These three secondary colors are placed equidistant between their two parent primary colors, thus redividing the color wheel into six parts.

Intermediate colors. A secondary color mixed with one of the two primaries of the secondary forms an intermediate color which comes between the secondary and the primary on the color wheel. For example, true green with yellow forms yellow-green. When more yellow than green is added to the mixture, the color is a green-yellow. The exact hue of the intermediate color depends on the proportions of the primaries in the mixture. This mixing and further dividing and enlarging of the color wheel can proceed limitlessly until the wheel resembles the rainbow.

Neutralized colors. Greyed or neutralized colors are made by adding small amounts of black for dark colors, white for light colors, or the one or two primaries not already contained in the color. For example, green is greyed with a little red, and yellow with violet (red and blue).

Neutrals. When all three primaries are mixed in approximately equal amounts, neutrals are formed. Black through lightest grey and browns through lightest ivory are commonly accepted as neutrals and used to enhance other colors. White, also a neutral, can not be mixed except with light.

Color Qualities

All colors have three qualities—hue, value, and intensity. It is only by describing these qualities that colors can be accurately indicated and given their proper place on the color wheel.

Hue. The name of a color usually indicates its hue. In fact, the word "color," as it is commonly used, is synonymous with hue, except that the hue name may be more accurate. For example, either blue or green-blue might be given the color name "azure" or perhaps "sky-blue." The hue of a fire might be yellow, red-orange, or orange, but its color name might be "flame." The color name "gold" might be applied to several hues from a greenish yellow to a yellowish orange.

In a two-word color name, such as green-blue, the second word indicates the dominant hue. Commercial firms select color names to attract attention. Color indicators such as "winging, swinging pink," "shocking pink," "luggage tan," "bittersweet," or "toast" may be currently fashionable. However, such names are not uniformly used and are not accurate color indicators.

Value. The lightness or darkness of a color is called its value. The range of values of any color may vary from almost white, the lightest value, to almost black, the darkest value. Pink is the lightest value and maroon is the darkest value of red. Light values are called tints; dark values are called shades. A color that has a value halfway between a tint and a shade, or between a light and dark value, is called a "middle value" of color.

Values affect the apparent size and distance of objects. A dark thundercloud will seem to be much lower and larger than it really is, and a white cloud will seem to be much smaller and higher. Dark-colored walls in a room have a tendency to seem closer, and light-colored walls to seem farther away.

To lighten a middle-color value, add white or water to it. To darken a middle-color value, add black to it.

Intensity. The brightness or dullness, the strength or weakness, of a color is called intensity. The word "chroma" is sometimes used as a synonym for intensity. Many a bathing suit begins the summer as a strong, intense hue, but after daily dips in the lake or daily sunbaths on the beach, ends the season as a very soft, grayed color that has almost no intensity at all. The yellow of a dandelion is brilliant, a color of high intensity. The yellow of a field of ripe wheat is dull and soft, a yellow of low intensity. A color that is so dull and soft as to have no intensity is a neutral. Sand, for example, is usually neutral.

Objects in intense colors, whether warm or cool, tend to advance and seem larger than they are, whereas objects in grayed, or neutralized, colors tend to recede and seem smaller. The colors of butterflies and hummingbirds are brilliantly intense. The colors of elephants and mountains are usually so soft that they are neutrals. These examples may help you

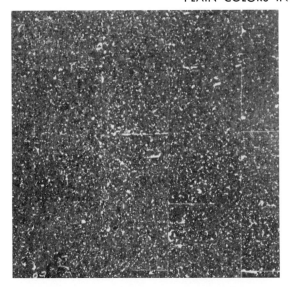

The texture of cork causes dramatic shadows and highlights which intensify the background color.

The strength of a grasscloth pattern depends on the coarseness of the fibers. The grasscloth effect can be created in simulated wallpapers.

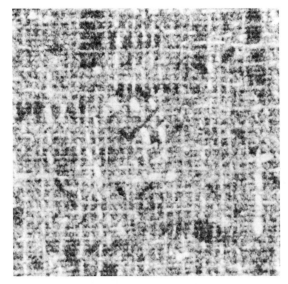

Random-tweed weave gives a dramatic or quiet effect, depending on the color and value contrast. It covers cracks and rough plaster especially well.

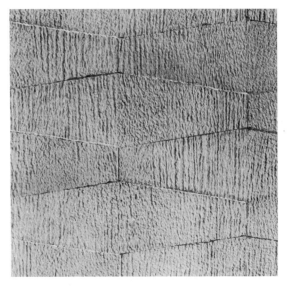

A softly textured plain-color effect can be obtained in printed wallpapers through use of closely related hues in an allover pattern.

Courtesy Wallcoverings Council, Incorporated

Plain colors are affected by the surface texture of walls and the fiber, weave, or finish of the wall covering.

REALISTIC DESIGNS

A scene used above a plain dado may dramatize a wall.

A stylized mural is frequently used to emphasize a dining room or a bedroom wall.

Realistic designs can be used to accent a specific area or to give importance to a room. No more than one realistic design should be used in a room.

168

remember a good working formula for using intensity: use high intensity for smaller areas; grayed neutral intensity for larger areas.

Color Expression

Tonight as you go home, look at the colors around you. Look for relatively plain color in large areas such as the sky, country fields or lakes in city parks. These areas of unpatterned color tend to be relaxing. Look also for areas of color which are broken into pattern by houses, office buildings, and streets with heavy traffic. Patterned colors tend to be stimulating. Indeed they may be so overstimulating as to become tiring.

Plain surfaces. Color is affected by the texture or character of the surface of an area or object. For instance, yellow paint on slick plaster or yellow dye in satin will look far more intense and bright than the same yellow on a rough plaster or corduroy where tiny indentations of the surface create shadows that produce a textured, softened effect.

Colors in nature also show the effect of texture. The green of grass or foliage is not an even green. Each blade of grass, each leaf on a bush, tree, fern, or plant is slightly different from the others in color, and each casts its own shadow. Thus the effect of the whole is of closely blended color that has interesting variety. The Japanese have worked out a complete concept around this natural phenomenon which they call *shibui* or *shibusa*. It is a system for bringing slightly different colors together in an interesting variety of closely blended hues and values to produce textural beauty. In this way they are able to produce the quiet, rich, soft background colors which make livable homes.

Many manufacturers follow this concept to produce rugs and fabrics with a tweedy effect, using yarns in many variations of the same hue or of closely related hues. As a result, these rugs and fabrics have softly blended colors which are easy to harmonize with other objects.

Patterned surfaces. There are three types of patterns: realistic, conventionalized, and abstract. Each has its own beauty and its own worth, but each needs to be separated from other patterns by plain or textured surfaces to show its beauty to full advantage.

Realistic, or naturalistic, pattern. This is the most familiar form of pattern. It is a picture-type representation of recognizable objects from the world around us. A house, a barn, trees, animals, or people, all form patterns against the landscape. A representation of any one of these can be used as decoration, either singly or in repetition. Used singly, this type of pattern might decorate an object such as a box top, a tray, or a book. If repeated, it could be used for rugs, fabrics, or wallpaper.

Conventionalized pattern. This is a stylized pattern originally inspired by natural forms. In such a pattern, realism has been sacrificed for arrangement and decoration. Artists create conventionalized patterns by eliminating or varying details of realistic objects so they will fit the space to be decorated or so they will work into a repetitive design more effectively. Conventionalized designs can often be used upside down or right side up equally well, because they have ceased to be realistic representations. This type of design is used frequently for fabrics and rugs which will be seen from many points of view.

Abstract patterns. This type of pattern includes all nonobjective or nonrepresentational designs. There are many opinions as to the different types of designs that fall into this classification, but the following two are generally considered basic.

1. The geometric pattern: This pattern is an exact, evenly repetitive type of pattern. It is perhaps the best known type of abstract pattern. In nature it is found in such forms as rock crystals, shells, the backs of turtles, and the skins of reptiles. In man-made patterns, this type of pattern includes plaids, stripes, checks, circular, and diamond-shaped designs.

2. Random lines and free forms: This pattern has no definite shape. In nature, it is found in the cracks of a dried mud bed, in cloud formations, and in the markings on the spotted cow or the mottled cat. This type of pattern is becoming very popular for modern interiors and is being used for fabrics, wallpapers, and carpeting.

Color Divisions

In addition to their relationship on the color wheel and their form of expression in plain

CONVENTIONALIZED PATTERNS

Conventionalized patterns have an obvious beginning in realism that has been submerged to produce a decorative design for a particular use.

A striking geometric design, while beautiful in itself, should be used sparingly in the overall room plan.

Highly dramatic conventionalized designs can be used to cover a small piece of furniture in an otherwise simple room.

or patterned surfaces, colors also have other qualities which distinguish and divide them. Qualities of warmth or coldness divide them according to their primary color content.

Warm colors. Colors which have a dominance of either yellow or red, the colors of sun and fire, are called warm colors. Warm colors tend to be stimulating and exciting. Objects in warm colors appear to be larger and closer than they really are. Check this by glancing quickly over your school auditorium, over the bleachers at a football game, or over the landscape as you ride by. You will notice that all the warm-colored objects—the red sweaters, the yellow and orange pompons, the red barns, and the yellow flowers—seem to enlarge and come toward you.

Cool colors. Colors which have a predominance of blue, the color of water, sky, and ice, are called cool colors. Objects in cool colors

have a tendency to recede and seem smaller than they really are.

Evenly balanced colors. There are two evenly balanced colors in which there is an equal amount of cool and warm color: the absolute violet, which is made up of exactly the same amount of red and blue, and the absolute green, which is made up of equal amounts of yellow and blue. Evenly balanced colors can look cool or warm, depending on the colors with which they are used.

Color Relationships

Colors, like people, are seldom seen alone, and like people, they are different, depending on their associates. Each time you place one object next to another, you establish a color relationship, whether it be a skirt and a sweater or a pillow and a sofa. The color of each is beautiful in itself, but when colors are used in quantity or placed with other colors, they may enhance each other or they may create discord, according to the human response. Such changes in appearance fall into three classifications.

Change of hue. The most surprising change that association produces is a change of hue. Have you ever had someone say, "What a beautiful blue sweater!" when you had chosen it because it was green? You may have thought the person who made the remark was color-blind, but if you had glanced around, you might have found that your sweater did look blue. This happened because you were standing beside someone who was wearing an intense green. An intense, true green will make a soft blue-green look blue by comparison. Colors of low intensity are more easily influenced by association than are bright colors. Experiment by holding a grayed color against several different intense colors.

Colors vary under different levels of light and under different types of light. Colored lights change colors completely. For this reason, when selecting colors, always be sure to check them under the lighting conditions that are to be used. Only in this way can you be sure.

Change of value. Another change in colors produced by combining one with another is a change of value. This change in value can frequently be seen in people. A girl who looks quite suntanned as she stands next to a fair-skinned blonde, will look delicately pale when she stands next to a deeply tanned lifeguard. In the same way, a color that is quite dark can be made to look several degrees lighter if it is placed beside black, or a dark color. A color that is quite light can be made to look darker if it is placed beside white or a lighter tint.

When you are selecting the value of each color for a room scheme, be sure to try it in the exact place it will be used. It will be strongly affected by the values of the colors surrounding it.

Change of intensity. A startling change of intensity occurs when color is used in large areas. Colors used over large areas, especially on the walls of a room which reflect back and forth on each other, increase in intensity. You must keep this fact in mind in selecting color for any large area or object. To obtain the color you really want for large areas, select a color that is lighter in value and lower in intensity than the one you desire, because the value and intensity will change when used in quantity on walls or on a large floor area. Prove this by working the experiment suggested in Learning Experience 7 at the end of the chapter.

COLOR SCHEMES

The crystallizing of color combinations into color schemes is the first step in adapting them to use in a room. By so doing, you can draw upon a whole body of knowledge about color as it has been professionally formulated, and use it to create color schemes that will help produce beauty in your home.

Finding Color Combinations

Choosing colors that will go together harmoniously seems to come naturally for some people. For others it is difficult, but skill can be developed with knowledge and experience. It is wise for the beginner to look for guidance in combining colors.

Pictures. The most obvious source of beautiful color combinations is in the pictures painted by artists of accepted repute which can be found in museums, in art galleries, in good art magazines and books, and in some art stores. In such paintings, you will find unusual combinations of color in every area of the color wheel.

Handcrafted objects of art. Other sources of color schemes are objects of art created by craftsmen through the ages. Handmade rugs—oriental or American Indian, hooked, embroidered, or braided—or a piece of handwoven fabric can be excellent starting points for a color scheme. A beautiful patchwork quilt or a coverlet can be not only a source of a color scheme but also a climax for the room whose colors have been inspired by its beauty.

Manufactured products. The original designs of many manufactured products are the work of talented artists and craftsmen.

Beautifully designed wallpapers, fabrics, carpeting, china or pottery, all are excellent points of departure for color schemes that can be individual and beautiful.

Abstract patterns may be subtle enough to be used over an entire room or dramatic enough to emphasize a particular area.

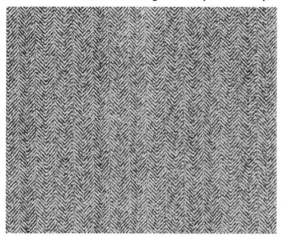

Herring-bone tweed forms an appropriate background for both contemporary and traditional furniture.

Color contrast often furnishes the main interest in a strict geometric design.

The color wheel. Many people feel that the color wheel alone can be a place to look for the colors we use in our rooms. However, colors picked from a color wheel can be correct but dully trite. That is why we have suggested the use of guides such as fine painting and the use of a color wheel as an aid in interpreting your color scheme.

Related Color Schemes

Related color schemes are made up of colors adjacent to or near each other on the color wheel. There are two types of related color schemes, both of which are especially effective in small rooms but also can be used in large rooms.

Monochromatic color schemes. One-color harmonies, using just one color in different values and intensities and one neutral in various values, are called monochromatic color schemes.

A seascape is an example in nature of a monochromatic color scheme. The sea and sky are made up of blues in different values and intensities. They are set off by the neutrals of white caps and white clouds. Another example

in nature is the forest where many different greens are set off by the neutral browns of the tree trunks, the old pine needles, and the dried leaves. In each example there is one basic hue plus the neutral color. Neither color scheme is monotonous because of the variety within the one color and the neutral.

Sometimes the plan is reversed in nature. The neutral then becomes the dominant, and the color is the accent. For example, the leaden gray winter sky, the white snow, and the gray leafless trees are a dominantly neutral scene into which the flame of the setting winter sun brings the accent color. When used in a room, the one color, or monochromatic, scheme produces a feeling of complete unity.

Analogous color schemes. A second type of related color harmony is the analogous color scheme. You begin with one dominant color and a neutral and add other related colors lying adjacent to the dominant on the color wheel. This color scheme includes one primary and one secondary color. Thus blue, blue-green, and green, the colors in a summer scene of water, hills, woods, and sky form an example of this type of scheme. When used in a room with one clearly dominant color, and the related colors and a neutral used as accent, the room will retain the unity of a monochromatic scheme but have the added drama of more color.

Contrasting Color Schemes

Contrasting color schemes are composed of unrelated colors. Because of their wider range, these color schemes are especially effective in large rooms. In contrasting color schemes, the accent colors should be confined largely to small areas used against a strongly established dominant of a grayed color.

Complementary color schemes. The two-color harmonies made up of unrelated colors—one primary and one secondary—that appear opposite each other on the color wheel are known as complementary color schemes. The red-green color harmony suggested in the color experiment in Learning Experience 7 is the easiest to check. Other examples are blue and orange, and yellow and violet. Complementary color schemes appear in nature in the red apple on the green tree, the gold sun in the violet evening sky, and the orange of late fall foliage against a blue sky. In using this type of scheme, you add a neutral just as is found in nature in the gray evening mist, the white clouds, and the brown tree bark. You begin with a softened or grayed form of one of the complementary colors or with the neutral as dominant, and then play the remaining colors against the dominant color.

Split complementary color schemes. A three-color harmony in which the colors on each side of the complementary color are used is called a split complementary color scheme. For example, instead of using the complementary green with red, you would use blue-green and yellow-green. You would use red-orange and yellow-orange with blue, and you would use red-violet and blue-violet with gold. You would also add a neutral and follow the same plan as with the complementary scheme.

Triadic color schemes. A three-color harmony in which the colors are equidistant from each other on the color wheel is called the triadic color scheme. For example, if you start with red, you use yellow and blue with it. If you begin with green, you use violet and orange with it. Here again you select one of the colors for a dominant and proceed as in complementary color schemes, adding a neutral if desired.

Dissonant color schemes. A less familiar, more difficult type of color scheme to use is being talked about currently. It is called the dissonant color scheme. If you enjoy this type of scheme, get a good reproduction of a picture that exemplifies it and hang it in a monochromatic room. The picture will stand out and you can repeat one or two of its colors in pillows without danger of upsetting the delicate balance of color existing in the picture.

USING COLOR IN ROOMS

The use of color in rooms is one of the most important factors in producing beauty. A well-chosen color scheme can make any room seem beautiful, regardless of the quality of the furnishings. Probably the most difficult colors to use are the intense ones. When used in quantity, they produce intense visual excitement. If you live in a home where these colors have been used, you may feel completely overwhelmed, because strong color in quantity demands your constant attention. You cannot forget it for a moment.

Adapting Color Schemes

To produce beauty in a room with color, you may find it wise to follow the pattern in nature. Each color should be chosen from one of two types—grayed background colors and bright intense foreground colors—and should be used as follows:

Choose a dominant color. The first step in putting color into a room is to choose one color as dominant and use it over 60 percent of the background areas. In nature, one color, grayed and softened, is used again and again in many different values and hues until it dominates a scene. Sometimes it is the soft grayed blue of the sky and water. Sometimes it is the soft green of the foliage. In the fall it may be the brown of dry leaves and dead grass, the dull gold of ripening grain, or the brown of bare earth. In the desert the dominant is the sand color. In the mountains the dominant is the many shades of gray rock. But wherever it is, one grayed color dominates—one color with infinite small variations in hue and value.

Abstract pattern in random lines may be contemporary or conventional in mood.

Courtesy Richard E. Thibaut, Incorporated

Free-flowing lines may be so demanding that they should be used very sparingly.

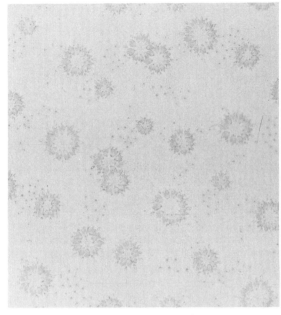

Courtesy Standard Coated Products, Incorporated

A delicate, randomly spaced pattern in neutral values may be especially attractive in small rooms.

Exotic colors. Colors such as aquas, violets, blue-pinks, and green-yellows, combined with grays and the whites, and used in grayed tints for background areas, produce a feminine effect.

Earth tones. Reds, oranges, and yellow-greens combined with browns and tans used in lower values produce a masculine effect. Used in middle values and in grayed form, earth tones are often pleasing to both men and women and so may be good choices when grayed for the background areas of the living room or master bedroom.

Select accent colors. The second step in putting color into a room is to select a stronger or more intense accent color or colors. At this point follow one of the color schemes you have studied. Every room must have a color climax in terms of bright sparkling color. This climax appears in nature in the bright colors of birds, butterflies, and flowers. In rooms, which are relatively small compared with the great expanse of nature, we must be careful to main-

tain that same proportion and to bring in accent colors in small areas. The easy way to introduce accent colors into a room is by the use of pictures, objects of art, books, and lamp bases. Accent colors can also be introduced in small areas of fabric, such as pillows and chair seats.

Balance color placement. The next step after the color is selected is to plan the placement of the dominant and accent colors. The large amount of grayed dominant color and the small amounts of bright accent color must be used and balanced in every area of the room and at all levels from floor to ceiling.

Backgrounds are the large areas (the floors, walls, and ceilings); it is on these areas that the dominant color should be used. If two of these three areas are done in tones of one grayed color, and if a sofa, a pair of lounge chairs, or a bedspread also repeats this hue, the 60 percent dominance will be met. Thus, if a living room that has a green rug and a lighter

CHART 3. USE OF PATTERN

Key: R = Realistic pattern
P = Plain
Tx = Textured
Tw = Tweed
G = Geometric
S = Stripe
Pictures = both matted and unmatted

Room	Floor Covering	Walls	Ceiling	Draperies	Upholstery	Wall Decoration
1.	R	P/Tx	P/Tx	P/Tx, and G P/Tx	P/Tx, and matching G RS or G and P/Tx	Mirrors, pictures, objects of art Mirrors, pictures, objects of art
2.	P/Tx, and Tw	P/Tx	P/Tx	R G Matching G and P/Tx	Matching R and P/Tx Matching G P/Tx and R	Mirrors, pictures, objects of art Mirrors, pictures, objects of art Matted pictures and mirrors
3.	P/Tx	G	P/Tx	P/Tx and Tw P/Tx	Matching G and P/Tx P/Tx and R	Matted pictures and mirrors Matted pictures and mirrors
4.	P/Tx and Tw	S	P/Tx	P/Tx trimmed with matching S Matching R	P/Tx and R P/Tx	Matted pictures and mirrors Matted pictures and mirrors
5.	P/Tx	R	P/Tx	P/Tx Matching R	Matching R and P/Tx P/Tx, Tw	Matted pictures and mirrors Pictures, mirrors
6.	P/Tx	P/Tx	R	P/Tx, Tw	Matching R and P/Tx	Pictures, mirrors
7.	P/Tx	P/Tw	P/Tx	P/Tx	P/Tx, S and G	Pictures, mirrors
8.	G	P/Tx	P/Tx	P/Tx and Tw	P/Tx and matching Tw	Pictures, mirrors
9.	S	P/Tx	P/Tx	R or P/Tx	P/Tx, G and Tw	Pictures, mirrors

FLORAL PATTERNS
Floral patterns vary in the quality of their realistic effect.

Courtesy Richard E. Thibaut, Incorporated

Provincial floral patterns often come with correlated paper for use on unaccented walls.

Courtesy F. Schumacher Company

Floral patterns may be arranged so that the dominant effect is geometric stripes.

A conventionalized floral motif can be arranged to form a delicately textured allover diamond pattern.

Courtesy Standard Coated Products, Incorporated

green wall also has a sofa covered with a tweedy or figured fabric of many values and hues of green, it will have achieved a dominance of green and a unity which no amount of accent color can upset. If a bedroom that uses white ceiling and walls, white bedspread and draperies, has a large rug of strong gold and additional gold in chairs or pillows, it will still have a dominance of white.

It should be noted that the dominant color was represented at all levels as well as in all areas of the room. In the green room, the green was used from floor to ceiling height and was repeated at middle level in the sofa. In the white room, the white was used from walls to ceiling and was repeated on the bed.

Accent colors must be repeated in all areas of the room. They can be used for pillow covers on the sofa, for upholstery on small chair seats, and for lamp bases or small pieces of pottery.

A picture may include all the accent colors on one side of the room, and a patterned fabric may serve to repeat them on the other side. In this way, no color is forgotten anywhere in the room.

Select a scheme of values. A plan for the use of values should be chosen, and here again we turn to nature for excellent examples. If we follow the normal plan of outdoor values, the lightest value would be in the ceiling, light and/or middle values would be in the walls and upholstery, and middle or darker values would be on the floor.

Using other examples from nature, you could use light values on the floor, just as there is light sand in the desert and on the seashore, if the other values of the room are very light. You can have dark values on walls and floors, just as there are dark values in the forest, if you use a light ceiling. You can keep everything in soft, misty middle values, just as there are gray misty days. And if you want to be very dramatic, you can use a dark ceiling, just as there sometimes are thunderclouds overhead. The whole thing to remember is that rooms must be so planned that they will be enjoyable for many years; sometimes too much drama is tiresome.

Using Patterns and Textures

The way we express color in terms of patterns and textures in rooms also affects the beauty of a room.

Separate patterned areas with plain. An effective way to show off any pattern to its best advantage is to separate it from other patterns with plain or textured areas. For example, a picture looks best on a plain or textured wall. A patterned drapery will show best against a plain or textured wall, a figured upholstery on a plain or textured rug and against a plain or textured wall, and a figured rug with plain or textured draperies and upholstery.

Plain or textured paper is a good choice for a hallway that may lead to some figured and some plain-walled rooms. Plain or textured draperies are usually best for the window that looks out onto a beautiful view. Plain lamp shades are best for interestingly designed lamp bases, plain pillows for patterned sofas, and plain upholstery on heavily carved chairs or sofa frames.

Combine different types of patterns. It is unwise to combine two patterns of the same type in one room, because it sets up an obvious comparison in which one of the patterns is bound to suffer. If, instead, one realistic pattern is combined with one geometric pattern, each will be judged separately and not compared with the other.

Express personality in patterns and textures. Your choice of patterns and textures determines, to a considerable degree, the personality of a room. Its mood can be masculine or feminine, casual or dignified, urban or rural, depending on the patterns and textures used.

Small patterns. If the colors are delicate, small patterns look very feminine. An excessive use of small patterns can make a room look fussy.

Large patterns. In strong contrasting colors and values large patterns are demanding and should be used sparingly. They should not be used as background areas in a home. They have a tendency to seem dramatic and urban. If they are predominantly straight lines, they have a masculine effect.

Textures. The personality of a color or of a room is influenced by texture. Smooth-textured walls, rugs, and fabrics have a tendency to look elegant and dignified. In light delicate colors, smooth surfaces produce a feminine effect. Rough, nubby textures in rugs, walls, and fabrics look informal and countrylike. An exceedingly coarse texture is distinctly masculine in appearance.

These general guides for the use of color and pattern in rooms are the tools with which you will start the specific work of planning color schemes for your rooms. The more you study, the more you will realize that there is no architectural beauty that color, poorly used, cannot destroy. But, by the same token, there is nothing so bad in a house or a room that color cannot improve. In fact, color can take its place quite creditably beside the magic of the old fairy tales, by which the good fairy waved her wand and turned the ordinary orange pumpkin into the glamorous golden coach.

1. Define the meaning of the following words and phrases as used in this chapter: hue, value, intensity, primary colors, secondary colors, intermediate colors, patterns, and color schemes found in nature.

2. Help build a class supply of reference material on home furnishings by sending for mail order catalogs and collecting discarded magazines from friends, beauty parlors, and doctors' offices, as well as advertising pieces from large companies.

3. Help create a class file on color by collecting discarded sample books of drapery fabrics, wallpaper, and paint colors from department stores and paint shops.

4. Give each sample its color-wheel name as well as any current commercial name it may have.

5. Using class reference material, clip for your own file or portfolio pictures of outdoor scenes, flowers, birds, fish, or butterflies which exemplify the color schemes you have just studied, and find a picture of a piece of ceramic, a reproduction of a painting, or a fabric sample that uses the same colors.

6. Create your own portfolio of attractive room schemes by clipping pictures which you would like to follow in planning your own room color schemes.

7. Try the scientific experiment of staring fixedly at an intense red square held against a white area. When your eyes feel strained, remove the red and, without moving your eyes, note the afterimage. Check its relation to red on the color wheel and identify the color scheme the two colors represent. Discuss the experiment in relation to the effect on living comfort of intense color for large background areas.

8. Compare the effect of two intense colors (a blue-green and a green) on a grayed blue in a lighter value. Discuss how this would affect the use of values and intensities in a room.

9. Borrow a prism from the science department and compare the colors created by the light that passes through it with those of the color wheel.

10. Use the three primary colors to mix the secondary colors, and then discover the way each color can be grayed by mixing it with its complement. Discuss this method for producing grayed background colors.

Well-chosen furniture is adaptable to many home situations. Bright furnishings
blend well with neutral furniture for a skillfully planned decorating scheme.

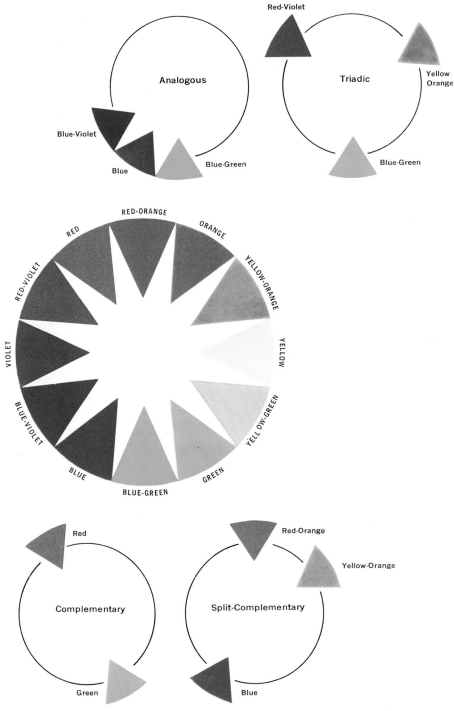

The standard color wheel with twelve standard colors is useful in identifying effective color combinations.

A warm monochromatic color scheme for the background areas skillfully blends traditional furniture into a Contemporary setting.

An analogous color scheme of blue, green, and yellow was chosen to blend
with the multicolor floral print of the sofa.

The complementary color scheme of the bathroom repeats the colors used in the adjoining living area.

Courtesy Gerhard C. Miller, Artist

Courtesy Better Homes and Gardens, © Meredith Corporation, 1963

When you use the colors of a fine painting for the fabrics and furnishings in a room, you are profiting from the expert color sense of the artist.

Courtesy PPG Industries

A dark color value will make the ceiling seem lower. A contrasting color emphasizes architectural features. Paint the wall and woodwork the same color in order to minimize the importance of overly heavy woodwork. Use a dark color value on the far wall of a narrow room to improve its proportions.

French Provincial furniture is adaptable to many color schemes. The bold cretonne fabric gives dramatic emphasis to the French Provincial setting.

Traditional furnishings coupled with modern furniture lend coziness and comfort to the rugged architectural backgrounds which display individual interests.

Courtesy Better Homes and Gardens, © Meredith Corporation, 1963

Contemporary metal furniture can be used either indoors or outdoors, depending on the fabric chosen for use with it.

Effective furniture arrangement allows for small group activities and individual interests as well as larger conversational groupings.

The wallpaper on one wall and the matching fabric cushions serve to unify adjoining rooms.

Inexpensive brightly decorated furniture can be innovatively combined to turn a back porch into a second living area.

A dramatic applique quilt and cornice board set the tone for an Early American bedroom.

The colors found in such accessories as pictures, lamps, and flowers can be skillfully coordinated with the color scheme of the room in which they are used.

Gaily colored fabrics for use in a child's room should be durable and colorfast.

11

Backgrounds
in the Home

You may be wondering just how much you will be able to do, or will want to do, about the backgrounds—the floors, walls, and ceilings—in many of the homes in which you will live. Of course, if they are clean and inconspicuous, you probably will do almost nothing.

However, if the backgrounds are wrong in color, or dirty, you will want to change them as promptly as possible. You can get an inexpensive wallpaper or a quick-drying paint to change them with little trouble. When you move into a home where you feel reasonably settled, you will want to make the backgrounds add all the personality and beauty possible. It is with both these situations in mind that you will want to study this chapter.

FUNCTIONS OF BACKGROUNDS

The primary function of the background areas of a room is to be exactly what they are called —backgrounds—against which the furnishings of the room will show off to the very best advantage. If the furnishings lack character, one of the three background areas can be made dramatically important in order to add personality to the room. In such a case, the furnishings, which would otherwise have been important, must inconspicuously match the remaining two quiet background areas to establish a clear dominance of plain or unifying color.

But whether the background areas are intentionally dramatic or intentionally inconspicuous, the ceiling, wall, and floor areas establish the tone of the room by their overwhelming size. Sometimes they do it in unexpected ways. For instance, a ceiling that has not been washed for years can give a dingy look to a room which no amount of clean furniture can dispel. Yet water and washing compound are readily available. A streaked, drab-colored wall can make everything in the room look "down at the heels." Inexpensive, quick-drying, water-based paint can be rolled on in a few hours. A soiled rug can cast suspicion on all the furnishings. Perhaps all that is needed is to scrub it with rug cleaner or, if it is too badly worn, pull it up, toss it out, and refinish or paint the floor. Area rugs that can be bought

Applying paint with a roller takes a relatively small amount of time and effort and makes the room look cleaner.

Prepasted, pretrimmed wallpaper can be used in small do-it-yourself projects.

inexpensively or made by hand will lend the softness and color needed. So, although backgrounds are large in area, they can be quickly changed by anyone who has knowledge and determination. And they should be our first concern in working on a room.

Establish the Personality of a Room

The first decorative function of background areas is to establish the personality of a room. This personality depends on color, texture, and pattern.

Color. Sometimes the choice of a color scheme is predetermined by something that must be accepted and worked with. It may be a rug, draperies, a sofa that can't be thrown out, or a floor tile or stone that can't be changed. If this is the case, accept it ungrudgingly. Treat it as though you liked it. Never ignore it! And, amazingly enough, you may find that the reason you disliked it originally was that it had not been properly harmonized.

However, if you are free to choose the colors you prefer, turn to some object of beauty which appeals to you and from which you can draw your colors, as was suggested in Chapter 10. The colors you choose can indicate whether the room is a boy's room, a girl's room, or an impersonal living area.

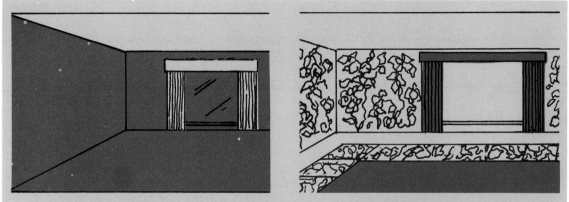

To make a room seem larger, use light, closely matching values on two of the areas. The use of demanding patterns on walls and in rug borders tends to make a room look smaller.

Pattern. In using pattern in the background areas of a room, follow the suggestions in Chapter 10. If one area is patterned, select plain or a texture for the other two. But because the floors, walls, and ceiling are the backgrounds for the other furnishings of the room, which frequently are patterned, it may be that all the background areas need to be plain or textured. Figured upholstery will show off best on a plain or textured rug. Pictures, books, collections, and objects of art look best against a plain or textured wall.

Improve the Architectural Effect of a Room

One of the important functions backgrounds can serve is to create illusions of space. In other words, how you handle backgrounds can determine whether a room looks larger or smaller than it really is. The choice of dark or light colors and their arrangement will to a large degree affect the apparent size.

Ways to make a small room seem larger. In these days of space-saving, compact housing, our big need is to create a feeling of spaciousness. Indeed, many bedrooms and bathrooms look considerably smaller than they are because of the current trend toward high windows, which gives the room an almost cell-like effect.

Use light values. As a starting point use light values for backgrounds. Walls and ceilings that are painted or papered in extremely light values tend to recede, regardless of their hue, and the room seems larger.

Use plain, unified surfaces. To further increase the effect of size use plain, unified surfaces. Plain or textured walls in light values with matching woodwork and draperies are so undisturbingly quiet that they do not stop the eye. They say in effect, "forget we are here."

Gabled ceilings, which slant down into the walls of a room, seem far less noticeable if they and the walls and woodwork are painted the same light color. The cut-up spaces of a room that has too many doors, cabinets, and window openings will run together and recede if walls, woodwork, and draperies are all treated in the same hue as well as in a light value.

Ways to make a large room seem smaller. Few people have the problem of rooms that are too large. Yet this problem does occur in some older houses and some houses whose architects have blended too many rooms into one.

Use dark values. Dark background areas make a room seem smaller. Use a dado treatment to cut the height of a wall, and vary the color of any alcoves or special-use areas to optically separate it from the main room, thereby cutting down the size.

Use pattern. A pattern with an attention-compelling quality on one background area will bring it closer. This will reduce the apparent size of the room.

Indoor-outdoor carpeting in colorful 12-inch squares may be used in the kitchen. The darkest square matches the adjacent area carpeting.

Harmonize Decorating with Architectural Styles

Whether the house is contemporary or traditional in style, present-day architecture has developed several new concepts which change the handling of backgrounds. Some of these trends have helped us move away from some of the artificiality erroneously called "decorator" styling.

Blend the indoors with the outdoors. Probably the most important new concept affecting the way backgrounds are handled is the close relationship between the indoors and the outdoors of many homes. Frequently, all that separates the indoor color scheme from the outdoor colors is a wall of glass in a door or picture window. If this is the case, the colors in these rooms must harmonize with the outdoor colors. Select the dominant color for such rooms from among the outdoor colors: the greens of grass and plants; the beiges, tans, browns, and terra-cottas of the earth; and the yellow-reds and golds of the sun.

If fireplace or planter walls are in the same brick or stone that is used outside, their color becomes a part of the interior scheme. If the color is rust or brown, all reds in the room must harmonize with it. If the color is gray, it must be repeated in the room; and yellow-beige and tan should probably be avoided. Only if a room is optically separated from the outdoors can the colors of the outdoors be disregarded.

Blend the backgrounds of merging rooms. If the rooms of a house merge, their background treatments should blend in color, texture, and pattern. If a kitchen opens with an arch into the living room or family room, everything possible should be done to make it blend with them. Avoid colorful kitchen floor coverings, kitchen wallpapers, and kitchen chintzes for the windows. Instead, repeat the living-room wall and drapery colors for a greater feeling of unity. Select a floor covering for the kitchen that blends smoothly with the living-room floor.

If a change in background is desirable, the backgrounds of the dining area of a living room may be treated like a game area, with dishes invisible behind wooden doors and the walls only slightly varied from those of the living room. The backgrounds of a powder room that opens off a downstairs hall or a bathroom that opens off a master bedroom must blend in color and tone with the related area. A hall that leads to several rooms must have backgrounds that will merge with them.

Having considered general relationships between the three background areas, you are now ready to study the handling of each area separately and in greater depth. Each has a wide range of possibilities both in materials and in handling.

FLOOR COVERINGS

Because of its cost, a floor covering is usually the first background area that is planned. Also, by its area and position, it takes a leading part

Rugs can be used to divide a large room into a cozy conversation area, an isolated passage way with a writing unit, and a dining area.

in establishing the tone and mood of the room. What we walk on has a definite effect on our mood. Deep, soft rugs or carpeting make a room seem warm and luxurious and make us feel elegant; matting, hard-surfaced floor covering, or painted floors make a room seem cool and make us feel energetic and brisk.

Floor Coverings According to Size

The range of size and shape of all floor covering is, of course, governed by the loom on which it is woven. The names of floor coverings indicate this size and shape.

Rug. The term "rug" is given to stock-sized floor coverings ranging from small throw rugs to room-sized rugs. (See standard measurements in Chart 4 on page 195.)

Carpet. The term "carpet" is given to floor coverings woven by the yard on a loom that is 9 feet, 12 feet, 15 feet, or 18 feet broad. Such carpeting can be cut into area rugs of room sizes or used for wall-to-wall installation. This type of carpet is frequently called broadloom—a term suggested by the wide loom. "Broadloom" is sometimes mistakenly thought to indicate high quality.

Runner. The term "runner" is applied to the narrow carpet woven on looms that are 27 or 36 inches wide. It is used mainly for stairways and hallways but can be sewed together into area or room-sized rugs.

Floor Coverings According to Fibers

The analysis of floor coverings according to fiber content is of primary importance. What they are made of affects not only their use, but their wearing quality and also their price.

Natural fibers. All floor coverings were originally made of natural fibers, and such floor coverings still form a large proportion of those sold today.

Wool. This fiber has always been the most favored fiber for floor coverings. It is generally durable, resilient, resists soil, and is easy to clean. It takes deep, rich dye colors. Sheep's wool and mohair are the two highest-quality wools used nowadays, and both are imported mainly from the Argentine. The initial price of floor coverings made of good quality wool is relatively high.

Cotton. Cotton cloth in the form of rags was used for rugs in early American homes. These rags were woven to form a flat rug fabric or hooked through a heavy backing to form a thick-pile rug. More recently, cotton fiber itself has been used to make bath mats,

183

Area rugs may be cut from broadloom carpeting. This can be an economical way to make use of little-worn areas of an older rug.

Inexpensive fiber-matting rugs are frequently found in checks which have a masculine effect.

and since 1949, when the first mill started weaving cotton on carpet-width looms, it has become increasingly popular for large rugs. Cotton fiber soils quickly and the pile crushes. Its popularity lies in its relatively low price and its wide range of color and sizes.

Grass, rushes, and wood pulp in the form of paper. These natural materials have found an increasing use as inexpensive floor coverings for studies, recreation rooms, bedrooms, and informal living rooms. Prairie grass and reeds are grown mainly in Europe and the Far East. All three fibers are being made into lovely one-color rugs in both plain and fancy weaves. They are also woven into checked and plaid rugs, and the cheaper ones sometimes have printed patterns.

Runners made in India from these fibers are most useful for stairways and halls. Other, more expensive, floor coverings are made from these fibers in China. These floor coverings come in natural-colored squares and oblongs which can be sewed together to form any shape or size of rug.

Man-made fibers. The development of man-made fibers began in about 1900 in the yard goods field. (See Chapter 15.) Since then, chemists have increased the strength and weight of these fibers so that they are now used for floor coverings. Man-made fibers are used separately or blended with natural fibers to meet the rapidly increasing demands of an affluent society for quantities of floor coverings.

Man-made fibers have widely varying qualities—some of which make them very attractive to the housekeeper and some of which make them less attractive than the natural fibers. The variety of man-made fibers is increasing

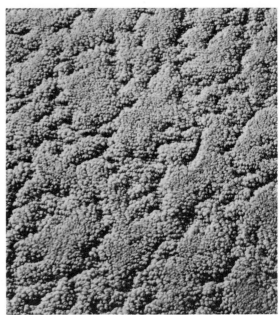

Shag carpeting has a casual contemporary appearance. Its long-cut pile shows footprints easily.

Random-sheared carpeting adjusts to contemporary or traditional furnishings. The indefinite textural pattern helps hide footprints.

each year. Scientists are working with every imaginable material—natural and chemical—to produce new and better fibers that will serve in better ways. Indoor-outdoor carpeting is one such recent innovation.

Nylon, acrylic, polyester, and olefin fibers. These man-made fibers have proved themselves durable enough for the pile fiber of floor coverings. The fibers are mildew resistant. Water-borne stains usually come off easily, but oil-borne stains are difficult to remove. As a rule, floor coverings of these fibers are less expensive than wool, which makes them attractive to people who move frequently and are constantly readjusting their floor coverings to new room areas.

Modacrylic (Verel). These fibers are often blended with other man-made fibers, as well as with wool, in floor coverings.

Rayon. In the high-strength carpet variety, rayon often appears in area rugs. Rayon is frequently blended with wool.

For a basic analysis of man-made fibers, see chart on page 278. A reputable store will help you choose the fibers best suited to your needs.

Floor Coverings According to Construction

The way a rug is made not only affects its value, but it can, in very important ways, affect its wearing quality and its appearance.

Machine-made floor coverings. The first machine-made rugs imitated handmade rugs. Then gradually, creative manufacturing methods made great changes in the field, producing new types of constructions, each with its own qualities and advantages.

Some floor coverings are woven on looms with the pile and backing produced in one operation. Standard weaving processes of this type include Chenille, Wilton, Axminster, and Velvet.

Other floor coverings are made by a tufting process in which rows of pile yarn are sewed to a backing material. When this process was first invented, it was used for cotton bathroom rugs, but in recent years the process has been expanded to include large floor coverings. To-

A modern hand-hooked rug in contemporary design forms a focal point for a conversation area.

day, the majority of floor coverings are tufted. A latex backing is usually applied to secure the tufts and to give body. A second layer of backing material may be applied to increase the body and give stability.

The texture of machine-made rugs is produced by using either a cut or uncut looping of the fiber, by twisting the fiber, and by varying the color. Pattern is put into rugs by cutting some of the loops in a design, by cutting or carving the fibers in different heights, and by using color in a set design.

Handmade rugs. Depending on the artistry of the weaver, handmade rugs can be priceless works of art or they can be simple, primitive ways to meet a need. Rug making can be a fascinating hobby. Handmade rugs can be room-sized or they can be small area rugs. With the increasing interest in area rugs, handmade rugs of many types are coming back into great favor and prominence.

Hand-tied pile rugs. Mainly Oriental and Scandinavian, such rugs are works of art which last a lifetime; they come in every size and shape. The Orientals, which are much the older, have such an established value that they can be readily exchanged or resold at auction until they are threadbare. Thus they are a good investment, as well as being a rug of great elegance. The Scandinavian rugs, frequently called Rya, are newer, and, depending on their design, are either contemporary or provincial in mood. The pile is longer and the wool is coarser than that used in most Oriental rugs, but, like Orientals, they frequently have a beauty of design and color that is timeless.

Needlework rugs. Rugs of this type are made in the Orient, in Europe, and in America. The Numdah rug from India is a beautiful, relatively inexpensive rug with a delicate, floral pattern embroidered on a felted goat's hair fabric. Needlepoint and cross-stitch rugs are favorite handwork in Europe and America. They lend themselves to beautiful personalized designs which can be elegant or informal.

Hooked and braided rugs. A simple type of floor covering that originated as an economy, such rugs have become works of art. Frequent-

Carpeting, woodwork, and accent wall in a plain, neutral color combine with off-white for the remaining walls and ceiling to form background areas which emphasize the furnishings and accessories.

Courtesy Sherwin-Williams Company

ly made from old fabrics that lend a mellowness of color, they may be a priceless climax for a room, especially when the color is coupled with beauty of design. Many girls and women make hooked or braided rugs out of new or old fabrics or yarn, following good antique or contemporary designs, thus adding great beauty to their homes with relatively small expenditure.

Flat woven rugs. These rugs are made both in Europe and in America. The French Savonnerie rugs have great delicacy of design. The American Indian rugs have a masculine quality because of their geometric design and color. Both are quite expensive.

The same basic weaving method in its simplest form was used by women who substituted old fabric for the filling yarn. These rugs were woven without pattern on a narrow loom. They are called "rag rugs." The narrow strips are used for hall or stair runners or sewed to-

gether to form area rugs or room-sized rugs. Rag rugs are most effective in simple interiors.

WALL TREATMENTS

Historically, walls were covered with wood, hung with tapestries, painted with murals or whitewashed. Then wall coverings were made from stretched fabrics. Scenic wallpapers originated in the Orient. They were imported for use on European and American walls. Then repetitively designed papers were made in Europe and the United States. Colored paint was introduced as a complete wall covering. Which covering we choose is basic to the effect of the room.

Wall Coverings

The range of wall coverings is great both in the final effect and in the cost of materials and labor. Each has its special decorative qualities and each its qualities of wear and service. In

Floral wallpaper may be combined with matching fabric to emphasize the under-the-eaves sleeping alcove for a young girls' bedroom.

order to choose wisely, the entire field should be explored.

Paint. Perhaps the most adjustable medium for covering walls is paint. Its cost depends entirely on the quality and type used, and on whether you are willing to supply the labor yourself or must hire it. It can be a permanent job or it can meet a temporary situation. It also is a most adjustable medium. It can be used over wood, plaster, brick, or cement. It can be mixed to harmonize with any color. If the color is a good selection, painted walls are the most undemanding background of all.

Wallpaper. Because of the wide variety of designs available and the various methods of application, wallpaper has tremendous potential for beauty. For this reason, its selection can be exciting or completely exhausting.

Plain or textured paper. This style of wallpaper is often overlooked. Beautiful papers are now designed to look like canvas, linen, silk, tweed, grass cloth, brick, and wood. Each has an interesting textural effect; many have subtle

color that is a perfect foil for pictures or objects of art. Many papers are produced with washable, vinyl surfaces that take tremendous wear. Some of these papers are a "no match" variety, which means that no paper need be wasted by pattern matching. A textural paper is an excellent choice to hide uneven or cracked plaster.

Patterned paper. Such wallpaper comes in an inexhaustible variety of designs. Most papers are printed, some are hand-blocked, and some are embossed. Most designs are planned for use over all the walls. Murals, however, are designed with some plain matching panels so the pattern can be used sparingly to emphasize the architecture of the room. Borders and appliqué designs are also available.

Surfaced coverings. There is a wide range of heavily surfaced or coated fabrics, such as canvas or burlap, which are far more expensive than the average wallpaper but are also far more durable. These are especially effective when used in areas which receive hard wear,

189

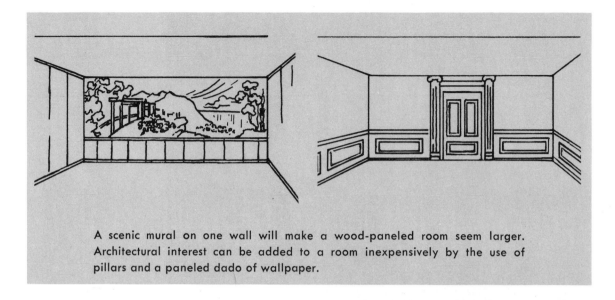

A scenic mural on one wall will make a wood-paneled room seem larger. Architectural interest can be added to a room inexpensively by the use of pillars and a paneled dado of wallpaper.

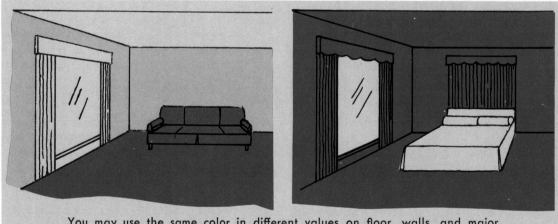

You may use the same color in different values on floor, walls, and major pieces of furniture in order to establish a dominant color. You may also establish a dominant by using one color in similar values for ceiling, floor, and walls and wall hangings.

such as halls and stairways, and are excellent for bathrooms and kitchens where there is apt to be steam and moisture.

Surfaced papers are now available that are designed to imitate all types of stone, brick, terrazzo, and marble and are about the weight of thin linoleum. These are being used in many bathrooms because they are less expensive than ceramic tile and have more softness and beauty than traditional plaster or other surfaces.

Paper-backed fabrics. Silk and grass cloth, backed by paper, are used for wall coverings, but they are extremely difficult to hang and very expensive.

Variety in Handling Wall Coverings

Many people think of the four walls of a room as one surface that must be treated uniformly. Actually, they can be handled in an infinite variety of ways.

Well-designed woodwork can be given importance by painting it to contrast with the walls. The woodwork color may also be used in the draperies and other home-furnishing fabrics.

Walls can be accented. The addition of wooden moldings or dados to walls is an inexpensive but effective method of adding beauty. Inexpensive screen-door moldings can be used to create panels. Wallpaper borders can be used at ceiling height and also to emphasize window and bed cornices. Wallpaper or plywood sheathing can be used either as a dado or to cover an important wall. Bed alcoves created with panels of bookshelves can be papered, painted, or sheathed for depth.

Beautiful woodwork can be emphasized. Homes built in recent years tend to have less woodwork than older homes. However, in many houses, woodwork is an important and beautiful part of the construction. If you are fortunate enough to have woodwork of that type, it can be emphasized. If the wood has been poorly finished or badly damaged through the years, it can be painted a contrasting color, as was done in Colonial days. Study the restorations of Williamsburg interiors for inspiration. If the wood is in good condition, it can be stripped and refinished to blend with the wood of the furniture in the room, and the effect will be beautiful.

Poorly designed woodwork can be blotted out. If the woodwork is uninteresting or clumsy, blot it out by painting it to match the walls. If the walls are papered, the woodwork can be painted to match the wallpaper background.

Drapery walls should blend with other wall coverings. Homes frequently have large-sized windows or window walls in the living areas. These must not be treated like windows but should match or blend with the walls. Otherwise they will completely unbalance the background areas of the room. To do this, buy the drapery material first and then match the paint to it, or select wallpaper to match the draperies.

CEILING TREATMENT

The ceiling is often overlooked in the planning of a room scheme, yet it is one of the large areas in a room and its effect is great. Whether it is to be inconspicuous or dramatic, the cost of handling it need not be excessive.

Ceiling treatment can be used to improve the existing ceiling. The ceiling must be considered an integral part of the background

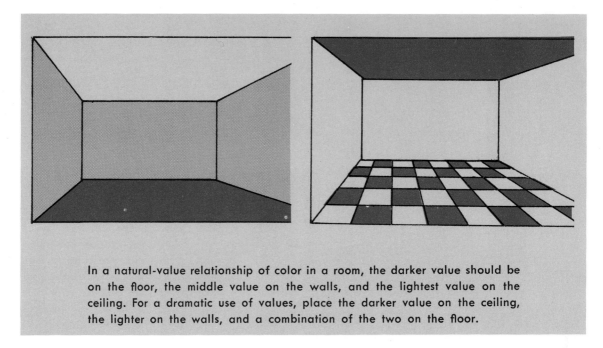

In a natural-value relationship of color in a room, the darker value should be on the floor, the middle value on the walls, and the lightest value on the ceiling. For a dramatic use of values, place the darker value on the ceiling, the lighter on the walls, and a combination of the two on the floor.

scheme for the room. Therefore, its condition and its handling are important.

Ceilings in Good Condition

Painting or wallpapering a ceiling that is in fairly good condition is the easiest way to treat it. To make the ceiling inconspicuous, match the color of the background of the wallpaper, provided it is pleasantly light in value. If the walls are painted with a light color, a slightly lighter value of the color can be used. A third possibility and a more usual one is to paint or paper the ceiling in an off-white to match other areas in the room, such as woodwork, draperies, lamp shades, or picture mats. This treatment has high light-reflecting quality which is often desirable. If the ceiling is to add decorative importance to the room, it can be painted a darker color, picked up from the dado or floor covering; or, if the walls and floor are plain, the ceiling can be papered in a dramatic pattern to match a fabric used for slipcovers, bedspreads, curtains or curtain trim.

Ceilings in Poor Condition

If the plaster is not in good condition. A thick, rough-textured, dull paper or, if the walls and floor are plain, a figured paper can be used on a ceiling to partially disguise cracks or rough plaster.

SHOPPING FOR BACKGROUND MATERIALS

Once the general work of exploring the market has been done, and tentative plans have been made as to color scheme, you are ready to begin the preparation for shopping. Assemble any colors that must be harmonized so you will have them in your hand. Review Chapter 10 about color, and then take measurements of the background areas of the room and draw them out on graph paper so a salesman can understand them.

Floor Coverings: First Choose the Type

The carpet or rug that is best for you depends on many factors, one of which is the size of your room and how it fits with stock-sized rugs or broadloom carpeting. Other considerations are whether you will be moving soon, whether you enjoy change, whether you like rooms to blend into each other or to have dramatic individuality, and how much you can spend.

Wall-to-wall carpeting. If you need to increase the apparent size of a room, you may decide to use wall-to-wall carpeting. Because

192

TYPES OF CARPETING

The increasing interest in decorative floor covering has encouraged the development of looped, textured, and shag weaves as well as realistic and geometric patterns.

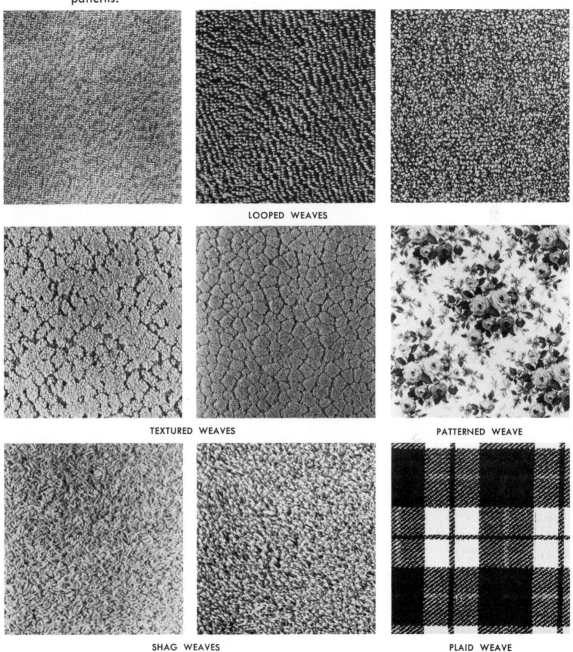

LOOPED WEAVES

TEXTURED WEAVES

PATTERNED WEAVE

SHAG WEAVES

PLAID WEAVE

Courtesy American Carpet Institute

A dramatic area rug may be made from carpeting samples.

Courtesy Better Homes and Gardens, © Meredith Corporation, 1965

this type of floor covering cannot be turned, it may show traffic patterns. If the room is a passage way to other rooms, wall-to-wall carpeting may be a poor choice of floor covering. It also can be expensive if the room width is not the same as broadloom widths, because the next width of carpeting must be bought and there will be waste. When you move, all of the cutting and installation charges will be repeated, even if you are fortunate enough to have sufficient carpeting.

Room-sized rugs. To have the maximum effect of size with a minimum cost, use the largest room-sized rug possible. This can be a stock-size rug, or it can be cut from broadloom carpeting. It may fit closely, or it may leave a narrow border of floor showing. This type of rug can be turned to distribute the wear, it can be moved without additional expense. Frequently, room-sized rugs give the appearance of wall-to-wall carpeting.

Area or accent rugs. For greatest economy and ease in moving and for great individuality and dramatic beauty, use area or accent rugs. They can be plain or strongly patterned if the floor is plain, but should be plain if the floor is a patterned tile, vinyl, or linoleum.

Get Your Money's Worth in Floor Covering

Because floor covering can be a big expense, it is especially important that the purchase be carefully planned, not only as to appearance but as to quality in relation to price.

Select price range according to situation. The best choice of floor covering for your situation may be in a low-price range if you expect to move shortly. It may be a moderately priced Oriental or Navajo which can be used in many situations or perhaps resold at auction when your needs change. If you like provincial furniture, it may be a room-sized braided or hooked rug. It may be low-price, candy-stripe broadloom carpeting cut in area-sized rugs or used wall to wall. Or your best buy may be medium-priced, good quality, room-sized carpeting which can be cut into smaller area rugs when it begins to show wear. In other words, what is best for you depends entirely on your particular situation, and this you must analyze for yourself.

Check the quality against the fabric price. In making a final decision, quality as well as price must be considered. Domestic pile rugs of any fiber—natural or man-made—can be

CHART 4. FLOOR COVERINGS

Type	Size	Use	Special Qualities
CARPETING			
Broadloom Standard indoor	12 and 15 feet	Wall-to-wall installation Cut into room or area-sized rugs Cut into runners	
Exceptional indoor	12, 15, 18 feet		Good for use in especially wide rooms
Indoor-outdoor	3, 6, 9, 12 feet	Outdoors and indoors in areas of hard wear, such as kitchen, bath, halls	Moisture, spot- and soil-resistant
Runners Standard indoor	27 and 36 inches	Halls and stairways	Available only in commercial quantities
Hemp	27 inches	Halls and stairways	Imported from India and occasionally available in home lengths
RUGS			
Small Area rugs	24 by 36 inches 27 by 48 inches 24 by 70 inches 3 by 5 feet	Accent or area emphasis	
Large Area and room-sized	6 by 9 feet 9 by 12 feet 12 by 15 feet	Area rugs in large rooms All-over carpeting effect in small rooms	
SQUARES			
Fiber	18 by 18 inches 12 by 12 inches	Sewed together to form area or room-sized rugs Use with metal or reed furniture	Imported from Orient
Carpet	12 by 12 inches	Cemented together for floors and walls—indoors and outdoors	Easy replacement
RUG PADDING			
Sponge rubber waffle mold	Same as rug or carpeting	Gives softness and longer wear to floor coverings	Extra buoyancy
Smooth rubber solid sponge	Same as rug or carpeting	Gives softness and longer wear to floor coverings	Hard wearing
Cattle hair and fiber	Same as rug or carpeting	Gives softness and longer wear to floor coverings	Less expensive
Hair and sponge rubber	Same as rug or carpeting	Gives softness and longer wear to floor coverings	

Plain-cut pile or plush-type carpet will show wear quickly. This type of carpeting lends itself to formal as well as informal furnishings.

A random-patterned, looped-pile rug helps hide footprints. It harmonizes with all types of furnishings.

judged on three points of quality: (1) the closeness of the weave, (2) the height of the pile, and (3) the quality of the yarn and the backing.

You can check the first two yourself. Examine the front and the back for closeness of the weave. You can compare pile heights by holding rugs of different qualities side by side. However, high pile alone does not indicate quality unless combined with a strong fiber and a close weave. As to the quality of the type of yarn, you are completely dependent on the word and reputation of both the manufacturer and the retailer you are dealing with. For that reason, it is necessary to deal with a reputable firm that will back up its statements. The word of a reputable merchant is worth far more than a written guarantee from an unreliable firm that may go out of business before flaws show up.

Check the total cost. The cost of wall-to-wall carpeting must include the waste, if there is any, plus any sewing and the installation. The cost of a room-sized rug cut from broadloom

carpeting must include serging the two ends. And to these costs must be added the cost of padding.

Consider the cost of upkeep. In figuring the cost of a pile floor covering, its upkeep must be considered. The pile rugs or carpets that are somewhat patterned, tweedy, or textured demand least care. They show footprints and soil less than a plain color. Any floor covering in the middle-value color range will be easier to care for than those that are very light or very dark. A multilevel pile requires a stronger suction cleaner than a single-level pile. The distance between the outside entrance and the carpet will also make a difference as to what will be practical. Whether a floor covering has been mothproofed and whether it is subject to mildew are also important in some climates. In any climate or situation, the type of care a carpet gets affects its durability.

Check a sample of the floor covering at home. Before you make a final decision on floor covering, take a sample home to see it in the room and in the light in which it will be

Plain walls, draperies, and upholstery help focus attention on art objects placed in an otherwise simple room.

Inconspicuous neutral tones in the walls, woodwork, floor, and ceiling allow the furniture and window treatment to dominate the room.

Courtesy Window Shade Manufacturers Assn.

used. If it is a braided or hooked rug, you may have to take a small throw rug of the same color scheme or a picture of it. Any good company will find some way of helping you, even though it may be necessary for you to call for it at the time the store closes and return it as the store opens in the morning. Decide on your purchase; if possible, do not order the floor covering until the other background areas are settled.

Wall Coverings: First Choose the Type of Treatment

Once you know what is available for wall coverings, you are ready to think about them in relation to the architecture of the room and to the floor covering you have already chosen. It is important to know the condition of the walls before final decisions are made. If the plaster is rough or a sand-float finish, painting or paneling is the simplest possibility. If the plaster is smooth, it can be papered or painted. If it is cracked, a rough-textured or patterned

wallpaper that has a dull surface will hide its defects best.

If you decide on paint. If the wall covering is to be paint, go immediately to the large display of paint samples that is part of the equipment of most paint shops. Study the special qualities of each type of paint, and then select six or eight color samples that seem nearest to the one you have in mind. They are there for that purpose.

Check the paint color samples. When you get home, hold the paint color samples directly against your floor covering and draperies (or your samples for these background areas) to be sure the colors are correct. Keep in mind the tremendous areas each represents and see them together in daylight and at night. The right sample will seem to blend with the other materials.

Check the accuracy of the paint mixing. Before you start the painting, apply a small patch of the mixed paint on the wall behind a piece of furniture or on a stick of wood which you

198

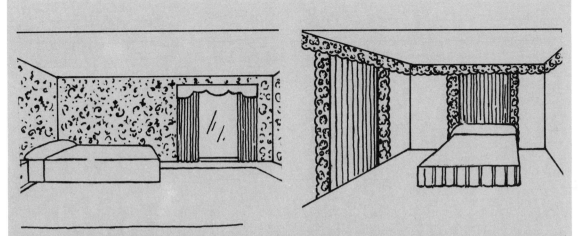

For a pleasant effect, contrast patterned walls with plain areas. Any additional patterned areas should be done in **exactly** the same pattern. A wallpaper border around the ceiling, the windows, and the area at the head of the bed, will add individuality to a room done in plain colors.

can hold against the wall. Dry it thoroughly with a heat lamp or fan, and then check the color in different lights. It is much easier to return the paint at this point to correct the mix, than it would be to repaint the wall, and it doesn't cost anything but effort.

If you decide on wallpaper. If you have selected a plain floor covering, you can use a plain, a textured, or a patterned paper. You will find you have a seemingly endless number of possibilities, but this need not be confusing to you. Place the samples of floor covering and drapery material directly on any piece of wallpaper that attracts you as you page through the books. It will be very obvious which ones blend best after you have done this with a number of papers. In choosing a pattern, hold the paper against the wall so you can judge it in a vertical position. After that there are certain guides for selection which you must keep in mind.

Harmonize the scale of the pattern. The pattern must be in scale with the size of the room. A large room can take a large pattern, provided pictures, books, or wall decorations are not going to be used importantly. A small room must have a small pattern or a fine-textured paper or the room will be overwhelmed and greatly reduced in apparent size.

Harmonize the type of the design. The personality of the room and of the people who will use it will affect the appropriateness of the design. Girls tend to like finer, daintier designs, while men prefer simple, bold geometric styles.

Some patterned wallpapers have a matching fabric which makes them especially useful. Using this fabric as a banding can make plain, ready-made curtains or window shades look expensively individual. A piece of it can be made into toss-on pillows to spark up an inexpensive bedspread, or it can be used to upholster a chair seat.

Know the Total Cost of the Wall Coverings

Before making any final decisions, be sure to find out exactly what you will have to pay for the total job—labor and materials—and what the probable cost of upkeep will be.

Paint and its application. Be sure to check the cost of the paint per gallon against the quantity you will need. Work this out by giving the salesman your wall sizes and the number and sizes of door and window openings, or estimate it yourself, using the paint chart. Then check the cost of application if the job is more than you can handle yourself. Most paint stores have painters they will recommend and for whom they can estimate prices. If you

CHART 5. WALL COVERINGS

TYPES

Paper
  Prepasted (brush with water to hang)
  Pretrimmed (edges fit together perfectly)
  Plastic-coated (washable and moisture-resistant)

Fabric
  Plain, coated, and some prepasted
  Decorative paper-backed — grass, jute, hemp, linen, canvas, silk

Vinyl film — three-dimensional imitation of wood, stone, leather
  Paper-backed   Fabric-backed   Adhesive-backed

STYLES

Plain colors   Textures   Tweeds
Patterns
  All-over (some with matching fabrics for draperies or slip-covers)
  Murals — for above dado or on one or three walls (have matching rolls of plain background color for walls, ceiling, or dado)
  Borders — pillars, dados — precut to use for architectural or decorative accent

QUANTITIES

Architectural makeup
  Count windows, doors, archways, fireplaces, cabinets, and deduct one single roll for every two average openings

Roll coverage
  Single rolls cover 36 square feet
  Double rolls cover 72 square feet
  Triple rolls cover 108 square feet
  Allow for waste in cutting and pattern matching by estimating rolls as:
  Single rolls — 30 square feet
  Double rolls — 60 square feet
  Triple rolls — 90 square feet
  For pasting, allow 1 pound of adhesive per six to eight single rolls

Architectural sizes

Size of Room, ft	Height of Ceiling			
	7 ft Single Rolls	8 or 9 ft Single Rolls	10, 11, or 12 ft Single Rolls	Rolls for Ceiling Single Rolls
6 by 10	7	8	11	3
6 by 12 or				
8 by 10	8	9	12	3
8 by 12	8	10	14	3
8 by 14 or				
10 by 12	9	11	15	4
9 by 12	9	11	15	5
9 by 14	10	12	16	5
9 by 16	11	13	18	5
10 by 14 or				
12 by 12	10	12	16	5
10 by 16 or				
12 by 14	11	13	18	6
12 by 16 or				
14 by 14	12	14	19	7
12 by 18 or				
14 by 16	12	15	20	7
14 by 18 or				
16 by 16	13	16	22	8
16 by 18	14	17	23	8
16 by 20	15	18	24	10

can do the job yourself, inquire about the cost of buying brushes, ladders, paint roller and tray, or of renting them along with canvases to cover the floor, and so on.

Wallpaper and its application. Estimate the cost of the paper by taking the measurements of your walls as you did for painting. Follow the wallpaper chart. Allow for loss in pattern matching and the cut length of the rolls. At the same time, get an estimate on the cost of the work if you are not able to do it yourself. The wallpaper retailer will have a list of paper

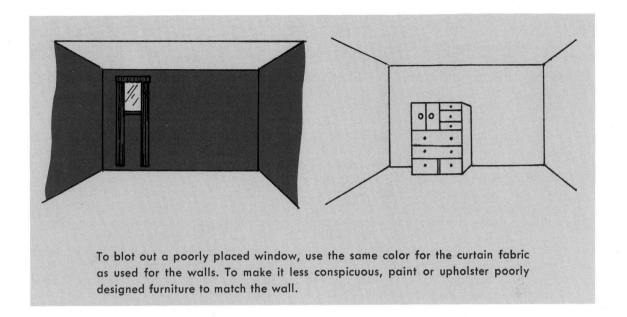

To blot out a poorly placed window, use the same color for the curtain fabric as used for the walls. To make it less conspicuous, paint or upholster poorly designed furniture to match the wall.

hangers and will probably be able to estimate their charges for you. If you are going to do the work yourself, inquire about making the paste and also about renting the necessary equipment either from them or from a hardware shop. Some paper is prepasted because of the increasing number of people who are doing their own decorating.

If the total cost is within your budget, ask to take the wallpaper book of samples out overnight to try the samples in your room. Only in this way can you be sure, because of the difference in light, and no professional decorator would dare buy without taking this precaution.

Ceiling Treatments

In order to determine the cost of materials and installation, you must be in a position to tell the salesman exactly the size and condition of the ceiling. If you are painting or papering, the same process as used for determining the cost of doing the walls can be followed.

PLACE ORDERS AFTER ALL PLANS ARE MADE

The importance of planning all three background areas before you place any one order cannot be overemphasized. *Always make all your plans at one time* for the floors, walls, woodwork, ceiling, and any window walls you may have. They should complement each other and blend as a unit. If you cannot afford to change all three areas at one time, this in no way diminishes the need to plan them at one time. Go ahead with the one unit that demands immediate attention and postpone the rest until you can afford to continue. If there is a long time lapse and your selections of fabric, wallpaper, or floor covering are no longer available, you can revise your original plans easily. You will know the approximate colors, textures, and types of patterns you need to keep the backgrounds of your room harmonious.

1. Define the meaning of the following words and phrases as used in this chapter: backgrounds, rug, carpeting, merging rooms, natural fibers, and man-made fibers.

2. Choose samples of wallpaper or paint for a bedroom for a girl who is (*a*) dramatic or (*b*) quiet and reserved. Explain your choices.

3. Measure a small room and figure out exactly how much paint would be needed to give it one or two coats of paint or how many rolls of wallpaper it would take. Discuss the wearing qualities and decorative values of each method of decorating and the problems of upkeep.

4. Using the figures arrived at in No. 3, check the cost of using the paint or wallpaper of your choice, including the cost of equipment you would need (rented or purchased) and the comparative effort involved.

5. Find a picture of a living room in which an intense color has been used for one of the background areas. Using material from the class file, show the class a more grayed version of the color that would be easier to live with and more beautiful.

6. Find a picture in which pattern has been used on two of the background areas. Decide which you would change to a plain or textured area in accordance with decorating principles, and explain how it would affect the apparent size of the room and the impact of the other furnishings.

7. Plan the background areas (pattern, textured, or plain) for (*a*) a room with many pictures, (*b*) a room featuring a large collection of dolls or books, and (*c*) a room with plain, rather uninteresting furnishings. Explain your decisions.

8. Clip pictures for your own portfolio of rooms in which (*a*) carpeting, (*b*) large rugs, and (*c*) area rugs have been used. Report to the class the advantages of each type.

9. Measure a small bedroom and figure the cost of (*a*) painting the floor using dribbling or stenciling for interest, (*b*) covering it with matting or carpeting, or (*c*) painting it and using area rugs you would buy or make.

10. Plan a color scheme for a kitchen or bathroom that blends well with a living room or a bedroom into which each might open.

12 *Knowing Furniture*

To MOST PEOPLE, furniture is either comfortable or uncomfortable, heavy or light, old-fashioned or modern. They never analyze it to see why they react to it the way they do. This is why so few people have furniture that truly expresses them. It may explain why people sometimes choose poorly designed furniture.

You will find that much traditional furniture which has survived from other times is not only beautiful but also appropriate for its time and for the houses in which it was used. Ideally, the furniture being designed today should be appropriate for today's times and homes. A study of traditional furniture and Contemporary furniture now on the market will familiarize you with furniture styles and will help you decide what types will give you the most comfort, beauty, and usefulness in your home.

TRADITIONAL FURNITURE AVAILABLE TODAY

Most traditional furniture styles that are on the market today are not exact reproductions of the pieces we see in museums. Instead, they have been adjusted to fit present-day production methods and present-day living. In most cases, this has meant only a little change in scale or in unimportant details. In general the wood, the designs, and the characteristic decoration have been retained.

Provincial Furniture

As a rule, furniture inspired by provincial or country life is comfortable and casual. There are two main types of Provincial furniture on the market: Early American, which developed in the New England settlements in the seventeenth century, and French Provincial, which developed in the central and southern provinces in France at about the same time.

The utility and adaptability of the style. Provincial furniture is well suited to an unpretentious, comfortable way of life. It has a forthright, direct simplicity and sincerity that is charming and informal. Early American furniture expresses the more austere, frugal type of life that existed in the hard-pressed New World colonies. French Provincial furniture has more elegance and comfort, reflecting the lux-

A.

B.

C.

D.

E.

F.

(A) The Early American home and its furnishings were informal and useful by nature. Modern adaptations retain this informality. The furniture fits well into modern multipurpose rooms. (B) A trundle bed which doubles the sleeping capacity of a tiny bedroom was a necessity for the early settlers. It is equally welcome in today's small bedrooms. (C) The Early American daybed (furniture that served for daytime seating as well as for sleeping) has been adapted as a modern sofa. (D) The Early American Windsor chair is used extensively in today's traditionally furnished homes. (E) The ladder-back chair is popular in present-day Early American interiors. (F) The Early American drop-leaf table style fits well in modern dining-room and living areas.

G.

H.

I.

J.

K.

L.

(G) The highboy chest furnishes maximum storage space in a minimum amount of floor space. (H) The versatile hutch cabinet can be used to display and store tableware and linens as well as to serve as a bookcase and storage space in living rooms and dining rooms. (I) Footstools frequently match the wood accent pieces of furniture in a well-planned room. (J) The oil lamp with its Early American tole shade furnishes the basic design for a versatile lamp used in bedrooms and study areas in traditionally furnished homes. (K) The Early American hand-made small rug has furnished the basic design for modern machine-made carpeting for Provincial homes. (L) Traditional sash curtains of natural-colored muslin, edged with ball fringe or braid, control light and provide privacy at minimum cost.

A.

B.

C.

D.

E.

F.

(A) Modern adaptations of the French Provincial house retain much of the country spaciousness of the original architecture. (B) This type of high cabinet, or armoire, originally served as a bedroom closet and chest. Modern adaptations may retain the original function; the addition of shelves makes the armoire suitable for living-room and dining-room storage. (C) A modern adaptation of a French Provincial lamp has a simple beauty which is appropriate in almost any traditional room. (D) Traditional hooked-rug designs have inspired modern machine-made area rugs and carpeting. (E) The upholstered arm chair is one of the most popular modern applications of French Provincial furniture design. (F) The rectangular shape of the French Provincial dining table may be squared off for modern use as a game table. A long, narrow form has been adapted as a desk or hall table and low styles are used as coffee tables and end tables.

G. H. I. J. K. L.

(G) The ladder back of the French Provincial chair has been adapted as a graceful headboard for a modern bed. (H) The graceful curved-front chest is suitable for living rooms and dining rooms as well as bedrooms. (I) A modern sofa adapted from the French Provincial daybed matches the ladder-back chair. (J) The French Provincial wall cabinet is an attractive accessory used for displaying small objects of art in traditionally furnished homes. (K) A French Provincial desk can also serve as a buffet or a dressing table. (L) The French Provincial ladder-back chair frequently has tie-on cushions for added seating comfort.

Early American furniture has been adapted for modern homes. These compact adjustable units meet the changing needs of a growing family.

uriant harvests and greater wealth of the middle-class farmers and small townsmen in this part of France.

The woods and upholsteries. Provincial furniture naturally used the woods that were found on the land close at hand. Walnut, maple, pine, and the fruit woods—primarily cherry—were commonly used in both America and France. Sometimes several different kinds of wood were used in a single piece of furniture. Handwoven fabrics of wool, cotton, or linen served for upholstery.

The designs. Simple and informal designs were used for Provincial furniture. The frugal use of even the small branches made the design of spindle-back and ladder-back chairs both natural and practical. Three-legged stools that would stand steadily on uneven floors were also popular. Drop-leaf tables were a standard method for conserving space in small rooms. Chests to hold things came in all sizes; low chests served for seats as well as storage, and high ones saved floor space; closets were unknown.

Early American chairs were apt to have higher backs which would cut off the cold New England winter drafts. They tended to have small seats appropriate to people who wore simple clothing. French chairs had lower backs because of the milder climate and wider seats to accommodate the fuller skirts that more prosperous women wore. This affluence was also reflected in the thick cushions and pads on the seats and backs of French chairs. In hard-pressed New England, the seat pads were quite thin; frequently the rush-bottomed or splint-bottomed chairs had no pad at all.

Present-day adaptations. The present-day manufacturers of Provincial furniture use the same woods and types of upholstery fabrics and the same general designs as the originals. In general they have deepened and lowered chair seats for greater comfort. They have also added springs and cushions to some chairs and benches. The trundle bed that slides under another bed, the drop-leaf table, the secretary desk, the hutch cabinet, and the chests which were so appropriate for the provincial age that produced them are equally practical in certain homes today.

Present-day settings. Provincial furniture fits well with informal living. The traditional

Courtesy Window Shade Manufacturers Assn.

Early American furniture is simple in design, reflecting the busy, frugal lives of the New England settlers.

Courtesy Royal System, Inc.

Although French Provincial furniture is basically simple in design, it reflects the more affluent conditions in the south of France.

A.

B.

C.

D.

E.

F.

(A) Eighteenth-Century English architecture has a gracious dignity that reflects the affluent living of its era. (B) This wing chair with the claw-and-ball foot borrowed from Oriental furniture design is an example of the influence of expanding trade interests on the furnishings developed during the eighteenth century. (C) The four-poster bed may effectively support a canopy when used in a large bedroom. (D) The open-arm chair can be used in any room of the house. The straight, untapered Chinese leg fits well with either traditional or Contemporary furniture. (E) The comfortable occasional chair with its pierced, splat-back and cupid's bow was a special design contribution of Thomas Chippendale. (F) The double-pedestal dining table can be extended for extra space.

(G) The camel's hump sofa is formal or casual in tone, depending upon the material used for the upholstery (H) The swan-necked pediment at the top of this highboy is a characteristic feature of Eighteenth-Century furniture design. (I) Straight-line draw draperies with matching valance may be used with or without glass curtains in a modern setting for Eighteenth-Century furniture. (J) A versatile flat-topped desk may be used as a hall piece, a buffet, or a dressing table. (K) An Eighteenth-Century mirror with swan-necked pediment is a decorative accessory which fits well above a chest, desk, or table in a traditionally furnished room. (L) A candlestick lamp base, made of brass, glass, or fine wood, looks well with the period furniture for which the candlestick was designed.

A.

B.

C.

D.

E.

F.

(A) The modern adaptation of the eighteenth-century French chateau maintains an air of spacious elegance. (B) Modern designers have combined the delicate straight lines of the Louis XVI period with the Tuxedo design to create a sofa which fits well in a modern formal living room. (C) Formal window treatments complement modern pieces in Eighteenth-Century French court styles. Draperies may be sheer material to match the glass curtains or they may be made of a heavy contrasting material. (D) A Louis XVI side chair displays tapered legs and an oval back, typical design feature of the period. (E) A Louis XVI daybed retains an air of formal elegance yet serves in a modern room both as a bed and as a sofa. (F) The fluted lamp may be made of gilded metal, china, or marble. A silk shade is appropriate to the elegance of this style.

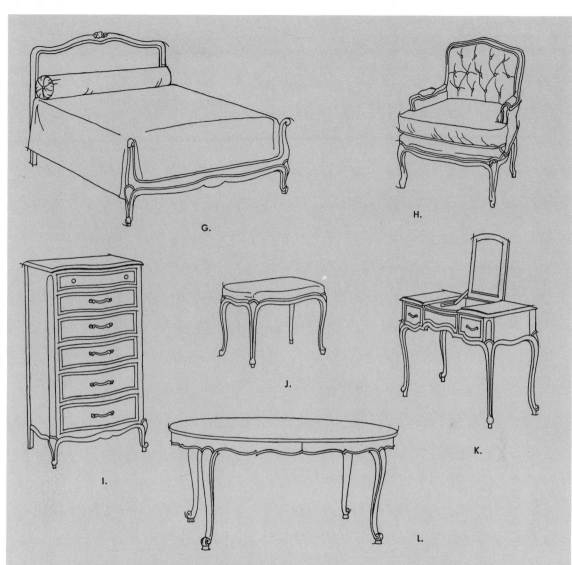

G.

H.

I.

J.

K.

L.

(G) The low footboard of the Louis XV bed makes the bed appropriate for a small bedroom. The headboard may be upholstered to match the bolster and spread. (H) A Louis XV upholstered chair is designed so that it does not crowd a small bedroom, yet it is important enough to be used in a living room. (I) A lingerie chest shows the delicate lines of the Louis XV period. Lower chests of this type may serve as end tables. (J) A Louis XV bench may serve as seating for a desk or dressing table. (K) The Louis XV dressing table, with its hinged lid, can also be used as a desk or tea table. (L) The designs of the Louis XV period are often appropriate to several sizes of furniture. A full-sized dining table suggests designs for smaller breakfast tables and for low-legged coffee tables.

Wallpaper patterned to resemble early tiles can be used as an effective background for a modern adaptation of French Provincial dining-room furniture.

Eighteenth-Century furniture styles are highly adaptable. A low chest may serve appropriately as a buffet, as an entry-area table, or as a game cabinet.

The dignity and grace of the Eighteenth Century secretary-desk and desk chair make these pieces attractive in modern small homes as well as in larger, more open rooms.

whitewash for the walls may be replaced with soft pastel paint or with wallpaper of simple fabric textures or chintz designs. Floors can be bare. Small hand-hooked or hand-woven area rugs can be used to soften the floors. Candy-striped broadloom carpeting reminiscent of rag rugs or room-sized machine-made hooked or braided rugs are also attractive, inexpensive, practical, and appropriate.

Coarse cotton, chintz, wool, and linen are appropriate for curtains, upholstery, and bed-spreads. Accessories of wood, wrought iron, pewter, and brass are always appropriate in an informal setting for Provincial furniture. Because they are simply and functionally designed, they seem to fit the informal living provided by Provincial settings.

Eighteenth-Century English and American Furniture

Just as Provincial furniture fits into present-day homes, so does English and American furniture from the eighteenth century. It can add beauty, dignity, and an individuality which some people greatly enjoy.

The utility and adaptability of the style. Designed for the affluent world of eighteenth-century England and America, this furniture met the needs of ambitious people who were making fortunes in trade. Furniture bought for modest homes frequently ended up in elegant ones. This furniture was light enough in scale to fit small rooms, yet so beautiful that it looked well in the larger ones. Many present-day young people who may also be moving

215

(A) The scrolled brackets used to support the eaves and door pediments of a Victorian house are typical of much of the ornamentation of the period. (B) Lamps, in either glass or china, with glass prisms and silk shades, are contemporary adaptations of a Victorian style. (C) Authentic Victorian pieces such as this desk with its side drawers can be refinished and featured in today's home. (D) The lyre-shaped pedestal and carved drawer handle exhibit the types of ornamentation so common in the Victorian period. (E) The small-scale Victorian side chair provides extra seating while using the minimum amount of floor space. (F) Traditionally, both mirror and picture frames in the Victorian era were heavy, elaborately carved, and gilded.

(G) The Victorian sofa frequently lacks the comfort and versatility required by modern home makers. (H) The Victorian ladies' chair can be used as an accent piece in present-day living rooms. (I) Ruffled net curtains, topped with a ruffled valance, make an effective background for Victorian furnishings. (J) This chest, usually combined with a wood or gold mirror, is a simplified version of the large, elaborately designed chest which served the big bedrooms of the Victorian period. (K) The heavy pedestal base of this dining table is an example of the Victorian trend toward over ornamentation. (L) The headboard on this bed is a contemporary adaptation of the Victorian style. Because of its simple lines, as well as its lack of a footboard, this bed is especially good for use in a small bedroom.

from small apartments to larger homes find that the present-day reproductions of this furniture suit their needs well.

The woods and upholsteries. The materials used in Eighteenth-Century furniture reflected the far-flung business interests of the period: mahogany from the West Indies and ebony from Ceylon, printed chintz from India and France, and silks and damasks from China and Italy.

The designs. Eighteenth-Century furniture designs had great dignity and beauty. Handsomely designed dining-room chairs were equally usable as side chairs, desk chairs, or game chairs. Fine chests and highboys could be used in halls, living rooms, dining rooms, or bedrooms. Dining tables were made in individually beautiful sections. The consoles could be used against the walls in halls or living rooms as well as in dining rooms. They could be combined to make a game table or a small breakfast table, or they could be added to the big table to make a banquet-sized table. Beds were designed to be used with canopies in larger rooms or as four-posters without the canopy in smaller rooms. Breakfronts were found in dining rooms, halls, or living rooms, as desks, china cabinets, or bookcases. Chairs and sofas looked equally attractive upholstered in damask or in handmade crewel; their lines were simple enough to be effective when slipcovered in chintz. These designs were created by the important furniture designers of this period: Thomas Chippendale, Robert and James Adam, Thomas Sheraton, George Heppelwhite, and Duncan Phyfe.

Present-day settings. Fabrics used for bedspreads, draperies, and upholstery range from the simplest to the most elegant: chintz, linen, needlepoint, crewel, and damask. Silver, glass, brass, porcelains, and tole may be used for lamp bases and objects of art. Oriental rugs, fine carpeting, and painted, paneled, and papered walls are all appropriate.

It is possible to change the tone of this style of furniture from informal to formal through the choice of fabrics and accessories. For this reason, Eighteenth-Century furniture is considered to be the most flexible and useful traditional furniture style. It is beautiful in itself, and it can be used harmoniously with furniture of other periods, including our own Contemporary style.

Eighteenth Century French Furniture

Sophisticated French furniture of the eighteenth century (and early nineteenth century) divides into two groups: the court styles of Louis XV and Louis XVI, and the Directoire furniture. They are beautiful in line and are light enough in scale to be appropriate in present-day homes.

Louis XV and Louis XVI furniture. The furniture of both periods was designed for French courts that were dominated by women —particularly Madame de Pompadour and Queen Marie Antoinette. Although the periods differ in design, they share a daintiness and delicate scale that lends itself to limited space. Furniture of these styles available today tends to be designed for dining rooms and bedrooms. Frequently the woods are painted in light colors and gilded, and the upholstery fabrics are delicate in color and light in weight.

Fine cotton toiles, taffetas, and damasks were used for upholstery. Glass, china, polished silver, brass, and gold were the preferred materials for accessories. Lace, sheer nets, and taffetas were considered appropriate for curtains.

Directoire furniture. French Directoire furniture is in great demand today, especially that which is based on Napoleon's earliest years. This furniture had much in common with that designed at the same time in America by Duncan Phyfe and in England by Thomas Sheraton and George Hepplewhite. The pieces most widely reproduced today are consoles, chairs, and benches which lend themselves to use with Eighteenth-Century English and American and with Contemporary furniture.

The fabrics most effective with this furniture are elegant and thin. Semitranslucent, filmy, voile glass curtains and fine-textured draw curtains combine well with silky, smooth-surfaced upholstery. The accessories should be elegant in feeling. Glass, gold, brass, and decorated china are all appropriate.

Nineteenth Century Victorian Furniture

The Nineteenth Century furniture is memorable for its Victorian designs. Many of these

Elegant Eighteenth-Century French court styles such as these open-arm chairs may be effectively combined with formal furniture of other types.

original pieces still exist in homes, attics, and antique shops and reproductions are readily available.

Early Victorian. There was much that was good about the Early Victorian furniture, inspired by the beautiful early Eighteenth Century French with its curved line and good carving. The ladies' chairs were comfortable for women, and the scale of the bedroom furniture was delicate enough to fit into small rooms. The small sofas were graceful, but many lacked comfort; the small wooden-backed chairs frequently had great charm but little strength; the marble-tops of the living room tables were easy-to-clean and decorative, but the pedestals were sometimes over-ornate.

Late Victorian. Much Late Victorian furniture was clumsy and inartistic. Based on the Late Empire Period in France, it reflected the increasing prosperity of Victorian times. The principles of good line, proportion, and restraint were apparently forgotten.

Both Early and Late Victorian furniture came to us overwhelmed by the fussy "decorating" of the ladies of that era who let their homes become inundated with knickknacks.

Is it any wonder that the men rebelled? At first, the rebellion took the form of demanding size and stability in furniture and simplicity in decoration. Mission furniture and over-stuffed furniture were developed. Both styles were massive in proportion. They tended to be lacking in beauty and to overwhelm small rooms. Both styles enjoyed comparatively short periods of popularity.

CONTEMPORARY FURNITURE

The Contemporary, or Twentieth Century, furniture style began as a general rebellion against historic design, both in Europe and America. The first examples appeared at the 1925 Paris Exposition; they contributed little toward meeting twentieth-century needs or expressing twentieth-century art. The style has gone

219

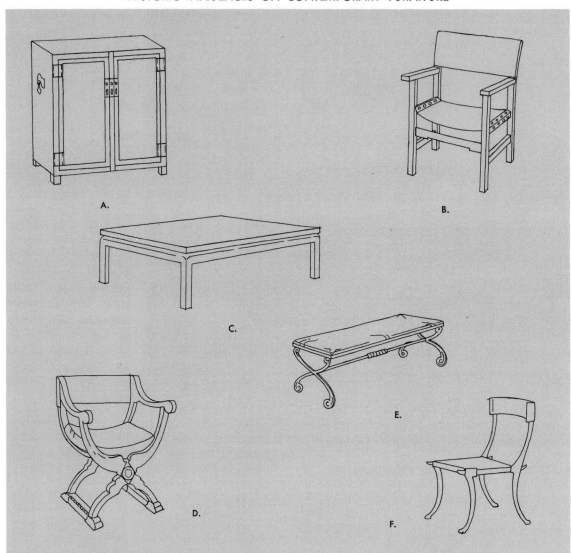

(A) Chinese chests with their straight, simple lines and beautiful brasses influence the design of most contemporary chests. (B) The basic design of the Italian and Spanish Renaissance has influenced many contemporary designers. (C) Ancient Chinese tables, used by people seated on floor cushions, serve perfectly for contemporary coffee tables. (D) The influence of the folding X chair of Greco-Roman design can be seen in Contemporary furniture for both indoor and outdoor use. (E) Greek metal benches influenced Eighteenth-Century furniture as well as the metal and wood furniture of today. (F) The ancient Egyptian metal chair also influenced Eighteenth-Century and Contemporary designs.

The multipurpose use of many rooms in modern homes has led designers to develop storage furniture which will fit as well in formal dining rooms as it does in bedrooms.

through a series of violent changes, and has been since slowly and painfully evolving into the smooth, low-slung, functional simplicity we know and use today.

It is well to realize that all furniture styles go through a similar evolution. But since you are a part of this twentieth-century one, you must buy carefully or you may choose some of the doomed-for-oblivion pieces.

Influence of Historic Designs on Contemporary Furniture

Some aspects of the furniture of the past have gradually been reinstated as an integral part of the design of some of the best Contemporary furniture, just as many historic designs developed from earlier designs.

The Ancient Oriental influence. Certainly the oldest and strongest influence in contemporary furniture design is that of the Orient. The straight-leg motif inspired Chippendale in the eighteenth century and even more strongly inspired our contemporary designers in their handling of tables, chairs, and sofas. The Oriental chest has influenced the designs for

Materials from many regions may be combined successfully in modern furnishings.

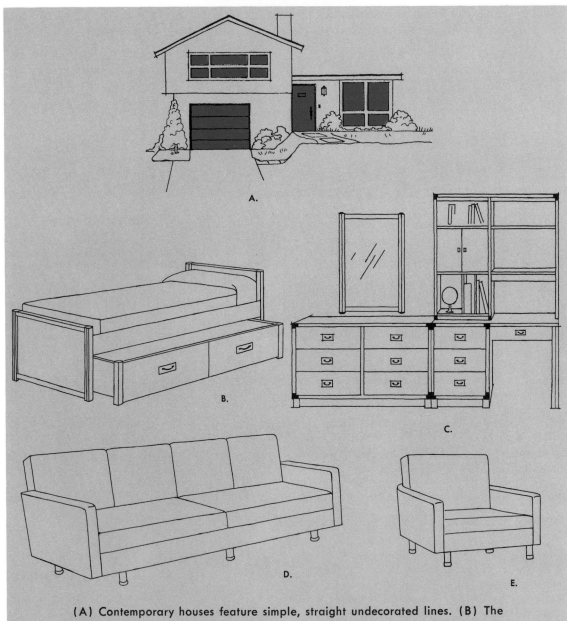

(A) Contemporary houses feature simple, straight undecorated lines. (B) The Contemporary trundle bed doubles the sleeping potential of a small room. (C) Separate units of similar Contemporary design can be assembled in many ways or used separately in any room in the house to serve many different functions. (D) The set-back legs and straight lines of this Contemporary sofa are inspired by Oriental designs. (E) Contemporary style lounge chairs can be used with matching sofas or with sofas from other periods.

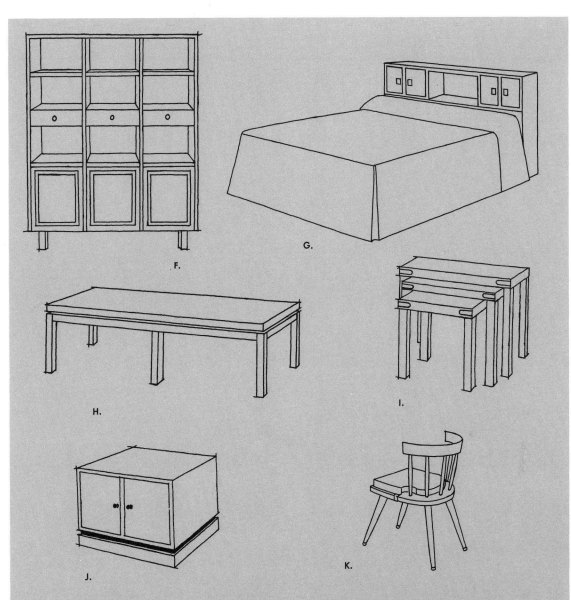

F.

G.

H.

I.

J.

K.

(F) Contemporary styles feature multipurpose pieces such as this storage piece which can be used as a room divider or an against-the-wall cabinet. (G) The versatility of Contemporary design is evident in this bed with bookcase headboard. (H) The slim lines of a Contemporary bench make it adaptable for entry ways or other types of living areas. (I) Nested tables are especially efficient for small rooms where a few pieces of furniture must serve many functions. (J) The simple lines of the Contemporary cabinet end table reveal the influence of ancient Chinese designs. (K) The modern curved-back chair may be used as a desk chair, a dining chair, or an occasional chair.

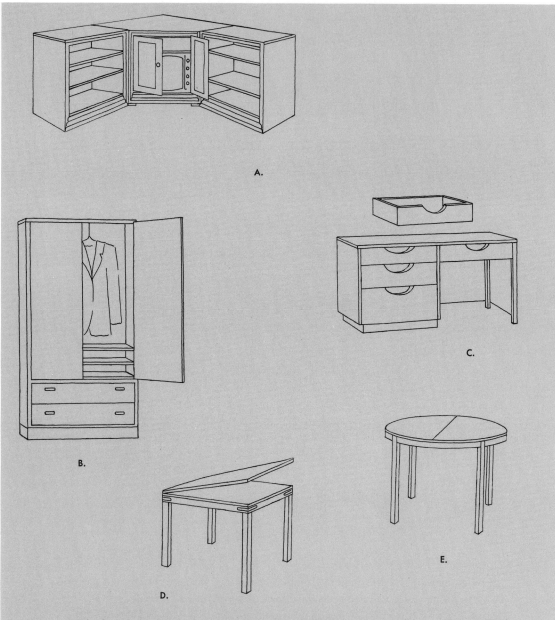

A.

B.

C.

D.

E.

(A) Contemporary storage pieces are designed to use all available wall space. (B) Storage ideas from earlier times have influenced Contemporary cabinets. (C) Contemporary furniture designs may often be adapted for use in do-it-yourself projects. (D) A well chosen flip-top game table can be used as an extra dining table for entertaining a large group. (E) A small breakfast table can be extended for extra space.

(F) The separate cushions make it relatively easy to change the upholstery of a Contemporary sofa. (G) A similarly designed Contemporary lounge chair may be upholstered to match the sofa or to blend with it. (H) A folding lounge chair may be used either indoors or outdoors in casual settings. (I) A straight chair, with rope back and seat, can serve in the dining room, living room, or bedroom. (J) Matching end tables may be used together to serve as a coffee table. (K) Low upholstered benches can be used for footstools or for extra seating as necessary.

Much Contemporary furniture has a simplicity of design which fits equally well into formal arrangements or informal multipurpose rooms.

Courtesy Armstrong Cork Company

our cabinets and chests. Bamboo, lacquered woods, important brass hinges and locks, and the clean, smooth, undecorated line which is basic to all Oriental art have become a hallmark of good Contemporary furniture.

The Ancient Mediterranean influence. The oldest European influence in contemporary furniture design is that of the Mediterranean countries—Greece, Italy, and Spain.

The Greek X-chair found a warm reception in Medieval Italy and Spain and in later European furniture. Recently, it inspired both Scandinavian and American Contemporary chair designers. The barrel-back chair of ancient Greek origin finds a warm welcome in our contemporary period. The use of leather for upholstery and the use of simple boxed pillows to turn benches into sofas came from the Greco-Roman days.

Influence of World Contacts on Contemporary Furniture

As a result of better communication and transportation, we know almost as much about

Africa, Tasmania, and Indonesia as we do about Chicago and Kalamazoo. Today's market places sell products from all parts of the world. In consequence, Contemporary furniture is a world style to which each country makes its contribution.

Natural stone, slate, and marble from everywhere and man-made glass, plastics, and lightweight metals make it possible for us to have furniture styles never thought of before. Primitive chairs and stools from every country are imported for use in our homes. Exotic primitive fabrics hang at our windows and are made into our bedspreads and slipcovers; primitive designs from remote areas have strongly influenced those designers who search for the exotic. Color combinations from the Far East and from India affect the fabrics created for our upholstery. Leathers, furs, and special wools from every corner of the world change the whole look of our upholstery. Man-made synthetics in the form of fillings and fabrics supplement feathers, down, springs, and natural fabrics in making furniture comfortable.

Influence of Contemporary Needs on Contemporary Furniture

Reread Chapter 9 and try to visualize exactly the type of furniture which would meet your needs effectively. Then study the line drawings on pages 222–225 to see how Contemporary furniture designs meet these needs. By knowing these styles, you will be able to avoid many of the "doomed-for-oblivion" pieces which are in fashion today but do not meet these needs.

PERIODLESS UPHOLSTERED FURNITURE

The cost of sofas and chairs is one of the biggest furniture investments because the development of this furniture in styles which are durable and comfortable involves expensive designing and manufacturing skills. A whole group of seating furniture has been designed that can be used with any style of furniture. Because it is produced in quantity, such periodless furniture can be sold for less than similar quality in period styles. Customers can sometimes choose upholstery from fabric swatches supplied by the manufacturer and plan minor tailoring changes without extra cost. In this way periodless furniture can be harmonized with the furniture styles of the wood accent pieces in the room.

Types of Periodless Sofas and Chairs

In periodless seating furniture, the designs for sofas and chairs are harmonized so they can be used together. The sofas in the seating groups may be made in sections, allowing great versatility in room arrangements.

The Lawson sofa and lounge chair. Perhaps the best known of the periodless styles and the most versatile is the Lawson style. With its slim straight lines it can give complete comfort in minimum space. The Lawson style ranges from a love seat size to an extra-long size to seat four. The usual size seats three and has one, two, or three cushions. The Lawson has a slim, trim base and medium high legs. Frequently the Lawson comes in two sections, and occasionally it is designed to open into a bed. The Lawson chair has the same simple arm line and slim base.

The club sofa and chair. A distinctive, wide, flat-topped arm and a heavier appearance characterize the club, or Charles of London, style. Consequently, these sofas and chairs tend to look best in large rooms that are masculine in tone.

The Tuxedo sofa and chair. Simple in line, the tuxedo style is especially useful with formal furniture. It comes with either a single cushion for greater elegance or two cushions which are easier to handle. The high arms of the sofa necessitate high end tables. Low chests may be used instead of end tables, or a long narrow table may be placed behind the sofa for lamps.

The armless sofa and chair. Armless sofas and chairs are especially good in small rooms, because they seem to take up less room than those with arms. The sofa comes in one or two sections, and sometimes it is slightly curved for use in rooms with oval rugs or with furniture that emphasizes the curved line. One of the most useful armless pieces is the studio couch, because it furnishes both sleeping space and seating space at a minimum cost.

Upholstery for Periodless Furniture

A periodless piece of any of the designs mentioned (with the exception of the Charles of London style) can be made to harmonize with any style of wood furniture if it is upholstered in the correct fabric and if the details of tailoring are properly planned.

When ordering any upholstered pieces, order an extra yard or two of fabric from which to make arm and back protectors, and to hold in reserve for repairs. It will save a far bigger expense later on.

Informal upholstery. Chintz, cretonne, coarsely woven cotton, wool, and man-made fibers can be used for informal upholstery. The thinner fabrics may be made with ruffled skirts for a feminine effect. Either ruffled or pleated skirts may be attractive with Provincial furniture.

Formal upholstery. Smooth, closely woven, or quilted fabrics are appropriate for more formal urban-style furniture. Such fabrics are best made up in simple lines either without a skirt or with one that is straight, with a kickpleat at the corners and at the center of a long sofa skirt. Seam cordings add elegance.

Masculine style upholstery. Leather, coated fabrics, and heavy tweeds produce a masculine

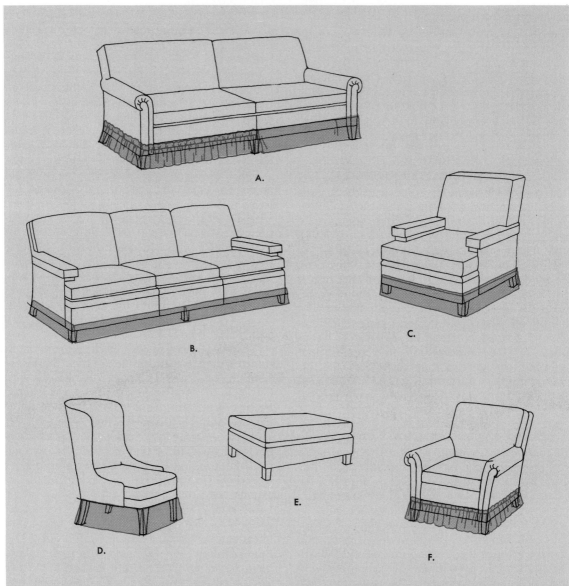

(A) The Lawson sofa, showing both formal and informal upholstery styles, illustrates the adaptability of periodless upholstered furniture. (B) The lines of the Club sofa make it especially appropriate in a man's room. (C) The Club lounge chair requires more space than the compact Lawson lounge chair. (D) The curved-line side chair can be used with formal or casual furniture, depending upon the upholstery used. (E) A foot stool may be designed to match the lounge chair with which it will be used. (F) The Lawson lounge chair gives a maximum of lounging comfort in a minimum of space.

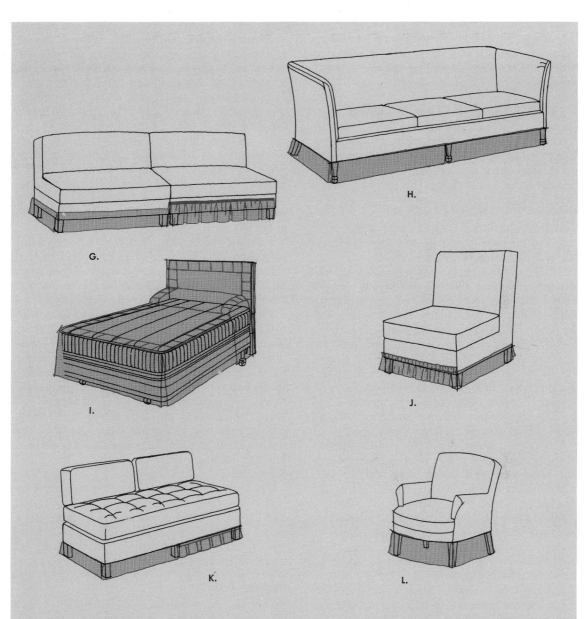

(G) The armless sofa is particularly usable in small rooms because of its slim lines. (H) The Tuxedo is a slim, dignified sofa that fits well in formal rooms. (I) A separate headboard can be combined with a mattress and box spring for an economical, adaptable bed. The headboard may be slipcovered to match the bedspread. (J) The armless lounge chair, like the sofa, adapts well to use where space is limited. (K) A studio couch is an inexpensive way to furnish seating and sleeping space in a small home. (L) Lounge chairs can fit into any room, depending upon the style of upholstery used.

upholstery effect, as for office or club-room furniture. These coverings are best made up with no skirt; they should be very simply tailored.

SPACE-SAVING FURNITURE

Furniture that has hidden functions, furniture that can be stored easily, and multipurpose furniture can be used to conserve valuable space. Such furniture tends to leave the room free for general activities.

Furniture with Hidden Functions

Furniture with hidden functions must be simple and easy to handle if the conversion features are to be truly convenient.

Hidden beds. Many Lawson sofas, studio couches, and some chairs nowadays are so designed that they can be opened up to form a single or double bed. If they are well designed, they are not only beautiful but comfortable both for sitting and for sleeping, and they are easy to unfold and to close up. Some are clumsy to look at, uncomfortable both for sitting and sleeping, and take a mechanical engineer to operate. Hidden beds are heavier to move and usually cost more than an ordinary sofa or chair. Check them carefully, and weigh the cost against other types of supplementary sleeping equipment plus a regular sofa or chair. The regularity with which they will be used is an important consideration in evaluating the expense.

File cabinet tables. Some small chests are designed with file drawers that are styled to resemble standard drawer fronts. These small chests can be used as bedside tables or end tables in a living room.

Sewing table desks. Many manufacturers of sewing machines are installing them in knee-hole desks or lowboys. These pieces can be used as dressing tables or dining-room buffets, or as desks.

Folding Furniture

Folding furniture is a great space saver, but there must be a handy place planned for storage when it is not in use. Without this, the furniture will either be used too infrequently to justify its cost, or it will waste space, rather than saving it.

Folding tables. The folding table is considered an essential in many homes. These tables are now made in a great variety of colors, textures, and styles. There are, for instance, folding banquet tables and folding aluminum picnic tables. Both these types are especially good for those who like to have frequent dinners for large groups. Square tables are good for games and supplementary dining for four, but they are too low to be combined with a normal height dining table. Round folding tables are good for those who enjoy games for more than four people, and those who like to entertain six at informal meals.

Folding table tops. Smaller tables can be increased in size with a detachable top that takes up very little storage space. These tops are an excellent, inexpensive way to accommodate extra dinner guests with comfort.

Folding chairs. The family's first source of extra seating is the collection of small straight chairs purchased for the bedrooms, living room, dinette, and family room. Be sure your home has an adequate supply of this type of casual chair before you invest in folding chairs for temporary use. However, if your supply of casual chairs does not accommodate the large groups that you sometimes entertain, you may decide to invest in folding chairs. Well-designed modern folding chairs are both beautiful and comfortable.

Foldaway beds. The least expensive foldaway bed is the type that simply folds up on itself and can be rolled away into the back of a closet. Another type can be attached to a door, which, when opened, allows the bed to be dropped down for use.

Stacked Furniture

Furniture is sometimes designed for easy stacking. Tea tables which nest under each other until needed for casual serving are a common example of such furniture. Patio chairs and tables have been designed to stack up to be stored in a small area when not in use.

Multipurpose Furniture

Furniture that has versatility or multiple use has additional value. A table height chest can be useful in almost any room, but if in addition it is designed with a kneehole opening,

Well-chosen furniture provides both comfort and beauty within a home.

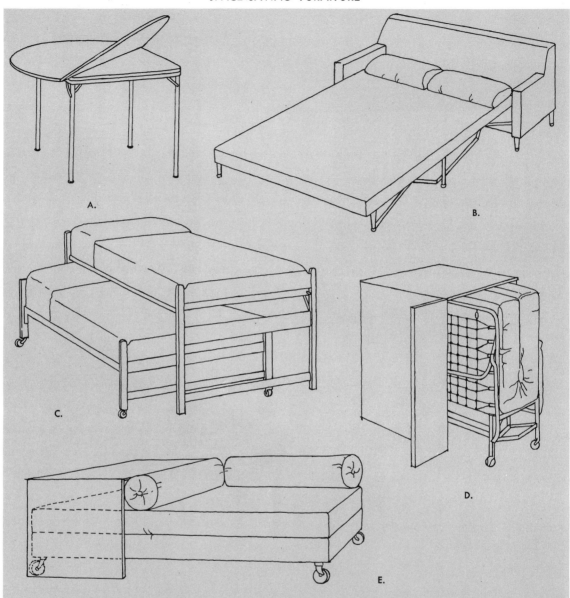

(A) The seating space of a standard folding table can be increased easily by the addition of a folding circular top. (B) A hide-a-bed can be converted from sitting space to sleeping space. (C) Trundle beds need space for only one bed by day, yet neither bed is overly high and each is completely separate. (D) A chestlike cabinet provides dustproof storage for a folding rollaway bed. (E) A twin bed that rolls partially under a corner table can serve as a sofa for daytime use.

it can be used as a desk or dressing table. A game table with a double top can also be used for dining for six or for a buffet table. This type of furniture saves space and saves money because it does the work of several pieces.

Seating. Box-style cushions which provide attractive upholstered seating at windows or along wall benches and which double as hassocks for casual entertaining are another example of space-saving multipurpose furniture.

Beds. Bunk beds that pile up above each other or can be separated to work as twin beds are excellent for saving space. The modern trundle bed, copied from the youth beds of early American days, can be rolled under its companion bed during the day. Trundle beds and other lower than average beds may be rolled under a corner table or corner storage area to save space in a small room.

Modular furniture. Many furniture manufacturers sell modular furniture which may be combined and stacked to adjust for maximum utilization of available space. Shelving may be stacked on a matching chest for use as a breakfront in one room, for a study area in another room, and for clothing storage in a third. Or two units of shelving may be stacked on each other and used as a bookcase, a room divider, or a china closet.

MONEY-SAVING FURNITURE

Everyone is interested in getting the best value possible for the money he has to spend. There are many ways of doing this in the field of furniture. Common methods include making furniture of readily available stock materials, remodeling old furniture, and finishing unfinished new furniture.

Do-It-Yourself Projects

There is a growing field of do-it-yourself furniture which can be made by almost any amateur with a few tools. This furniture can be amazingly smart and reasonable in price. The increasing interest in such furniture projects has brought onto the market a constantly enlarging supply of well-designed component parts that make the construction far easier than ever before.

Tables, benches, and desks. Most hardware stores and mail order catalogs now stock a wide variety of furniture legs, core doors, and plywood which can be combined into tables, benches, and desks. Legs are easily screwed on to core doors or pieces of heavy plywood cut to your measurement at the mill or hardware shop. The finish can be wax, a sprayed-on stain, or lacquer. This form of table construction can be used as a seat or a bed when covered with softening pads or pillows, or as a desk when or if combined with files or bookcases. This type of furniture is low in cost.

Beds. Six legs can be screwed into a box spring to make one type of studio couch bed. A metal bed frame on rollers to which a headboard can be added, can turn a mattress and spring into a beautiful bed.

Other projects. Aluminum tubing and framing can be combined with metal, plastic, wood, or wood-product panels to make cabinets, desks, and storage shelving. Extension poles may be combined with stock panels to make room dividers and storage shelves. Plans readily available at local libraries show how to use such components for chairs, patio furniture, and children's furniture.

Remodeled Furniture

Old furniture has limitless possibilities for remodeling. Evaluate the condition of the furniture before you undertake such a project. Is the piece structurally sound? Are the joints solid? Is the furniture warped or is the veneer peeling? Do the doors and drawers fit and slide easily? Estimate the amount of work necessary to put the piece into condition. Only after this is settled should you consider what can be done from a design and finish point of view. If you are planning to buy used furniture for remodeling, you must consider the cost of the remodeling and the time involved as well as the initial cost of the piece.

Simplification. The first need of most furniture is simplification. Perhaps legs should be lowered or cut off, backs cut down, mirrors removed, bad hardware replaced, or decoration removed. It is amazing how different a piece of furniture will look after it has been treated to this sort of rejuvenating process. Look at straight chairs, old dressers, radio cabinets,

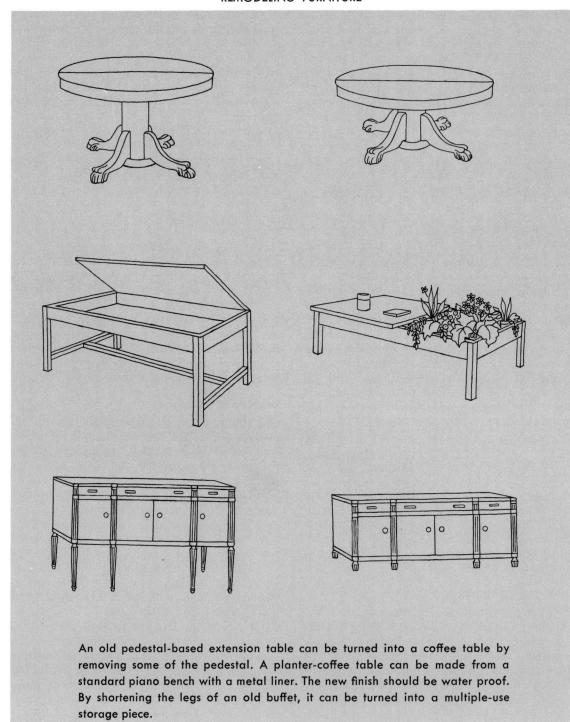

An old pedestal-based extension table can be turned into a coffee table by removing some of the pedestal. A planter-coffee table can be made from a standard piano bench with a metal liner. The new finish should be water proof. By shortening the legs of an old buffet, it can be turned into a multiple-use storage piece.

An old dresser of good quality can be transformed by changing the mirror, shortening the legs, and replacing the drawer pulls. An old bed of good quality can be converted by using the footboard for the headboard. A drop-leaf table can be divided for a bench and a wall console.

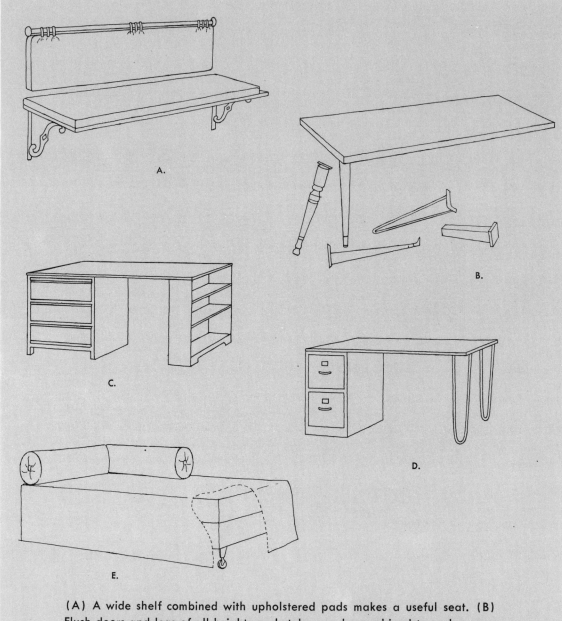

(A) A wide shelf combined with upholstered pads makes a useful seat. (B) Flush doors and legs of all heights and styles can be combined to make many types of tables. (C) An unfinished chest, bookcase, and flush door can be combined to make a desk. (D) A metal file cabinet, metal legs, and a flush door form a Contemporary work table. (E) A mattress and springs, combined with screw-on legs, plus bolsters and matching cover, make a versatile bed-seating arrangement.

and tables with this in mind. See if an old bed is improved by removing the headboard and allowing the low footboard to become the headboard.

Division. Can you separate an extension table to form two separate tables? Can you divide a dressing table to make a pair of low chests? In such ways you may use division to change what you have into what you want.

Refinishing. The final process in changing the total effect of an old piece of furniture is the refinishing. A little sanding and a coat of paint is the easiest finish. But if the wood is good, it may be worth stripping down, sanding, and refinishing with wax or with a stain and wax. If the piece is absolutely straight and simple, you might enjoy covering it with wallpaper or fabric.

Unfinished Furniture

The range of unfinished furniture has increased considerably in recent years. It comes in a wide variety of pieces and in several styles. It comes in standard sizes and designs. Some unfinished furniture is planned on the modular concept. Chests can be paired or used side by side. Matching chairs can be grouped around a table. Unfinished furniture tends to be made of soft woods. The quality of the wood and the quality of the construction must be carefully evaluated.

The design. Unfinished furniture is usually of two types of design—Early American and a periodless straight-line which can be used anywhere. The scale is usually small enough to be easily adjustable to the smallest rooms.

The finish. This furniture can be painted or given a natural wood finish. Since the wood and the design tend to be rather ordinary, it may be best to choose an inconspicuous finish. Bookshelves could be painted or stained to match the woodwork; chests in small rooms painted to match the wall or woodwork.

Outdoor or Casual Furniture

The contemporary emphasis on outdoor living has introduced a whole new type of furniture into our homes. The so-called porch or patio furniture has found its way into bedrooms, dens, and "young" living rooms in a charming, comfortable, and often inexpensive way.

An imported cane-tub chair is an attractive, relatively inexpensive piece of furniture.

Rattan furniture. The Orient has supplied us for many years with rattan furniture: chairs, tables, and small sofas. It is attractive, comfortable, and very inexpensive, but has a relatively short life under hard usage. The standard designs harmonize with traditional furniture. Several new designs have a more contemporary feeling. Rattan furniture can well be used as supplementary pieces anywhere. Such furniture is especially attractive when used with natural or painted wood tables and chests and with periodless furniture in casual, informal rooms. Rattan chairs are less expensive and more comfortable than the average metal folding chair; they make an attractive permanent addition to a room.

Outdoor wood furniture. The range of outdoor wood furniture runs from the very heavy redwood type to the light folding chair that has a canvas back and seat. These folding chairs may have a natural finish or a colored lacquer finish with white or colored canvas. Such chairs tend to have a nautical, masculine, breezy effect that is most attractive. These chairs can be combined with periodless wood chests and benches.

When several children share the same study area, individual study desks can be made from molding boards fastened to the wall. Shelving attached to the wall provides space for each child's interests.

Metal furniture for indoor use fits well into the casual pattern of the kitchen dinette or the family room.

Metal furniture. The range of metal furniture has grown tremendously in recent years. The outdoor type runs from the elaborate, expensive, and less comfortable New Orleans floral type to the inexpensive, comfortable folding chrome furniture that can be taken on picnics.

Sunroom metal furniture is somewhat expensive but is very durable and comfortable. The frame is of oxidized or painted metal; the cushions are covered in sail cloth or cretonne to give living-room elegance in an outdoor manner. The styles may be masculine or feminine, traditional or contemporary.

COMBINING FURNITURE

The most sterile, impersonal type of furniture is the completely matched set which is standard in public institutions. Furniture for a home should be selected far more thoughtfully.

Look for Variety with Unity

Furniture for a room in a home should be subtly unified and yet have interesting individuality. The question thus becomes: What is the best way to combine furniture to produce this?

Select a dominant style. The first decision that must be made about the furnishings of a

Furniture of various styles and periods can express your individuality in a total unified effect.

room is the style. Is it to be casual or formal in feeling? Is it to be contemporary or traditional? Is it to be masculine or feminine? Is it to be tailored or dainty? Most people have an innate liking for a certain type and style. A long-term liking for such a style should be the basis for the buying of most of the furniture. But each piece should be individually selected.

Select a dominant wood color. The furniture wood in any one room should harmonize, but it is not necessary to have either the finish or the woods identical. So long as two or more wood colors are harmonious, they can be used effectively in a single room.

Look for Lasting Beauty

The final step in choosing furniture is to be sure that it is beautiful. To do this you must train your eye to discriminate, to see good line and good proportion. Become acquainted with the best by looking through illustrations of fine furniture and visiting historic mansions and historic restorations such as the Williamsburg interiors. Watch the furniture in stage settings, in the movies and on television. Go to the museums and study the furniture. Visit furniture stores and study what styles attract you and why. You will learn to recognize good line wherever you meet it, whether it is in traditional, contemporary, or periodless furniture.

LEARNING EXPERIENCES

1. Define the meaning of the following words and phrases as used in this chapter: traditional, contemporary, and provincial furniture.
2. Clip pictures of furniture you would like to use in a living room of your own. Identify the style of each piece and tell why you would choose it.
3. Find the closest duplicate of two of the pieces of furniture you choose and check what they would cost, using a mail order catalog or a store near your home to determine prices.
4. Ask your librarian to suggest a novel with a background that is (*a*) Early American, (*b*) French Revolution, or (*c*) Eighteenth Century. Visualize the homes furnished in the furniture you are studying and see its relation to the life and clothing of those times.
5. Learn about furniture refinishing by experimenting with waxing, painting, or staining an unfinished wooden cigar box, an old jewelry box, or a chest for storing flatware that needs stripping and sanding.
6. Start a portfolio of pictures of traditional and contemporary furniture, discarding the less attractive as you find better examples, thus training your eye to see good line when you buy.
7. Clip and compare the lines and proportions of furniture in the ads that urge you to consider price with those that urge you to consider quality. Discuss the differences in class.
8. Show pictures and discuss the values of desks and end tables that have good storage space over those that are the table type.
9. Discuss multipurpose and single-use furniture, its functional value for those who move frequently, and its comparative price.
10. What piece of furniture would you like to buy for your own use right now? Check its cost new against its cost secondhand or unfinished.

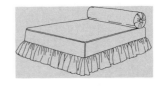

 Selecting Furniture

WITHOUT A DOUBT, the most difficult part of buying is deciding the amount of money to spend on anything. For instance, how important to you is a trip compared to a more expensive sofa? How important is carpeting compared to a new car? There is *no standard right answer* to these questions, because people differ so greatly in what they consider necessary for happiness and satisfaction.

If you are businesslike you may be able to stretch your money in several directions. Perhaps you can take a trip and slipcover the old sofa to make it look like new. You might buy a less expensive floor cover and a used car. You can get more from your money by planning your purchases.

SETTING UP YOUR OWN BUDGET

Buying according to a budget is important in every area of family living. It is especially important in buying home furnishings, because there is a wide range of choices and because a great deal of money is involved in each purchase. Only by deciding how much money you can spend and by dividing it according to what you need to buy can you hope to meet your furnishing needs.

Personal Basis

Many girls begin thinking about buying furniture by dreaming. Unfortunately no budget is ever large enough to buy the furnishings that will make a dreamer content. So check yourself and your probable income and plan to fit into your world which has few castles but many charming homes.

Your educational resources. As a rule, the greater your skills and educational background, the higher your income may be, and the more you can hope to have in your total budget to spend for home furnishings. Analyze objectively both yourself and any man you consider marrying and estimate the economic level you will probably reach. Higher education also tends to increase your general knowledge in fields which relate to home furnishing, with the result that you are able to make better choices and so get better value for your money.

Your aims. The furnishings of your home will also depend on your own personal stand-

A careful selection of individual pieces of furniture according to an overall pattern will help achieve individual rooms of beauty and usefulness.

ards of beauty and your idea of the relative importance of a home. To some people, a home is of utmost importance; to others it is secondary to travel, the theater, or some special hobby. Those who feel that a home is of primary importance will spend a larger proportion of their income on home furnishings than those to whom other things are of greater importance.

Family Basis

The proportion of the total budget assigned to home furnishings may not be the same two years running. The changing needs of the family must be considered.

The needs of early years of marriage. During your early years of marriage, when your living expenses may be relatively low, you will be able to assign a larger proportion of your income to home furnishings than at any other time. At that time, too, your needs may be greater because you will be buying the basic furnishings to set up your home.

The needs of middle years of marriage. During the middle years of your marriage, your budget for household furnishings will have to be planned to meet two situations. It will have to cover the buying of supplementary furnishings necessitated by the changing requirements of a growing family and it will have to meet the cost of repairs and replacements of furniture.

The needs of later years of marriage. During the later years of marriage many couples find they can raise their home furnishings budget to include furniture and accessories which might have seemed luxuries before.

Financial Basis

The actual figure to be spent on furnishings can only be decided by analyzing your total resources.

Personal resources. For many people, personal resources, aside from personal savings, means the amount of money which can be spent from current income without upsetting their way of life too drastically. Personal credit is another resource. By meeting all their charge accounts promptly, some people have built up personal credit that will permit them to charge

Comfort and a smart appearance for a one-room apartment may be achieved at comparative low cost with furnishings such as a sofa hide-a-bed, folding chairs, and an unfinished chest-bookcase.

Courtesy Window Shade Manufacturers Assn.

Courtesy Better Homes and Gardens, © Meredith Corporation, 1965

By buying wooden occasional chairs instead of upholstered lounge chairs, or a hide-a-bed instead of a bed plus sofa, you can adjust your furnishings budget to allow for special interests, such as an organ or an important painting.

Courtesy Drexel Furniture Company

In evaluating a furniture grouping, consider the possibility of multiple functions, the quality of the proportions, and the beauty of the wood graining.

merchandise and pay for it over a period of from three to six months with little or no carrying charge. Personal skills may also be considered as a personal resource. Carpentry, refinishing, remodeling, and sewing skills that can save labor charges may be as important to you as money.

Impersonal resources. Some people may wish to consider borrowing money. If you do so, do not make the mistake of automatically letting this money be furnished by the store that sells furniture—in other words, of doing installment buying. It may be that the total store's charges will be far higher than the cost of borrowing money at a bank because some stores actually make more money on their "carrying charges" than they do on their furniture. Check the total percentage that will be charged each year for the use of money by various types of organizations before you sign your name to anything, including a contract to buy furniture anywhere. Fine print in a contract may contain many legal entanglements.

Furnishing needs. A plan of financing begins with a list of what you will need to buy. When the list is completed, turn to the chart on page 345 showing a furnishings budget on a unit basis. This chart will be a tremendous help in giving you approximate figures to budget toward. The chart figures will be adjusted by actual circumstances: a good buy in a sofa allows you to spend more for a rug; a new slipcover for a chair that you have will leave more money for the new chair you still must buy. The unit system of planning your furnishings budget provides the basis for a sound initial estimate of your furnishings costs.

EVALUATING FURNITURE ACCORDING TO QUALITY

Price is not necessarily an accurate indication of quality. A knowledge of furniture will help you get better quality furniture in any price range.

Furniture Wood

Many people have absorbed a great deal of misinformation about furniture woods. They think that all maple furniture is inexpensive and all mahogany expensive, that solid wood is a sign of quality and veneered wood a sign

When buying furniture, be sure to read the tags carefully for information about the quality and construction, as well as for advice about its care.

of cheap construction. Instead, it is the appropriateness of the wood for the use and design, as well as the selection and method of preparation and the care in the furniture construction that determine the quality of the furniture.

Solid wood. The term "solid wood" indicates good quality in furniture only if the wood has been well selected and carefully dried. If, on the other hand, the wood has not been well selected, or if it has been inadequately dried, it can warp and crack in such a way that the piece can never be repaired.

Good-quality solid-wood furniture lends itself to carved designs. Such furniture is easier to refinish than veneered-wood furniture.

Veneered wood. The use of veneered wood in furniture construction is neither modern nor necessarily inexpensive. Some of the oldest known furniture found in ancient Egyptian tombs was made of veneered wood, and the most expensive piece of furniture in existence—a desk commissioned by Louis XV—is veneered. This type of construction makes it possible to match the grain on doors and table tops and to decorate with inlay. It helps prevent warping when used on large surfaces. But veneer can separate and cause trouble if it is not properly made and it can be harder to refinish than solid wood.

All new furniture is clearly tagged according to construction and the materials used. If the furniture is old, a careful inspection of the top edge of the front of the drawer or the top of the door will show a solid piece of wood or the fine lines of the layers of veneer. Frequently, furniture is a combination of both types of construction. Quality furniture can be made of solid wood, veneer wood, or a combination of both.

Hard wood. The term "hard wood" is applied to wood from any deciduous tree (the term applied to those trees that have broad flat leaves that drop in the fall). Not all hard woods are equally attractive. Birch, gumwood, oak, maple, cherry, walnut, and mahogany are a few of the best-known hard woods used for furniture. They are sometimes called cabinet woods. These woods take a good finish; they have an attractive grain, and a cell structure that permits them to hold glue, nails, and screws securely.

Soft wood. The term "soft wood" applies to woods from the trees with pinelike needles, such as the red cedar, Douglas fir, white pine, and spruce. Inexpensive furniture, such as unfinished wood furniture or rustic patio furniture is frequently made from these woods. This type of wood is also frequently used as the core for hard-wood veneers.

Furniture Construction

The service that a piece of furniture will give depends upon its construction as well as on the quality of the wood. In well constructed furniture, the legs will remain solid, the drawers will slide easily, and the doors will fit. Construction details that ensure these results should be checked wherever possible.

General. Details of general construction can easily be seen in chairs and case furniture. All furniture is joined together with nails or screws and with glue. Nails are used primarily for inexpensive furniture. Screws, because of their threads, will hold pieces of wood together far more securely than nails. Even the backs and the under parts of good-quality furniture usually contain screws. Glue is sometimes used alone, but on good-quality furniture it is used as a backup for nails and screws. Corner blocking and the use of dowels are also marks of quality.

Case details. In evaluating chests, cabinets, and dressers, check for dovetailed joints and for center guides on the bottom of drawers to make them pull straight. The finer grades of furniture will have dustproof construction between the drawers. Check to see that the pieces will be level when set on a level floor.

Finish. Although fashion influences the degree of gloss, a high gloss tends to indicate a cheap finish. A hand-rubbed finish is satiny smooth to the touch and seems to glow. A well-made piece of case furniture has no rough, unsanded wood anywhere, not even on the bottom of the drawers or on the back. Heat-resistant treatment of the top of tables has come to be very important. Various kinds of plastics are now being used, both as a finish and in thin, veneer-like layers, to make the surface impervious to water, alchohol, and even cigarette burns. In some situations, these finishes are excellent. In others, they have an artificial

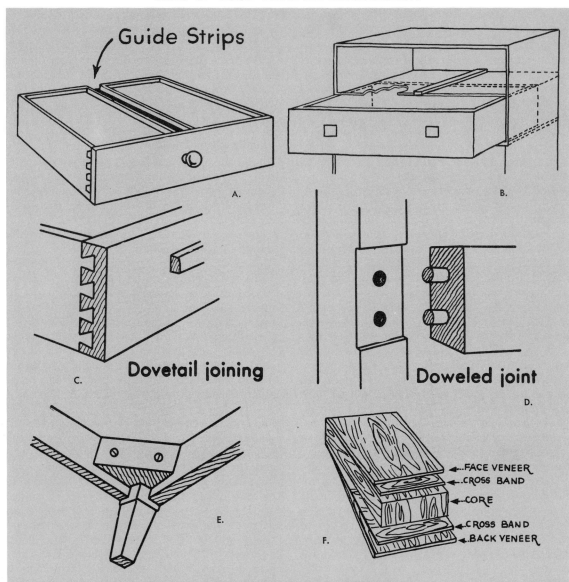

Guide Strips

A.

B.

Dovetail joining

C.

Doweled joint

D.

E.

FACE VENEER
CROSS BAND
CORE
CROSS BAND
BACK VENEER

F.

Screwed - in corner block

(A) Center glides on the bottom of drawers keeps them sliding in and out evenly. (B) Dustproof construction—a wooden shelf to which the second part of the center glide is attached—is another mark of quality. (C) Dovetail joining is the mark of good construction on drawers. (D) Doweled joints help to ensure continuing strength and rigidity. (E) Screwed-in corner blocking is another means of producing solid construction. (F) Veneer wood consists of a center core plus thin sheets of plywood with the grain running in opposite directions.

The quality of upholstered furniture is judged by the details of the stitching and by the firmness and the comfort of the padding and springs.

quality and seem rather institutional. Plastic veneer is irreparable in case of serious injury.

Hardware. In evaluating furniture, examine the hinges, magnetic catches, drawer pulls, knobs, and brackets. They should be heavy enough to wear well. They should be well designed and in harmonious proportion to the furniture they serve. They should be smoothly finished.

Furniture Upholstery

Shopping for upholstered furniture is a special skill, because the upholstery methods, the inside materials, and the frame construction are completely covered. The only wood finish visible is on the leg or possibly a small piece of the frame. This wood, the upholstery fabric, the tailoring, and the labels which identify the filling materials are the indicators of the total quality.

Fabric and tailoring. Strong indicators of quality can be found in the quality of the fabric and the tailoring. Even if the piece is being sold "in muslin" for slipcovering, examine the muslin itself as well as the tailoring. Small details such as good stitching or the careful placing of pleats or gathers, indicate general manufacturing attitudes about things you cannot see. Check both the quality of the upholstery fabric and its color. Avoid a fabric of

garish color or one of loose construction that will catch and pull. These features indicate poor quality.

As far as the inner construction is concerned, you are dependent on the integrity of the retailer. You will never know whether he has told the truth until it is too late to put in a complaint. Labels list only trade names, and filling and materials used. Consequently, your choice of store for upholstered pieces is more important than anything you can learn about how many times a spring should be tied and what kind of twine should be used.

Sitting comfort. The way a piece of upholstered furniture feels is another indication of quality. Sit on it. Feel of it. If it is hard and uncomfortable, it will not improve after use. If it is soft and luxurious but too inexpensive, it will go to pieces in no time. On the other hand, if it is firm and yet comfortable, if the price is reasonable, and the manufacturer and the retailer are reliable, there is a good chance that it will wear well.

BEGIN TO ACCUMULATE FURNISHINGS NOW

Accumulating furnishings is like cooking; if you wait to cook until the morning after you are married, it will be a rather grim first breakfast! In the same way, if you wait to begin buying

Gay importance can be given to a simple bed by means of a framed panel of floral applique, hung on the wall as a headboard.

Courtesy Better Homes and Gardens, © Meredith Corporation, 1964

your furnishings until you are faced with an apartment or house to furnish, you may make some mighty expensive mistakes. Practice by buying one or two pieces for a room that is already furnished. Each piece of furniture has many variations, and what is right for you depends on everything from your pocketbook to your physical makeup, the house you live in, and the length of time you will probably be living there.

Choose According to Personality

Personality traits show up early in life. They are apparent in your choices of friends and clothes, in your free-time activities, and in your studies. Sometimes your ideas may shift about quite rapidly as you meet new people and are exposed to new ideas, but generally only minor changes will occur; new knowledge and experiences will lead to deeper understandings and appreciations rather than to complete changes in your patterns of choice.

Quality need not be costly. You may find quantity is not necessary for your happiness if the little you do have is of top quality. You have a built-in insulation against the advertising pressures which push people into buying the wrong things. A knowledge of good line, good workmanship, and good materials will help you to be a discriminating shopper. You will be able to locate good quality furnishings whether advertised at sale prices or hidden in a little visited corner of the store.

Change can be practical. You may find that you are content to have less quality if you can have variety; you enjoy change. You will find that a long-term plan for home furnishings will allow you to achieve maximum change at a minimum cost.

The larger, more expensive wood pieces of furniture such as tables, cabinets, and chests can be permanent background pieces. The effect of change can be achieved through upholstered pieces. Bedsteads that have removable upholstered panels can be changed to match each new bedspread. Straight chairs with removable slip seats can be inexpensively and quickly recovered. Sofas and lounge chairs that have simple, slim lines can be bought in muslin for use with slipcovers or can be slipcov-

250

ered over the original upholstery. Sewing skills will be a great help if you plan to change room fabrics often.

Another way to achieve dramatic change is to change the location and use of your furnishings. Area rugs can move from room to room. A chest may be used for a buffet in the dining area or game storage in the family room or clothing storage in a bedroom, all with equal effectiveness. Portable TV sets and portable phonograph equipment which can move from room to room and from chest top to storage shelves offer many possibilities for change.

High-style can be moderately priced. You may find that more than anything else you want to lead in everything from hairstyles to dance routines and even to the dating of the newest boy in school. Later you may find it stimulating and exciting to lead in setting home furnishing trends. Most people feel that it is extravagantly costly to keep a home furnished in the newest style. Frequently this is true, but the cost can be decreased by careful planning and wise buying.

Home furnishings can be handled in much the same way as clothes. In clothing, modern high-style accessories such as hat, purse, and jewelry can make an older basic dress and simple pumps appear as the latest style. Similarly, good-quality periodless basic furnishings —chairs, sofas, tables, and chests—will seem fresh from the pages of the decorator magazines when set off by colors, fabrics, lamps, and accessories that seem to have been designed this morning.

Be stubbornly adamant in refusing to buy too much. A few new accessories will be far more effective than quantities of them. Do not keep your old accessories; sell them immediately. Resale value is greater for pieces which are well cared for. Good original quality and relative newness of style are also important factors in resale value. It is true that the resale value will be lower than your original cost. This is the money you have spent to enable you to keep up with fashion. But the money from such sales can be added to your furniture budget to increase the amount available for new furnishings.

If you are to be a leader in home furnishing styles, you must be willing to constantly study

A smart folding chair, a painted molding board on top of a cabinet, and a good lamp can add the comfort of a desk to a small room.

trends. You must be willing to spend a great deal of time in planning for and shopping for your furnishings. You must have a canny judgment and a businesslike attitude toward money and the home furnishing budget.

Choose According to Physical Needs

All people have individual physical qualities which determine what furniture will be comfortable or uncomfortable for them. Weight, height, posture, and health conditions such as allergies affect your furnishing decisions.

Weight. Your weight and the weights of the other family members are a basic factor in furniture buying decisions. How much you weigh will determine the firmness of the mattress you will need and the type of upholstery springs you will find comfortable in chairs and sofas. The wrong degree of firmness may result in furniture which sags too quickly or which never softens for comfortable seating.

Relatively inexpensive but well-designed, lightly scaled furniture adjusts well to many uses. Such furniture may be bought either in finished or unfinished forms.

Height. In selecting furniture, height also is a most important factor in determining comfort. Extra length is necessary in both the bed sideboards and the mattress for tall people. A lounge chair for a tall person should have a deep enough seat and a high enough back so he can sit comfortably and yet have head support. The height and position of the arms also affect the comfort of a chair. A short-legged woman will be miserably uncomfortable on a deep-seated, high-armed sofa or chair. Therefore, a sofa should be selected primarily for the comfort of the shortest regular user; taller people can sit on the diagonal to get the greater seat length. A chest of drawers can be too high or too low for maximum efficiency for the user. A mirror hung low over a low chest of drawers may be attractive in the room, but also a constant source of irritation to the tall occupant of the room. Desks for tall people must be high enough to use comfortably without slumping.

Allergies and skin conditions. Many people have allergies or skin conditions that must be considered in buying furniture. An allergy to feathers or cow hair necessitates man-made fillings. A skin that is irritated by wool or by coarse weaves restricts the type of upholstery fabrics which can be selected. Keep such factors in mind as you make your buying plan.

Choose According to Functional and Aesthetic Needs

Before you go near a furniture store, make out a list of all the functions you will want served in your room or home; list the major and minor pieces which will serve each need.

SHOPPING TECHNIQUES

To some people, shopping is recreation. To others, it is a dreaded chore. Efficient shopping should avoid these extremes.

Choose Where You Will Buy

Choosing the place where you intend to do your buying is not as easy as it might seem. There are many possibilities. Consider them all.

Wholesale buying. "I can get it for you wholesale" has the sound of a great bargain. Many people eagerly accept a card of intro-

Special furniture displays in retail stores can give you an idea as to the total effect of the furniture in a room setting.

If the outline of a piece of furniture is simple and the design is pleasing, the furniture may be given a new finish: cover it with wallpaper, paint it and stencil it, or decorate it with cut-out designs.

duction, travel to a distant city to use it, only to come home poorer but wiser. They have seen more furniture than they might have, but they have found the experience more confusing than helpful. They learn that there is no such thing as *one* wholesale price. The wholesale price depends on the relative buying power of the person who sends them, plus his service charge, plus a showroom fee, plus the crating and shipping. This total *wholesale* price can be larger than the *retail* price found in some large-volume furniture stores.

The wholesale salesman will earn more money selling to a department buyer, who is purchasing quantity, than to a retail buyer.

He cannot afford to spend a great deal of time with you, and he will not offer you the services a retailer will offer in order to get your return business. If there are any mistakes in your order, there is little recourse and if things do not wear, no one cares.

Retail stores. By contrast, the retail stores are built on service to you—the retail customer. They can only stay in business if they make you happy so you will come back. Each store has its own level of merchandise, its standards of ethics, its type of salespeople, and its way of handling service in general. No store, not

253

Be sure that the furniture you are planning to buy fits the furniture you already own. The step table is too light in scale for this Early-American arm chair, but the height, scale, and design of the storage table make it an excellent choice to use with this chair.

even the wholesale showroom, pretends to have all the furniture in stock. They show those pieces which are representative and which sell rapidly and use catalogs and swatches of materials for the rest. Each pictured piece has its measurements listed; you can compare these measurements with those of similar furniture on the sales floor. You can borrow swatches of material to check with other furniture or furnishings, or with furniture at home.

Catalog houses. Another important source of home furnishings is the catalog house. Because of their quantity of sales, they are in a position to buy advantageously, so it is frequently possible to get better prices on standard things like mattresses, rugs, plain draw curtains, and some furniture. When comparing costs, you must add cost of transportation to the basic cost. Be sure to send for the special furniture catalog in checking this market.

Discount houses. Urban centers usually have discount houses and railway and trucking salvage houses which sell furniture. There will be less customer service in such stores than in retail stores. Usually all sales are final; you will be unable to return a purchase because of errors in purchase or of flaws in the merchandise, but the prices are usually less than in retail stores. There frequently is a delivery charge.

Used-furniture market. The value of the used-furniture market often depends on the size of the community. Antique shops, resale furniture columns, and radio swap ads also should be checked. Prices in this type of buying are based on a cash transaction; the customer is responsible for delivery.

Plan the Buying Trip

It is important not only to know what you need but also to keep accurate records of merchandise, sizes and prices, and buying terms instead of depending on memory. By comparing this information, you can begin to make decisions as to where you will buy and approximately what it will cost.

Assemble all the information. Know your needs; if colors must be harmonized, take samples, even if you have to carry a pillow, a book cover, or a piece of color torn from a magazine. If size is important take measurements.

Choose the time carefully. No customer can expect good service from a salesman just before closing time or in the midst of a hectic sale. Plan your timing.

Select your salesman. Never let yourself be selected by a salesman. This is of primary importance if you are going to enjoy and profit by the transaction. Instead, look the salesmen over when you are doing your comparison shopping. At that time you will have explained that you are not ready to buy but wish to look around by yourself and you will see how they handle other customers. Then, when you are ready to buy, step right up to the one you have chosen and say, "I know you are busy now, but when you are free, could you take care of me?" The salesman will be flattered, he will know you are in earnest, and he will be eager to wait on you.

Take advantage of decorator service. If decorator service is offered by the store you have chosen to deal with, use it. The service costs you nothing additional. Such service can add great beauty to your home; it can save you time and money. But do not expect decorator advice unless you have decided to buy merchandise from the store, any more than you would expect a gift of furniture from the store.

Present all the information. You can help the salesman or decorator work effectively if you present him with all the information to start with. Tell him your needs and exactly what you want to spend. Never try to evade this point, because it is hard on everyone. If the salesman knows what you have to spend, he can save your time by showing you immediately the range of merchandise within your budget. He will respect your frankness and be interested in helping you do as well as you can.

Ask questions. Never hesitate to ask about anything you do not understand. The sales-

Courtesy Better Homes and Gardens, © Meredith Corporation, 1964

The decorator service offered by some retail stores can help you save both time and money. This is especially true when you wish to combine old furnishings with the new pieces you are planning to buy.

man will be glad to show his knowledge. Inquire about credit, carrying charges, special order merchandise which is pictured in catalogs complete with upholstery swatches. Ask about storing furniture with them until you are ready for delivery and about the costs of delivery.

Buy slowly. Probably the most important thing to keep in mind is to buy slowly. Prepare the salesman by saying, "This purchase is very important to me, and I may want to think about it overnight or for several days before deciding." Always be willing to wait to get the right thing. Having a piece of furniture for Saturday's party is not as important as the long term effects of the purchase will be.

And above all, leave immediately if pressure is exerted on you to make a quick decision. "I can give you this price only if you buy to-

Chart 6. Approximate sizes of furniture in inches

Furniture	Width	Depth	Length	Height
Beds				
Twin	41		80 with footboard	38 (headboard)
Double	56		80 with footboard	38 (headboard)
Queen	64		80 no footboard	38 (headboard
King	80		80 no footboard	40 or more (headboard)
Bunk	30–39		76	67 double
			86 (bookcase headboard)	73 triple
Crib	30		53	42
Dressers				
High chest	54	20		47
Double dresser	64	20		32
Triple dresser	72	20		32
Night stand				
Average	23	16		24
Sofas				
Love seat and average sectional	56	34		27–30
Standard 3-seat	78	34		27–30
Longer (4-seat)	84	34		27–30
Extra long	96	34		27–30
Studio couch	74	30		27 with bolster
Hide-a-beds	86	38		30
	64	38		28–30
Tables				
Long coffee	22		54	16
Individual coffee	18		18	17
End tables	20		26	22
Game	30		30	28
Dining extension	44		64	29
Desks				
Flat top	25		48	30
Flat top student	20		31	30
Piano				
Upright				
Baby grand	60		24	
Chairs				
Lounge	30	32		27–30
Pull up	26	28		27–30
Dining or game	19	21		27–30

day," is high-pressure selling which usually goes with low-grade merchandise. Never allow it! Remember an appointment—have a sudden headache, but *get out!*

HIDDEN DANGERS IN SHOPPING FOR FURNITURE

Furniture comes in all grades or qualities but usually the most loudly advertised furniture has the least quality per dollar cost. Scare headlines about a "gigantic saving," "less than half price," "low, low, one day offer only," or "special, spectacular manufacturer's closeout," frequently indicate such poor quality that price is the only thing a salesman can talk about to make it attractive.

This very cheap furniture is usually poorly designed and poorly constructed and the finish, as a rule, is brilliantly shiny. The decoration is frequently oppressively ornate and the

Matching furniture pieces which are separately priced but designed to be used together are frequently very good buys. Furniture such as this is not the same thing as a "room of furniture" which is priced as a single unit and usually cannot be bought separately.

size is ponderously large. "Look how *much* you are getting" is the standard sales talk.

"Rooms of furniture" is another favorite method of selling low-grade furniture. A lamp or two and possibly an end table are usually thrown in as buying bait. In such cases, you may be fairly sure that the original purchase is overpriced. No company can consistently give away good merchandise and stay in business. In the long run, moderately priced furni-

ture that will hold up under normal wear is less expensive because it will give you years of satisfaction and comfort. This does not mean that you must beware of all sales. Real sale situations do exist. You can tell the difference by the moderation of the advertising claims and the comparative price differences. A knowledge of furniture quality and reputations of various dealers helps you recognize true sales savings.

1. Define the meaning of the following phrases as used in this chapter: personal resources, impersonal resources, solid wood, veneered wood, hard wood, and soft wood.

2. Make a representative list of stores that sell furniture in your area. Check the type of merchandise and services they offer and discuss in class the advantages and security of local buying as against catalog, out-of-town, or discount house buying.

3. Talk with a loan officer in a bank and report to the class about the comparative costs of borrowing money to pay cash for furniture instead of buying it on an installment plan.

4. Interview the assistant buyer or the interior decorator of a furniture store and report to the class about ordering semi-custom-made furniture at no extra cost by selecting from manufacturers' fabric samples.

5. Analyze pictures and store displays for the relationship as to line, mass, and height of chairs and their accompanying tables. Report findings to class.

6. Join with one or two others to present a skit based on an imaginary shopping trip to buy an area rug or a piece of furniture. Ask for class criticism based on shopping techniques analyzed in the chapter.

7. Choose a studio couch or a table, and then do comparative shopping using other resources in your community or mail order catalogs. Report differences discovered in price and quality.

8. Make a list of the minimum furniture you would need for a bedroom-study. Make tentative selections in (a) minimum price range and (b) middle price range, and discuss in class the comparative quality and price differences.

9. Make a list of the minimum furniture needed for a one-room apartment for two people. Using the same resources as for question 8, determine the approximate cost of the furniture you would like to select for your own use.

10. If you could buy one piece of bedroom furniture tomorrow, what would you choose? Report to the class on how it could add function, comfort, and appearance, and what it would cost.

14

Arranging Furniture

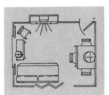

MANY PEOPLE talk about furnishing a house as if the space to be filled was more important than the needs to be met. They buy a sofa for a "long wall" or a chair for an "empty corner" and end up with furniture lining the walls of a room and with no notion of how the use the yawning center. In the homes of today we have fewer, larger rooms, each one serving several functions. The decision of just what functions must be served by each room should be dictated by the individual needs of the family members, as well as by common needs such as eating, sleeping, conversation, and entertainment.

PRINCIPLES GOVERNING FURNITURE ARRANGEMENT

The placement of furniture in houses today should be based on "use groupings," each serving a specific function. The exact placement of furniture within those groupings, and of the groupings themselves, is dependent on two general considerations: the comfortable functioning of the group and the beauty of the group.

For Comfortable Functioning

The comfortable functioning of a furniture grouping is dependent primarily on whether it meets our behavior patterns and our physical needs. If it does, we find that the grouping automatically attracts use, and we use it constantly.

Content of groupings. Each use grouping must be made up of major and minor furniture pieces plus important accessories.

Major pieces. The pieces that determine a group's primary function are called major pieces. A desk is the major piece for a writing or study group; a table for a game group; comfortable seating furniture for a conversation group; and a bed for a sleeping group. A cabinet style TV set or a large combination radio phonograph is a major piece of furniture which is usually placed to be an addition to other functional groups rather than a part of any one grouping.

Minor pieces. All groups include several other pieces of furniture without which the major piece could not function. These are called minor pieces. A desk group would in-

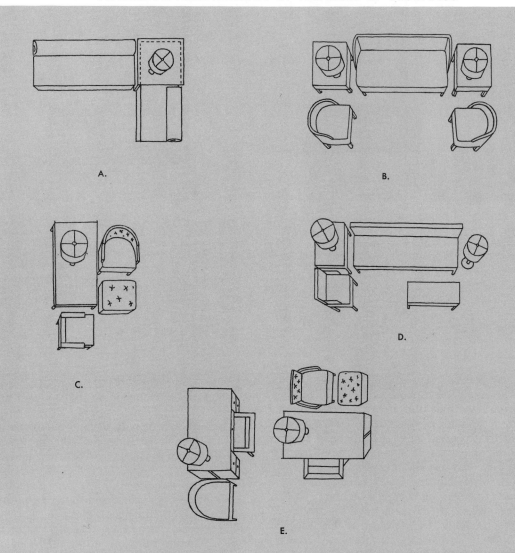

(A) Two twin-sized mattresses and springs, with corner table to cover half of one bed, forms a grouping that serves for conversation during the day. (B) A love seat with pairs of chairs, tables, and lamps form a semicircular conversation-and-reading group. (C) Two chairs, an ottoman, and a long table with a lamp form a grouping that serves for conversation and reading. (D) A sofa, chair, and coffee table plus end table, table lamp, and floor lamp form an L-shaped conversation-and-reading group. (E) A study grouping can be arranged with the desk against the wall. Another study grouping places one end of the desk against the wall with a reading chair beside the long end of the desk.

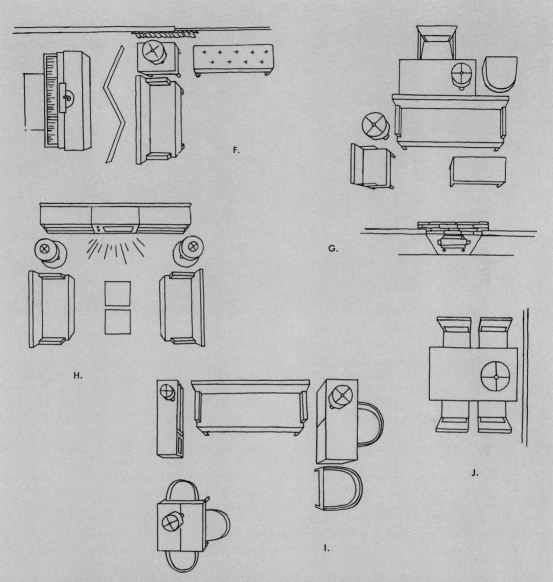

(F) Music and conversation groups, separated by a screen, can be placed end out from a short wall in a room lacking long wall space. (G) A grouping of desk and chairs and a sofa-and chair grouping can be combined to form a study-conversation unit centered in front of a fireplace. (H) A bookcase holding the TV completes a conversation-and-recreation grouping of pairs of love seats, coffee tables, and floor lamps. (I) A large recreation grouping may be made from a study group, a conversation group, a TV set, and an extendable game table. (J) A dining table, used end out from the wall, with four chairs and a table lamp, serves for dining, study, and games.

The furniture in this one-room apartment is well arranged to serve many needs for personal and social occasions.

clude a desk chair. Additional minor pieces might be a bookshelf for reference material and a reading chair. The minor pieces of a sofa group would include at least one comfortable chair and a table with a table lamp or an appropriate floor lamp. A low coffee table to hold between-meal snacks, magazines, a low bowl of flowers, or a small object of art could also be included in a sofa group. The minor pieces to accompany a chair in a reading group would include the light source. A small table or bookcase might also belong here. Or it could include a table to hold a lamp, a footstool, and a bookcase. A game table must have comfortable game chairs. Perhaps a chest or cabinet to hold additional game equipment would add to this grouping.

Size of groupings. The size of the major piece of furniture in the grouping will probably control the size of the grouping. The main conversational grouping of a living room may be more elastic in size than any other functional grouping. The only limitation on size is the fact that we cannot converse with anyone seated more than five or six feet away. Conversation becomes public speaking if the group takes up more space than that.

Shape of groupings. The shape of any grouping involving seating space for more than one person is determined by the fact that communication between people is a matter of facial expression as well as words. Consequently, a grouping must be arranged so that people can face each other comfortably. See the line drawings on pages 260–261, showing the different types of furniture groupings, and analyze them carefully to see just how each functions.

For an Effect of Beauty

In furnishing a room, the effect of beauty can be ruined or increased by the way the furniture is arranged within each grouping, and within the room itself.

Placement of major pieces. Large pieces of furniture such as a sofa, a desk, a bed, a cabinet, or a long coffee table should be placed parallel to a wall. Such furniture can be placed in the middle of the room away from all walls, or end out from a wall as long as it is parallel to one of the walls of the room. A lounge chair, when used as a major piece in a reading group, can be placed at an angle to relieve a feeling of rigidity.

The L-shaped conversation grouping is interrupted by the natural traffic from the doorway. A simple rearrangement of the furnishings allows the traffic to pass on the side of the conversation group.

An unimaginative arrangement of seating furniture around the walls of the room creates a grouping which is too large for conversation. A more intimate conversation group formed around the fireplace leaves a free entry lane from the door.

By alternating the placement of upholstered and wood furniture and by contrasting heavy groupings with lighter ones, a spacious effect can be created in relatively small rooms.

Placement of minor pieces. The placement of all minor pieces is determined by their relation to the major piece in the group. A table to accompany a major piece should be placed parallel to it—at the side, behind it, or in front of it—no matter where the major piece is placed. A chair can be placed to form a comfortable conversational grouping in relation to major pieces without considering its relationship to the walls of the room.

Placement of wood versus fabric. The placement of furniture is also affected by the principle of alternating hard and soft pieces. A hard wood table should be placed between an upholstered sofa and an upholstered chair. An upholstery-seated chair is very effective with a wood desk. Upholstered-back host and hostess chairs add color and softness to a large dining area.

Placement of furniture for balance. There are two types of balance: absolute, or formal balance, and occult, or informal balance. Formal balance consists of balancing identical objects. Twins seated on a teeter-totter are an example of this type of balance. Informal bal-

ance refers to the balancing of unlike things. An example of informal balance would be one boy on one end of a teeter-totter balancing two girls on the other end. Formal balance is somewhat stiff in feeling and is usually elegant in effect. The more flexible informal balance is most frequently used in multifunctional rooms where a variety of furniture is needed. Informal balance makes it possible for us to balance unlike pieces of furniture within a group as well as to balance unlike groups of furniture within the room.

EFFECT OF ARCHITECTURE ON ARRANGEMENT OF FURNITURE

The placement of individual pieces or groups of furniture within a room is based on the functional needs of each group and the architectural makeup of the room. For example, the shape of the room, the way it merges into other rooms, the way it is accentuated with architectural features, what areas are open and what areas are isolated, must all be considered. A group for reading and studying must have light and it must be away from traffic lanes.

A conversation grouping in a natural traffic lane can be a constant source of irritation whether you are moving from room to room or trying to hold a conversation. When the furniture is rearranged to open up the traffic lane, the room appears to be more spacious.

Conversation areas should be close to the center of the room where they can be easily expanded. The placement of the TV set depends on the size and interest of the family and the amount of use they make of it. All these personal and functional matters must be weighed along with the aesthetic considerations before the final placement of the groupings is determined.

Effect of Space

One basic consideration in the placement of furniture is the floor space in the room and how to make the best use of it. You must recognize and handle such problems as the clearing of natural paths from room to room and from room entrances to closets; the planning for uncluttered open spaces in small rooms to create a feeling of space; and the division of large open spaces.

Natural paths or traffic lanes. The way to analyze natural paths or traffic lanes is to review the steps taken in a normal day's routine. Paths from one room to another, to closets, and cupboards and to the telephone and outside doors all should be uncluttered and fairly direct. These traffic lanes are natural room dividers; they must be kept in mind when furniture groupings are being placed.

Hall furniture should be placed along one wall so there will be a straight, uncluttered path through the hallway. If the living room acts as an entrance hall, or as a hall to a stairway or another area of the house, the furnishings should be so arranged that a direct path is open. In bedrooms keep the natural paths between closets, dressing areas, and the room entrances open and unblocked by furniture.

Natural space divisions. Furniture groupings must be placed according to natural space

A comfortably - sized conversation grouping in the center of the room leaves the wall free for other activities.

divisions. If one part of a living room is cut off from the rest of the room by a traffic lane or an archway, a furniture grouping that can function in isolation should be assigned to it. A desk group, a lounge-chair reading group, a piano or game group would work well in such isolation. Conversational groupings should be centered so they can expand. They should be planned so they are not crossed by traffic lanes.

Natural light areas. The placement of furniture should take advantage of natural light. Turn a flat-top desk out from a window so the light falls on the desk instead of in the writer's eyes. Place reading groups near windows, if possible. Place dressing table mirrors where the natural light will fall on the person reflected.

Open living spaces. It is important to the beauty and usefulness of a room to have open living spaces. A small bedroom will look much larger if twin beds are arranged at right angles in a corner, leaving the center of the room clear. To avoid blocking the center of a small living room, use large end tables or a nest of end tables instead of a large coffee table. Can you think of other space making arrangements?

Effect of Architectural Features

Some rooms have an architectural feature of great beauty. It may be a fireplace, a picture window, or a built-in bookcase. Whatever it is, this architectural feature should be accentuated by the furniture arrangement.

A fireplace. If you have a fireplace, the furniture should be arranged around it to give it importance. The inside of an artificial fireplace should be painted dull black so the fireplace appears to have been used. Real logs arranged as if they will be lit later on will be more attractive than an electric fire.

A picture window. A picture window becomes particularly important if it overlooks a fine view. If the window goes to the floor, the groupings around it can be the same as for a fireplace. A picture window with a higher window sill can become the center of a conversational grouping by placing a bench or

A TV set placed in a built-in cabinet is visible to most of the room for viewing, yet hidden away when the room is being used for other purposes.

low sofa below the window. Do not block a picture window with a table and lamp.

A bookcase. A built-in bookcase can be a focal point for a functional grouping. This is especially true if the shelving holds electronic entertainment equipment such as a TV or a phonograph in addition to books and objects of art. The furniture arrangement can be similar to that suggested for the fireplace or picture window.

Effect of Architectural Faults

There are very few houses or apartments that do not have some architectural faults. It may be the proportion of a room that is wrong or an archway that is too large. It may be a complete lack of separation of an important functional area. Whatever it is, the careful placement of furniture can help to minimize these faults.

Widen a narrow room. If a room is too narrow, it can be made to appear wider by placing large pieces of furniture at the extreme ends of the room and by keeping high pieces near the corners. Placing furniture arrangements out from the wall to break into the room length will also make the room appear to be wider.

Reduce a wide archway. Some rooms have a large archway that makes it impossible to

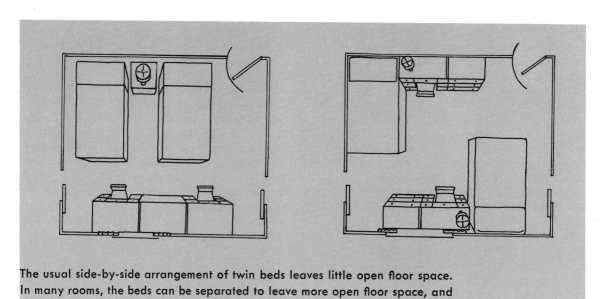

The usual side-by-side arrangement of twin beds leaves little open floor space. In many rooms, the beds can be separated to leave more open floor space, and each person has his own area.

The arrangement of furniture in functional groups can give a sense of architectural division in a large room, yet still retain the feeling of natural spaciousness.

Courtesy California Redwood Association

use an entire side or end to advantage. By filling in the archway on each side with bookshelves or with folding screens, it is possible to create protected space. This space can then be used for chair or desk groupings that require some feeling of isolation from general household traffic.

Create hallways and room divisions. In many homes, the living room serves as entrance hall. A hall grouping of chest and chair and hall mirror on the wall nearest the outside door will create the effect of an entrance hall. If the living room furniture grouping on the opposite side of the door turns its back on the entrance area, the people in the living area will feel even more separated from those entering and going through to other parts of the house.

Need for a Focal Point

A room is more effectively arranged when there is one specially important spot to which attention automatically turns. If there is no architectural focal point, it is possible to effectively create one with furniture. By reason of its size, a sofa grouping can become the focal point in a room, if the wall above it is dramatized. This can be done with a large picture, a picture grouping, or wall shelves that catch and command the eye. Similarly a pair of chairs plus a table, a lamp, and a footstool can become the focal point. A screen, a bookcase, or a high chest placed behind the chairs will raise the eye level and give height and emphasis to the grouping. A secretary desk that rises high on the wall, a flat-topped desk, or a phonograph or TV cabinet with a hanging bookshelf or a grouping of pictures on the wall above it can be developed as the focal point of a living room or family room. The focal point in a bedroom is usually a bed. For real importance, the wall above the bed should be dramatized with a picture or picture grouping or with a canopy treatment that, by its height, dominates the room.

269

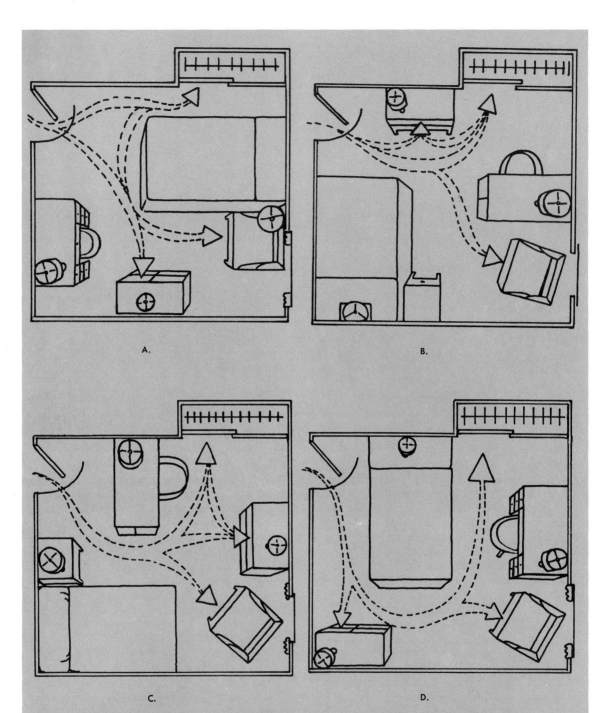

A.

B.

C.

D.

Analyze these four possible arrangements for a study-bedroom. Consider traffic paths, daylight, and appearance of space to see which would serve best for daily living.

FURNITURE ARRANGEMENTS
TO INCREASE ROOM FUNCTIONS

Adding new functions to a room can encourage a whole new set of activities that will enrich the entire life of the family. The easiest way to go about the job of adding new functions to a room is to measure the floor space carefully, noting every door, window, and heat outlet. Next measure the furniture in the room. Make a scale drawing of the room and of the furniture on graph paper. Cut out the pieces of furniture so you can move them about on the room diagram. Only after that are you ready to start planning how to convert a single-purpose room into a multipurpose room.

Making a Multipurpose Room Out of a Bedroom

Your bedroom can serve many functions. To be suited to you, the changes must start in your interests and your dreams and then be planned according to your resources.

Decide the functions desired. Would you like to have music in the room? Do you have a special talent you want to develop? You may need an easel, a drawing table, a sewing machine, a musical instrument, or a work table. Do you want to be able to entertain close friends? You would need extra chairs and probably, if the room is small, a bed that would serve as a couch for daytime lounging. You would probably want a small phonograph or a radio. For overnight guests you would need some sort of extra sleeping arrangement such as a trundle or a rollaway. Would you like to study here where you would be more alone and quiet? You would need a flat-top desk or table, a bookshelf for resource material, drawers for desk equipment, a comfortable desk chair, and a good light. Check both the cost and the measurements of all the special purpose pieces of furniture to see whether they can be fitted into your room.

Evaluate your present furnishings. Before you go any further, evaluate the furnishings you now have and how they might work into the new scheme. They may have much greater potential than you think.

Your dresser might serve, when remodeled, as a part of a chest-desk combination. Perhaps your bed is a single bed; it could be remodeled for daytime lounging. Such remodeling may be as simple as adding cushions and bolsters to make a more comfortable seating arrangement or perhaps it may involve lowering the bed, adding a new headboard, or remodeling the old headboard.

Decide what needs to be added. Study newspaper advertisements and mail-order catalogs; look for furniture in secondhand stores and regular retail stores, and consider specialty shops, such as art supply stores, as you plan to add furniture to supplement your present furniture and serve the new functions planned for your room. Perhaps you can build some of your needed additions, such as new shelving or a simple cabinet in which to store a rollaway guest bed.

Plan the arrangement. With the remodeled furniture in mind, plan the way you would arrange your room to serve the additional functions. The measurements you have taken will make it possible for you to place both new and old furniture accurately on your floor plan, and to see what supplementing pieces, such as bookcases and additional storage chests you will be able to use.

Change the tone of the room. In considering the use of color, fabrics and accessories, treat a multipurpose bedroom as you might treat a livingroom. Choose fabrics that will be wrinkle resistant and easy to care for. A tailored bedspread of a heavy fabric will be more practical in a multipurpose room than a ruffled organdy spread. Straight draw curtains will help give a living-room atmosphere. If you can sew, you may be able to make some of these and save money.

Making a Multipurpose Family Room Out of a Dining Room

In a small home, a room used only for dining may be an inefficient use of space. In such cases, it is important to see how this area could be rearranged to serve additional functions.

Decide on the functions desired. Usually, this area of the home is easily accessible for everyone and may therefore serve for family recreation or as a study area. The area could serve for temporary guest sleeping and for daytime lounging if a studio couch is added. If

Storage units which include a drop-leaf desk section can help you adapt a dining room to multiple use. The table serves for extra desk space as well as for dining.

the living room already has too many functions, the dining room might relieve the living room by serving as the TV viewing area. Extra storage space could house a portable sewing machine and sewing equipment; the dining table might serve as a cutting and sewing table. However, the new functions for the room must be planned to allow its continuing use for family and company meals.

Evaluate the present furnishings. Before making any changes, it is well to analyze the present furnishings. Frequently, a little readjustment will turn what you have into what you need. A dining table can be converted into a study table or a game table without much expense or effort. The table top may need protecting with a set of table pads. By moving the table to one wall, you will gain space in the room. If you arrange chairs around the table on three sides, it will serve as a game table yet be available for family meals at any time. A large table lamp, floor lamp, or hanging wall lamp will supply good light for all these activities. A china cabinet with adjustable shelves can usually be converted to hold a TV set or reference and study books.

Explore the market for additional pieces. Furniture to supplement what you have can often be found inexpensively. Consider buying a new studio couch or rejuvenating a used one with a slipcover that will harmonize with the color scheme.

Additional storage space is needed when you add new functions because of the equipment necessary to serve them. A bench, wide enough to hold a TV set and magazines, as well as reference books, can be built under the windows. If long enough, this bench may provide extra seating also. A table-height cabinet or chest could be used to separate the dining area from the living area in a home where the two merge. If the cabinet faces the living room, it can serve as an extra wall in the dining area, against which a table or studio couch may be placed, thus providing a greater sense of separation from the living area.

Making a Family Room Out of a Kitchen

In a house with a large kitchen area, you may wish the kitchen to serve functions other than food preparation or eating.

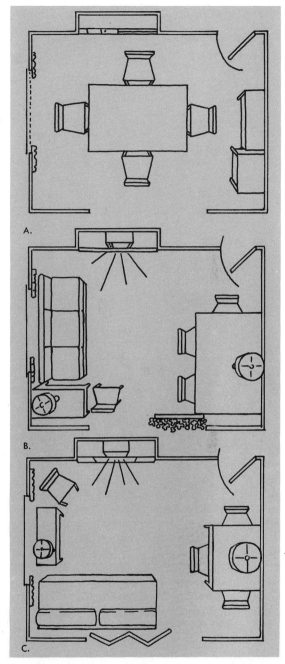

A usual single-use dining room (A) can be adapted for recreation (B) or for an extra guest (C). A planter or a screen can be used in the archway to extend the wall space and add privacy.

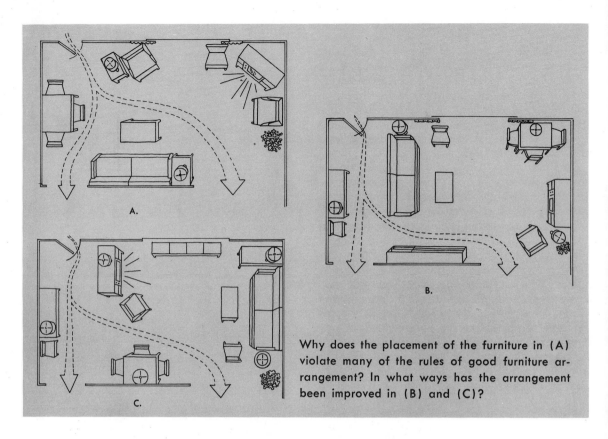

Why does the placement of the furniture in (A) violate many of the rules of good furniture arrangement? In what ways has the arrangement been improved in (B) and (C)?

Decide on functions desired. The kitchen is an ideal place for young people to entertain. The floor is planned to withstand wear, the refrigerator is handy for snacks, and the furniture is usually scratchproof. The kitchen dining area has a natural potential as a study area, or an extra game space. Many kitchens can be closed off from the rest of the house as a noise control measure. Is there room in the kitchen for a TV set? Should a laundry center be part of the kitchen area? Does the family record-keeping center belong here?

Analyze changes that need to be made. To implement these functions certain changes are needed. You may wish to change the mood of the room. You may need to cover the table with fabric and soften the chairs for long hours of study or games. A pair of wall bracket lamps or a pull-down fixture with a metal shade can be hung over the table to concentrate the light on the table. An inexpensive area rug can be put under the table or in the center of the room, tailored draw curtains will add privacy, and pictures can be added to the wall to produce a living-room mood that will be inviting and warm.

You may need to change the storage plans if the room is to meet these new functions. A TV set can be placed in a cupboard or put on a slideout shelf; one cupboard shelf and one refrigerator shelf could store "treats available without additional permission;" extra shelves near the table could hold books, desk equipment, and household records. Shelves or cabinets could be planned for temporary clothes storage if a laundry center is planned.

274

1. Define the meaning of the following phrases as used in this chapter: use groupings, major and minor pieces, formal or absolute balance, informal or occult balance, traffic lanes, and focal points.
2. Start a portfolio of furniture arrangements that have multiple functions as well as beauty.
3. Using sheets of ¼-inch squared graph paper, experiment with drawing accurate floor plans of several bedrooms you know.
4. Either send for furniture templates from a furniture company or make a set following dimensions suggested in chart 6, using a scale to match your floor plans.
5. Using templates and one of the bedroom furniture arrangements from your portfolio, reproduce the furniture arrangements on graph paper.
6. Be ready to discuss both the weaknesses and the strengths you discovered when you analyzed the arrangements on graph paper and any corrections you could suggest.
7. Using one of the floor plans drawn for question 3 and templates, work out one good arrangement of furniture, keeping in mind use groupings you admired and analyzed and traffic lanes in the bedroom you know.
8. Analyze one of the living-room furniture arrangements from your portfolio by arranging it with templates, and be prepared to suggest any changes that would improve it.
9. Draw a floor plan of a living room you know, and plan a comfortable arrangement of furniture for it.
10. Get the floor plan of the living area of a one-room apartment, and show how you could arrange furniture to serve all its necessary functions.

15

Fabrics

FABRICS ARE a dramatically important factor in creating comfort and beauty in our homes. Our windows look stark till framed with draperies, our seating furniture is uncomfortable and unattractive without the color, softness, and charm of upholstery, and our beds look undressed without a bedspread. Indeed, only after fabric has been used in a room does it look homelike and inviting.

Traditionally, fabrics have always been important. Silks from the Orient, cottons from Egypt and India, linens from Ireland, and wools from cool countries all have been as effective in stimulating trade in bygone centuries as they are now. In Chapter 15 we will study both the use of fabrics and the special qualities each fabric possesses—qualities that depend on the method of construction, the type of yarns, and even more basically, the fibers from which these yarns were constructed.

FIBERS ANALYZED

Traditionally, fabrics were made from natural fibers. In recent years, scientists have worked to supplement these natural fibers with man-made fibers. Man-made fibers may look and react like natural fibers or they may have new qualities not to be found in the traditional natural fibers.

Natural Fibers

The natural fibers are usually divided into major classifications: animal and vegetable. Silk and wool are the major animal fibers; cotton and flax are the principle fiber producing plants.

Silk. Many people consider silk to be the most beautiful and valuable of all fibers. This animal fiber is usually classified in two catagories: cultivated and wild. Since cultivated silk has been unwound from whole cocoons, the fibers are very long. Single strands of cultivated silk may range from 1,000 to 4,000 feet in length. These highly lustrous fibers are beautifully responsive to jewel-like dye colors. Cloth woven from cultivated silk is delicate and expensive. Wild silk fabrics are woven from shorter, broken strands of silk fiber. Yarns

Simple fabrics, properly handled can give individual character to a student's room. The tailored draperies set the tone, which is continued by the coordinated plaid fabric of the quilted bedspread and headboard.

The use of sheer material and ruffles gives a room a dainty, feminine air that is both cool and delicate in feeling.

CHART 7. TEXTILE FIBERS FOR FABRICS AND FLOOR COVERINGS

Fiber	Chief uses	Characteristics	Care
NATURAL FIBERS			

Cotton	Household fabrics
	Carpets
	Drapery and
	  upholstery fabrics
		Versatile Durable
		Withstands frequent, hard laundering
		Easily ironed at high temperature
		Inexpensive
			Limited only by finish, dye, and construction
			Generally may be machined-washed and
			  dried
			Avoid risk of mildew

Linen	Table linens
	Drapery and
	  upholstery fabrics
	Other household
	  fabrics
		Beauty and luster endure through
		  frequent, hard laundering
		Does not shed lint
		More expensive than cotton
		Wrinkles easily unless treated to resist
		  wrinkling
		Resistant to dye-type stains
			Limited only by finish, dye, construction of
			  item
			Iron at high temperatures; avoid pressing in
			  sharp creases
			Avoid risk of mildew

Silk	Drapery and
	  upholstery fabrics
		Natural luster Strong Dyes well
		Moderately resilient, naturally resistant to
		  wrinkles, readily returns to shape
		More expensive than man-made (filament)
		  silky yarns
			Dry cleaning usually preferable
			Careful hand laundry possible with some
			  items
			Protect from prolonged exposure to light
			Can be attacked by moths, carpet beetles

Wool	Blankets
	Carpets
	Drapery and
	  upholstery fabrics
		Springs back into shape; requires little
		  pressing
		Great versatility in fabrics
		Has insulating capacity increasing with
		  fabric thickness; hence fabrics can be
		  warm
		Long-wearing
			Dry cleaning usually preferable
			Will shrink and felt in presence of moisture,
			  heat, and agitation, as in laundry
			Must be protected from moths and carpet
			  beetles

MAN-MADE FIBERS			

Acetate	Drapery and
	  upholstery fabrics
	Fiberfill
		Drapes well Dries quickly
		Inexpensive
		Subject to fume-fading
			Will glaze and melt at a low temperature in
			  ironing or pressing

Azlon	This experimental protein fiber group has not yet been used for decorator fabrics. Scientists continue to search for better fibers in this group which might be used for such fabrics.		

Metallics
  Gold
  Silver
  Lurex
	Drapery and
	  upholstery fabrics
		Decorative threads	May tarnish
			May melt at low temperatures

Rayon
(conventional)
	Drapery and
	  upholstery fabrics
	Some blankets,
	  carpets, table
	  coverings
		Absorbent
		Inexpensive
		Moderately durable
		Lacks resilience; wrinkles easily
		Flammability a danger in brushed or
		  napped fabrics
			Dry cleaning often required
			Can be laundered, but does not withstand
			  treatment that can be given cotton or linen
			Tends to shrink and stretch

Rubber Lastex*	Stretch slipcovers	High degree of stretch and recovery Damaged by oils and light	Wash frequently with mild soap or detergent Avoid constant overstretch

Spandex
  Glaspan*
  Lycra*
  Vyrene*
	Stretch slipcovers	High degree of stretch and recovery
		Resists abrasion
		Resistant to body oils
			May be machine laundered with warm water.
			  Dry lowest heat, shortest cycle

General Characteristics of the Man-made Fibers Listed Below:

Moderate to high strength and resilience
Resistance to moths and mildew
Sensitivity to heat in ironing
Dimensional stability; resistance to shrinking or stretching
Tendency to accumulate static electricity in cold, dry weather
Nonabsorbency; easy to wash, quick-drying
Resistance to nonoily stains, but body oils penetrate the fiber and are hard to remove
Pleat retention because of thermoplastic qualities

Nytril and Vinal fiber groups are still in experimental stages.
Nytril has been tried in blends where an elastic fiber is desirable and Vinal has been tried where a wool-like texture is desirable, but no serious application of these fibers to decorator fabrics has yet been developed.

Distinctive Properties

Acrylic Acrilan* Creslan* Orlon* Zefran* Zefkrome*	Carpets Pile fabrics Blankets	Soft hand Resistant to wrinkling High bulking power Silky texture, if desired Resistant to effects of sunlight	Remove oily stains before washing Waterborne stains easily removed
Modacrylic Dynel* Verel*	Deep-pile and fleece fabrics Carpets (in combination with acrylic)	Soft and resilient Resistant to wrinkling Resistant to chemicals Nonflammable	May be ironed at extremely low temperatures only
Nylon	Carpets Upholstery fabrics	Exceptional strength Excellent elasticity Permanent shape retention Woven fabrics often hot and uncomfortable to wear	Oily stains should be removed before washing Washes easily Care must be taken to maintain whiteness Press at low temperature
Olefin DLP* Herculon* Vectra*	Seat covers for autos, outdoor furniture Carpets	No water absorption Low melting temperature	
Polyester Dacron* Fortrel* Kodel* Vycron*	Curtains Fiberfill	Sharp pleat and crease retention Some have resistance to pilling Exceptional wrinkle resistance	Oily stains should be removed before washing Easily washable Care should be taken to maintain whiteness Needs little ironing or pressing
Saran Rovana* Saran*	Seat covers for autos, outdoor furniture Screening; awnings Luggage	Resists soiling and staining Resists weathering Flame-resistant	Blot stains; rinse with clear water Sensitive to heat
Vinyon	Mixed with other fibers for heat bonding	Resistant to chemicals, sunlight Nonflammable	
Glass Fiberglas*	Drapery fabrics	Nonflammable Resistant to wrinkling, sunlight Permanent shape retention	Drip dry Avoid all rubbing

*Trademark name.
Source: American Home Economics Association.

The coarse texture of the plain linen bedspread and frame cornice, the texture of the Rya rug, and the geometric shapes of the adjustable wall shelves and cabinets combine to create a masculine effect.

Courtesy Royal System, Inc.

made of wild silk are rougher and coarser than yarns from cultivated silk. Wild silk yarns can be woven into fabrics such as pongee, shantung, and raw silk. Wild silk fabrics have interesting uneven textures as well as vibrant colors.

In general, silk is more expensive and less durable than other fibers. Silk fabrics are very absorbent, but they water-spot easily, are very sensitive to heat and to sunlight, and they abrade quickly. Japan, Italy, and China furnish most of the silk fibers used today; some silk is grown commercially in Brazil and in the United States.

Wool. The most common animal fiber, wool, is produced in most countries. However, the main commercial sources for this fiber are Australia and the United States. Wool possesses several characteristics which make it an ideal home furnishings fabric: it is naturally water resistant; it has great resilience and elasticity, it takes dye beautifully; it cleans easily; it is warm when compared to other fibers of similar weight; and it can be chemically treated to become mothproof and stain resistant.

Wool fabrics may be found in every weight from a sheer gauze which makes beautiful semitranslucent curtains to the heavy durable fabrics used for fine upholstery and carpets. The cost of woolen fabrics varies with the weight of the fabric and the quality of the wool; in general woolen fabrics tend to be expensive. The high initial cost may be somewhat offset by the durability of woolen fabrics.

Cotton. This common vegetable fiber is used in fabrics for many household purposes. Cotton is grown on a large commercial scale in the United States, India, China, Brazil, Peru, Persia, Mexico, Russia, and Egypt. Many other countries produce cotton for local use, or are developing cotton as an important part of their agricultural economy. Cotton fibers are comparatively short fibers, ranging from ⅔ inch to 2 inches in length depending upon the variety of cotton. Long-staple cottons such as Egyptian and American-Egyptian are considered to be the finest cotton fibers.

Cotton is comparatively absorbent. It is strong, washes well, and takes color beautifully. Cotton fibers may be blended with man-

280

made fibers to produce wrinkle-resistant and quick-drying fabrics. Chemical treatments are also used to produce similar qualities in all-cotton fabrics.

Cotton fabrics range in weight from the thinnest gauze to heavy upholstery drill or canvas. Medium-weight cottons are frequently used for curtains, slipcovers, bedspreads, and the entire range of household linens. Cotton fabrics tend to be less expensive than other fabrics of comparable weight.

Flax. The fabric we call linen is woven from the fibers of the woody stalk of the flax plant. Although many countries produce linen, Ireland and the northern European countries still produce most of the world supply. Ireland has cultivated flax and woven linen for more than two centuries. Fine linen is considered to be a household treasure. Flax fibers lack elasticity, so linen fabrics hold a tailored shape beautifully. They take color well or can be bleached to a dazzling white.

Linen is one of the oldest fabrics known to man. It has a natural crispness, strength, and luster which are especially good for draperies and upholstery. It is naturally absorbent and wrinkles easily. Today linens may be treated so they are wrinkle- and moisture-resistant. Linens are available in a wide range of weights. Those used for curtains, slipcovers, bedspreads, and upholstery are usually heavy, fairly coarse fabrics.

Other natural fibers. Animal fibers such as mohair, alpaca, angora fur, or goat's hair may be combined with wool or with man-made fibers and used for articles such as bedspreads and pillow tops. Vegetable fibers such as ramie may be used instead of linen. Coarse vegetable fibers such as hemp and jute, grasses, reeds, leaves, and even barks may be braided, woven, or felted to form fabrics which may serve some special household need. Check the natural durability and comfort characteristics of such fibers; be sure that the fabrics in which they are used are appropriate for the intended use.

Leather. While leather is not technically a fiber or a fabric, it is used so frequently in upholstery that it should be considered in connection with decorator fabrics. Leathers dye beautifully, are durable, and moisture-resistant. Such leathers as cowhide and steer hide are very expensive. An imitation leather made of plastic-coated fabric is also available.

Man-made Fibers

When a silkworm disease threatened the large European silk industry in 1878, scientists were asked to develop fibers to replace the natural fibers. They developed a method of preparing a liquid from natural products such as wood chips and cotton linters. Forcing this liquid through the small holes of a spinnerette, they produced fibers which became solid on contact with the air. They called this first man-made fiber artificial silk. Our modern rayons and acetates are descendants of this first development.

More recent research has developed many different types of man-made fibers. Chemists now combine simple chemicals to produce fibers having characteristics not found in any natural materials. In a continuing program of research and development, scientists seek to improve existing fibers and to provide new ones. They study the results of blending and combining various man-made fibers with each other and with the natural fibers in order to produce fabrics with specialized characteristics. In addition, these research programs have developed many finishes which provide additional desirable features in fibers and in the yarns and fabrics made from them.

All this development has given us a range of fabrics which can meet almost any need. It has also led to rapid changes which make it difficult to keep up with the field. Since 1960 the Textile Fiber Products Identification Act has required that all fabrics be labeled with certain basic information. The man-made fibers had been classified into 16 generic groups. The exact fiber content of any fabric (whether natural or man-made) must be listed on the label and the percentage by weight of each fiber must be stated. (Fibers which make up less than 5 percent of the content may be grouped together and listed as "other fibers," and certain types of fillings, paddings, trimmings, and so on need not be specified.) Special identifications of the natural fibers, such as "virgin wool" or "pure dye silk" and identifications of special finishes such as

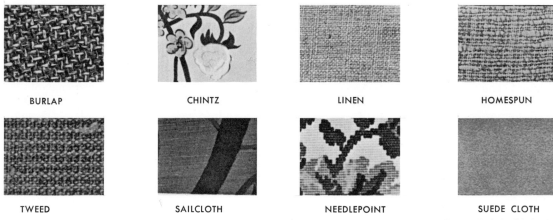

BURLAP   CHINTZ   LINEN   HOMESPUN

TWEED   SAILCLOTH   NEEDLEPOINT   SUEDE CLOTH

Courtesy Nettle Creek Industries

The effective use of fabrics depends in part on the characteristics of the fabric itself. Coarse, simple fabrics are perfect for Contemporary, Provincial, or simple traditional rooms.

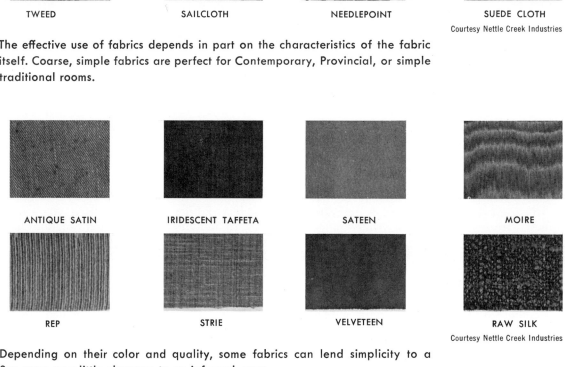

ANTIQUE SATIN   IRIDESCENT TAFFETA   SATEEN   MOIRE

REP   STRIE   VELVETEEN   RAW SILK

Courtesy Nettle Creek Industries

Depending on their color and quality, some fabrics can lend simplicity to a fine room or a little elegance to an informal room.

"durable-press" are subject to the provisions of the Wool Products Labeling Act and to special rulings of the Federal Trade Commission.

The Textile Fiber Products Identification Act allows a manufacturer to use a brand name along with the generic classification of a fiber, but does not require this identification. Such brand names help in identifying the special characteristics of a particular fabric. For example, Dacron, Kodel, and Fortrel are brand names which identify polyesters produced by different manufacturers. As polyesters, they have common characteristics and properties, but there may well be variations among the brands which may guide your choice in a particular situation.

Chart 7 on page 278 lists the major natural fibers and the sixteen generic groups of man-made fibers, and gives information as to the special characteristics, special requirements in caring for fabrics made of these fibers, and appropriate uses for each. You may need to

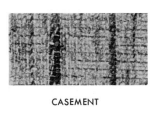

CASEMENT

MARQUISETTE

NINON

VOILE

BATISTE

PRINTED NINON

Courtesy Nettle Creek Industries

The effect of the semitranslucent fabrics and the sheer fabrics depends on their color and their tailoring. They can add a feminine or an informal tone or a provincial simplicity to a room.

BROCADE

DAMASK

MATELASSE

SATIN

TAFFETA

CUT VELVET

Courtesy Nettle Creek Industries

The most elegant, elaborate fabrics are seldom appropriate in rooms that must serve an active family life.

check recently printed articles for new developments in the textile industry.

YARNS ANALYZED

The yarn, or thread, from which a fabric is made determines, to a great extent, the characteristics of the fabric. Yarn can be made of a single fiber or of a mixture of several fibers. When fibers of different origins are twisted into a single homogenous unit, it is said to be a blend. When two or more fibers are twisted into individual strands before they are twisted together, a combination yarn is created. The texture and thickness of yarns can also vary. Thus the yarn, as well as the fibers from which it is made, affects the various qualities of a fabric.

Yarns made by twisting together long fibers, such as linen or long filaments such as silk or nylon, can be very smooth in texture. This smoothness is seen in yarns used in fine silk brocades and in table linens, as well as the yarns used for rayon and nylon satins. Long-staple cottons and wools make smoother yarns than do the shorter staple fibers.

The preparation of fibers for spinning into yarn also affects the smoothness of the yarn. Staple fibers must be arranged for spinning. Some staple fibers go through only two steps before spinning: they are carded and drawn out before being spun. If such fibers are combed after carding, the staples are arranged to be nearly parallel to one another. Combed yarns are much smoother than carded yarns. This smoothness is important in some fabrics while roughness adds to the characteristic beauty of others.

The thickness of the yarn depends upon the number of fibers or strands twisted together to form the final yarn. Both the texture and the thickness of a yarn are also affected by the amount of twist in the yarn. Special effects may be obtained by varying the twist within a yarn. Thus, soft untwisted sections within the yarn give the characteristic texture of shantungs while the texture of a bouclé yarn is formed by twisting tight and loose strands of yarn together.

FABRICS ANALYZED

Finally, the basic qualities of any fabric depend on the method of fabric construction used. This construction, when combined with color and the final finishes applied to a fabric, produces the finished appearance of the fabric.

Construction of Fabrics

The method of fabric construction used affects the appearance, the texture, the durability, and the cost of the fabric. Thus, handmade fabrics tend to be of a more interesting texture than a similar machine-made fabric. They may also be more expensive and less durable than machine-made fabrics of the same type. Such factors must be considered as you decide whether a particular fabric is appropriate for a particular use.

Weaving. There are three basic weaves and three exotic weaves used in the weaving of fabrics. In all weaving, the warp yarns that run lengthwise are crossed by the filling yarns which interlace the warp yarns at right angles. The three basic weaves are called the *plain weave,* the *twill weave,* and the *satin weave.* All basic weaves can be given added interest by variation of the weight, type, or color of the warp or filling yarns. The three more exotic weaves are the *pile weave* (cut, uncut, or velvet), which produces a fabric of great depth; the *leno weave* (marquisette), which produces a net or porous fabric; and the *figured weave,* which produces jacquard or tapestry fabric.

Knitting. Knit fabrics are formed by looping together a continuous yarn, rather than by crossing two sets of yarns as in weaving. Knitted fabrics are very elastic. This elasticity makes them very adaptable for inexpensive slipcovers, soft towels, and dishcloths.

Lacemaking. Manufacturers have developed a method of making lace, as well as a patterned lacelike fabric, which lends itself to an elegant and rather feminine type of glass curtain material. This fabric is mainly used in very feminine bedrooms.

Felting. The process by which fibers are made to mat and interlock with each other to produce a heavy material is called felting. It is admirably suited for padding of all kinds. Felt fabrics make interesting covers. They may also be used to decorate other fabrics.

Color in Fabrics

There are several methods of coloring a fabric. Each method has its own particular values. There are also several effective ways to decorate fabric with additional color.

Piece dyeing. The easiest and least expensive process of coloring a fabric is called piece dyeing. As the name indicates, the fabric is colored after it is woven; thus it is of a single hue. Some color variation in piece-dyed fabrics may result from the fabric weave and from the nubbiness or the luster of the fibers.

Yarn dyeing. Greater potential for delicate color variation is possible when the yarns are dyed before the fabric is woven than when fabric is piece dyed. There can be interesting close color relationships between warp and filling. There also can be lovely color variations such as tweed effects, distinct geometric patterns, or patterned tapestry effects.

Printing. The process of stamping color onto one side of a fabric is called printing. Because

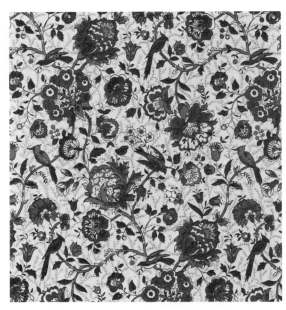

Printed fabrics are of three basic types. **Chintz** is characterized by a fine detailed design printed on fine cotton.

Toile de Jouy or **toile** is a repeated picture-type pattern, usually printed in one color on fine off-white cotton.

this treatment can add any number of colors to the fabric, it has infinite potential for variety.

There are three general groups of printed fabrics for home furnishings use. *Chintz*—a fine cotton fabric printed in delicate detail and many colors—was first produced in India. The word "Chint" is the Hindu word for "painted calico." The direct European adaptation of Chintz is *toile*—also a fine cotton printed in delicate detail. Usually printed in just one color, it was first produced in the French town of Jouy and so was called Toile de Jouy, meaning fabric made in Jouy. The third group of household prints is called *cretonne*, a coarser fabric printed in a bolder multiple-color design. Cretonne was first produced in the French town of Creton from which it derives its name. When printed on linen, this bolder cretonne printing is called hand-blocked linen. It is especially beautiful and expensive.

Modern chintzes, toiles, and cretonnes may be found in traditional and contemporary designs. They are produced both by hand and by machine. Their value depends on the qual-

Cretonne has a strong design done in broad brush strokes. It is usually printed on heavy cotton.

Courtesy "What's New in Home Economics"

In shopping for fabrics for use in your home, be sure to examine the tags or the selvage markings for information on the fiber content and on care and use specifications.

ity of the fabric, the ability of the designer, and the durability of the printing.

Embroidering. Matching or contrasting colored decoration may be added to fabric by embroidery. This is an expensive means of applying color to a fabric. Crewel embroidery is perhaps the most colorful and elaborate version of this process. Fabric so decorated is used mainly for hangings, upholstery, or very expensive draperies.

Finishes of Fabrics

Modern research has developed many new fabric finishes which may increase the ease with which a fabric may be cleaned, improve the function of a fabric, and improve its general appearance. Study the hang tags and information on the fabric selvages so as to make proper use of these modern developments.

Finishes which increase ease of care. Fabric finishes in this classification include durable-press treatments, permanent glazes, water- and spot-repellent treatments, crush-resistant impregnations, and completely opaque surface coatings. All of these finishes have helped to change cleaning from a laborious process to a relatively quick and easy one. These kinds of easy-care finishes have made it practical to use far lighter, more delicate-colored fabrics without lowering standards of cleanliness or complicating the job of housecleaning.

Finishes which improve function. This classification includes finishes which improve the functions of fabrics by adding greatly to their areas of usefulness. For instance, there is a finish which makes fabric moth- and mildew-repellent. Another finish provides permanent crispness which makes it possible to use sheer fabrics in steamy moist climates. A flame-resistant finish makes it possible to use fabric draperies where none would be safe otherwise. A controlled-shrinkage finish makes it possible to use fabrics for draperies or slipcovers where proper fit must be retained after cleaning. A napping finish makes many fibers heat-retentive and much warmer than would otherwise be the case.

Finishes which improve appearance. Many finishes are purely decorative in their purpose and effect. Moiré engraving gives an absolutely plain fabric a watered silk effect that is very beautiful. Mercerizing gives cotton more luster, makes it stronger, and more effective in absorbing dye. Sizing is a temporary

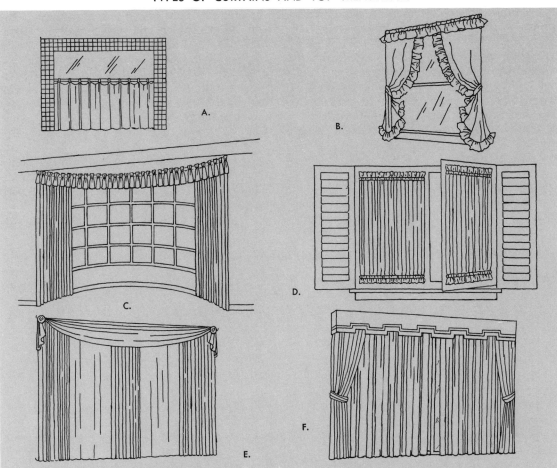

(A) A cafe curtain and a frame of plywood or pressed wood covered with a colorful fabric give daytime privacy and decorative accent to a kitchen, dinette, or family-room window. (B) Shirred and ruffled net glass curtains with a ruffled valance lend a dainty, feminine effect which many girls enjoy for their bedrooms. (C) Translucent or semitranslucent glass curtains, as well as heavy draw draperies, can be pleated and made to draw. With their matching pleated valance, these draperies follow the lines of the bay window. (D) Stretched sash curtains give practical privacy to inswinging casement windows, French doors, or doors with inset windows. The addition of shutters painted in the accent color lends decorative interest. (E) Pleated glass curtains, combined with fixed draperies and topped with a swag, lend daytime privacy and decorative accent to a pair of windows. (F) Fixed draperies, looped back, and a fitted and shaped lambriquin are combined with draw glass curtains for use on large windows. They are also appropriate for sliding doors and French doors.

starch finish that gives an appearance of a closer, firmer weave, or gives a shine to the surface of a fabric such as chintz. Weighting is a somewhat similar treatment of silk. Weighting weakens the fiber and impairs its wearing quality. Heavy, opaque coatings completely disguise a plain, rather thin cotton fabric, to make it look like leather, grass cloth, and other interestingly textured materials. Decorative finishes may be permanent, semi-permanent, or temporary. Some may be renewed as desired.

WINDOW TREATMENTS

Curtains and draperies are to a window what clothes are to a woman. They can cover faults or accentuate beauty; they can lend privacy like the face veils of the Orient, or, like a picture hat, they can frame a window. They can be elegant or inconspicuously practical; they can be dramatically important or quietly basic. But dramatic or quiet, framing or covering, the window fabrics in a room are of great importance both in the way they function and in the way they emphasize the tone and mood of the room.

Types of Curtains

As you look through home furnishing styles, there seem to be endless ways of curtaining windows. Actually there are a few general types of curtains and draperies. These plus a few ways to treat the spaces above the windows are the basis of all window styles.

MEASURING FOR CURTAINS

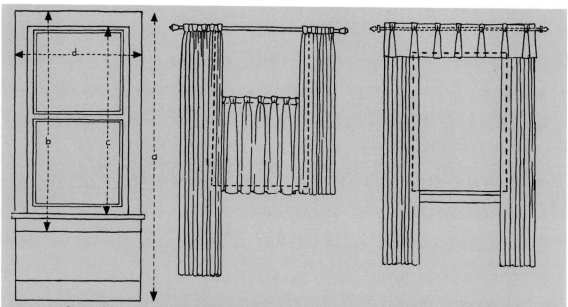

Draperies can hang from the top of the window casing to the floor(a) or the apron (b). Draperies must be wide enough to cover the casing (d). Glass curtains can be hung in the same way or they can be recessed inside the casing and hung to the sill (c). Both long and short heavy draperies can be hung beyond the window over the wall to increase the apparent size of the window and to admit more light. Half curtains provide privacy while allowing light to enter the room. Low windows can be raised and different height windows can be made uniform by placing a top treatment on the wall above the window.

Glass curtains. The curtains that are rather sheer and that hang next to the window glass are called "glass curtains." When glass curtains are shirred onto rods, top and bottom, and attached directly to the window sash, they are called "sash curtains." Sometimes sash curtains are gathered onto a single rod placed within the window casing and are either hung straight down or looped back. Cottage curtains and double Dutch curtains are other common types of glass curtains. When glass curtains overlap each other and are tied back, they are called crisscross or Priscilla curtains. If these cover the window and casing, they assure daytime privacy or blot out a bad view.

Draw curtains. These are panels that are attached to a rod in such a way that they can be drawn back and forth to cover the entire window. They may be lined or unlined, opaque or translucent, depending on the needs of the situation. Draw curtains may be set on the window casing or they may be placed out on the wall so that maximum light may enter when they are drawn open. Sometimes they are made in one or two tiers of short curtains which draw (cafe curtains).

Over-draperies. Over-draperies are panels of decoratively important fabric that hang on each side of the window to outline and decorate it; they may or may not draw. Over-draperies are usually used with glass or draw curtains which control the light and privacy; their function is to give the window color and decorative importance. Straight over-draperies are frequently used with cafe curtains in Provincial rooms. Fixed over-draperies may be looped back for an elegant effect. This style is frequently used for circular-topped windows. Occasionally they are combined with shutters or venetian blinds.

Styles of Window Treatments

The style of a window treatment is determined not only by the fabric and type of curtain but also by the length and the width of the panels, the way the fabric is decorated, and the way the space above the windows is treated.

Length. Curtain lengths can affect the tone of a room in the same way that a dress length can determine the tone of a costume. All window curtains should end at an architectural detail. For most curtains, this means the floor, the window apron, or the window sill. Sometimes special architectural features such as baseboard heating, window seats, or cupboards may affect the curtain length.

Width. Curtain widths depend on the weight of the fabric and the width of the space to be covered. A sheer fabric needs triple fullness to seem adequate when drawn across a window, but a heavy fabric or a lined curtain looks bulky if more than double fullness is used. Curtains are usually set at the outside edge of the window casing, or if the fabric is heavy, from 6 to 12 inches out on the wall on each side. It is usually unwise to cover any more of the wall with fabric than is necessary. A wider curtain is expensive to buy and extra work to keep up.

Decoration. If a window treatment is made of a patterned fabric, it is likely that no fur-

A frame cornice, such as this braid treatment, is an excellent way to save housekeeping effort and to beat the high cost of draperies for a home you may live in only briefly.

A strong decorative unity can be achieved by the skillful use of the same cretonne for the draperies and the chair upholstery.

ther decoration should be added. If, however, the fabric is plain, it is possible to add great beauty and individuality to it with decoration such as tapes, bandings, fringes, tassels, beadings, ruffles, plaitings, or edge shapings. As a general rule, the more curtains there are in a room, the plainer each one should be.

Top treatment. The framing of a window is completed by the treatment of the space above the window. If this top treatment is made of curtain fabric, it can be handled in several ways: it can be an informal shirred or pleated *valance;* it can be a draped *swag;* or it can be a more formal fitted and shaped *lambrequin* in which the material is stretched over buckram, plywood, or wallboard. All three can be attached to a shelflike board placed on the wall above the window, or they can be hung like a curtain from an extra rod outside the one holding the curtains. If the top treatment is made of wood, metal, or mirror, it is a *cornice.* It can extend across the top of the window, or it can frame it on three sides.

Color and Pattern in Window Treatments

When choosing window coverings, all the guides governing the use of color, pattern, and design should be reviewed and applied. Curtains should be chosen on the basis of the way they will look when closed and therefore covering the largest area.

Contrast to emphasize. If a window is well proportioned and well placed in a room, it can be made the focal point by curtaining it in a fabric that presents a strong contrast to the wall in color, value, intensity, or pattern. This treatment is effective when there is only one window or window grouping to be handled.

Match to deemphasize. If windows are poorly proportioned, poorly placed, or numerous, they should be reduced in importance by matching the color of the curtain fabric to the wall color. Such treatment blends them into their surroundings, making them less offensive.

Isolate pattern with plain. A plain color in curtains can always be used with plain colored walls. If the wall covering, floor covering, bedspread, or sofa in a room is figured, the curtains should exactly match the pattern or be plain, in order to allow the one pattern to be dominant.

Reduce intensity with area. Compare the total area to be covered by curtains with other large areas of the room to evaluate the impact the curtains will have. If the area is large, avoid pattern, and select a grayed, soft color that is closely related to another major color so that it will not unbalance the room.

EFFECT OF ARCHITECTURE ON WINDOW TREATMENTS

There are many factors that affect the curtaining of windows, but probably the most difficult and expensive to change are the architectural details of the window construction, its placement, and the view it reveals. These usually must be accepted with all their advantages and disadvantages.

Window Construction

The way a window is constructed will often predetermine what type of curtains must be used on it. If it does not open, it presents no problem except for outline, but the moment any part of it moves, the manner of its moving and the effect of the incoming air must be carefully considered in planning the curtaining. However, the problems of window movement and air currents have been somewhat removed by the use of year-round air conditioning in many modern homes.

Sliding sash. There are two types of sliding windows: those which slide up-and-down, called double-hung sash, and those which slide sideways, frequently called ranch windows. Both these types of windows can be treated with any type of fixed curtain or draw curtain and any type of top treatment.

Swinging casements. Out-swinging casements can be treated with any kind of curtains that can be drawn back and any type of top treatment. But fixed curtains that would blow in the wind are a poor choice. In-swinging casements and hopper windows can be treated with draw curtains only if there is wall space on each side on which the curtains can hang when the window is open. Top treatments for these windows must stop above the height of the sash frame. All fixed curtains should be set back on the wall, hung on swing-arm rods, or attached to the sash itself.

Awnings and jalousies. Neither awning nor jalousie windows interfere with draw curtains or top treatments. Fixed glass curtains should be avoided to allow free passage of air.

Courtesy Better Homes and Gardens, © Meredith Corporation, 1963

Simple sash curtains on each window can be framed by a pair of decorative panels for an inexpensive way to handle a window grouping. A slipcovered sofa in matching cretonne will supply additional color.

In-swinging glass doors. Like in-swinging casements and hopper windows, all in-swinging glass doors can be treated with draw curtains only when there is wall space on which the curtains can hang when the door is open, and top treatments must stop above the top of the door frame. Any fixed curtain must be attached to the door itself or hung on a swing-arm rod.

Out-swinging or sliding glass doors. Like out-swinging casements, out-swinging or sliding glass doors can be given any kind of top treatment, but any draw curtains must have wall space on which they can hang when the door is open. Fixed curtains are a poor choice unless they are hung on a swing-arm rod.

Window Shapes

In general, a window in pleasing proportion to the walls of a room should be accepted and worked with regardless of current style. Many poorly proportioned windows which

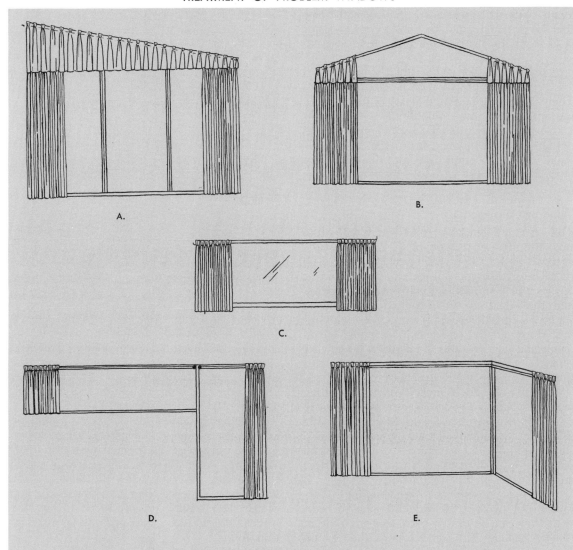

(A) Clerestory windows usually are left uncurtained, but where privacy or warmth is desired, a fixed pleated valance, shaped to fit, can be used. (B) Clerestory windows with a peaked roofline can be left uncurtained, covered completely with a fixed valance, or softened with a partial valance which is the width of the opened draperies. (C) Ranch-type windows, placed high on a wall, will look better if treated with simple traverse curtains that match the wall. (D) Irregularly shaped windows, planned as architectural accents, should be accepted and curtained as they are, blending drapery and wall in color. (E) Contemporary curtaining emphasizes the airiness of corner windows by placing draw curtains at the outside edges of the grouping.

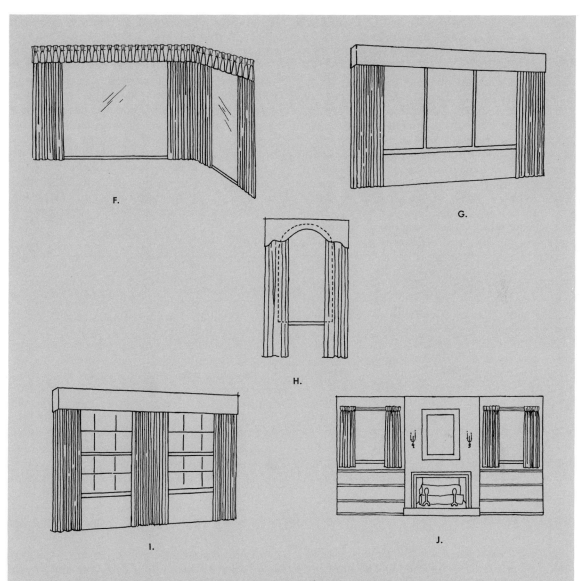

F.

G.

H.

I.

J.

(F) Traditional curtaining of corner windows emphasizes the structural corner with draperies. Occasionally the whole corner is unified with a valance or a lambriquin. (G) Groups of windows should be treated as one wherever possible. (H) When draw curtains are desired on an arched window, the rod is placed on the wall and the wall is masked with a shaped lambriquin or valance. (I) Windows separated by a wall space that is smaller than the width of a single window can be treated as a grouping by covering the wall with drapery and unifying the whole with a single top treatment. (J) Windows on each side of a fireplace should be inconspicuously draped with draw curtains that match the wall.

need to be changed can be easily treated to give the effect of good proportion.

Effective changes. The window that is too tall for its width can be either widened by placing the curtains out on the wall or shortened by a top treatment that covers part of the top. A window that is too short can be given height by a top treatment that is placed on the wall above it and by full-length curtains. Windows of different heights in the same room can be equalized by the use of top treatments that raise or lower them to a harmonious even level. Irregular widths which clash can be made less apparent by widening the narrow windows, and narrowing the wider ones. In many rooms, however, irregular widths may be pleasing. Round-topped windows can be squared with a top treatment which makes the room less formal in tone while rectangular windows can be given height and a formal effect with a semicircular top treatment.

Acceptable compromises. Clerestory windows can be a difficult curtaining problem. If they are rectangular, they can be curtained separately with draw curtains. If they are triangular and if they must be covered for privacy or light control, they can be treated with a fixed drapery that is shaped to exactly fit the window. Needless to say, the fabric and design of curtains for clerestory windows must exactly match that used on the other rectangular windows.

Grouped Windows

When windows are grouped together with no wall space between, they are usually considered and treated as one window. If, however, the expanse of the group (as on some window walls) is so great that both mechanically and from the point of view of light control it is impractical to treat them as one, they can be divided. Where windows are cornered or separated by wall space, special handling is necessary.

Cornered windows. The draperies on cornered windows may be placed at the outside edges of the grouping and at the corner itself. This treatment is often used with traditional styling. For a more contemporary effect, draw curtains or draperies draw from the outside edge of the window group to meet at the corner.

Separated windows. There are two ways to handle windows separated from each other by wall space. If separation is not great, the space may be covered with a panel of drapery or it may be left open. In either case the entire area of wall spaces and windows can be unified with a single top treatment. If the separation is larger, the windows should be treated separately and inconspicuously, and the space between should be used importantly for bookshelves, a mirror, or pictures.

Window Light and View

A window's most important function is to bring in light and air. In air conditioned homes, only light must be considered. In many cases, a window also frames a view. All curtain treatments should aid in these functions rather than detract from them.

Light control. If privacy must be provided as well as light control, you may cover the entire window with semitranslucent curtains. If privacy is the main need, you may use either translucent or opaque curtains to cover only the lower portion of the window. All the windows of the room must be treated in the same manner, even though a particular problem affects only some of the windows.

View control. Some windows face a garden or a pleasant view that should be framed by plain draperies that in no way detract from it. In other cases you may prefer to blot out the view with a semitranslucent draw curtain that has texture or design interest. Analyze your situation carefully before you choose your fabrics or your type or style of curtaining.

BUDGETING FOR WINDOW TREATMENTS

Any budgeting for curtains brings up not only the matter of quality but also the question of whether they will be professionally tailored or made at home. Curtains made at home may meet certain individual needs better than other curtains. Whether or not they save money depends on many other factors.

Consider Curtain Quality According to Permanency

One of the important and determining factors in the budgeting for and the selection of window treatments is how long they will be used. Will there be a move within a year or two, or is the home a more permanent one? Answers to questions of this type will help you decide on the quality of curtains that fit the situation.

A temporary situation. Curtains for a student's room or for a young couple's first apartment are bound to have temporary tenure. There are two ways to plan for such temporary situations. You may spend as little as possible so that the cost can be ignored. However this method is apt to be unsatisfactory and uneconomical. Instead, you may plan to buy curtains that could fit in with a change. For example, good-quality curtains that are impersonal in style can be given temporary individuality with easily removed personalized decoration. If all curtains in a temporary dwelling are made of the same neutral colored fabric, but decorated differently for different areas, they can be used together in a bigger room in the next home.

A more settled situation. When the home becomes somewhat permanent, greater individuality can be considered in the selection of curtains for each room. In this case, better quality in curtains is both justifiable and advisable.

Compare Professionally-made and Homemade Curtains

The decision as to whether to have professionally-made or homemade curtains is no longer a simple one. Manufacturers now buy fabrics in such large quantities and streamline their tailoring so efficiently that the finished curtain frequently costs less than do curtains you make. You will have to decide how important it is to have your own selection of fabrics and style and your own quality of workmanship. You must also consider the time you have available, the magnitude of the job in terms of window sizes, and what is available in fabrics and professionally made curtains in your area.

Costs of professionally made curtains. There are three types of professionally made cur-

A gay window treatment of relatively little cost consists of sheer cafe curtains and a semitranslucent window shade, both decorated with a sprinkling of butterflies.

tains: the ready-made, the semi-custom-made, and the custom-made. The first two are usually available in department stores and catalog houses at fairly standard prices. The latter is individually made in drapery shops, and the cost varies with the season, the pressure of work, the locale, and the size of the workroom.

Ready-made curtains. These curtains are mass-produced in one or two lengths and widths and in a limited range of fabrics and colors. You may need to adjust lengths and join widths to meet your situation. Ready-made curtains generally cost less than the fabric and other materials you would need to buy in order to make curtains.

Semi-custom-made curtains. These curtains are also mass-produced. They can be ordered in a range of standard lengths and widths that

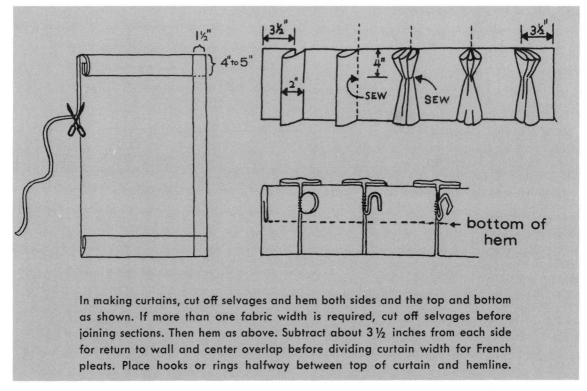

In making curtains, cut off selvages and hem both sides and the top and bottom as shown. If more than one fabric width is required, cut off selvages before joining sections. Then hem as above. Subtract about 3 ½ inches from each side for return to wall and center overlap before dividing curtain width for French pleats. Place hooks or rings halfway between top of curtain and hemline.

will probably come close to meeting your needs. The workmanship is better, the range of fabrics and colors greater, and the cost higher than for the ready-made curtains. Most stores will install them for an additional fee.

Custom-made curtains. These curtains are individually made to fit your windows. They are usually the most expensive professionally made curtains. The cost usually includes the measuring; the rods, hooks, and installation; and the cost of the fabrics as well as the cost of making the curtains. It is wise to check exactly what any quoted price covers and to establish a specific delivery date before ordering.

Costs of homemade curtains. Once the cost of fabrics and other materials has been checked, you must consider the need for special equipment. For example, picture window curtains may require special tables and machines in order that large quantities of fabric may be handled properly. Community resources, such as vocational schools or commu-

nity workshops, may provide such equipment. The fact that work space, equipment, and unusual fabric resources are available can open up the entire field of beautiful and individual fabric furnishings and provide a tremendous personal delight to the person who can sew well enough to make curtains and draperies.

Evaluate Other Types of Window Treatments

Frequently it is desirable to find means other than curtains for controlling light, air, or privacy and occasionally it is necessary to supplement curtains in special situations. Fortunately, there are many possibilities available.

Window shades. Coated fabric window shades that roll onto a small inconspicuous roller, which is easily hidden under a top treatment, are probably the most inexpensive and adjustable means of controlling the light in a horizontal manner. They can be decorated and used by themselves, or they can be used as a supplement for curtains. They are available in *semitranslucent* or *semiopaque* weights

The cost of draw draperies to fit each window can be avoided by using adjustable drapery panels and decorative window shades.

Courtesy Window Shade Manufacturer's Assn.

and in a *black undercoated* quality which lends nighttime darkness for naps and daytime viewing of slides or movies. All shades are available in a wide range of colors; the opaque ones may come in double colors—one on the outside to harmonize with the exterior house trim, and another on the inside to match the curtains or walls of the room. The use of shades for decoration as well as light control has increased tremendously in recent years.

Shutters. Because they serve as curtains and as a means of controlling light and privacy in both a perpendicular and a horizontal manner, wooden shutters are a practical window treatment. They may be painted for a casual look that is appropriate in either traditional or contemporary rooms. When finished in natural wood tones to match furniture or paneled walls, they have great dignity and are appropriate in elegant or simple interiors.

Venetian blinds. Venetian blinds of wood, metal, or plastic control the light like a shutter.

They are less expensive to buy and install. They provide privacy and at the same time permit air circulation. Like shutters, venetian blinds present a housekeeping problem.

Split bamboo and match-stick curtains. These curtains can be spray painted to match a color scheme or used in natural color in almost any informal room. Although they are attractive, they may not provide complete privacy.

Screens. Wallboard screens, painted or covered with fabric or wall-paper, can be used dramatically as shutters to control light and serve as curtains as well. When used as floor screens, they can blot out a poorly designed or inconveniently placed window, while allowing air to circulate as needed.

OTHER USES FOR FABRICS IN HOME FURNISHINGS

In planning fabrics for a room, there are two dangers—that of using too much of one kind so it looks like a "sale on fabrics," or of not using enough and thereby missing the opportunity to soften and unify the room. If a fabric is plain and quiet in color, it can be used far more liberally than if it is figured or strong in color.

Upholstery

Upholstery fabrics have been discussed in relation to furniture in Chapter 12. As a rule, upholstery fabrics are heavier and stronger than other fabrics used in a room, although in recent years there has been a trend toward the use of both plain and quilted linen, chintz, and cretonne for upholstery. Should you decide to tackle an upholstery job, courses in reupholstering are often given in adult education classes. Also there are some jobs of reupholstering which are so simple that anyone with a tack hammer can manage them.

Removable chair seats. Some dining-room and desk chairs are constructed with an upholstered seat which can be removed by unscrewing four screws and can be reupholstered with a square of fabric and tacks. These chairs can be adjusted quickly to any new fabric scheme. Because they are small, they can be covered in bright sparkling colors, or decorated with embroidery or appliqué.

Plain walls and rug furnish a unified background for a dramatic use of chintz in the bed alcove.

Removable paneled headboards. Many bed headboards which can be attached to a metal spring and mattress frame have removable panels that can be reupholstered as easily as a chair seat. Extra bedspread fabric can be used in this way. You may also cover the headboard with a plain fabric which is repeated in the dust ruffle, thus allowing the bedspread to act as the accent.

Screens. Wallboard screens can be most effective when upholstered with fabric over an undercovering of soft materials. The screens are then edged with a braid or other decoration. This type of screen can be used in the corner as an accent, behind a sofa for decoration, or in an archway, or between beds, thus adding both beauty and privacy.

Slipcovers

Historically, slipcovers were beautiful and important. In the nineteenth century, the French made slipcovers of taffeta and used them in very elegant rooms. In England they were frequently made of crewel-embroidered fabrics and were considered most desirable. In hot countries where cool, smooth, light colored upholstery is desirable, they have always been used. And now, with the appearance on the market of chairs, sofas, and even bed headboards "in muslin," slip covers are taking a place of importance in many homes.

Professionally made slipcovers range from the inexpensive stretch type, through the ready-made ones which must be individually adjusted to fit, to the expensive ones which are tailor-made to measure. The woman who can sew well has great opportunity to add beauty to her home and to save considerable money in this field.

Bedspreads

Bedspreads come in a great variety of colors, fabrics, and styles, and in a wide range of prices. Because of the large choice available and the difficulty faced when working with large quantities of fabrics, bedspreads are generally bought from the ready-made selection in department stores. Matching the color of the floor or walls is an easy way to reduce the apparent size of a bed in a small room.

It is frequently advisable to buy one or two extra bedspreads for other uses in the room. They can be made into bed curtains or window curtains—delightful ways of balancing and unifying the room. They can also be used for bolsters, for upholstery, for slipcovering a headboard or a chair, for banding curtains, making a window seat pad, making a dressing table skirt, or making the dust ruffle on the bed.

Other Uses

Fabric-covered pads and pillows will change an unattractive, hard-looking bench or chair into an invitingly comfortable place to sit. Fabric pasted on an ordinary straight-line chest can make it a decorative focal point in a room; while fabric pasted on tin or cardboard containers can turn them into attractive

TYPES OF BEDSPREADS

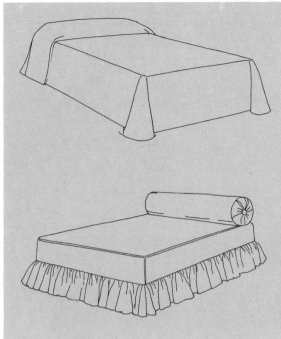

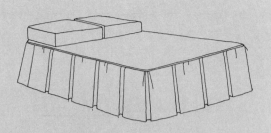

The sheet-style bedspread is long enough to fold over pillows. It usually has rounded corners at the foot of the bed to hang even with the sides. A two or three-piece bedspread can be made with box pleats and matching pillow covers. Another type of two- or three-piece spread, made with a separate bolster cover, has a fitted top with a shirred dust ruffle. The dust ruffle can be attached to the spread or placed between the springs and the mattress.

DRESSING-TABLE SKIRTS

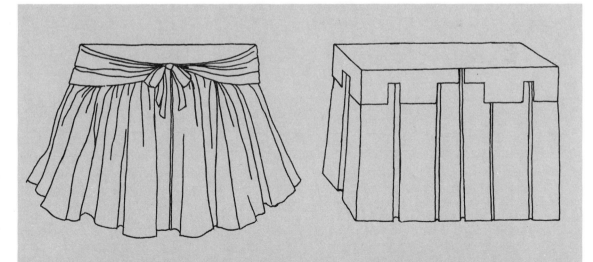

Dressing-table skirts are more effective when the fabrics and design match the other fabrics used in the room. The soft fullness of a semicircular dressing-table skirt is appropriate with ruffled feminine window treatments. A box-pleated dressing-table skirt may repeat the styling and fabric of the bedspread shown in the second drawing at the top of the page.

An interestingly textured, spongy soft bedspread that needs no ironing can be given additional smartness with a row of colorful pillows that pick up and add to the other colors of the room.

Courtesy Morgan-Jones, Incorporated

and useful wastebaskets and storage boxes. Indeed, fabrics, creatively and ingeniously used, can work miracles of inexpensive changes in the appearance of any room.

SHOPPING FOR HOME FURNISHINGS FABRICS

Smart buying demands an exploratory attitude of mind. Less expensive fabrics, or their equivalents, can often be blended with or used in place of expensive drapery fabrics. The average department store or catalog store has many resources suitable for drapery, slipcover, and upholstery fabrics other than the drapery department itself.

Preparation for buying. The first step in preparation for a shopping expedition is to know the window or furniture measurements. Turn to the drawings on page 288 for help in figuring the exact yardage you will need. Al-

ways carry samples of the other room colors with you. Finally, know your community resources and explore them carefully.

Precautions about hidden costs. Most people check the tags and selvage markings to learn about strength, firmness, soil- and spot-resistance, and wrinkle resistance, but there are other less obvious qualities which are easy to overlook. The appropriate width for your needs; the size of the repeat which must be matched or centered in a patterned fabric; and the cost of decorations, additional materials, and hardware, all can add to the total cost in a startling way. Be sure you know the complete costs before you start buying—not after you have gone too far to change your plans.

Need for patience. To get what you want, you must frequently be willing to wait. Never let temporary inconvenience push you into buying something that is not right.

300

1. Define the meaning of the following phrases as used in this chapter: yarn-dyed fabrics, piece-dyed fabrics, custom-made curtains, ready-made curtains, draw draperies, and glass curtains.

2. Visit a high school or vocational school class in weaving to understand the construction of fabrics, the potentials of yarn-dyed color, and the decorative qualities of handwoven fabrics.

3. Using the classified directory, find and visit a small drapery and slipcover workshop and report how some of its work methods could be adapted to the making of curtains and slipcovers at home by a student.

4. Make a plan for a window treatment and a bedspread for (a) a feminine type or (b) a tailored type of girl's room, showing pictures or sketches and samples of fabrics to make it clear.

5. Make another plan for a boy's room, using window shades, shutters, and/or coated fabrics to emphasize the masculine styling.

6. Compare homemade and ready-made curtains for a bedroom as to individuality, beauty, workmanship, and cost, being sure to include the cost of findings and the estimate of time spent on adjusting or making.

7. Make the same comparison on bedspreads.

8. Plan the window treatments for a living room, dinette, kitchenette apartment so they could be reused in rooms with more windows in a larger apartment in two or three years.

9. Measure the windows in one room in your school and plan a treatment for them using curtains, window shades, or shutters or any combination of these. Include cost of any hardware needed and indicate how you could cut costs with your own ability in sewing, woodworking, remodeling or installation.

10. Compare the cost of buying a ready-made or custom-made slipcover with the cost of making one for a chair you own, and report to the class.

16

Accessories

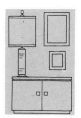

A Room that has no personalized accessories looks impersonal and institutional; a room that is overloaded with accessories, no matter how fine they are, looks restless and tiresome. So, in studying accessories, you need to find out how to distinguish worthy accessories from unworthy ones, how to use them effectively, and finally, how to buy them.

RECOGNITION OF GOOD ACCESSORIES

As you grow up, your interest in accessories changes. As a high school student, you are no longer content to stake out your area of possession with a beaten-up stuffed animal or doll, as you did in the early grades. You may still enjoy a stuffed animal if it is a little unusual, but you find you want to indicate your area with accessories that are more important and more indicative of your personality. You begin to develop discrimination. Exactly how you develop that discrimination differs with each person, but there are certain tests which you can apply as a check and a guide for your choices.

Tests of General Values

Some accessories, like clocks or pillows or bookends, have important practical functions that are so basic that they are the first and main source of value. Other accessories, like pictures or ornamental objects of art, must be evaluated solely on their decorative value.

Will it work? In the case of an accessory with a practical function, it is essential to apply a functional test first of all. Does the clock keep time? Can the pillow be leaned on comfortably? Does the lamp give a good light? Unless the object meets these practical tests, it is a failure.

Is it really beautiful? All accessories can and should be beautiful. Study the best that is shown in books, magazines, and shops, so that you recognize beauty wherever it exists.

Look at its form. Begin by considering the form of the object without regard for its decoration. Is it simple and well balanced, or is it a weird shape created to attract the unwary buyer? Good artists and craftsmen seldom distort an object. In general, beauty of proportion, simplicity and grace of line, and the material

302

A fine painting, growing garden flowers transferred to a bowl, and a candlestick lamp add accent to the simple informality of a room.

Courtesy Harmon Studios

itself are sufficient to win attention and give pleasure to the discriminating person.

Look at its color. Are the colors lovely and well blended? Do they clash with each other? Are colors shown in pleasing proportions?

Look at the decoration. If an object is decorated, is the decoration a structural decoration that seems to fit and be a logical part of the object? If the decoration appears to be stuck on and does not harmonize with the shape or the function of the object, turn your back on it firmly.

Tests of Specific Personal Values

You need to develop an understanding of yourself and of your own home, so that you begin to feel, automatically, what things express you and are appropriate in your home. Many accessories can be beautiful in themselves but utterly inappropriate for your use.

Is it appropriate for the individual? Everyone has natural interests which can be used as a starting point for study and growth. Ask yourself what naturally attracts you? Is it china, horses, dolls, fans, plants, or books? Whatever it is, encourage your interest; don't be content with just collecting. Whenever you are in a library or a museum, or when you travel, study your interest, learn about its historical background in your own and other lands, make a file of clippings about it, and then begin to incorporate that interest in the decoration of your room.

Accessories that reflect your natural interests will reflect your personality and enhance your personal growth. On the other hand, an accessory chosen simply because it is for sale or is inexpensive will probably add little to the real decoration of your room. Thus, a map or travel poster may be less expensive than a reproduction of your favorite artist's work, but if you really like the artist and are not interested in travel, the less expensive map is inappropriate for you.

Is it appropriate in the room? In selecting accessories for a room, you should take into

Courtesy Better Homes and Gardens, © Meredith Corporation, 1964

Special interests often provide unusual accessories. A shell collection may be framed and hung above a sofa as an interesting focal point in a conversation area. A conch shell makes a unique container for a special flower arrangement.

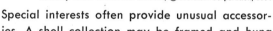

consideration the room's style and scale. A lamp with a cut-glass-vase base and a silk shade is obviously not a good choice for a room furnished in rough tweeds and heavy oak furniture. The textures and the style would not harmonize. In the same way, it would be just as unwise to select a huge clock or lamp for a tiny room. It is important to harmonize style, textures, and the scale of the major accessories with the room in general. A minor accessory need only be personally interesting to be appropriate.

THE USE OF ACCESSORIES IN THE HOME

Many people accumulate beautiful things as an investment, while others acquire them be-

A careful arrangement of different accessories provides a unified focal point. Pictures of different styles and shapes, a candle sconce, and a statuette combine to form an unusual sofa wall.

The hanging of pictures in a trim rectangle can be accomplished by following the directions on page 309.

cause they cannot resist their beauty. Both types of people are making collections which may give them much joy and satisfaction.

Pictures

The use of pictures in homes has gone through a fascinating process of development. At first the only pictures available were original paintings; only the very wealthy could afford to buy these, especially when they were works of major artists. With the development of printing, black and white and sepia reproductions of paintings and photographs came into general use. And finally, as printing methods improved, reproductions of fine pictures in good color became available at reasonable prices so they could be used in any home. The color process developed a new interest in pictures, and gradually, as the affluence of our society increased, it also developed an interest in moderately priced originals. In consequence, many young people are able to rent originals from art institutes. They also buy inexpensive originals at art fairs and save to buy really good paintings.

In hanging pictures in any room, it is desirable to use different styles, sizes, subjects, and types of media. If you combine a small picture with others in a grouping, it is quite all right to include pictures of several types. If a picture is big, you may hang it alone to give it a chance for importance; other walls in the room can be used for the placement of groupings of secondary importance.

According to medium. Original pictures are painted mainly in oil, tempera, acrylic, or wa-

Courtesy Better Homes and Gardens, © Meredith Corporation, 1966

Place pictures in relationship to the furniture they accompany. The arrangement of pictures to follow the lines of the sofa and the chest is more pleasing to the eye than the unrelated arrangement.

A narrow frame and a mat are used to frame a watercolor or etching. Place the widest mat margin at the bottom. Use a heavy frame for an oil painting. A liner may be used, but oil paintings are not matted. While an elaborate frame may be successfully used to emphasize a mirror, it may detract from a picture.

tercolor. Original prints are created by such methods as etching on metal or carving on wood to make a design which can be imprinted repeatedly. Each of these methods (or media) of creating pictures has its merits and no one is more permanent or more valuable than another. Each depends for its value on the ability of the artist. Reproductions are made by a photographic process; their value depends on both the quality of the original and the faithfulness of the printing process.

According to style of work. Pictures can be divided according to style into three large categories: the realistic, in which the picture is made up of recognizable objects arranged in normal relationships; the nonobjective in which there are no recognizable objects; and the imaginatively realistic, in which the artist takes liberties with both representation and relationships to create his composition. No one of these types of work is considered more acceptable than the other. The value of the picture depends entirely on the skill and ability of the painter. So in selecting a picture for your home, look at each picture with an open mind and let each speak to you itself. All three types of work can be used together in the same room in the same way that all media can be hung together.

According to subject matter. Some people mistakenly feel that certain subjects are appropriate only in certain rooms—for example, fish and fruit in a dining room; architecture, landscapes, and marines in a living room. Actually, a good picture is good anywhere and a poor one should not be hung anywhere. The determining factors in the hanging of a picture are its art quality and the interest it holds for you, your family, and your guests. Consequently, pictures which are mainly personal in their appeal, such as enlarged photographs of family and friends, are better hung in the more personal rooms—the bedrooms or the den—where their personal interest will compensate for possible lack of art value. Hang the pictures of established art merit in the living rooms of a house, where you and your guests will enjoy them equally.

According to framing. The framing of pictures is of greatest importance; a great picture can be ruined by the wrong frame and a very simple picture can be given importance with the right one. The selection of a frame is dictated, first of all, by the medium; next, by the

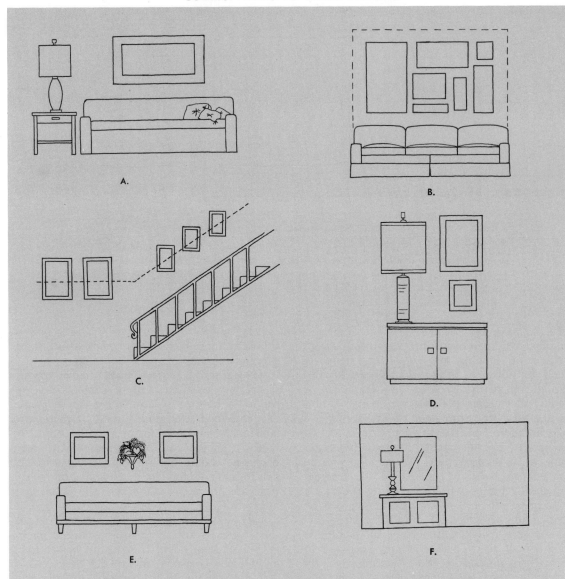

(A) Center a picture or a picture grouping which is to be placed above a piece of furniture. (B) Try to form a rectangle when arranging a grouping of pictures of various sizes and shapes. (C) When they are not hung in relation to furniture, pictures should be placed at average eye level. (D) If a lamp takes part of the wall space above a piece of furniture, treat it as part of the picture grouping. (E) Small pictures can be amplified with a bracket and plant to decorate a large wall space. (F) Hang mirrors or pictures in relation to the furniture, rather than to the size of the wall.

To plan a grouping of pictures, begin by placing a piece of paper on the floor and outlining the grouping on it. The total effect can be checked and adjusted before one tack is driven. Attach the paper to the wall, pound in hooks, and hang the pictures before removing the paper pattern.

style and color of the picture; and finally, by the tone of the room in which it is hung. Watercolors, temperas, etchings, and wood blocks are matted and glassed. Oils are framed without a mat and are varnished for protection. The color of a painted frame should complement the dominant color or tone of the picture. Natural wood and gold and silver frames need not reflect the colors of the picture, but the style of the frame should reflect the mood of the picture and should never detract from it by its importance. An extremely informal room demands simple informal-type frames of natural wood or of color. An elegant room can use pictures framed in antique gold or silver or smoothly polished woods.

According to placement. The placement of a picture or a group of pictures on a wall is determined by several factors. The first is average eye level—the position at which the picture was painted; the next is the relationship to furniture or architecture; and the last is balance—either formal or informal.

Height. If a picture is hung in a hallway, on a stairway, or in a room where it is away from any furniture, the average eye level determines its height. In other cases, the deter-

mining factor is the relationship to the height of the furniture or to an architectural horizontal, such as the top of a fireplace opening or mantel shelf.

Horizontal placement. If the arrangement of furniture with which the picture is hung is based on formal balance, the picture or group of pictures is centered on the largest piece. If the furniture group is arranged according to informal balance, the picture or group of pictures may be moved to one side or another to achieve a balance.

Individual versus group placement. Avoid the monotony of placing one picture above each piece of furniture or on each wall space. Instead, use variety in hanging pictures. Place one big picture on one wall, a grouping of two or three on another, and possibly a large grouping of quite a few pictures on still another. Do not overlook the possibility of combining pictures with objects of art, plants on brackets, or hanging bookshelves.

Portable Lamps

Portable lamps have gone through many transitions since early days. The basic reason for using them is to place light where it is

309

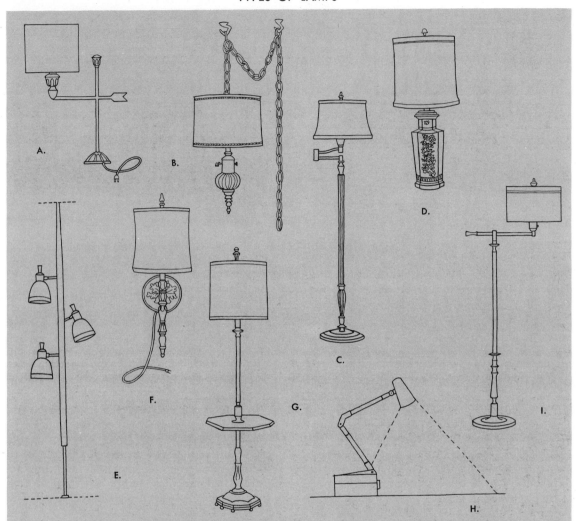

(A) The traditional student lamp gives good light for study and general desk work. (B) The hanging lamp is a versatile supplement for inadequate fixed lighting. (C) A swing-arm bridge lamp acts as both a floor lamp and as an extended-arm bridge lamp. (D) The vase-type lamp is found in a wide range of heights. It can be used on tables, desks, and chests. (E) The pole lamp, which extends to fit different ceiling heights, is especially useful for lighting bunk beds or pictures hung at varying heights. (F) The portable pin-up wall lamp is a good supplement for fixed lighting. (G) A junior floor lamp with an attached table serves a double purpose and therefore saves floor space. (H) A functionally designed high-intensity lamp adjusts to give concentrated light for especially demanding work. (I) A bridge lamp brings light more directly over the reader than does the floor lamp.

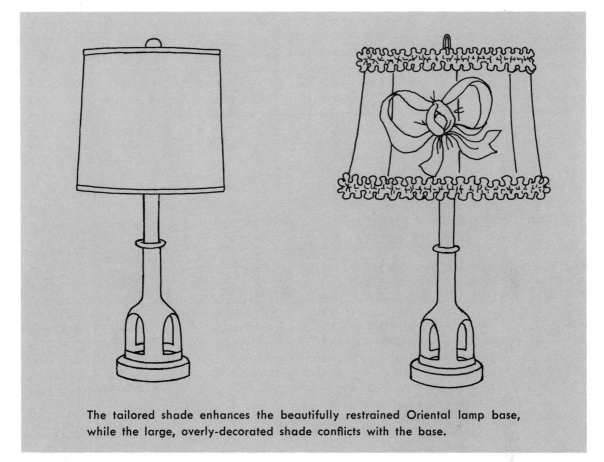

The tailored shade enhances the beautifully restrained Oriental lamp base, while the large, overly-decorated shade conflicts with the base.

needed in the room and in the intensity needed for varying functions. Because lamps also lend a friendly, intimate atmosphere, they should be decorative as well as functional.

According to type. Portable lamps can be roughly divided into the following categories: table lamps, desk lamps, floor lamps, junior floor lamps, swing-arm lamps, bridge lamps, wall lamps, and pole lamps. Each of these is produced in a wide range of styles to harmonize with different styles of furniture. They are produced in a variety of heights to adjust to various ceiling heights, table heights, and chair and sofa back heights.

Lamps of several different types add interest and variety to a room as well as meeting the various functional needs of the room. More than one pair of lamps in a room tends to become monotonous unless the room is exceptionally large.

According to base. The base of a lamp is of great importance, because it will be highlighted all the time the lamp is lit. Therefore, consider the base as if it were a separate shaft, vase, or object of art. If it is not in itself beautiful in material, color, design, and workmanship, don't buy it. A good, simply designed lamp has lasting beauty.

According to the shade. The beauty of a shade must be considered both as a unit in itself and as it relates to the base. The shade should be simple in outline and decoration. For most uses, a semitranslucent shade should be white or a light neutral, so that light passing through it is not distorted. Such a shade colored red or green can make a healthy person look on the point of death. If the shade is opaque metal or paper, only the inside color of the shade needs to be an off-white. If all the lamp shades in one room are semitranslu-

This drawing shows the correct relationship of the height of table lamps and tables to the eye level of a person when seated.

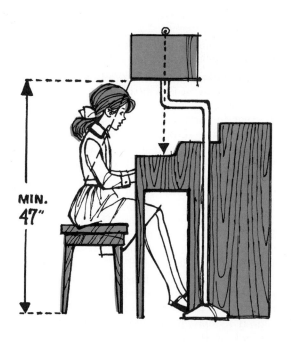
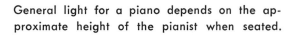

General light for a piano depends on the approximate height of the pianist when seated.

The height of a desk lamp depends on the approximate eye level of a person when seated.

cent, they should all be approximately the same color, so the overall effect of light in the room is harmonious.

It is necessary to judge the size, shape, color, texture, and decoration of the shades as they relate to the bases. The more decorative the base, the plainer the shade should be, in accordance with the principle of alternating pattern and plain. Coarse-grained wood and rough pottery bases should have heavily textured shades; bases of glass, polished metal, or polished wood require shades of smooth paper, metal, or fabric.

According to placement. In order to have adequate and individually controlled light, each functional grouping of furniture should have its own portable lamp. If this plan is followed, the lamps will be well spaced throughout the room; the room will have a general spread of light with concentrated areas of intensity contrasting with cozily shadowed areas that add charm.

Objects of Art

The trend in the use of objects of art was toward scarcity during the beginning of the contemporary era. But now we are again adding enough of the personal objects of art to make a room pleasingly interesting and individual. However, to keep from adding too much, it is necessary to remind ourselves of the fact that the mere process of living involves equipment or "things."

In planning what you will use on a dresser top, a desk, or a coffee table, remember that you will add things the moment you enter a room. Not only will you bring them with you, you will get them out of cupboards and drawers. Your cosmetics, your mail, the daily paper, the telephone book, the note pad and pencil, and your school books, all will be constantly in use, and space for them must be planned or you will have to clear a space to accommodate them. You don't want a room to look bare when you walk into it, but neither do you want to crowd things together in order to use the room. So ask yourself before you add one thing, "Is this object needed? Does the room look bare without it?" If the answer is "Yes," use it. If it is "No," take something away before you add anything more.

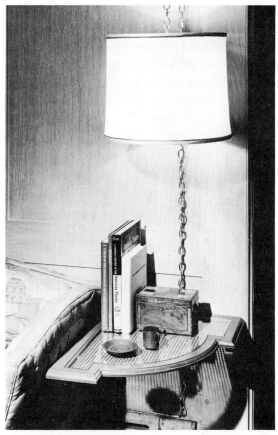

A hanging lamp above a small wall shelf leaves space on the shelf for the placement of other accessories.

According to interest. There is a Chinese axiom which says that native jade can only be polished by stones from other mountains and a biblical statement about lifting your eyes to the hills from whence cometh your strength. Literature implies that everyone needs the enrichment that comes with distance and perspective; it is this quality which you can put into a room with objects of art.

Your desk should always have one thing on it that is so beautiful that it will take your mind to other worlds. It may be a carved wooden figure that reminds you of a wonderful vacation day or a beautiful shell that takes your mind to the quiet of a remote seashore where you walked and dreamed. A glimpse

Courtesy Wallcoverings Council, Incorporated

A well-arranged harmonious group of accessories such as a Chinese wall panel, simple Chinese pottery lamp and figurines, and Oriental brass box, will lend interest to an obscure corner.

of one of these will give you the perspective of a look into the distance, and perhaps you will return to your studies refreshed and with a new insight that will speed your learning.

In the same way, the coffee table, the top of the chest, and the shelf in the bookcase, all should have their mind-stretching objects that take you to other worlds.

According to need. There are many objects of art which add greatly to your comfort. A pillow can fit into the small of your back or prop your head to the right angle. An attractive wastebasket can be an aid to neatness. Paperweights, bookends, letter openers, clipping scissors, and file boxes are needed constantly; if they are beautiful, they can also be objects of art.

According to beauty. The arrangement of objects on the top of any table or chest is an exercise in composition. The same rules of balance that apply to furniture placement apply to the placement of accessories. The same need to vary color, texture, hardness, and softness exists here. Too many figurines on a table will look cluttered. A collection of one figurine, a plant, some books, and a letter opener can have functional value as well as beauty.

A mantel shelf is a logical focal point for an entire room and should be one of the most carefully arranged areas. If the fireplace wall is informal in architectural design, the decoration of the mantel shelf should be informal. If, however, the fireplace wall is formal in balance, the arrangement can be either informal or formal depending on your resources.

Mirrors increase the size of a small room or widen a hall exactly as though you had opened a window; hang them low enough to be used comfortably and to reflect interesting objects in the room, and frame them to blend with the room furnishings. Pillows should harmonize in color and texture with the sofa, the bed, or the chair they rest on, and they should be grouped carefully as a part of the total composition. Books and magazines can be stored so as to add to the room decoration, or they can be a messy cluster. Learn to take advantage of their rich bindings and varied shapes while you place them for practical use.

Plants and Flowers

Every room in the house, and especially the dining area, can be beautified with flowers or growing plants or vines. Conversely, there is nothing more unattractive than sad wilted flowers or a dried-up plant fighting for its life in an unsuitable receptacle. Plants should be strong and vigorous, large enough to decorate importantly but not overwhelmingly. Plant containers should be easily movable as the needs of the plant may dictate. Remember to use plants or flowers that are geared to the ability of the one who cares for them. If you are not skilled, use plants sparingly so they can be replaced without too much expense.

According to placement. The first step in using flowers or greens is to decide their placement. This, in turn, will determine the container, the size, and the shape of the finished arrangement.

314

Terrarium planters
need little or no spe-
cial care once plant
growth is well estab-
lished.

315

(A) A simple, undecorated, wide-necked container takes no attention away from the flowers and allows them to spread out naturally. (B) A terra cotta pot, when scrubbed clean and set in its matching saucer, is both functional and beautiful as a container. (C) A simple, low container such as a pyrex or aluminum pan makes a convenient container for flowers set in a frog. Interest can be added if the floral arrangement is placed on a trivet. (D) A distortion of nature, such as the back of an animal, detracts from the interest of the plants or flowers it is to contain. (E) A narrow-necked vase, especially a decorated one, should be used **only** as an art object. Its beauty is ruined by the addition of flowers. (F) A low, ornate bowl allows flowers to be arranged well, but fights them for attention.

In the living room. The mantel shelf, the coffee table, the piano, the end tables, and the chests are all good places for medium-sized plants or bouquets. In some rooms it is possible to stand a big plant or floral arrangement on the floor near a window.

In the dining room. The size of the dining room table makes it seem bare if there is nothing on it between meals and any meal becomes more attractive if the table is decorated with flowers or a plant. Between-meal and buffet table decorations can be as generous in size and height as the table will permit, but any decoration for the center of a table around which people will be seated must be low so it does not block the view or conversation of those around it.

In the personal rooms. Plants and flowers for bedrooms, dens, bathrooms, and kitchens must be considered from a practical point of view. Plants for kitchen and bath must be chosen to thrive on heat and steam. Plants for bedrooms should withstand cool nights and those for dens may need to adjust to a lack of sunlight. A careful selection of the type of plant for each room can result in especially beautiful houseplants. Talk to a good florist before you make any decisions. He has the information necessary for wise plant selection at his fingertips.

According to container. An important factor in the use of plants and flowers is the selection of the container. It, like the frame on a picture, must be simple in form and undemanding in color or decoration so that attention is focused on the flowers or plant rather than on the container that holds them. For example, strong green may be a poor color choice for a container, because it may make the foliage look dull, or yellow, or sickly by comparison.

Glass. Water-growing plants and cut flowers look especially well in shallow bowls or glass containers that show off the interesting stems or root structure. Such different containers as a low serving dish, a mayonnaise jar, a glass battery box, a fish bowl, a table glass, or a goblet will work beautifully.

Pottery. The simple terracotta pots that come from the greenhouse are suitable for most plants. Their color, texture, and shape are excellent, and they have a hole in the bottom which is essential for proper drainage. Such pots may be scrubbed clean and used as received or they may be set into containers of wood, metal, or china which may be more distinctively decorative.

According to arrangement. The world has learned much about beauty from the Orient, especially in decorating with foliage and flower arrangements. The basic principle is to use as few flowers and as little foliage as possible but to make each flower and leaf important. Many excellent books have been written on this subject which you will find very helpful.

Foliage plants, flowering plants, cut foliage, flowers all have a tremendous range of possibilities. Study the flower arrangements done by members of your local garden club. Get books on this art at the library and make it a point to notice flower arrangements and the use of cut foliage and foliage plants in model rooms arranged by recognized decorators. Train your eye to see where they have used arrangements that are formal or informal, casual or stylized. Frequently this is determined by the flowers or foliage you have to work with; but a skilled hand can make a bunch of field daisies formal or a bunch of camellias informal, depending on the need of the moment.

THE BUYING OF ACCESSORIES

If you apply the tests of good accessories, you will be able to evaluate and buy accessories no matter where you find them. You will be able to select a well-designed vase in a junk shop with the same confidence you would feel if it came from the best shop in town. You will be able to evaluate the strange and lovely things in distant countries as well as the more familiar objects in your own home town. Knowledge frees you from the tyranny of place, of prestige, and of price. It admits you to the fraternity of those who enjoy the beauties of the past as well as the present. Museums, art institutes, antique shops all become familiar places where you go to study and to admire. The things you learn there will keep you growing in your awareness of beauty everywhere. Since no room is ever finished, and since your rooms will change with each

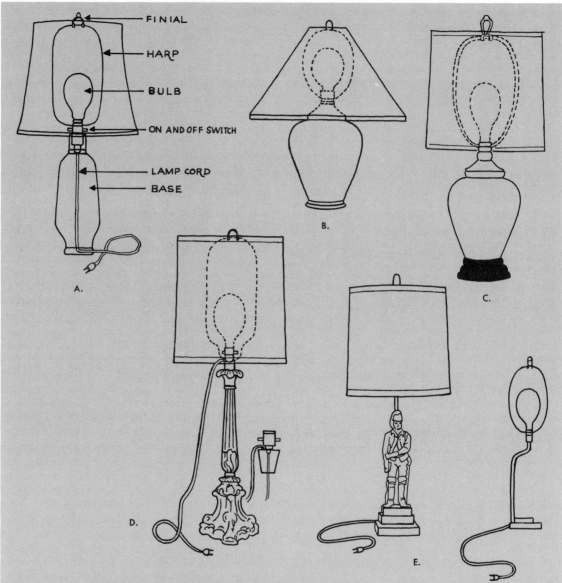

FINIAL

HARP

BULB

ON AND OFF SWITCH

LAMP CORD

BASE

A.

B.

C.

D.

E.

(A) Many of the parts that make up a lamp are available at hardware stores. (B and C) A poorly designed lamp of good quality can be completely re-modeled by the addition of a black wood Oriental base, a larger harp, and a well-designed shade. Such changes show off the real beauty of the old lamp base. (D) Any candlestick can be changed into a lamp by using a converter kit available at most hardware stores. (E) A favorite figurine or a potted plant can be made into a decorative lamp by mounting it on a wired base.

An unusual background for pictures is formed by a split bamboo shade which covers poorly spaced windows on one wall. Pole lamps with special fixtures inserted into the lamp track give support and light for the pictures.

Courtesy Better Homes and Gardens, © Meredith Corporation, 1967

change in your family situation, you will constantly be replacing your accessories with those which meet your new needs. Some things you admired a year ago will not satisfy you this year; sell them to a secondhand shop or give them to a rummage sale to make room for the more beautiful things you admire today.

In buying any accessory, never hesitate to admit to yourself or a sales person that there is a limit to the money you can spend. But never put a limit on your mind, your creativity, or your ingenuity. In the field of accessories, these qualities will be more important, perhaps, than in any other, and your knowledge will open doors that people with considerably more money and less knowledge can never enter.

Pictures

If you love pictures, you should start now to collect a file of them. You can buy art magazines and clip reproductions from them. Some calendars specialize in reproductions of fine paintings. Good reproductions are available inexpensively at museums and art institutes. You can buy originals at art fairs where young artists sell their work quite reasonably. If you

Courtesy Ebony Magazine

Many reproduction of fine paintings are registered in the Arts Section of the Library of Congress.

319

do this, you will always have pictures on hand and ready for framing.

According to quality. If you love pictures, you will be primarily concerned with the quality of the picture as a whole rather than with color, size, subject matter, or framing. Fine pictures, either reproductions or originals, add permanent beauty to your surroundings that cannot be otherwise achieved; you will always want them. You will also want pictures that have personal or family interest value.

According to color. Once standards of quality have been met, color becomes important. An uninteresting picture that "picks up" the colors you have already chosen for your furnishings will remain an uninteresting picture, while a room color plan which enhances the colors of a well-loved picture will be interestingly warm and personal. There are some cases, however, when a well-loved room color scheme seems to require a "blue" picture to complete the room. In such cases, wait to find a picture that you truly love which has the color you desire.

According to size. The size of a picture in relation to the space where it will hang affects the importance of the picture in the room. It is dangerous to guess at sizes. Often you will find that pictures seem to shrink on the wall and that you can use a bigger picture than you had first thought possible.

Measure the area available before you start to shop. When you find a picture that seems to be the proper size, take measurements of the picture including the frame. When you get home, cut out a brown paper shape of your measured size and tape it to the wall in the place where you intend to hang the picture. If the size is not right and if you are considering a reproduction, you may be able to find the same picture in a more appropriate size. If you cannot find the same picture in an appropriate size, you may try a picture grouping that will be suitable to the space. Or you may need to continue your search for a well-liked picture which also suits the wall space for which it is intended.

According to subject matter. Pictures according to subject matter may be originals or reproductions, they may be scenic views or portraits, and they may be in any of the media. You may find that a local artist has painted a favorite scene in a manner you enjoy. If you are this fortunate, you will have a picture that is valuable for both personal and artistic reasons. It will be a joy to you all the rest of your life. You will also want a constantly changing assortment of photographs of your family and friends, of places you have been, and of things you have done. Put them in frames with removable backs and group them on the walls of a hall, your bedroom, or a family room.

Lamps

You can begin the gradual accumulation of beautiful lamps immediately. Any beautiful object, such as a vase, a candlestick, a figurine, which comes your way can be made into a lamp of great individuality. There are many ready-made wiring devices and lamp shades on the market which enable you to make such individual lamps. Fine lamps that have been discarded because they were too small can be found in secondhand shops. By fitting them with a larger harp or a riser and a new shade, they can be made into taller, useful lamps which may exactly fit your needs.

As you shop for a table lamp, place those you are considering on a table the height of the one it will be used on in your home. If possible, move the table next to a chair or sofa that closely resembles the one you have in your home. In this manner, you will be able to be sure that your selection is right for your use. The more you know about furnishing a home, the more care you will take to check your judgment against facts.

According to style. Lamps may be traditional or contemporary, informal or formal. Some lamps are so simply designed that they adjust to several different types of rooms.

According to size. Try to take a tape measure along to check in feet and inches the exact size of a lamp. The high ceilings in most shops are apt to dwarf even a tall lamp and make it impossible for you to judge its height without measuring it. If the base of a table lamp is large, it must be used only on a table large enough to accommodate it and other accessories without crowding.

Courtesy Better Homes and Gardens, © Meredith Corporation, 1964

The beauty of a lamp is affected by its use in the room and its relationship to other furnishings. Which arrangement is more harmonious? Why?

Courtesy Drexel Furniture Company

The careful placement of pictures in relation to the lamp, the importance given to the foliage plant, and the discriminating choice of objects of art emphasize the graciousness of this formal room.

According to intensity of light. Several methods have been devised to reduce the glare and diffuse the light of the high wattage bulbs. Some of them have been especially recommended by lighting experts. The tag of approval will give you a standard by which to guide your judgment of other lamps that give good light but do not have the tag.

Small Objects of Art That Primarily Add Beauty

If you buy art objects such as figurines, fragments, china, glass, or carvings in regular retail stores or antique shops, the cost will be high. It is hard to find objects of true art quality in tourist souvenir shops. However, if you train your eye to recognize beauty, and if you enjoy prowling around in small shops off the beaten path, you may find great beauty at surprisingly low prices. You may be able to see value where others do not, and you can find a treasure that will enrich your life for years to come at a price which is a true bargain. Never be afraid of a crack or a chip. Some of the most valuable pieces in museums are mere fragments of beauty from another time.

Furnishings That Add Decoration

Nowadays, in our affluent society, we have some furnishings that are primarily decorative but that also have functional value.

Screens. Floor screens, which are so practical, should add beauty no matter how utilitarian their function. Inexpensive ones made of three, four, or five panels of wallboard hinged together can be bought in drapery departments. With ingenuity these can be upholstered in fabric; decorated with wallpaper, maps, or interesting documents; or painted in plain colors or designs. The more expensive shutter screens can be bought in furniture stores. They can also be made of antique shutters bought from a salvage company or antique store.

Pillows. Pillows which are bought to add comfort to a sofa may be found in drapery departments. Such pillows should be covered with well-tailored, attractive fabrics that blend well with the other fabrics of the room. Avoid the fancy pillows which cannot be leaned against and which do not harmonize in tone with the room. The most individual pillows are those made at home, using coverings that match or harmonize with the draperies, the

Pillows should harmonize with the upholstery of the sofa both in texture and in shape. The print upholstery is complemented by the smooth texture and formal shapes of the quilted pillows. The rough textured square pillows are more appropriate for a less formal room.

upholstery of the sofa or chairs, or the bedspreads.

Mirrors. Because mirrors are both functional and decorative and can be bought in fairly large sizes at reasonable prices, they are an excellent, comparatively inexpensive way to decorate a hall or a bedroom. Begin by testing what size will be right for the room. Cut several different sizes out of brown paper and tape them to the wall to test your decision. You may find a ready made mirror to meet your needs. For a more individual mirror, find a picture frame in the correct size in a secondhand shop. They usually have quantities in every possible size and style for a reasonable price. Only after you have the frame in your hand are you ready to go to the glass company and have a mirror cut to fit. Make sure it is plate glass that will give a clear reflection. The difference in cost between a plate glass mirror and a window glass mirror is usually not enough to compensate for the irritation of a wavy, distorted reflection.

Books. If you love books, you will easily acquire a large collection of them. You may find

them in secondhand stores and the sale tables in the book shops of big cities. As your collection grows, you may buy more slowly and spend more money for each book. No matter where or how you find them, your books should reflect your interests and your growth as well as adding great beauty to your home.

Plants and Flowers

The world of the garden or the greenhouse is a delightful one where money goes unexpectedly far. Fruit and flower seeds grow into beautiful plants and flowers. Tiny inexpensive plants grow with care to become important in size and beauty. Make your money stretch by buying a flowering plant which lasts for weeks and yet costs no more than the cut flowers that wither in a few days. Look for the less popular plants. Often they are half hidden behind plants that are in constant demand or they may be forgotten on a lower shelf. Frequently these plants are charmingly different and individual; they are always less expensive than the currently most popular plants.

Accessories may sometimes solve an architectural defect. This mirror, set in an old picture frame, has decorative importance. No one would suspect that it hides a problem window.

Courtesy Better Homes and Gardens, © Meredith Corporation, 1966

An old picture frame for a mirror, a long coffee table, and a well-arranged high bouquet may provide a sense of welcome as you enter a formal home.

Courtesy Better Homes and Gardens, © Meredith Corporation, 1966

A small bouquet of fresh or artificial flowers adds a mind-relaxing touch of the outdoors to this study area.

There are so many types of plants and flowers that, obviously, it is impossible to properly catalog them all. But there are a few general groupings of different types that are common, inexpensive, and beautiful.

Water- and earth-growing plants. Sturdy, bushy vines such as philodendron, grape ivy, and the sweet potato vine can be grown in water in almost sunless rooms. Small, fast-growing flower bulbs such as the inexpensive paper-white narcissus, daffodils, and colorful narcissus will grow rapidly in water after a few weeks in a dark closet. Their fresh beauty and perfume will put new vitality into the most sterile room. Tiny fruit plants can be grown from the seeds of the dates, lemons, oranges, and grapefruit which may be in your refrigerator right now. Quite a few of one kind, planted in a pot of earth and watered, will produce interestingly bushy little plants. These can be used to make any dining table or end table interesting and attractive.

Cut flowers . To many people, cut flowers mean a gift box from the florist. Yet field daisies, black-eyed Susans, or thistles arranged with interesting green leaves will add a lovely note in the dullest room. Learn to see flowers where they grow, whether it be in a vacant lot or along a country roadside. A well-arranged bouquet made up of the "weed-of-the-week" and driftwood can be a note of great beauty. Many states have strong conservation laws; be sure that the "free" flowers you find are truly free to be picked.

Bare branches. Bare branches cut from a tree or bush in the winter are another source of inexpensive beauty. They will form a beautiful pattern against an otherwise plain and uninteresting wall; if they are put in water, the heat of the room will soon bring out the soft fresh green that is so thrillingly springlike. If you have cut a flowering bush or tree, you may have the additional bonus of flowers earlier than the natural season.

Artificial flowers and greens. For many years, artificial flowers and greens were anything but satisfying to the person who loved the real ones. But in recent years, there has been a complete change. Plastics and new manufacturing processes have produced flowers and greens that are difficult to distinguish from the real plants, even at close range. They are especially convincing if they are combined with some real foliage. Good artificial flowers are expensive, but if you use them for brief periods as you would use real flowers, and if you store them carefully between uses, they will last for years. Such extended use may well turn them into an inexpensive accessory of great value.

LEARNING EXPERIENCES

1. Define the meaning of the following phrases as used in this chapter: personalized accessories, functional accessories, and objects of art.
2. Start a portfolio of pictures of lamps clipped from magazines and newspapers that have bases that are (a) urn shaped, (b) cylinder shaped, (c) vase shaped, and (d) candlestick shaped.
3. Find two pictures showing lamps that harmonize in style and size with the furniture they serve and two that do not.
4. After studying the lamps shown with furniture styles in Chapter 12, report to the class the type of room in which one of each of the types of lamps clipped for question 2 could be used appropriately.
5. Find a good reproduction of a watercolor, etching, oil painting, or wood block and frame it, selecting from the stock of inexpensive ready-made frames in a chain store.
6. Tell where you would hang photographs of your friends or relatives and why.
7. Based on the principles listed in this chapter, bring to class pictures of ash trays, pillows, bookends, and vases which you think are functionally and effectively designed and indicate the type of room in which each could be used appropriately.
8. Collect a group of natural objects, such as leaves, shells, fossils, or butterflies. Mount them on dark-colored cardboard panels with holes placed in upper corners so they can be hung in groups on a wall and changed as the collection grows.
9. Cut out six or eight rectangles of various sizes representing pictures, and arrange them in a rectangular grouping (following the instruction in the line drawing on page 309) that could be hung over a 72-inch sofa.
10. Cut out four rectangles 7 by 9 inches representing pictures and one rectangle 22 by 24 inches representing a three-shelf bookshelf. Arrange them in a grouping to be put over a studio couch.

17 Tableware and

Household Linens

THE TABLEWARE and household linens you choose for your home should express your own personal taste. Your choices should also be based on the factors affecting your life today, such as shortened housekeeping time or fewer formal meals. Because tableware is used two or three times a day, your choice in this area may be a more constant source of joy or frustration than other furnishings in your home. It should be thoroughly studied.

FLATWARE

The term "flatware" has replaced "silverware" as an inclusive word meaning the knives, forks, and spoons used at the table, because several other metals are now being used most effectively in their construction. Which metal you choose should be influenced by its specific qualities and how it will affect your household work, your comfort, and your satisfaction. Fortunately, each metal is available in a tremendous range of qualities and designs.

Types Available

Most flatware is made of silver, stainless steel, or Dirylite. Silver is available in many weights

of either solid or plated construction. Stainless steel comes in many weights but only in solid construction. It may have a bright finish or a dull pewter-like finish. Dirylite comes in one quality in solid construction.

Sterling silver. Sterling silver in any weight is 92.5 percent pure silver. It has heirloom quality and can be handed down from one generation to another. The imprinted word STERLING on each piece is your guarantee, and the weight, as well as the design, is the indication of its value. The more sterling silver is used the more beautiful the finish becomes, but it requires care to keep it in shining condition. Tarnish-proof boxes and bags help cut down on the time required for this care, but the oxidizing effects of certain foods and the natural dimming of the shine from contact with the air necessitate polishing. Sterling silver is so expensive that many people feel it is not a good investment unless you plan to use it at least once a day.

Plated silver. The words "double," "triple," and "quadruple" plating indicate the thickness of the silver coating that covers the base or core metal of each piece. Some manufacturers

An attractively set table does not need to be very expensive. The relationship between the various elements is more important than cost.

Courtesy Extension Service, University of Maine

imbed cubes of silver at points of heavy wear to lengthen the life of plated silver. Many manufacturers use the same stainless steel blades used in sterling silver flatware, so the danger of wear-off at the knife edge has been removed. However, the more diligently plated silver is polished, the sooner it will wear out. Check carefully, therefore, the guarantee of service and the reputation of the manufacturer when buying this type of flatware.

Stainless steel. Stainless steel is a solid alloy composed of steel, nickel, and chromium which wears endlessly and does not tarnish or dull with use or age. The range of weights and designs now available is nearly equal to that of sterling. One of its great attractions, its carefree quality, adjusts well to the demands of the present-day household.

Dirylite. The metal called Dirylite is a solid gold-colored metal alloy. It tarnishes somewhat but holds its shine and its color with less care than silver. Because it is a solid metal, there is no wear-out and it therefore is a lifetime purchase.

Novelty handles. Flatware also comes in a variety of novelty handles with stainless steel

The teaspoon, luncheon fork and knife, dessert spoon, salad fork, and butter knife are the most used pieces of flatware. The dotted lines indicate the dinner fork, dinner knife, and cream soup spoon, which are more limited in use.

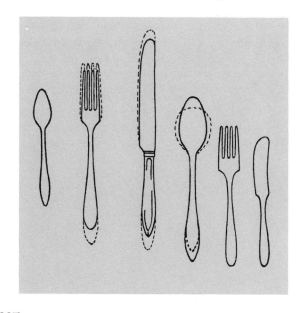

Timelessness marks the silver and the linen on this table, allowing china and glass to supply the novelty that can change with the course or meal.

These four basic handle outlines are used for both contemporary and traditional designs of flatware.

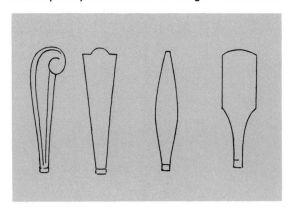

or other metal forming the knife blade, fork tines, and spoon bowl. China, wood, ivory, bamboo, pearl, and plastic handles are most common. Each must be evaluated according to how it will stand wear and the high-temperature water of either a dishwasher or a sterilizing rinse.

Designs

It is important that you not only consider the types of metal available, but that you realize the wide range of flatware designs available in each. For this reason, it is advisable to start a file of these designs in all metals. Study them until you become familiar with all the styles before making any choice.

Contour. The general outline or shape of each piece, its weight, and the way it balances and feels in your hand should be important considerations when you choose flatware. Before your final decision is made, actually lift each piece, hold it, and go through the motions of using it. You will quickly find that the weight and shape of one contour will be far more enjoyable than another. A well-designed piece will feel strong and well balanced in your hand. Some beautiful flatware is absolutely plain. It depends on its contour for its total decorative impact.

Decoration. Most flatware makes its decorative impact by a subtle combination of contour and decoration, and the skill of the craftsman shows up immediately in the blending of the two. As a result, the first test of good decoration is how it has been harmonized with the structural shape of the handle. A good design seems an integral part of the shape. A poor design is sprinkled around haphazardly. The placement of such a design does not harmonize with the contour.

Style. Your choice of the style of your flatware will establish the general style of all your tableware. Many designs can be used with almost any style whether it be contemporary or traditional, informal or formal. Other designs are quite specifically geared to one particular style or type. Your choice of style is a personal matter. Do not hurry your choice. Study the designs with an open mind for several months to test your judgment with time and familiarity. If the pattern is good in quality, you will come to like it better each time you see it.

How to Buy

You may, like some girls, begin to buy flatware with the first money you earn. Friends and relatives often are glad to give you individual pieces in your pattern, feeling that each gift has permanent value. Flatware may be the most expensive portion of your tableware. If you choose your pattern and begin to buy your flatware now, you are choosing the basic style for all your tableware, so make your selection carefully.

Method. Most good designs produced by reputable houses can be bought both in open stock and in place settings. If you buy place settings, you can immediately serve a certain number of people adequately. If you buy by the piece from open stock, it will probably take more time to accumulate place settings, and the total cost may be higher, but individual purchases can be made more frequently, since less money is required for each purchase. Your decision as to how many place settings to buy will depend on how many people you want to be able to entertain at one time.

Choice of pieces. The decision as to which pieces of flatware you will buy should be made on the basis of multiple use. For example, an oval bowl soup spoon can be used for breakfast food and dessert as well as soup; a round bowl soup spoon or cream soup spoon is used only for soup. Luncheon-sized knives and forks are appropriate for all meals, but the dinner size is large and seems appropriate only for dinner. Whenever possible, it is wise to buy as many as possible of the dual service pieces rather than single-purpose flatware.

Variety in type. There is a growing tendency to use a novelty type of flatware for a separate course, such as fruit or cheese and crackers at the end of a meal, or for coffee in the living room. When eggs are standard on the breakfast menu, some families use breakfast flatware that will not be discolored by them. Special variety flatware may appeal to you either as a work saver or for the pleasure of variety.

Comparative cost. An important consideration in planning what you will buy is how much it will cost. The price range in flatware is great. Take time to check catalogs, jewelry shops, and china houses carefully and figure out what you would have to invest to serve eight or ten people before you make your decision.

DINNERWARE

Your choice of dinnerware—your second step in choosing tableware—is as thrilling and involved as is your choice of flatware. Dinnerware may be bought in metal, fine china, earthenware, pottery, or plastic. The range of shapes, styles, colors, and decoration is dazzling, and the price range is equally wide. The material of which it is made has great bearing on the relative permanence of your

The curving lines of the silver, glassware, and china harmonize well with the circular mats in this table setting.

Courtesy 1847 Rogers Brothers Silverplate

choice. Consequently, the cost of replacement because of chips and cracks should be considered as you make your decision.

Types Available

In early periods, gold, silver, and pewter were the only materials used for tankards and plates; they are still used occasionally and effectively. But to most people, the term "dinnerware" means some form of ceramic material. Ceramic dinnerware reached Europe from China, which explains our general name "China" for this type of dinnerware, regardless of where it is produced.

Chinaware. The finest white clay, when shaped delicately and fired at an extremely high temperature, is called china or chinaware. It is almost translucent when held to the light. It is highly durable, chip-resistant, and nonporous, and has a bell-like tone when struck. It is quite expensive. When the white clay is mixed with crushed bone, as was first done in England, the product is called bone china. Porcelain gets its name from the Italian

word "porcellana"—the name for a pearl shell. Fine chinaware has heirloom qualities.

Earthenware. Slightly coarser clay shaped in slightly heavier pieces and fired at a slightly lower temperature than chinaware is called earthenware. It is opaque, somewhat more porous than chinaware, and is sometimes called semi-vitreousware. It is more subject to chipping and breaking than china, and it has a flatter tone when struck. It is less expensive than china but still quite costly in its best quality. It has a wide range of qualities, many of which are extremely and lastingly beautiful.

Pottery. A much coarser clay, formed into considerably heavier shapes than earthenware and fired at a low temperature, is called pottery. It is susceptible to chipping and breaking, and its finish, even after glazing, is apt to be rather rough and porous. Its general tone is charmingly informal and provincial, but with hard use, it will have to be replaced frequently.

Plastic ware. When first produced, plastic ware was an economy dinnerware planned to meet the most rugged conditions. It was made

Increasing interest in outdoor eating, as well as casual indoor meals, makes a well-designed plastic ware a practical tableware.

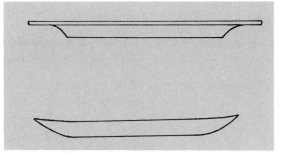

Both contemporary and traditional china use plate contours of the flange style (top) and the coupé style (bottom).

Contemporary cup shapes (bottom row) vary only slightly from the traditional (top row).

of melamine. Plastic ware has been gradually improved and beautified to the point where it is available in a wide range of shapes and styles. It has found great popularity in homes where children help with the work and breakage might otherwise be very high. Most of it can withstand the high temperature of dishwashers or a boiling water rinse. Although it will not break, it can be cracked by dropping, scratched by knives with serrated edges, and stained by food.

Designs

The artistic quality that goes into the shape and decoration of dinnerware is almost as important as its material. So here also it might be well to start a file of patterns so you can study them over a period of time and not be tempted to make a hasty selection.

Contour of plates. The variation in the contour of plates is wide, but in general, the shapes divide into two classifications: the coupe, without a lip or flat edge; and the rim, with a flat edge or rim to hold while serving. The unbroken line of the coupe plate seems contemporary, whereas the rim plate seems more traditional in appearance. Variations in the rim plate style are the fluted rim, the shaped rim, and the molded edge rim. The width of the rim in relation to the center varies greatly.

Contour of cups and bowls. The general contour of cups and bowls is rounded, fluted, or straight-lined. The overall design is either footed or plain. The contemporary styles frequently incorporate the handle into the overall contour, whereas the traditional designs usually do not.

Decoration. Much dinnerware, in both the traditional and the contemporary styles, depends for its beauty on its glaze, its contour, and its natural clay color to which is occasionally added low molded decoration. Other dinnerware depends upon a beautiful overall body color or on colored bandings. However, patterned dinnerware is most common. The pattern may be abstract, geometric, or realistic. The best patterns are placed so they relate to the contour.

Your final decision on a choice of dinnerware should be based on how each piece will look with food on it or liquid in it. Since dinnerware is used for serving food rather than for display in empty cleanness, a final judgement should be based on this factor.

How to Buy

There is an even stronger tendency toward the use of variety in dinnerware than in flatware. It is common practice, nowadays, to buy only a minimum of one pattern of dinnerware and to supplement it with glass or metal for variety. It is no longer good style to straightjacket a table with the unimaginative monotony of one single pattern used from soup bowl and saltcellar to dessert plates, cups, and coffeepot.

Many women buy a best dinnerware for dinners and party meals and an inexpensive set to use for family meals. They realize that an inexpensive set chips and breaks readily, but they rather enjoy the thought of occasionally replacing this with a new style after a period of constant use.

Place settings or open stock. Most good china patterns can be bought in place settings of a minimum number of pieces or from open stock. Fortunately, the better the china, the more assurance you have that the set will continue to be manufactured, so you will be able to add to what you have and to make replacements over a period of years. Even so, it would be well to buy extra pieces, especially of cups and large plates, as rapidly as possible to protect your investment. These are the most essential pieces and the ones that are most apt to be broken. China that can only be bought in complete sets will probably be produced for only a season or two at most.

Multiple-use pieces. Essential dinnerware pieces which should be bought first include plates in the dinner size, plates in the dessert size for desserts, luncheons, and salads, and plates in the bread and butter size. Cups and saucers are equally important, as are cereal bowls which can be used for soups, tossed salads, and some desserts.

Relationship to other tableware. Since the flatware has already been selected, check the relationship between it and a tentative selection of dinnerware. There should be a feeling of harmony between the two as to style, contour, and decoration. Check for this by arranging them together as they will be on a table. Most good shops will encourage you to do this, knowing that only in this way can you know that your selection is right.

Comparative cost. In figuring the total cost of dinnerware, get information on all grades and weigh the differences against the relative permanence of the various types of ware and the cost of replacement. Dinnerware that will craze in the high-temperature water of a dishwasher or in a boiling water rinse is a poor investment at any price.

HOLLOW WARE

The term "hollow ware" includes both the bowl and tureen type of serving dish for food and the pitcher and pot type of server for liquids. These pieces may be bought to match dinnerware, but because matching pieces are expensive, fragile, and difficult to store, they are less popular today than they were traditionally. Unmatched hollow ware which harmonizes with dinnerware adds beauty to the table, is far less expensive than matched pieces, and can be used with more than one set of china.

Types Available

Currently, popular hollow ware is unmatched. Each piece is beautifully and practically designed to harmonize with dinnerware, but also to lend interesting variety to a table or a buffet. Some of the pieces are designed in two parts: an ovenproof or flameproof part in which food can be cooked, and a second part into which the first can be slipped for table or buffet service. Others are designed with the heating element incorporated so that food can be prepared at one heat, and then kept at a constant temperature during an extended serving period. Most modern hollow ware is manufactured to provide for greater heat retention than is china. These serving pieces can be used effectively for any occasion.

Metal pieces. Silver, pewter, stainless steel, and aluminum used by themselves or combined with pottery, heat-resistant glassware, wood, or enameled metal, all make practical hollow ware serving pieces. Some have been available for years and others are quite new. Their durability makes them easy and practical to store and to move. Metal pieces do not need to match each other. They can be purchased gradually as the need arises and as designers' ingenuity presents the right piece for a particular need.

Glass. Glass hollow ware will be discussed further on page 334, but is mentioned here because it is frequently combined with metal or wood in hollow ware pieces. In general, glass hollow ware should harmonize with the other glassware on the table. Naturally, these pieces are less durable than most metals or wood, but they are usually less expensive.

Wood. The use of wood for trays and bowls for salads, fruits, cheese, and breads has be-

Courtesy David Douglas Company

Trays, salad sets, and snack sets should be chosen to complement your other tableware. Plastic hollow ware is especially practical for informal meals which may be served away from the table.

Courtesy 1847 Rogers Brothers Silverplate

Careful selection of china, silver, glass, and sheer embroidered organdy creates a unified table setting with a feeling of delicacy of design and texture.

come increasingly popular. The designs range from the painted and carved traditional type to the severely plain contemporary style. The durability of wood is one of its important advantages.

Pottery. The use of a pottery serving piece for some special course or food can add a very pleasing table accent. A salad bowl or a group of small dishes for serving jelly, olives, or pickles might be interestingly important in specially designed, yet harmonizing pottery serving pieces.

How to Buy

In buying, great care should be exercised to harmonize hollow ware pieces with the style and design of the dinnerware and flatware. These pieces should be considered as part of the table setting as a whole. Whether it be by color, shape, or tone, hollow ware should be tied to the entire table service to give a general unified effect. Highly colored novelty pieces, while attractive alone, seldom blend harmoniously.

GLASSWARE

Glassware is another important part of your tableware selections. One of the oldest man-made products, legend tells us that glassware was produced from the desert sands of Egypt before history was recorded and that it was considered as precious as gold or semiprecious jewels. Glassware adds height, sparkle, and exciting beauty to your table setting and should be very carefully selected.

Range Available

Glassware is available in a wide range of quality, styles, and prices. Clear plastic is also sold along with traditional glassware. Glassware designs change even more rapidly than do dinnerware patterns. But, like dinnerware, good quality glassware of a specific design is usually available in open stock for a number of years. It is wise for the interested young person to start a picture file of styles from which to make a final selection.

Types according to material. Lime glass, which was developed some five thousand years ago, is the least expensive and the most brittle glass used for tableware. Lead glass, an expensive glass which was developed in England in the seventeenth century, has great brilliance and a bell-like tone when struck. Heat-resistant glass was developed in America in 1910; it is used on the table chiefly in the form of serving dishes.

Types according to production. Tableware glass falls into categories according to the method of forming, or production. There is blown glass and pressed glass. About 250 B.C. someone discovered, almost accidentally, that glass could be blown into shapes, much as children blow soap bubbles; but like bubbles, there could be no regularity of shape or size. Some Venetian glass is still formed in this way, and its irregularity is considered its distinction and beauty.

Later on, it was found that blown glass could be controlled, to a certain extent, by blowing it into a metal form which dictated a uniform shape. Most of the blown glass on the market is formed this way. Its thickness varies slightly. Occasionally a bubble is blown into the stem to form a teardrop—a mark of beauty and quality.

As glass making methods improved, a process was invented whereby the glass was forced or pressed into a mold with a plunger. This process assured that all pieces would be of absolute uniformity. Most of our modern day tableware glass is produced by improved versions of these simple glass making processes.

Attractive glassware ranges from the very delicate to the very heavy. Either type may be both graceful and useful.

Shapes. Glasses divide according to overall shape into stemware, footed tumblers, and tumblers. They also divide according to their general style, their capacity, and their use.

Glassware for tables nowadays includes glass hollow ware, pitchers, bottles, serving bowls, glass platters and plates, individual glass bowls or sauce dishes, and glass cups and saucers. These pieces, as well as the different types of glasses, can be found in all styles—heavy or delicate, elegant or informal, traditional or contemporary.

Decoration. Glass can be decorated by adding color to the molten liquid, by blowing bubbles into the liquid, or by adding patterns to the surface of the glass. Patterns can be molded into the shape, cut, engraved, etched, or blasted into the surface, or painted on the surface. Most manufacturers produce a complete line of glassware so that the same style is available in all the table glassware, if desired.

How to Buy

Your selections of glassware must depend, first of all, on how it harmonizes with your flatware and dinnerware. To check this, actually arrange a place setting so you can try out any glassware styles that appeal to you. There should be a harmony of weight and contour, as well as a harmony of feeling in any decoration. Thus all pieces combine into a single artistic unit.

In addition, your decision to choose a certain glassware pattern should hinge on such practical matters as how it will fit into a dishwasher or how it will store in a limited shelf space. In deciding quantity, it is well to consider the danger of breakage. The more fragile the pattern, the more important it is to get several extras of each type of glass to be sure that you have the required number for a given table setting. Otherwise, you may be forced to buy an entire new set because the pattern has been discontinued.

The low centerpiece, while effective in the middle of the table, isn't strong enough to balance the table arrangement when placed against the wall. The more dramatic tall arrangement serves as a focal point in this situation.

Courtesy Better Homes and Gardens, © Meredith Corporation, 1965

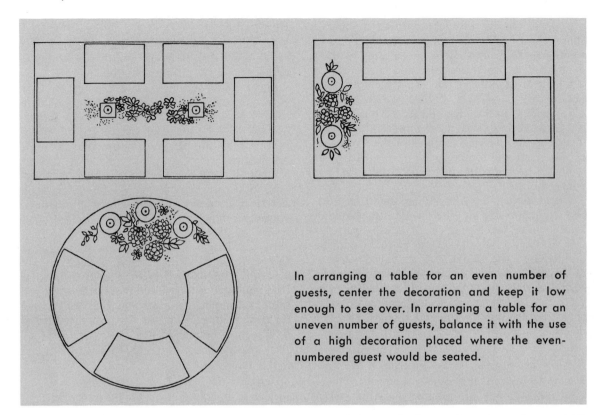

In arranging a table for an even number of guests, center the decoration and keep it low enough to see over. In arranging a table for an uneven number of guests, balance it with the use of a high decoration placed where the even-numbered guest would be seated.

TABLE SETTINGS

Setting a dining table is like composing a picture, except that the elements used are tableware and decorations. There are guides for achieving composition and balance that must be followed just as there are in placing the objects in a painting.

Placement of Tableware

The proper placement of tableware has both practical and aesthetic value. Each piece of flatware, glassware, and china is in a position that makes its use comfortable and natural, and the accurately repeated pattern at each place is beautiful and satisfying.

According to occasion. Established guides for table settings are simple and easily followed for each meal and for each type of occasion. As you use and memorize these patterns, they will become automatic, and therefore easy to follow.

According to seating. The spacing of people at a round table is simply a matter of even spacing around the entire circumference. If there are just two or three people, they can be grouped and the group balanced by decorations. If, however, the table is rectangular, the situation is quite different.

If the number is even. An even number of people can be seated in a balanced arrangement around four sides, or opposite each other on two sides of a table. The decoration, in that case, can be centered or evenly divided between the two ends.

If the number is uneven. In this situation, the extra person can be seated at one end of the table. The other end of the table is balanced with offsetting decorations.

Decoration

The use of one note of decoration as a part of each table setting should be as standard as the tableware itself. This need not be difficult or expensive if you learn to recognize your resources.

A perishable accent. The use of cut or growing flowers, plants, fruit, vegetables, or even

336

African violets grouped closely on a Lazy Susan provide a fresh and constantly changing centerpiece for family meals.

A centerpiece made of fruit can be used both at mealtime and when the table is not in use.

A table or desk takes on an appealing quality when a cherished object of art is combined with a flowering plant.

a newly baked and frosted cake set high on a compote can be a delightfully fresh note of decoration that will interest everyone. It will be a focal point that gives accent to the entire table and makes the meal a thing of pleasure rather than a physical necessity to satisfy hunger.

An object of art. When there is no fresh object available, an object of art can serve beautifully as a center of interest. It can be a small figure, a group of lovely shells, leaves, or pine cones, a chunk of coral or anything else that has become a family treasure. It may be used alone or combined with a little foliage for a softer effect.

Special lighting. Concentrated light from a group of candles or a candlestick lamp that highlights the table and allows the rest of the room to lie in shadow will add glamour and make a simple meal seem like a party occasion.

Sherwin-Williams Company

A tablecloth which matches the kitchen curtains adds a bright note to family meals.

TABLE LINEN

The term "table linen" includes everything that is used either to cover the table or as napkins. Until rather recently, most fine table coverings were made from flax fibers; this consistent use of linen cloth has furnished the name, table linens, to all table covers no matter what material is used.

Types Available

The complete covering of a table was standard procedure for many years. This is probably still the most common way to prepare the table for a meal, but in recent years there has been a growing trend toward using partial covers, exposing the beauty of the wood and sparing the housewife the care of large tablecloths.

Tablecloths. Fine tablecloths, woven or lace, of linen or rayon, are used without question for formal occasions such as weddings, anniversaries, and other important occasions. The color is almost always white or ivory, but some few cloths now come in delicate pastel colors. The size of the cloth is determined by the size of the table. Authorities usually agree that a cloth should hang down at least 6 or 7 inches on all sides. For very formal occasions and for a buffet table, an even greater overhang is desirable.

Because many people still feel that a tablecloth is necessary even for family dinners, there is a demand for a wide range of quality, type, and price in what are commonly called every day table covers. Fortunately, there are new finishes which minimize their care. Also, there is a wide range of plastic-coated and all-plastic tablecloths available. These need only be wiped off with a damp cloth to be absolutely clean for the next meal.

Luncheon and breakfast cloths. Because they are smaller than tablecloths and therefore more easily maintained, luncheon and breakfast cloths have retained their popularity. The range of size, quality, and type is almost endless. They can be bought with or without matching napkins.

Card table covers. There is no longer one standard card table size or shape, so card table covers also vary in size. It is important to measure your own table before you buy covers for it. It also is important to consider the room

A colorful printed tablecloth is very attractive for a small table.

The use of plastic and other types of washable materials for place mats is increasingly popular today.

Courtesy International Sterling

in which the table will be used as well as the tableware. There is a growing trend toward the use of a wide range of fabrics and colors that are specifically harmonized with the furnishings of the room. This type of cover is frequently made by hand and can be very personal in decoration.

Place mats. Individual place mats, (usually about 11 by 17 inches in size), are made in rectangular, round, oval, and wedge shapes. They have been responsible for one of the major revolutions in the handling of a dining-room table. Made of everything from plastic to linen, and from cork to lace, they make it easier to maintain a higher standard of cleanliness than ever before. No longer need the spot where Johnnie dropped the jam return to the table for the next meal. Instead, Johnnie's place mat can be replaced by a fresh one, and the entire table setting is once more completely clean with a minimum of housekeeping effort.

Place mats adjust to tables and counters of all sizes and shapes. Since place mats require

less yardage than full tablecloths, you may be able to buy a higher quality fabric for your budgeted amount.

Side runners. These are another form of table linen which is easier to handle than a tablecloth. Side runners are most attractive on any rectangular table. They usually are made about 12 or 13 inches wide and approximately the length of the table.

Fabric napkins. Needless to say, a white linen napkin will probably be the quality mark of a dinner or of any special occasion for many years. Cloth napkins in different fabrics and colors, in plain and in patterned fabrics, are currently in style. When used, these colors or patterns should be carefully blended to each other, to the tablecloth or place mats, and to the tableware, or they will look unrelated and ruin the general unified effect.

Paper napkins. Paper napkins are becoming more and more popular for family meals. They are inexpensive, save labor, and make it possible to have napkins that are absolutely clean at each meal. There has been a great improvement in the quality of paper napkins in recent years.

Buying Table Linens

Colored table coverings or napkins must be carefully harmonized with the color of the dinnerware and glassware. If the dinnerware is patterned, the rule of isolating pattern with plain makes it necessary to use plain colored or plain white table linen. If the dinnerware is plain or banded, you may wish to use patterned cloths or mats.

HOUSEHOLD LINEN

The term "household linen" includes bath and bed linens and all linens used in the kitchen as well. At one time linen was the preferred fabric, but it has been replaced largely by cotton because of its lower cost and easy care qualities.

Sheets and Pillowcases

The same creative designing that has brought such variety to table linen has also brought variety to sheets and pillowcases. The need for housekeeping shortcuts has changed the shape of sheets, and it also has dictated the introduction of new fabrics and finishes.

Fabrics. Cotton is the preferred fabric for sheets and pillowcases. It looks fresh for a long time and feels crisply cool to the touch.

The highest quality of cotton is called percale. It is the lightest to handle and to iron, and it feels silky smooth. The fibers from which percale is made are longer, more smoothly combed, and more closely woven than are those in cheaper cotton fabric. Thread counts will approximate 180 or 200 per square inch. (Thread counts tell the total number of crosswise and lengthwise threads in a square inch of sheeting.)

Muslin sheeting is made from shorter, rougher fibers which are more loosely woven than percale. Thread counts will approximate 112, 128, or 140 per square inch. The fabric is heavier to handle and wrinkles more quickly than percale. Muslin is sometimes filled with a starchy substance to make it look finer and smoother in the store.

There is a growing trend to combine polyester fibers with cotton to produce a material

Courtesy Springmaid

Plain white or monogrammed bed linen is still the most common choice. Many people enjoy having a few sets of decorated or bordered sheets and pillowcases for variety.

for sheets and pillowcases that has a durable-finish. Rayon combined with cotton produces a sheet with a soft, smooth feel. Wrinkle-resistant finishes are also gaining in popularity. Eventually, these qualities may become as important in bed linens as in wearing apparel.

Type and size. There are two types of sheets: flat and fitted (or contoured). A fitted bottom sheet with corners that are gusseted, or gathered with elastic, makes for easy bed-making. Sleeping is more comfortable, because the sheet is constantly taut. A fitted top sheet is available. Because it cannot be reversed to even the wear, it is not as popular as are fitted bottom sheets. Fitted sheets are harder to iron, to fold, and to store than are flat sheets.

The standard flat sheets should be bought 24 inches wider and longer than the mattress in order to allow ample tuck-in. Pillowcases

341

CHART 8. HOUSEHOLD LINEN

TABLE LINEN

Tablecloths
Full size: extend 6″ below edge of table
Stock sizes:

    36 by 54 inches 54 by 54 inches 72 by 90 inches
    45 by 54 inches 64 by 72 inches 90 by 108 inches

Place mats: stock size, 11 by 17 inches
Breakfast cloths   Bridge table covers

Napkins
Fabric, stock sizes:
  dinner: 24 by 24 inches
  breakfast: 18 by 18 inches
  luncheon: 15 by 15 inches
  tea: 12 by 12 inches
  cocktail: 7 by 7 or 5 by 8 inches
Paper — to save work — for family meals

Fabrics
Damask: widths — 36, 42, 54, 58, 64, 72, 80, 90 inches
Pure linen is 95 percent linen — frequently blended with cotton
Part linen is 25 percent linen plus cotton
Manmade fibers in various weaves are used for place mats
Lace used for tablecloths and place mats is made from linen, cotton, nylon and other manmade fibers

Quantity
Tablecloth: 1 — linen, lace, damask
Place mats: 2 sets — fabric or plastic with napkins
Breakfast cloths: 2, with napkins unless paper preferred
Dinner napkins: 6 to 12, depending on quantity of other tableware

BATHROOM

Towels and washcloths
Stock sizes:
    Bath towels: 24 by 28 and 40 by 52 inches
    Face towels: 16 by 26 and 18 by 36 inches
    Washcloths: 12 by 12 inches

Preferred fabric
Cotton terry cloth — firmly woven edges, fluffy loops
Huck toweling — preferred by some for face towels

Quantity
Bath towels: 4 per person
Washcloths: 4 per person
Face towels: 4 per person

Bathmats
22 by 36 inches in heavy terry cloth, or manmade fibers in a pile weave
At least 2 per bathroom

BED LINEN

Sheets
Flat: 24 inches wider and 24 inches longer than mattress
Fitted: tight but not enough to buckle mattress
Sizes: (all quoted torn and unshrunk — finished size 10 inches less)
    Crib: 45 by 77 inches
    Twin: 72 by 108 to 113 inches
    Double: 90 by 108 to 113 inches
    King: 108 by 120 inches
    Extra length: all 120 inches long

Pillow cases
Standard measurement: 2 to 3 inches wider and 10 inches longer than pillow
Standard size: 21 by 27 inches

Blankets
Standard measurement: 10 inches longer and 18 inches wider than mattress
Standard sizes Twin: 65 by 90 inches
              Double: 80 by 90 inches
              King: 90 by 108 inches

Preferred fabrics
Cotton
  Muslin: heavy yarns — thread count per square inch: 112-140
  Percale: fine yarns — thread count per square inch: 180-200
  Blend: nylon and percale — wrinkle-free, no iron
  Knitted: cotton and blend — preferred for crib
Wool: warmest, most expensive, used for blankets
Acrilon-Orlon blends: warm, mothproof, shrink and felt resistant, excellent for blankets
Cotton: used for summer blankets

Quantity
Sheets: 4 per bed (6 better)
Pillow cases: 2 per pillow (3 better)
Blankets: 2 per bed
Spreads: 1 per bed

KITCHEN LINENS

Towels
Preferred size: 18 by 30 inches
Preferred fabric:
  Linen or part linen for glassware
  Bleached cotton
Quantity: 6 to 12

Other kitchen linens
3 knit or terry cloth dishcloths, stock size: 12 by 12 inches
4 quilted or terry cloth pot holders, stock size: 5 by 5 inches

should be bought a little wider than the bed pillow and from 6 to 10 inches longer. Zippered protector cases should fit snugly in both width and length.

Decorative style. White sheets and pillow cases are considered to be the most economical choice of bed linens, but the use of color and printed patterns is growing in popularity. If these colored linens are well chosen and carefully coordinated with bedcovers and the color scheme of the room, the effect is charming. However, it is difficult to be specific in the room assignment of bed linen, so most of your supply should be white.

Warm Bedding

The field of warm bedding, other than electric blankets, falls into three classifications: Blankets, comforters, and quilts. Which will most effectively meet your individual needs depends on two factors: climate, frequently affected by air conditioning, and personal differences. In general, most people like the greatest warmth with the least weight, and they want cleanliness, beauty, and durability. A comfortable size is 10 inches longer and 18 inches wider than the mattress size.

Blankets. Wool—the fiber which of itself is warm and light—is still considered one of the finest fibers for blankets. This type of blanket requires careful washing so it will not mat or shrink. Man-made fibers, such as the acrylics, modacrylics, rayon, or nylon used alone or blended with each other, when napped heavily, will hold much warmth. The acrylics are noted for their washability. Cotton—the lightest and coolest fiber—can be made to have light blanket warmth by napping slightly or by mesh weaving. Mesh weaving, because of its air holes acts as insulation to hold in the body heat. A mesh woven blanket is called a thermal blanket.

Because of our demands, all of these types of blankets are available in a wide range of delicate colors as well as in white. They usually are bound with a wide satin binding top and bottom. All of them are reversible.

Comforters and quilts. Basically, all comforters and quilts consist of a fabric case and a filling. The filled case has been quilted or tied to keep the filling evenly distributed. The

A figured blanket is a welcome novelty. Such a blanket should be used with plain sheets and pillowcases. It is most effective when used in a room with little or no pattern.

quilt is thinner than the comforter. It is frequently used for a bedspread in Provincial rooms as well as for warm bedding. Quilt cases are usually made of patchwork or appliqué. Cases made of cotton sateen, rayon, acetate, or silk and filled with down, feathers, wool, or man-made fiber fillings make puffy, elegant comforters. Cotton used as a comforter filling is apt to become lumpy with use. Like blankets, comforters and quilts should be selected to harmonize with the room color scheme. Plain colors blend more easily into the room decor if walls, floor covering, draperies, or bedspreads are figured.

Bathroom Linens

Linens for the bathroom fall into several categories. The two basic considerations for all bathroom linens are durability and absorbent qualities. Only after these qualities are properly provided does the decorative quality become important as a factor in selection.

Type of fabrics. The family linens—face cloths, bath towels, and face towels—are usu-

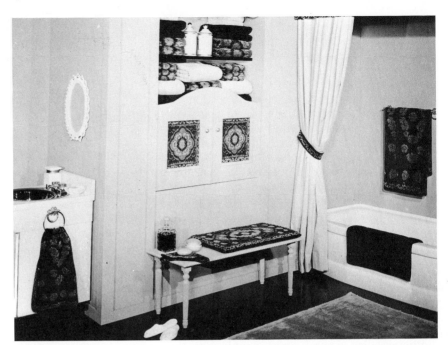

Courtesy Cannon Mills

Towels and toweling can be used for decorative purposes in a variety of ways — not only in the bathroom but in other rooms as well.

ally of terry cloth, or Turkish toweling. If terry cloth is heavy and firmly woven, it is more durable and less apt to have the loops pull out. To judge the comparative firmness of the different qualities, check the selvage or hems where there are no loops. For decorative interest, these towels can effectively be monogrammed in contrasting color or value.

Because guest and fingertip towels are small and little fabric is involved, it is possible to use fine-quality linen without undue extravagance and without complicating the housekeeping work to any great extent. Handwork can be added in hemstitching and monogramming. Lace edgings can be used if you want a touch of elegance. These towels can add an important decorative accent to your bathroom. Attractive guest towels are also available in terry cloth and cotton huck toweling.

Color. Color can be an important consideration in bathroom linens. Because strong color is often used for the wall tiles and floors in bathrooms, it is difficult to be sure that colored towels bought to accent one bathroom will not clash badly with the color scheme in your next bathroom. Unfortunately, you cannot do a colorfast job of stripping and redyeing towels to harmonize with the new backgrounds. If you try this you are apt to end up with ugly grayish towels that appear to be the result of poor housekeeping. Consequently, it is best to buy face cloths and guest towels in color, and use them with white bath towels and face towels. In this way you will need to replace only these smaller, less costly pieces if a change in background colors occurs.

Kitchen Linens

Changing housekeeping techniques are making great changes in the area of kitchen linens. Both the use of a boiling water rinse to sterilize and dry dishes and the increasing use of dishwashers limit the need for dishtowels. However, pots and pans, bulky serving dishes, and some glassware and flatware still must be hand dried. And towels must be on hand for emergency clean up situations. Linen, or linen and cotton huck toweling, is the most lintfree and the most absorbent toweling. Cotton squares are the most reasonable in price. Many kitchen hand towels are now made of terry

CHART 9. FURNISHING BUDGET ON THE UNIT SYSTEM*

Three-room Apartment	Relative Unit Value	Number of Units in Apartment
Living room and dining room:		
Bookcase (unfinished)	1½	1½
Curtains (2 windows)	½ (each)	1
Easy chair (2)	1 (each)	2
Large table	2	2
Rug	1	1
Side chairs (3)	½ (each)	1½
Small table (unfinished)	¼	¼
Sofa	3	3
Total units		12¼
Bedroom:		
Chest (unfinished)	1½	1½
Curtains (2 windows)	½ (each)	1
Double bed	1	1
Mattress, spring, pillows	1½	1½
Mirror	¾	¾
Rugs	¾	¾
Side chair (unfinished)	¼	¼
Total units		6¾
Kitchen:		
Glass and china	1	1
Kitchen equipment	1	1
Linen (complete apartment)	1	1
Total units		3
Accessories:		
Blankets	1	1
Lamps (2)	¼ (each)	½
Pillows (2)	¼ (each)	½
Vases and pictures	1	1
		3

Method of using Chart:

A. Deduct all units already obtained or not desired from number of units to be bought.

B. List remaining total number of units to be bought ....

C. List total budget for furnishings $........

D. Divide C by B for budget allowance for each unit $........

*Leon Pescheret's Estimate of Proportions and Costs of Furniture.

cloth for greater absorbency. The increasing use of paper toweling has almost entirely done away with the use of hand towels in the kitchen. The use of sponges and brushes is reducing the number of dishcloths needed. But the spongy knitted fabrics and absorbent chenilles continue to be a perennial favorite when dishcloths are used.

LEARNING EXPERIENCES

1. Define the meaning of the following words and phrases as used in this chapter: sterling silver, plated silver, stainless steel, contour, hollow ware, plastic ware, and decoration.
2. Visit a store that stocks sterling and plated silver as well as stainless steel flatware. Ask about the relative merits and cost per place setting and the best way to start buying flatware for a home.
3. Visit a shop that handles china and glassware or study mail order catalogs to learn about styles, qualities, and comparative costs of the different qualities.
4. Contribute to a class file by clipping pictures of styles of flatware, china, and glass. Be ready to join in a class discussion about combining the three to produce a harmonious table setting.
5. Study fabric resources in the dress goods, drapery, and trimming departments, as well as the ready-made table linens, to see what table coverings you could make or buy for the different types of table settings.
6. Make two tentative choices of flatware, china, and glass for yourself. Discuss how the three in each group relate to each other and to the table linen you might use.
7. Interview an employee of a small greenhouse or garden center about the planting and care of house plants, and talk with a member of a local garden club about decorative arrangements.
8. Start your resources for table decorations by planting fruit seeds (grapefruit, lemon, dates, oranges, etc.) in earth and putting slips of philodendron and cuttings of sweet potatoes and beets in water.
9. Start a collection of driftwood, figurines, large shells, simple terra-cotta pots, fish bowls, and baskets (with tin cans fitted inside) which could be used as planters, containers, or terrariums. Bring your favorite arrangement to class.
10. Make a collection of dried grasses, weeds, gourds, fruit, vegetables, or flowers from which you can make table decorations. Report on two table arrangements you produced.

PART

III

By Virginia Guthrie

Household Equipment

18

Equipment for the Home

Part III contains information on the selection, use, and care of household appliances. By and large, this information is stated in terms of the ideal. These ideal standards will not always be followed; we do not always do "the right thing", even though we know what the right thing is. The reader may feel at times that she is being told more than she wants to know. However, she is reading a source of information on recommended practices and recommended criteria for judgment.

Part III is approached from the consumer standpoint. It presents what the consumer needs to know in order to ask the right questions of the dealer and to evaluate the information given in advertising claims and by the sales personnel. Since the total dollar costs of the gas and electrical appliances used in a home can amount to one thousand dollars or more, it is important to know how to select, use, and care for this equipment. In most cases, intelligent selection, use, and care require an understanding of how the appliance works.

GENERAL BUYING GUIDES FOR APPLIANCES

The seven buying guides discussed in this chapter should enable you to select appliances which best fit your needs.

Guide 1

Buy on the basis of the quality of performance of the appliance's basic job. Too often the factor which determines the final choice of appliances is the color of the model on display or some special gadget which has nothing to do with how well the appliance will perform its basic job. To illustrate: a few years ago there was a range on the market which played the popular tune "Tenderly" when the roast was done, and a clothes dryer which played "How Dry I Am" when the load was dry. The wise consumer will ignore such gadgetry and instead will look for construction features which contribute to the efficient functioning of the appliance. When buying a refrigerator, one should be most interested in one with as large a capacity as available money and space

The lasting qualities in a given appliance depend on its adaptability to your changing situations. For instance, a refrigerator with movable shelving will be more adaptable for a family whose needs for milk and large containers of fruit juice are suddenly increased.

will allow. The fact that a refrigerator makes the ice cubes automatically should be of less importance, unless your main purpose in buying a refrigerator is to make ice cubes.

Guide 2

Know the relationship between price and quality. It is a common misconception that to get the best one must buy the most expensive. While a "bargain" may be false economy, one need not buy the top-of-the-line in order to get acceptable performance.

There is value in selecting a well-known brand put out by a manufacturer who has been making the particular appliance for a long time and has built a reputation for high-quality products. One would do well to recognize, however, that there is no one "best" brand. There are many good brands.

Any good brand will feature a wide price range. The larger the appliance is and the greater its capacity, the more expensive it will be. For example, there may be as many as nine different models ranging in price from the bottom-of-the-line model, priced at around $100, to the top-of-the-line model, priced at

$500. Is the latter five times better than the former? No. Aside from size and capacity differences, the more "convenience" features a model has, the more it will cost. Service calls are more frequent in connection with the extras than with basic performance.

Guide 3

Buy in terms of your situation and needs. Since many appliances can be expected to last ten or more years, one's needs in the foreseeable future should be taken into account as well as one's immediate needs, unless other factors, such as space and money, impose restrictions on one's choice.

Often the features which add to the price of an appliance are the automatic controls. A homemaker who is employed or active in community work may welcome the features available in certain appliances which will enable her to meet the demands on her time with a minimum of strain. For her, the least expensive model may not be the most desirable.

The size of the family as well as the frequency and number of guests entertained at home will influence the choice as to size of

The decision as to whether to buy a built-in or a portable dishwasher will depend in part on the kind of home you are living in and on how long you expect to live in the home.

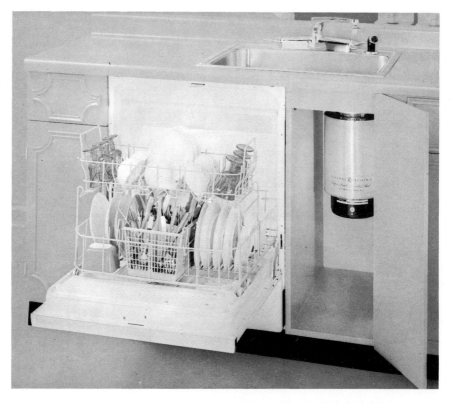

range, refrigerator, freezer, and perhaps even dishwasher. And the work habits of those who use the equipment will determine how durable the construction needs to be. Durability is always highly desirable, but the careful worker who is "protective" of her equipment will be able to get satisfactory service from an appliance that is only moderately durable. Some people need to select the most durable equipment available.

Guide 4

Find out as much as possible about the piece of equipment before you buy. There are many consumers who may be said to do their shopping *after* buying. What does this mean? It means that they discover after taking the appliance home that it does not fit their needs, or that it does not operate as they would like it to or as they expected it to. This practice leads to abuse of the return privilege, inconvenience to both the buyer and the seller, waste of time or money or both, and/or dissatisfaction in use of the appliance.

Here are some suggested ways for acquiring information *before* buying: (1) Read printed information about the equipment; (2) ask questions; (3) find out firsthand by examining the appliance and, if possible, have a trial use; and (4) determine in advance what are the special requirements, if any, of the appliance. Let us consider each of these.

Read printed information about the equipment. Textbooks such as this one and others of a more technical nature are one obvious answer. The well-known consumer organizations, Consumers Union, of Mount Vernon, New York, and Consumers' Research, of Washington, New Jersey, give information by brand name and model in their monthly publications *Consumer Reports* and *Consumer Bulletin.* One purpose of both organizations is to make recommendations to their subscribers as to the "best buys." There are certain limitations to this practice. One is that the shopper-reader will be unable to find in the magazine information on every model and every brand on the market. However, these publications do have several useful purposes. Most important, they serve as a substitute for firsthand experience, especially when a new product or appliance is being introduced. The criteria by which the testing organization evaluates the appliance are even more important than their final ratings concerning "best buys." Facts which a consumer cannot obtain by examination can be obtained by reading the results of the organization's laboratory tests. When using these magazines as a guide for buying, it is desirable to allow for some passage of time because it is not uncommon for the magazine to make a correction or addition to the earlier findings several months after the first results are published. As useful as these two consumer magazines are, they should not be a complete substitute for individual responsibility in making a choice.

Another printed source of information is a specification sheet, sometimes referred to as a "spec" sheet. Dealers receive from the manufacturer a specification sheet for each model they make, not for just those models which the dealer has chosen to stock. Specifications list the exact measurements; the weight; any special features; such relevant information as capacity, wattage, electrical or gas requirements for installation, and horsepower; and any other information a dealer needs concerning that specific model. Most dealers are glad to share this information with the consumer who asks for it, and even to order an available model if he does not have it in stock.

Advertisements, both in print and on radio and television, alert the consumer to new features and often indicate where the equipment is available locally.

Ask questions. In addition to printed sources of information, there are such human sources as salespersons and other owners. Perhaps the reader can recognize on her own the advantages and limitations of these sources.

Examine and try out the appliance. Armed with information from all these sources, the consumer is at last ready to go to the stores to start shopping for the item. If a home trial is available, it is desirable to take advantage of this offer. However, due to so much misuse of this privilege or for other reasons, a trial period of use in one's home may not be avail-

able. Find out, then, while in the store as much as possible about how the appliance is to be used, how it can be disassembled for cleaning, and any other aspect which affects one's satisfaction in use or protection against damage to the appliance through misuse. Study the instructions and see whether you can understand how to use and care for the appliance. Some instructions are very vague and lack clarity, while others are stated simply and specifically.

Determine in advance any special requirements. These include such things as the drain, the wiring, the type of gas, the quantity and condition of the water supply, whether an outside vent is required, the exact measurements of the space into which the appliance will be placed, the width of the passageways through which it will be carried, the upper and lower limits of temperature in the area where it will be used, and, in some cases, the strength of the floor which must support the appliance. Some of these points are self-explanatory; others will be taken up in more detail in connection with the discussion of a particular appliance. However, some explanation of wiring requirements and types of circuits used in a house seems in order here.

1. *Wiring requirements.* Since no appliance is better than the wires carrying the current, one must determine whether the wiring in the house is adequate for operating the appliance in question.

Electrical circuits can be classified into three categories: namely, general-purpose circuits; appliance circuits; and individual circuits.

A general-purpose circuit is the one which serves small motor-driven appliances and lighting needs. These circuits are usually wired with number 14 wire. They supply 120 volts and have a load capacity of 1800 watts. (Voltage is the force of electrical current. It is to electricity as pressure is to the water system in a home. Wattage is the amount of electricity used.)

An appliance circuit would be one into which such small electrical appliances as toasters, waffle-bakers, coffee makers, frypans, and rotisseries would be connected. An appliance circuit requires number 12 wire, or better yet, number 10 wire. Appliance circuits have a

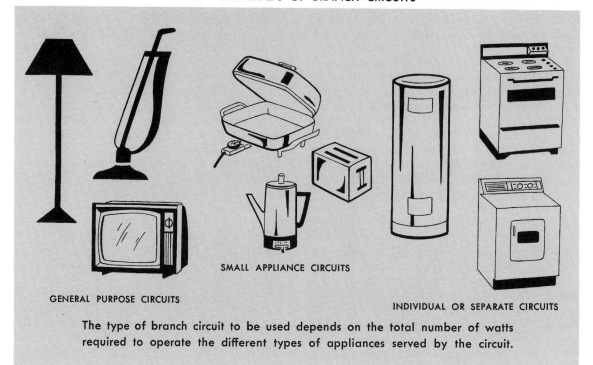

GENERAL PURPOSE CIRCUITS

SMALL APPLIANCE CIRCUITS

INDIVIDUAL OR SEPARATE CIRCUITS

The type of branch circuit to be used depends on the total number of watts required to operate the different types of appliances served by the circuit.

120-volt rating. They are able to carry a maximum load of 2,400 watts.

There are two classifications of individual circuits: 120-volt supply and 240-volt supply. The 120-volt circuit uses a number 12 wire. Appliances connected to 120-volt individual circuits include the electric refrigerator, freezer, and automatic washer. A dishwasher and food waste disposer may share one individual circuit. The 240-volt circuit uses a number 6 or 8 wire. Appliances which use the 240-volt individual circuit are the range, water heater, clothes dryer, one horsepower air conditioner, or any other appliance rated at more than 1800 watts.

2. *Fuses.* Fuses are safety devices used to protect the wiring against an unsafe load. They may be plug or tube type. If there is a greater demand for current than the circuit can safely carry or if there is a short circuit, which will cause a surge of electricity, the fusible metal strip will overheat, melt, and drop away; thereby "breaking" or opening the circuit.

Fuses are rated in amperes. A general-purpose circuit uses a 15-ampere fuse, an appliance circuit requires a 20- or 25-ampere fuse, and an individual circuit uses a 30-, 50-, or 60-ampere fuse. The amount of current is expressed in amperes.

To use a larger amperage than that recommended, or to put a penny behind the fuse to prevent the fuse from "blowing," is to tempt fate and possibly cause a fire. If an unsafe load of electric current flows over the wires, the insulation around the wires which prevents them from coming in contact with each other will eventually melt, permitting the wires to touch. When this happens, fire is the result.

As an added safety measure some homes and apartment houses are equipped with fustats, which are constructed in such a way that they will take only the size fuse which is safe for that circuit. One cannot replace a 15-ampere fustat with a 20- or 30-ampere one. Fustat fuses can be used in any Edison base

COMMON 15-AMPERE PLUG FUSE

FUSTAT

FUSATRON PLUG FUSE

TUBE FUSE

FUSTAT ADAPTER

FUSETRON TUBE FUSE

Fuses come in varying shapes. They may have special features but their overall purpose is to protect the house from overheated wiring.

Courtesy Bussman

fuseholder through the use of an inexpensive adapter that screws in like a fuse and locks in place.

Fusetrons and circuit breakers are other forms of safety devices placed in the circuit for protection against fire and damage to the appliance. Fusetrons, like fustats, are time-delay fuses, which can handle a temporary upsurge of demand of current without "blowing." Fustats, fusetrons, and fuses must be replaced when they burn out. This is done by unscrewing them, just as one replaces a light bulb. In some tube fuses the link may be replaced rather than the whole fuse. A circuit breaker works like the electric switch on the wall. But whenever the circuit is opened by one of these various safety devices, the trouble, which caused the safety device to work, must be determined and corrected before replacing the fuse or flipping the switch.

3. *Name plates.* A user of electrical appliances can often prevent the inconvenience of

a "blown" fuse by using the information found on the name plate of the appliance. The name plate will state either the wattage or the amperage requirement. If it is stated in amperage, one can determine the wattage by multiplying the voltage by the amperage. Thus, if the name plate gives the amperage as 12 and the voltage as 120, the appliance needs 1,440 watts to operate at maximum capacity. By multiplying the amperage and voltage of the circuit, one can also determine the wattage load of the circuit. Thus 15 amperes $\times$ 120 volts $=$ 1,800 watts, the maximum capacity of a general-purpose circuit.

Other information found on the name plate includes the model and serial number, which is important to know when parts or service are required, the name and address of the manufacturer, and the AGA, UL, or CSA seal.

4. *Wiring for appliance centers.* To accommodate the simultaneous use of as many as six small electrical appliances at full efficiency,

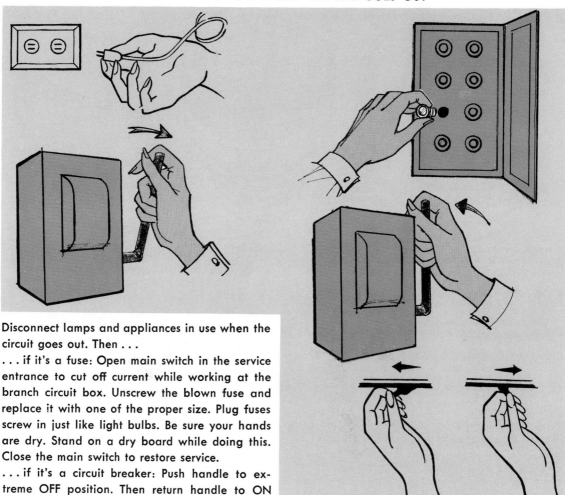

Disconnect lamps and appliances in use when the circuit goes out. Then . . .

. . . if it's a fuse: Open main switch in the service entrance to cut off current while working at the branch circuit box. Unscrew the blown fuse and replace it with one of the proper size. Plug fuses screw in just like light bulbs. Be sure your hands are dry. Stand on a dry board while doing this. Close the main switch to restore service.

. . . if it's a circuit breaker: Push handle to extreme OFF position. Then return handle to ON position.

Adapted from "Getting the Most from Your Home Electrical System," by permission of the National Electrical Manufacturers Association

some homes use an appliance center with a single control panel. Such centers require the same amperage as an electric range, since as many as six circuits may be in use at one time. Each circuit will have a 15- or 20-ampere fuse or circuit breaker. The control panel will often contain a time-clock for automatic control of the appliances.

Guide 5

Know the meaning of seals of approval. The two most important seals for which to watch when buying appliances for the home are the American Gas Association's Blue Star seal and the Underwriters Laboratories seal. An explanation of these organizations and their tests which precede the issuing of the seals will help to show what their seals signify.

American Gas Associaton. This is an organization of manufacturers, distributors, architects, contractors, plumbers, representatives of different departments of the federal government, and users of gas-burning equipment. Consumers are represented by the third group, the users. The chief purposes of the organization are to carry on research, establish standards, and sponsor testing, examination, and inspection of gas-burning equipment. Standards for installation are included as well as standards for construction. A complete examination of a gas range, for example, may require as many as 550 tests, which includes a thorough inspection at the factory of each approved *model* at least once a year. Inspection is also carried out on sales floors, in warehouses, and in customers' homes. When models conform to all requirements of the standards, a certificate of approval is issued for the remainder of that year, and the manufacturer is required to use the seal of approval on the tested model. (Models found to be defective in any part which does not conform to the AGA standard must be corrected before approval is granted.) Approval may be renewed annually for a period of five years. After that a retest is required, following the current standards.

Pieces of equipment bearing the Blue Star Seal show that they have met the Association's requirements as well as the American Standard for safety, durable construction, and satisfactory performance. Performance tests might include such requirements as the following: (1) ability to raise the temperature of a given amount of water to the boiling point in a certain number of minutes; (2) ability of the oven to bake four one-layer cakes at one time; (3) accuracy of the oven temperature at any given setting, both when the oven is used separately or with all four burners going.

Even though the Blue Star shows that the appliance was built to be safe, proper installation and use are also required. An open flame is always a potential hazard. Gas fuel is explosive and poisonous. The user should be aware of these potential dangers. Good judgment in use may avert the danger.

Underwriters Laboratories, Inc. This organization was originally sponsored by the National Board of Fire Underwriters, and its original purpose was to assist the fire and casualty insurance industry by establishing standards and certification of products, materials, and systems which complied with these standards. This remained its purpose for about the first twenty years of its existence. Its work was financed by contributions from capital stock

The American Gas Association seal indicates conformity to the Association's standards as well as to the American Standard for safety, durability, and performance.

Canadian homemakers should look for the Canadian Gas Association Seal of Approval. This seal on gas appliances manufactured and sold in Canada signifies conformity to standards of safety, durability, and performance.

property insurance companies which made use of the Laboratories' findings in evaluating property insurance rates. The property insurance companies ceased their financial support about 1916.

Today Underwriters' Laboratories' findings are made available to all who are concerned with public safety from fire, casualty, and

Appliances which carry these seals have been factory inspected to assure that they were manufactured according to safety standards. These seals indicate built-in safety but they do not assure continuing safety of electrical parts.

theft. Although it was first concerned primarily with electrical products, the scope of its work today is much broader than that.

Testing is done on a fee-for-service basis at one of their many laboratories in the United States and in some foreign countries. Manufacturers who wish their products tested make application and, if accepted, provide samples and pay for having the tests made. If the sample meets the UL standards, it is approved for "listing."

In addition to having a sample tested in the Underwriters' Laboratories, inspection takes place in the factory to see that the factory is complying with the approved standards. A label which reads "Underwriters' Laboratories, Inc. Inspected" signifies that the product has been produced under factory inspection and that it meets the UL standard. Under the UL's Re-examination Service, samples are obtained from the open market or the factory and are tested one or more times a year to determine compliance with the UL standards.

When buying electrical equipment of any kind, make sure the UL approval appears on the appliance. Fuses, too, should indicate compliance with the UL standards.

As important as the UL approval is, because it indicates the product has passed the tests for safety against electrocution and fire from a "short" in the wiring when used as directed, the UL seal is not an indication of the quality of performance. It stands for built-in safety. A worn appliance may no longer be safe. Also, judgment in use is required to prevent injury or electrocution. For example, one should never use an electrical appliance while in contact with water or a water faucet.

The Canadian Standard Association, which issues the CSA Seal, is the Canadian version of Underwriters' Laboratories.

Magazine seals. Several widely read household magazines, *Good Housekeeping*, *McCall's*, and *Parents'*, for example, give seals when their standards have been met. These are good guides for the consumer.

The Good Housekeeping Institute's Consumer Guaranty in essence means that those at the Institute believe the product to be a good one and that the advertisement of the product, which appears in the magazine, is truthful. Only by reading the advertisement bearing the Good Housekeeping seal can one determine what is claimed and how useful the information is. The Good Housekeeping Guaranty also states that if any guaranteed product or service (with certain listed exceptions) proves to be defective, upon request and verification the product will be replaced or the money the consumer paid for it refunded.

Parents' Institute seal reads "Commended by Consumer Service Bureau of Parents' magazine as advertised therein." The United States Testing Company (not an agency of the federal government) is hired to make tests as needed. Medical consultants and other professional advisers in various fields also give assistance (some based on their personal use).

McCall's magazine seal states "Laboratory and USE-TESTED and accepted (for advertising) by McCall's." Family performance tests supplement laboratory tests. McCall's Use-tested Tag carries the statement "We used it and we like it."

Guide 6

Judge the equipment in terms of how easy it is to use and care for. Ease in use refers to convenience in location of switches and controls. Controls should be easy to read as well as easy to get to for operation. Name-plate information which has the lettering embossed and is of the same material as the background is especially difficult to read. Thermostats for automatic operation contribute much to the ease of operation of many of the appliances discussed in the chapters which follow.

How easy the appliance will be to care for is partly a matter of design and partly a matter of the choice of material used. Design for easy care includes accessibility to all areas that require cleaning for efficient operation of the appliance or for lubrication. Many appliances are lubricated during construction and the gears are sealed so that oiling by the user is unnecessary.

The finish used on the exterior of any accessible part is a major factor in how easy the appliance will be to clean and keep looking attractive. Finishes used for the exterior of household appliances include one or more of the following: (1) enamel, either porcelain or baked-on; (2) stainless steel; (3) aluminum; (4) chromium; (5) glass; and (6) wood.

Enamel and glass are similar and may often be cleaned in the same way, that is, sponged with a solution of mild detergent, rinsed, and buffed to restore the gloss. Harsh abrasives (such as "scouring powder") should never be used, since the glasslike finish is easily scratched by the coarse particles of crystalline rocks. However, a paste made of baking soda is safe and effective for stubborn spots. For the exterior of enameled appliances, a commercial cream wax which contains a solvent for removing greasy film may be safely used. Check the label to see whether it is combustible and not to be used near an open flame such as a constantly burning pilot light. It should be applied and removed according to the directions. Care of the enamel interior of such major appliances as ranges and refrigerators will be discussed in Chapter 20.

Any shiny metal finish, whether stainless steel, chromium, or polished aluminum, requires more care than do other types.

To clean stainless steel, often soap and water, followed by buffing, is all that is needed. Scouring powder or steel-wool pads containing soap may be used for more stubborn soil.

Shiny aluminum may be cleaned with steel-wool pads containing soap. When aluminum is used in the trim of an appliance it often is *anodized*—that is, plated by an electrolytic method to give it a nonshiny appearance or a frosty effect. Sometimes dyes are added, such as copper-tone or turquoise. An anodized finish is less likely to water spot when air-dried. It should never be scoured with scouring pads or powders. Washing with a mild detergent solution and rinsing is all that is needed to preserve its beauty.

Chromium is used for trim on major appliances and for the outer shell of some small appliances such as toasters, waffle bakers, and some food mixers. Occasionally it is used as the finish for an oven lining. Since the chromium plating is about paper thin, it must be handled gently during cleaning so that it will not become scratched. Wiping off with a solution of soap and water and then buffing dry is the best way to preserve the gleaming finish of chromium. This method is ineffective on burned-on soil.

Wooden trim requires care to prevent water damage. If water is allowed to stand on wooden finish, the color will be faded. After successive or prolonged contact with water, the grain of the wood may be opened and the gloss of the finish damaged. Usually oiling with mineral oil or sweet oil is all that is needed to protect and preserve the original natural beauty. Once damaged and spotted, a small amount of wood stain may be needed to restore the color.

Guide 7

Buy from a reliable dealer. Your dealer is your key to satisfaction. Two factors enter into your assurance of satisfaction, the warranty and the guarantee.

The warranty is the manufacturer's written statement of responsibility for replacement of parts that fail within a specified period of time. Thus, such appliances as electric ranges, room air conditioners, refrigerators, and freezers carry the manufacturer's one-year warranty to protect the customer against the possibility of defective parts. In addition, the refrigerating mechanism is usually covered for an additional four years, and will be replaced if it fails sooner than this. Automatic washers carry the manufacturer's one-year warranty on all parts, and in some cases, an additional four-year warranty on the transmission.

It is the dealer, however, who largely determines how satisfied you are with the choice you make. The dealer who services as well as sells appliances and who has built a reputation for prompt and fairly priced service deserves

your patronage. It is the dealer through whom you will want to work to see that the warranty is fulfilled. The inconvenience of having to crate an unruly appliance and ship it back to the factory in order to have it put into working order is more than most people wish to undergo.

Thus, it is important to ask in advance of the purchase who will service the appliance, if you have trouble with it, and who will pay for the service. For example, the dealer may absorb the costs of service for the first thirty to ninety days.

The dealer who is eager to satisfy his customers will come to your home after the appliance has been installed and show you how to operate it. He will provide you with an instruction book which will reduce the number of service calls required if you keep the book handy and read it from time to time. During the warranty period it is a good idea to try out the various tasks the instruction book says the appliance is capable of performing so that if trouble does arise the purchaser may not have to pay for the service call.

Do not expect automatic appliances to give as many years of trouble-free service as the nonautomatic ones. Wringer-washers and coal-fired cook stoves are less complicated than their automatic counterparts. The more auto-

---

CHART 10. WAYS TO REDUCE SERVICE CALLS

1. If the oven won't heat, check to see whether (a) the heating element was pushed in all the way after being removed for oven cleaning or (b) the oven controls are still set on "automatic"; if so, turn the control to "M" (manual).

2. Check to see whether a fuse on the circuit has "blown" or the circuit breaker has tripped.

3. Find out if the neighbors are also without current; there may be power failure on the line.

4. Make sure the cord is plugged in all the way.

5. If the garbage disposer does not respond when the switch is turned on, check to see whether the overload switch has been tripped. The instruction book will tell you how to reset it.

6. If the clothes washer hums, but the water is not running in, check to see whether the faucets are turned on. (They should be turned off after use.)

7. If there is an unnatural noise in the vacuum cleaner or the smell of a hot motor, check to see whether the dust intake opening has become clogged. In a tank-type cleaner the blockage may be in the flexible hose. In an upright model, disconnect the cord at the wall outlet, turn the cleaner over, remove the plate covering the opening, and remove the blockage.

8. The strong odor of dust or the failure of the vacuum cleaner to pick up dirt may be due to the fact that (a) the dust container needs emptying or replacing, (b) the fan belt has broken or slipped off (upright model), or (c) the dust filter is not fastened securely.

9. In any gas-burning appliance with an automatic pilot, check to see if the pilot light is out. Use a flashlight when checking.

matic an appliance is, the more solenoids, timers, relays, thermostats, and the like there are to need adjustment. It is the accurate adjustment for the delicate interplay of the functional parts that must be maintained. Car owners have by and large come to accept routine service as part of the cost of auto ownership; owners of home appliances need to readjust their thinking also.

Once the local dealer absorbed many of the costs of servicing the appliances he sold, but today's price squeeze and competitive discounting practices have so narrowed his margin of profit that these costs are now largely borne by the purchaser. A repairman must be reimbursed for his time for making a service call even if no repair is made. To prevent unnecessary service calls, reread the instruction book and try some of the suggestions given in chart 10 on page 358 before calling the repairman.

To summarize, since some repair and maintenance are to be expected and since service calls to the home are expensive, it is important to select durably built appliances from reputable dealers and then to follow closely the instruction book to minimize the need for service.

A WORD ABOUT SOLID STATE

"Solid state" is a term being used more and more frequently. What does it mean? In connection with today's household equipment, solid state refers to an electrical control or switch which uses transistors and semiconductors to function. Appliances which are labeled electronic and transistorized make use of such solid state switches. These new switches are smaller, more reliable, and operate more efficiently than conventional switches. They also have a longer useful life. Their high efficiency is an even greater asset than their durability. Solid-state devices can perform in ways that conventional appliance switches can't.

Chart 11 below shows examples of the technological advances made possible by the invention of these electronic, solid state, semiconductor, or transistorized devices.

STANDARD OF LIVING, VALUES, AND ATTITUDES

One's personal set of values, or what is important to him, grows out of the influences of his childhood home, the influences of his circle of friends, and the influence of advertising. One's standard of living consists of those material things, as well as services and intangibles, which he considers *essential*. Many who are establishing homes today place high value on material things. They may take for granted that their homes will be equipped with appliances that their parents still do without or have only recently acquired. The standard of living of many young Americans includes most

---

CHART 11. EXAMPLES OF SOLID STATE DEVICES

1. Wall-lamp dimmer
2. A speed control on an electric mixer which can maintain a desired speed irrespective of batter thickness.
3. Semiconductor battery chargers for cordless appliances. The solid state device converts AC current to DC to recharge the battery.
4. Gas igniters which replace the match-lighted pilot flame on gas ranges.
5. Water-level control in self-filling ice trays in some refrigerators.
6. Controls for electric clothes washers and dryers which provide for a wider range of speeds in washing, suited to particular fabrics, and for a more accurate timing in the drying of fabrics, especially desirable for durable-press type fabrics.
7. Increased efficiency variable speed controls for hand tools, blenders, mixers, and electric knives.
8. Wide-range speed controls for floor care equipment. Slow speed prevents splashing when scrubbing or applying wax, middle-range speeds are desirable when shampooing rugs, and high speeds are desirable for buffing and polishing.
9. Solid state thermostats for electric, gas, and oil furnaces.
10. Timing circuits for cordless clocks.

Adapted from John E. Mungenast, "These Things Have Solid State in Common," What's New in Home Economics, vol. 30, no. 6, pp. 98–100, September, 1966.

of the appliances discussed in Chapters 19 to 22, plus others beyond the scope of this book.

Most users of this book will have grown up in the United States in what is characterized as the period of the "affluent society." Waste of resources seems to be of less concern to today's youth than it was to their grandparents. Young people now largely take for granted that things will wear out and that they will be replaced when they do.

The homemaker's attitude toward how much equipment she needs in her home and toward its care is influenced by her values, that is, by what is important to her. If the homemaker values the *time* saved by careless use of her equipment and omission of proper care more than she values the *money* saved in careful use, this is a choice she is free to make. She would do well, however, to consider the total cost of this choice and decide whether she is willing to accept the consequence of shorter service life from her equipment.

Even in an affluent society, all resources (time, energy, money, materials) are limited. The challenge is to balance the use of these resources so that by not spending excessively in any one area fewer desired things will need to be given up entirely. Thus, the user who prolongs the life of her equipment as much as it is within her power to do so frees dollars which can be devoted to other uses rather than to frequent replacement of poorly chosen and carelessly used equipment.

LEARNING EXPERIENCES

1. Define the meaning of the following words as used in this chapter: electrical circuit, amperes, volts, watts, fuse, circuit breaker, solid state.

2. Examine fuses, fusetrons, and fustats exhibited in class. Of what amperage are they? Look for the fusible metal strip. What are the similarities in the three types of safety devices mentioned above? Explain why it is unsafe to use a 30-ampere fuse on a 15-ampere circuit.

3. Select any electrical appliance in the home economics laboratory and locate its name plate. Write down all of the information given on the name plate. Explain how this information would be useful to a homemaker.

4. (*a*) Locate the Gas Association seal on a gas clothes dryer, range, or water heater. (If the appliance was manufactured in the United States, it should have the Blue Star American Gas Association seal; Canadian-made appliances will have the Canadian Gas Association symbol.) What do these Gas Association symbols indicate about the appliance? (*b*) Locate the Underwriter's Laboratory or Canadian Standards Association seal on several electrical appliances. Where, besides on an electrical appliance, have you seen or can you find the UL or CSA seal? What does the seal signify?

5. Prepare a bulletin board display of Seals of Approval found on household equipment. Include the seals mentioned in Number 4 above. Add magazine seals. Give a short talk to the class on the comparison of standards used as a basis for issuing each of the seals in your display. Include in your talk the purpose of the seal, that is, what it means or stands for and why you think it is used. Is it attached to the appliance, stamped or printed on the instruction book, or included only in the advertisements?

6. (*a*) Make a list of all of the gas and/or electrical appliances one might find in a modern American *kitchen*—not necessarily in any one home.
   (*b*) After each appliance listed in 6(*a*) write the price one could expect to pay. Use newspaper advertisements and mail order catalogs. Where there is a wide range of prices, list both lowest and highest. Total the cost.
   (*c*) Place an "X" in front of all appliances on the list in 6(*a*) which you consider the basic *minimum* for preparing

and storing food. Total the cost. State your reactions to these findings.

7. Explain how the following factors could influence one's decisions concerning which appliances to own: (*a*) type of home (apartment, mobile home, house, other); (*b*) number of people in the family; (*c*) physical condition of the homemaker; (*d*) whether frequent moves are anticipated; (*e*) personal values.

8. Obtain some specification sheets on different makes of any appliance of your choosing. If possible, obtain at least three of each—a bottom-of-the-line, middle-of-the-line, and top-of-the-line model. Study the "spec" sheets and discover the type of information given. Explain the various ways the information would be useful.

9. What are some "conditions" of water supply, referred to on page 351, which will have a bearing on the way an appliance performs. Name the appliance and explain the conditions and results one might expect. If you are a tenant in rented property, what can you do to improve the performance of the appliance? Tell what conditions would be beyond your control. How could the factors be corrected by a plumber or the landlord?

10. One popular source of information is a friend's experience. Explain the limitations and drawbacks to relying on a friend's experience as a source of information concerning an appliance you are considering buying. How valid is one person's experience?

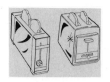

19

Small Electrical Appliances

for the Kitchen

ELECTRICITY HAS BEEN harnessed to perform almost every task from brushing teeth, polishing shoes, and shredding wastepaper, to rolling up the paper toweling or wax paper, peeling potatoes, and sectioning grapefruit.

This chapter will not attempt to deal with every portable device now known, nor will it attempt to predict what man's inventive genius will produce tomorrow, but it will deal with the more widely used portable electrical appliances for the kitchen and dining areas.

CLASSIFICATION OF PORTABLE ELECTRICAL APPLIANCES

Portable electrical appliances may be classified into three types: (1) heating appliances, with high wattage ratings; (2) motor-driven appliances, which use a small amount of electric current; and (3) appliances that are a combination of the heating and motor-driven types.

Included in the first group are coffee makers, toasters, frypans, waffle bakers, grills, griddles, roaster-ovens, and heat trays.

The second group includes food mixers, blenders (without a cook-and-stir attachment), can openers, and slicing knives.

Rotisserie-broilers represent the third group.

Thermostatic Controls

Most of the heating appliances which will be discussed are of the automatic type. This means that they are controlled by a thermostat which may be either built-in or removable. If the thermostat is built in, the appliance must not be immersed in water, as this will damage the thermostat. In some cases, where the thermostat is located in the handle, the pan may be immersed partially with the thermostat out of the water.

Built-in thermostats have a bimetal strip which opens the electric circuit as the metals heat and expand. Metals are used which have a different coefficient of expansion. This expansion difference causes the strip to curl, which breaks the electrical contact, thereby opening the circuit and shutting off the flow of current. As the curled metal cools, it straightens and closes the circuit.

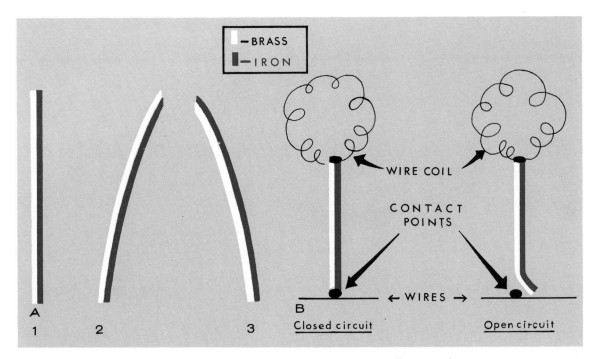

A thermostat with bimetal strip works because of the differing coefficients of expansion for the two metals. For example, a flat strip of brass and a flat strip of iron can be welded or riveted together. The brass will expand more than the iron when heated and will contract more when cooled. Diagram A shows such a strip at room temperature (1), heated above room temperature (2), and cooled below room temperature (3). Diagram B shows how an electrical circuit may be opened by the expansion of the bimetal strip when the temperature rises above the desired setting. The open circuit will cause the appliance to stop heating.

Most probe-type removable thermostats contain a liquid which expands and contracts, thus opening or closing the electrical circuit.

An indicator light is a desirable feature for any thermostatically controlled appliance.

Cordless Appliances

Some portable appliances are cordless—that is, they are powered by batteries. These are an outgrowth of recent improvements in battery technology. They have two major advantages: (1) They are almost completely shockproof and fireproof. (2) They may be used anywhere, since they do not rely for their operation upon an electrical outlet.

There are some disadvantages to cordless appliances: (1) They usually cost more than plug-in models. (2) The rechargeable batteries are expensive. (3) They may have less power than a plug-in model. (4) The length of time they will operate is limited. (5) There is no way of predicting when the batteries will fail; this may be before the job is completed.

ELECTRIC COFFEE MAKERS

A cup of "good" coffee can be made by a number of methods, including the use of non-electric coffee makers. The objective is a full-bodied brew which is clear and free from sediment, without objectionable coffee oils and bitter taste. The quality and quantity of the coffee used, the temperature of the water, the

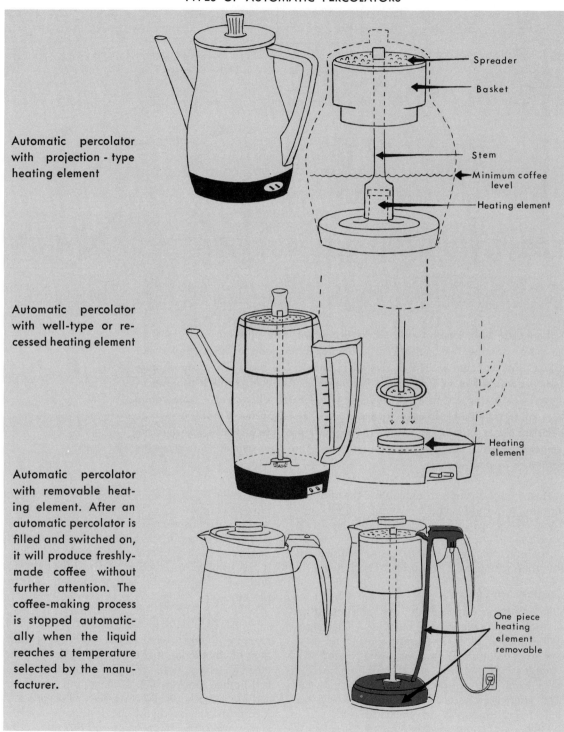

Automatic percolator with projection-type heating element

Spreader

Basket

Stem

Minimum coffee level

Heating element

Automatic percolator with well-type or recessed heating element

Heating element

Automatic percolator with removable heating element. After an automatic percolator is filled and switched on, it will produce freshly-made coffee without further attention. The coffee-making process is stopped automatically when the liquid reaches a temperature selected by the manufacturer.

One piece heating element removable

length of time water is in contact with the coffee grounds, and the condition of the interior of the coffee maker all play a part in the quality of the brew.

Factors over which the manufacturer, not the user, has control include the range of temperature, the design of coffee basket and spreader, and the accessibility of all parts of the coffee maker for thorough cleaning.

Electric coffee makers are now all of the percolator type. Percolators may be automatic or non-automatic.

Coffee makers may be made of aluminum, chromium, plastic, Pyroceram, or stainless steel. Some plastic ones are insulated for heat retention.

Percolators

The Coffee Brewing Institute recommends a brewing temperature range of 145° to 205°F and a holding temperature range of 185° to 190°F. Higher temperature would cause the coffee to boil which gives a scorched, bitter taste. Brewing the coffee for too long a time removes more of the oils from the grounds. The objective is to remove the flavor and aroma from the grounds without removing the undesirable oils.

Operating principle. In the bottom of a percolator is a heating element. It may be in a well, in a projection, or in a removable unit. The bottom of the stem fits into or over the heating element. A minute amount of water passes through a tiny hole close to the bottom of the stem. As the water in the base of the stem boils, the pressure forces the water up the stem, where it flows back through the spreader (basket cover) and is filtered through the ground coffee in the basket. The design of both the spreader and the basket, including the size of the holes, their number and spacing, affects the quality of the brew. To get maximum flavor from the total amount of coffee in the basket, the water must be distributed evenly over all of the coffee, not filtered through only the coffee immediately surrounding the stem. If the holes are too large, the water will pass through too fast. The basket must be large enough to permit the coffee grounds to expand when wet without overflowing into the brew. This poses no problem when less than maximum capacity of coffee is being made, but it can be a problem at full capacity.

The length of time the coffee percolates is controlled in an automatic percolator by an indicator marked mild, medium, or strong. The proportion of dry coffee to water, as well as the grind of the coffee, also affects the strength of the brew. Some guides recommend that the controls be kept on the strong setting and that the coffee-water ratio be varied until the desired strength is achieved.

Use and care. A nonstick finish on the lining of the percolator contributes to ease of cleaning. Since coffee oils become deposited inside the stem too, this area must be cleaned as well. An easy way to clean the inside of a nonaluminum coffee maker is to place one tablespoon of baking soda or nonprecipitating water softener in three or four cups of cold water and allow it to perk as if coffee were being made. Cream of tartar or a commercial cleaner may be substituted for baking soda if the coffee maker is of aluminum.

When all areas of the inside of the coffee maker, including the spout, are large enough to be accessible for cleaning, and there are no crevices in which coffee oils can be deposited, the flavor of the brew is likely to be better than when the percolator cannot be cleaned adequately.

Features to Look for in Coffee Makers

Design is not a matter of appearance alone. The handle should be of heat-resistant material. It should fit one's hand comfortably, without danger of the hand coming in contact with hot metal or of the coffee maker slipping during pouring. Some models have plastic knuckle guards. The lid should fit securely so that it will not fall off during serving.

A dial or lever for automatic control of strength of brew and a signal light are convenience features found on several brands. An especially desirable feature is that for keeping the coffee at serving temperature without boiling.

Immersibility is another desirable feature. This means that because the thermostatic unit is sealed in and watertight the percolator can safely be placed in the dishpan for washing.

Never put a coffeepot into water unless labeled "immersible." Note the design of this handle which protects knuckles when serving hot coffee.

However, only models labeled "immersible" should be immersed. If not immersible, water should be dipped into the coffee maker when washing it. The label or the instruction book will indicate whether or not the percolator is immersible. To immerse a coffee maker which is not immersible could create a serious shock hazard the next time it is used. Even in rinsing out the nonimmersible type, care should be taken to prevent water from seeping into the base.

The manufacturer's indication of capacity in cups refers to serving cups, not measuring cups, of brewed coffee and not to the amount of water put into the coffee maker. The National Electrical Manufacturers' Association specifies that capacity be measured in five-ounce cups, but there is some variation among coffee makers..

Serving markings on the coffee basket of a percolator as well as on the pot are useful. They are not always included. When the markings are on the outside of the pot, they are

Well-designed handles are especially important for party-size coffee percolators. Detachable cords are also desirable, since they make it easier to move coffee urns.

easier to read than when they are on the inside only.

Electric Coffee Urns

Twenty- to seventy-five-cup automatic coffee makers are popular in any situation where one entertains large groups of coffee drinkers. Much that has been said earlier about the smaller models of automatic percolators applies to the larger models as well.

Cup markings on the coffee basket as well as on the inside and outside of the urn are even more important on coffee urns because of the inconvenience of having to measure the dry coffee one measure at a time.

Although it is advisable to avoid trying to move the urn when it is full of hot coffee, there may be times when it is necessary to do so. For this reason one should take note of the size and design of the handles in terms of ease of carrying the urn. The handles should be large enough and designed in such a way that one can get a good grip on them without touching hot metal. A detachable cord is especially desirable when carrying the urn.

It is very important that it be cleaned after each use. Cleaning the urn is not easy since the size and weight of the urn, as well as the fact that it is not immersible, make it cumbersome to handle.

It is relatively easy to examine the urn in the store and make a judgment as to the accessibility for ease of cleaning of the coffee basket, the spigot, the inside of the urn, and the hollow tube which gives an indication of the amount of coffee in the urn.

TOASTERS

Two types of toasters still may be found on the market—the nonautomatic and the automatic.

The nonautomatic toaster has one heating unit in the center. Generally, two slices of bread can be toasted simultaneously on one side but must be turned by hand to toast the second side. Careful watching is required to avoid burning the toast. Even though this type is less expensive than the automatic type, it is less popular.

In a nonautomatic toaster (left), the bread is toasted on one side, then flopped and toasted on the other side. Well-type toasters (center and right) toast both sides of the bread at the same time. Such toasters cut off the heat source automatically when the toast has reached a preset color. The two-slice well-type toaster may come with a long well which will hold either one wide slice or two regular-size slices of bread, or it may have the more familiar double well for two single regular-size slices.

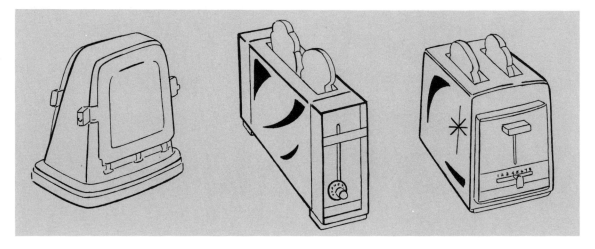

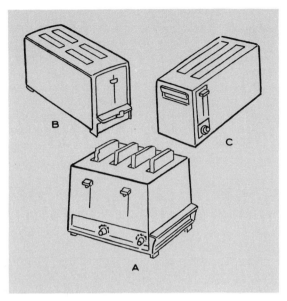

The automatic toaster operates by a thermostatic control. The thermostatic control usually has a bimetal blade which shuts off the current automatically when a given temperature is reached, when a given time has elapsed, or when a given amount of radiant heat is reflected from the bread. With the latter type of automatic toaster the more moist the bread the longer the toasting time.

Well-type Automatic Toaster

The well-type toaster has heating elements of flat or round nichrome wire wrapped on asbestos or mica. The elements are protected by wires to keep the bread from touching the heating element. It also has heat reflectors, a switch, a timer, a color control, and a crumb tray, as well as the cord and the thermostat which stops the toasting time automatically.

Sizes of the well-type toaster vary so that from one to four slices of bread can be toasted at one time. The bread is lowered, either manually by a lever or automatically, and both sides are toasted at once.

Some four-slice models have a dual-color control which will toast two of the slices to a different degree than the other two. Four-slice

Well-type four-slice automatic toasters may vary in the ways brownness is controlled. View A shows a dual color control and two levers for lowering the bread. Color may also be controlled by a lever (view B) or a knob (view C).

A special four-slice well-type toaster may be mounted in the wall between studs. It can also be used as a table-top toaster. The toaster will operate only when the door is open; a safety switch inside prevents it from operating while in a closed position, shutting off the toaster instantly if the door is closed.

Courtesy Nautilus Industries

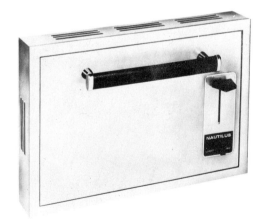

models are available in extra-long or extra-wide shapes. In the extra-long model all four slices are lowered at once. In the extra-wide (square) model there are two levers for lowering the slices two at a time.

Some color range in toasting is desirable, but a wide range is important only to a family with a wide difference in color preference. Some people may find a rotary control easier to operate than a lever. The controls should be conveniently located, easily read, and easily operated. Some toasters will reheat cold toast without darkening it—even without changing the color control. In others, the color control must be changed to a lighter setting to reheat without browning.

It is important that the toast rack lift the toast high enough to be removed easily. A hinged crumb tray makes crumb removal easy.

Handles should be large enough to grasp comfortably without touching hot metal. They should be located above the midline for stability and safety in moving a hot toaster.

A wider-than-average slot is important only if muffins or thick slices of bread are to be toasted. In this case, perhaps the oven-type toaster or the combination well-and-oven model will have greater appeal than the well-type.

Oven-type Toaster

The oven-type toaster toasts buns, muffins, or thick slices of bread, and warms rolls. In addition, some models can be used to bake certain foods in small quantity, to defrost bakery products, and to reheat small quantities of cooked food.

The reflector-type oven toasts or bakes by reflected heat. In some, an uninsulated, broiler-type heating element is located at the back of the rack. In models using the sealed-rod elements, the elements can be used independently or together. The highly polished top and bottom surfaces must be kept shiny in order for the oven to work properly and reflect the heat to both sides of the food. Any spattering of grease or other food residue should be removed with a nonabrasive cleaner. The area to be cleaned is often hard to get to.

Use and Care of Toasters

The use and care of all types of toasters is similar. Care must be taken to avoid being burned whenever it is necessary to reach in

Courtesy General Electric

An oven-type toaster usually has an adjustable thermostat which times the heating operation.

to retrieve the toast. This may be more likely to occur with some models of the oven-type toaster. With the well-type toaster there is sometimes a temptation to use a fork to retrieve a piece of toast that is jammed. Always disconnect the toaster if you must try this. Electrical shock can result if the toaster is plugged in, even if its switch is turned to OFF. There is also danger of damaging the heating element. A toaster should not be shaken in an attempt to remove crumbs, as this can damage the heating elements and the fine adjustment of the thermostat.

Finger smudges can be easily removed from the chromium case by the method described earlier under care of chromium. (See page 357.) However, the toaster should first be unplugged.

FRYPANS OR SKILLETS

Skillets of earlier days were usually round, made of iron, and heated on a range or open fire. Today's electric skillets may be rectangular, round or square, of aluminum, stainless steel, or ceramic. Best of all they allow the user more control of the temperature. Heating elements of the metal skillets are built in or plugged into the pan. Ceramic skillets rest on a separate heating unit, which is thermostatically controlled. The "skillet" serves as a casserole or serving dish.

Portability makes these skillets popular for patio cooking. Indoors they add an additional unit to the range, or they may be preferred to nonelectric skillets because the heat is thermostatically controlled. Today's electric frypans can also be used for some types of baking and roasting.

Sometimes the cover is included in the quotation price of electric frypans; sometimes it must be bought separately. A cover is necessary if one is to get the full range of uses of which the frypan is capable. A dome cover gives extra space for poultry and thick cuts

A special feature on some electric frypans is a warming tray where buns can be warmed by radiant heat from the underside of the frypan while the hamburgers are cooking.

Many frypans are immersible. Special features found in some frypans include nonstick coatings and an extra element in the lid to serve as a broiler.

Courtesy The Hoover Company

Courtesy Westinghouse

of meat. The high-domed buffet-server is an example of a frypan with a wide range of uses. Some models have a notched device for holding the cover at different angles to act as a splatter screen. A vent in the cover is necessary when the pan is used for baking, and it is useful during other types of cooking as well. Covers with a broiling unit in them are available. If the frypan controls are plugged into the cover, these must be removed before the cover is washed.

Square skillets have a larger cooking area than round skillets of the same diameter. The corners should be slightly rounded for easier cleaning. A square skillet will be somewhat harder to pour from than a round skillet.

The thermostat may be the removable probe type, or it may be built permanently into the frypan handle. Some temperature overshoot is not uncommon. If it is excessive, or if the thermostat is too inaccurate, it should be repaired or replaced. The removable type of thermostat can also be used in other removable-control appliances of the same brand.

The wattage requirements for electric frypans range from about 1,000 to about 1,300 watts. No other appliance should be used on the same 15-ampre branch circuit while the frypan is in use.

The handle or handles of electric frypans should be of heat-resistant material. They should be comfortable to use. If food is to be served directly from the frypan, two handles of comfortable size and shape will make it easier to move the pan when full of hot food.

Nonstick coatings have been added to frypans to reduce sticking of food and to make them easier to clean. Some instructions claim that they may be used without cooking fat, while others recommend that a small amount of fat be used to enhance the flavor and to eliminate sticking. Pancakes may brown more evenly when no fat is used. Most instructions recommend that wooden, nylon, or rubber spatulas or spoons be used with appliances that have a nonstick coating. Some newer nonstick coatings may mar less easily.

One should be sure to check on whether an electric frypan can be used without damage to the surface on which it will rest. If not, some type of heatproof mat should be used to pro-

tect the counter or table under the pan when it is in use.

OTHER APPLIANCES WHICH USE THE INTERCHANGEABLE CONTROL

Electric saucepans, pressure cookers, Dutch ovens, and grills are also available to use with the interchangeable removable control. Because they are thermostatically controlled, once the temperature has been set on the control dial, a minimum of attention is required.

Waffle Baker Grill

Waffle bakers may be round, square, or rectangular in shape. Rectangular bakers may make rectangular or square waffles. Some square waffle bakers make rectangular waffles.

Material. Waffle grids are usually of cast aluminum, which has been preseasoned at the factory to reduce sticking or has been treated

A removable probe-type thermostat may be used on a frypan, a griddle, a portable oven, and an electric pressure cooker of the same brand. An interchangeable control saves money when purchasing electrical appliances of the same brand.

Courtesy National Presto Industries

with fluorocarbon finish. The outside is usually of polished chromium.

Grid design. The design and spacing of waffle grids contribute to the degree of crispness of the baked waffle. However, the ingredients of the batter—for example, the amount of sugar—play a part also. Grids which are high and close-spaced give a crisper waffle than a baker with low grids that are wide-spaced.

Selection features. An expansion hinge on a waffle baker is essential, since waffles expand as they bake. An overflow groove is desirable for catching batter if the baker is filled too full. Not all bakers are automatic; those that are will have a signal light or other means to indicate when the waffle is ready for removal. Handles and feet should be of heat-resistant material.

Combination models. Some models have waffle grids on one side and a smooth-surface grill on the other. Others have interchangeable plates for grilling or waffle baking. There should be a drain and a receptacle for grease from grilled meat. In some combination mod-

Some combination-model grill and waffle bakers have a nonstick finish on the reversible grids.

Courtesy General Electric

els the lid flattens down to provide two open grilling surfaces. When closed, it can be used to grill sandwiches on both sides at once.

Use and care. Even though the feet of the baker should be of heat-resistant material and the bottom should be insulated, it is desirable to protect the counter or table top against any possible heat damage.

If the baker has been preseasoned or coated at the factory with a nonstick finish, the grids will not need to be brushed with fat, since the shortening in the batter should prevent sticking. (Some directions suggest one-fourth cup of fat per cup of flour; others say one-fourth cup of fat to two cups of prepared waffle mix.) Sticking sometimes does occur because of overheating of the grids or from a buildup of residue when certain vegetable oils are used in the batter.

If the baker has not been preseasoned, this can easily be done at home by brushing the grids with unsalted shortening and allowing it to heat at medium setting with the cover closed until the light goes out. Bake one waffle and discard. In subsequent uses, the first waffle should be edible, since there will be no excess fat on the grids.

Noncoated waffle grids should seldom if ever be washed. If the buildup of sticky residue does make removal necessary, let the waffle baker stand overnight with a cloth or paper towel soaked in ammonia between the grids; then brush with a stiff brush. Reseasoning will be necessary to prevent sticking. If the grids are coated with a nonstick finish, washing them after each use is recommended.

When finished with the baker, disconnect it, and leave it open to cool before storing. This preserves the seasoning. Then close the baker before storing.

Finger smudges can be easily removed from the chromium finish by wiping with a sponge wrung out of soapy water, followed by buffing with a soft cloth or paper. Silver polish or a paste made of powdered whiting may be used for more stubborn soil.

Griddles

The automatic griddle is closely related to the grill described above, as well as to the frypan. It may be made of heavy aluminum or of stainless steel with a heat-conducting core. Electric griddles are used for the same things that nonelectric griddles are used for.

The handles of griddles should be large enough to be gripped securely and should be of heat-resistant material. There should be no screws exposed where they can come in contact with fingers and cause burns when the griddle is moved while hot. If the griddle is to be used on a counter or table top, it must have heat-resistant feet of sufficient height to hold the hot metal away from the table top. Protecting the table top with a mat is a good precaution against possible heat damage. It is important that there be a receptacle on the griddle for catching drippings. The receptacle must be easy to empty when full. Removable receptacles have this advantage.

A removable, probe-type heat control makes the griddle immersible for easier washing. Unless the electric griddle has a thermostatic control, it has no real cooking advantage over a nonelectric one.

Roaster-Oven

The roaster-oven is usually rectangular in shape, roughly 24 by 12 by 12 inches. Although portable, it is cumbersome to move about, so it is customarily used on a special cabinet or stand. Without the insert racks and pans, it may be used for serving large quantities of soup, cocoa, meat, or vegetables for meals involving large groups of people.

With its racks and insert pans, it is used like any other oven. With the separate, stationary broiler unit in place, it may be used for broiling, grilling, or toasting. Some models have a rotating spit for rotisserie broiling, described later under combination heating-and-motor-driven appliances.

Small Portable Electric Trays

Small portable electric trays go by a number of names, such as heat trays, hostess trays, hot butlers, and electromatic platters. They are especially convenient when one wishes to hold cooked food at serving temperature for an hour or so without its cooking or drying out. Such situations include buffet meals, patio meals, circumstances where some member of the family is delayed past the regular meal-

A heated serving tray keeps hot food appetizing at serving temperature for an hour or so.

A serving cart with electrically-heated-tray surface may be rolled to any location where food is to be served.

time, or any meal in which some of the food being served tends to cool rapidly.

Types. Choices of trays range from small trivets 6 to 8 inches square to serving carts with an electrically heated tray surface. Some have removable cords, may be used as a hot

373

platter with the food placed directly on it, and are completely immersible for washing. Others provide a hot surface on which serving dishes, a casserole, a teapot, a nonelectric coffeepot, and the like may be set to retain the heat. This type is usually not immersible but is wiped off with a damp cloth when cool. Some have a Lucite dome-shaped cover.

Selection features. Trays with a removable cord and an outside temperature control knob or dial provide more flexibility than those in which the temperature is automatically predetermined at a certain point (usually about 200°F, which is below the boiling point of water and above the coagulation point of fat).

A tray should be fully insulated to protect the table top from damage. It should be UL-approved for built-in safety and freedom from shock hazard.

Care. A brass trim can be kept attractive by cleaning occasionally with brass polish. Wooden handles or trim will waterspot if liquid is dropped on them. Rubbing the wood with a small amount of medicinal mineral oil or with salad oil should restore the original beauty. Anodized aluminum requires no special care.

FOOD MIXERS

Electric mixers are available as portable models, which are hand-held and light-duty, or as stand models, which will do heavy-duty mixing. Stand models are considerably more expensive because they are built to perform a wider range of mixing tasks. If the intended use includes even occasional mixing of stiff batter or dough, a stand model may be preferable to a portable.

Common Selection Features

Design and construction features vary among brands, whether one is shopping for a portable or a stand model. Wattage, as shown on the name plate, is one important point to check. The higher the wattage, the more demanding the mixing job the motor can handle. Portables tend to use 100 watts. Some stand models have motors as high as 150 watts.

A governor on the motor enables it to adjust automatically and to maintain a uniform

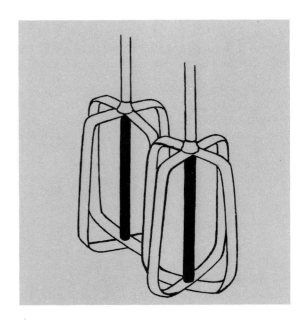

Whether the mixer is a portable or a stand model, well-designed beaters will give better performance and longer service. A strong center rod adds stability to a well-designed beater.

speed irrespective of the consistency of the food being mixed.

Speed controls should be located for maximum ease of operation, and the markings should be clear and easily read. This is even more important for a portable mixer where the motor switch is turned on with the thumb of the hand holding the mixer.

An ejector device is highly desirable for easily removing the beaters. It should be located where it won't be accidentally activated when operating the speed controls. Beaters should be easy to insert as well as easy to eject.

The design of the beaters is significant for maximum efficiency. Fairly large rectangular beaters are more efficient than small ones of another shape. An exception to this is the large looplike beaters which move in a planetary pattern through egg whites or batter. Beaters of the rectangular shape are stronger when they have a center rod.

With either type mixer, the frequency of use will probably be in direct proportion to the convenience of storage. Most portable models come with a bracket for wall storage,

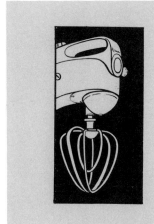 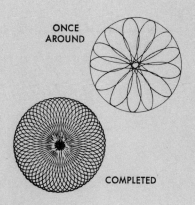

ONCE AROUND

COMPLETED

In a mixer with a single beater, the beater is set off-center, rotating clockwise, while the bowl rotates counterclockwise, creating a planetary action.

but storage in the original carton or in a drawer, if these are convenient, may be even more desirable. A stand model which can be left out on the counter will be used more frequently than one which must be brought out with effort.

If the cord is of synthetic rubber, it will not absorb grease or moisture.

Safety

The power of any motor-driven appliance creates a chance for injury, so naturally when using an electric mixer caution should be used to make sure that neither fingers nor spatulas get caught in the moving beaters. Since it is an electrical appliance, it should not be used near water. The mixer should be disconnected when not in use and before removing the beaters. Where slight electrical leakage is noticed, it can be corrected by unplugging and then reversing the poles by turning the plug over.

Portable Mixers

Portable mixers usually have three speeds and are built to do such lightweight tasks as beating eggs or light batters, mashing small amounts of potatoes, or whipping cream. Some have a special attachment for mixing drinks.

A heel rest is an important convenience feature not found on all models. It should be stable enough to support the beaters against the rim of the bowl without tipping.

Since the mixer must be held in the hand throughout its use, it should be comfortable in weight, balance, and shape. To lighten the weight, high-impact plastic is often used rather than metal.

Stand Mixers

Stand mixers have up to twelve speeds and are built to perform a variety of jobs in addition to mixing heavy dough and large quantities of food. Since the stand supports the mixer, this leaves both hands free for adding ingredients. The mixer can be left running unattended briefly.

Some models have a removable head which enables them to be used at the range, thus adding to their flexibility of use, but they are much heavier and more tiring to use in this way than the lightweight portables. The head should be easy to remove.

When the beaters are tipped back, for removal of beaters or bowl, the mixer should remain stable and well balanced. Ideally the beaters should be so designed that they automatically rotate the bowl for more thorough mixing. There should also be some device for changing the bowl's position to bring the beaters close to the edge of the bowl, since more than one size of bowl may be used with the mixer. Bowls ordinarily are standard equipment with the stand model. These should fit the beater shape and have straight sides so that the batter can be moved by the beater

REMOVES FROM STAND FOR
USE AS A PORTABLE, TOO

Attachments for a standard-model mixer may include a meat grinder and food chopper, a blender, and a juicer.

action rather than by scraping the batter from the sides of the bowl with a spatula. Steel bowls are more durable than glass ones.

Some models have a timer which rings after a preset number of minutes.

With the aid of special attachments, stand mixers can grind meat, shred or chop certain foods, and freeze ice cream. Other attachments include juicers, blenders, drink mixers, and dough hooks. Some of these attachments call for a power adapter.

Although the attachments add to the variety of uses possible, they may also add to the cost and should be purchased only if they will be used frequently. They can add to the storage problem as well, especially if storage is unusually limited.

KITCHEN BLENDERS

Blenders are frequently confused with food mixers, yet the tasks they perform are significantly different. A blender can supplement a mixer but not substitute for it. The unique functions of a kitchen blender are to puree fruit, vegetables, or certain other foods, especially for infants or anyone on a soft diet; to reconstitute powdered milk and to mix beverages; to aerate fruit juices to improve their flavor; to liquefy or pulverize solids; to chop, shred, grind, and grate; and of course, to blend, or homogenize, ingredients into a smooth sauce, dip, or spread. Liquefying solids and dry grinding are more demanding tasks than mixing or aerating, so a blender should be judged on its ability to perform these tasks.

One type of blender combines a ten-speed blender with a cooking appliance that has a thermostatically controlled temperature. It can be set to cook and stir unattended.

Operating Principle

The blender consists of a glass or plastic container which fits into a base that houses a powerful motor and the motor control. The control may be a knob, a lever, or a push button. Since some of the demands made on the motor are great—for example, for some grinding or crushing—the motor should have a high wattage. Since the sharp blades operate at very high speed, timing precision is important. Blending for a few seconds too long can result in a smooth paste rather than the desired chopped form. The push-button models partially, but not completely, overcome this problem.

Selection

Safety is always a primary factor to consider. Any safety device which prevents the motor from being accidentally turned on while one's hands are inside the container is highly desirable. Models that do not have such a device should be avoided.

Some models have been found to be a potential electrical-shock hazard if liquid is splashed out of the blender and gets into the motor housing. High humidity also contributes to current leakage in some models. Any spilled liquid should be wiped up so that the blender never operates while it is standing in liquid. Liquid can sometimes be drawn up into the motor housing through ventilating holes in the bottom of the base. Also, to prevent the

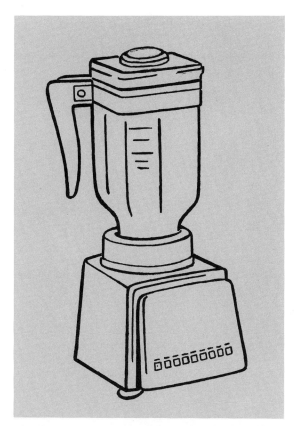

Blenders are available in a variety of styles. Some have solid-state controls. Push-button models have a preselected speed for the desired action.

possibility of moisture seeping into the motor housing, liquid should not be allowed to stand for any length of time in the container. This can cause corrosion of the metal parts. If moisture does find its way into the motor housing, the blender should be unplugged and allowed to dry out before reusing.

Convenience, both in use and in care, is desirable too. With the dealer's permission, many of the following features can be identified and evaluated by trial and examination in the store before purchase. Some of the factors which contribute to convenience in use are these: a cover with a removable center so that food may be added while blending; a container that can be removed from the base easily; a removable bottom in the container so that food is more easily removed; stability so that the container rests firmly on the base instead of rocking, tipping, or vibrating; a base that can be moved across the work counter easily without the necessity of lifting. Push-button controls have some advantages in that the desired speed can be reached immediately (without having to turn the speeds on in sequence). When a standard, screw-top canning jar can be substituted for the blender container, it adds convenience in making up several jars of baby food at a time. Weight is a factor in convenience in carrying, but if the blender is to be used frequently, it is even more important that space be available on the work counter for it to be readily available without having to be lifted. A handle, pouring spout, and measuring marks on the side of the container are other convenience features. Removable blades are more easily washed than those permanently attached. If the blades are permanently attached, a small amount of detergent solution can be added to the container with the blender turned on briefly. In any case, the container and blades should be washed promptly after each use.

Tips on using are given in the instruction book and should be followed carefully. Since the cutting blades are very sharp and operate at a very high speed, great care should be used in scraping the edges of the container while the blades are operating. Only a rubber spatula should be used.

A blender should never be filled too full. If incorrectly used, excessive splashing and overflowing are likely to occur. This creates a potential danger of shock hazard, as pointed out earlier. Also, better blending results when small portions are added at a time. The size of the ingredients and the order in which they are added also affect the quality of the finished product.

Recipe books tend to exaggerate the range of uses. Better results may be obtained with other pieces of equipment—for example, whipping cream and shredding cabbage.

Special attachments are available with some makes of blenders. The ice shaver is one example. Ice cubes, added a few at a time, can be shaved quickly. Juicers, coffee mills, and knife sharpeners are other attachments that are sometimes available.

Cost

A chrome-finished base tends to cost more than one with plastic or baked-enamel finish. Plastic containers are more likely to be found on the low-priced models. Glass containers are considerably heavier than plastic ones, but they seem easier to clean and less likely to scratch or crack. A removable cutter assembly is more likely to be found on high-priced models. Multispeed controls add to the cost as do special attachments. With the exception of the knife sharpener, the attachments mentioned here add $15 or more to the cost.

DRINK MIXERS

Drink mixers resemble blenders but are less powerful and limited in their uses to that of mixing. They are available in the form of an attachment to a mixer as well as a separate appliance.

CAN OPENERS

With the advent of self-opening cans of the flip-top variety, the electric can opener may lose some of its popularity. If one seldom uses canned food, the expense of an electric can opener is surely not justified. However, they are a convenience for anyone whose hand and wrist strength are limited by such things as advanced age, arthritis, a sprain, or a broken bone.

Types

Electric can openers are available in table models for use on a counter top or mounted on a wall. Some can be used either way. Some have built-in knife sharpeners or both knife and scissors sharpeners.

Selection

It is difficult to evaluate some of the important factors to consider unless one can actually use it on cans of different heights and shapes. Unfortunately, this is seldom possible in the store. A counter-model opener should be tall enough to accommodate a large can. A wall-model opener must be mounted high enough above the counter to allow for such cans. The opener should also be heavy enough or be supported well enough so that it will not tip in use.

Courtesy General Electric

An electric can opener opens cans more quickly and easily than other can openers. Be sure that a particular model will work well on cans of different sizes and shapes.

Some models have a rotating cutting wheel; others have a stationary cutting blade, either circular or punch-type, which cuts off the lid as the can is rotated automatically by the toothed drive-wheel.

In some models the user must keep the lever or button pressed down throughout the operation. When the pressure is released, the cutting motion stops. In others, the lever is depressed by the user only long enough to puncture the can and start the cutting action. These models shut themselves off when the can has been opened. Young children should be kept away from electric can openers, especially the fully automatic shut off type.

Children are less likely to get injured on the type in which the lever must be kept depressed manually in order to operate. If they do get a finger caught in this type, they are likely to instinctively release the lever or button.

Some openers require greater effort than others to puncture the can and start the cutting action. If one is selecting an electric can opener because of physical disability, it is especially important that the opener be easy to operate.

Two convenience features to watch for are a magnet to hold the lid when it is cut off and a niche at the back for storing the cord when the opener is not in use. Some models show electrical leakage in high humidity. In buying a can opener, it is safer to select one that has been listed by Underwriters' Laboratory.

Care

Although it should never be immersed in water to wash, the drive wheel and cutting blade should be wiped clean after each use. If juice or other food is allowed to dry on these parts, they will not work properly. Disconnect the can opener when not in use.

ELECTRIC SLICING KNIVES

Electric carving or slicing knives are acclaimed in the advertisements for their slicing versatility. However, no advertisement claims that the knife will replace all kitchen knives; it is primarily for slicing.

Operating Principle

Most brands use two blades, inserted into the handle where the motor is located. They move in opposite directions in a sawing motion at the rate of 1,400 to 3,000 strokes per minute. The higher the number of strokes, the better should be the slicing performance. No sawing motion is required by the user, only pressure. At least one brand uses a single blade with sawing motion supplied by the user. The power center in the handle, causes the handle to be bulky and heavy. Probably this is noticed more by women with small hands than by men.

This type of electric slicing knife with two serrated blades is operated by an on-off switch usually located under the handle. The special advantage of electric slicing knives is that they enable a person to cut uniformly thin slices without exerting a large amount of sawing pressure.

Selection

The quality of the steel in the blades is a factor in durability as well as in slicing quality. Most desirable is a blade which will hold a sharp edge for a reasonably long time. Since the blades have serrated edges and cannot be sharpened, they have to be replaced when dull unless a self-sharpening provision has been built in, as at least one brand claims. Tungsten carbide retains a sharp cutting edge longer than a blade of stainless steel. Blades that are sharp to the tip allow for easier trimming and piercing. If replacement blades are required, their availability and cost should be considered at the time of purchase.

A desirable feature, found at least in the most popular brands, is that the blades operate only while the switch button is held down. This means that the action stops when the pressure is released so the user can shift position or lay the knife down. It would be highly desirable to have a safety lock which could be switched on to prevent the slicing action from becoming accidentally activated or turned on by children. If such a device is not provided, the cord should be disconnected even during temporary disuse other than momentary rest periods. Since the pressure on the button must be maintained in order for the blades to operate, one should handle the knife and evaluate its balance, comfort, and controllability while the switch is held down. This design feature is important in determining how tired the hand and fingers become. One should also attempt to evaluate the convenience in use during both horizontal and vertical slicing.

Blades should be easy to insert and remove; they should lock firmly and fit snugly. The wider the space between blades, the greater the chance for food to get lodged there. The amount of space can be judged by holding the blades up to the light with the cutting edge forward.

Provision for convenient storage should also be considered when making a selection.

Use and Care

If one is using a plug-in type of knife, it must be disconnected, of course, before the blades are removed. The blades should be handled carefully, not only to protect the fingers but to protect the cutting edge from being nicked or blunted. Blades should always be returned to their case after being washed and dried carefully. Only the blades can be washed under water. One should avoid cutting against any surface which would dull the blades.

Some knives require greater pressure than others. It would be highly desirable to be able to try the knife in actual use in the store before making a purchase. Unfortunately, this is seldom possible, so a use-test rating will have to be substituted for one's firsthand experience. Another alternative is to ask a friend who owns one to let you try it out on a variety of foods.

ROTISSERIE-BROILER

Some top-of-the-line ranges have as optional equipment a rotisserie which broils meat as it turns on a motor-driven spit. An electric rotisserie-broiler is also available as a separate portable appliance. Some are round or oval, some are open-hearth, and some are enclosed in a case with a door.

Operating Principle

The rotisserie-broiler demands approximately 1,650 watts. It should be used alone on a separate circuit. A fowl, roast, or other food to be broiled is held in place on a spit which turns slowly and is cooked by heat radiated from the element.

Advantages and Disadvantages

The rotisserie-broiler provides a supplementary or even a substitute cooking facility. Its usefulness is increased when it is large enough to accommodate a 20-pound turkey or roast.

Storage could be a limiting factor in many homes. Since the rotisserie-broiler is bulky and cumbersome, a special cart or similar space would need to be provided.

Because rotisserie-broilers are not so well insulated as a conventional oven, there is heat loss into the room, metal parts become very hot, and baking efficiency will be lower than for a range oven.

Selection

The rotating spit on a rotisserie may be a single, horizontal skewer, or there may be several

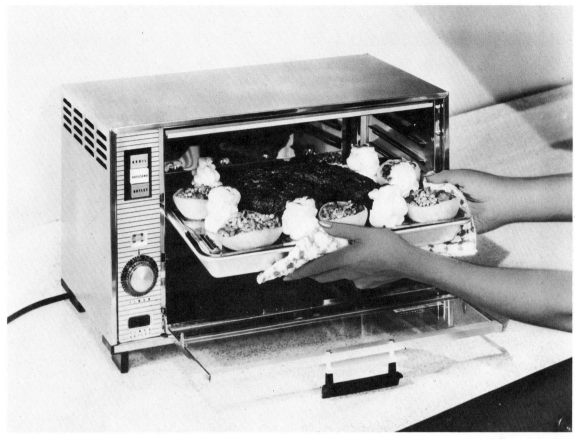

An electric rotisserie-broiler that is available as a separate appliance provides a supplementary or substitute cooking facility. It can be an effective outdoor cooking appliance or can serve as an additional oven space for special needs.

vertical spits. The one with several spits is recommended for broiling weiners or kabobs.

Some combination models are a rotisserie-grill or a rotisserie-broiler-baker.

A thermometer on the end of the spit which indicates the internal temperature of the meat takes the guesswork out of the cooking. So do an automatic timer and signal.

Some of the features to look for are infinite heat controls, a signal light, a switch to turn off the rotisserie when the oven is in use, and a hinged lid which opens wide enough for easy access.

Cleaning

The instruction book should be followed for cleaning as well as for use of the rotisserie. It should be disconnected and cooled before cleaning. The more parts there are that are removable, the easier it will be to clean. Racks and pans can be washed in the dishpan. Other areas should be wiped off—first with soft paper to absorb the grease, then with a cloth or sponge wrung out of soapy water. Burned-on grease or other residue should be removed by the method recommended earlier for chrome, steel, enamel, or aluminum.

1. Define the meaning of each of the following words as used in this chapter: thermostat; bimetal; probe; immersible; vent; preseasoned (metal); governor (motor); ejector; planetary (mixer); serrated.

2. On different days at home or in your home economics laboratory all on the same day, cook bacon by as many of the following ways as possible: (*a*) skillet on range top; (*b*) skillet on thermostatically controlled unit or burner of range; (*c*) oven; (*d*) broiler; (*e*) electric skillet. Write down your observations regarding: (1) the quality of the cooked bacon (for example, was it crisp? burned? greasy? browned evenly or unevenly?); and (2) the amount of attention required to achieve the desired results. Give your appraisal of the alternatives you used. What conclusions do you draw concerning your observations?

3. Using what you learned in Chapter 18 concerning the wattage load capacity of various circuits, list the *small* electrical appliances which could be used *simultaneously* on one general-purpose circuit in preparing either a breakfast or lunch without blowing the fuse. State what food you would serve.

4. How could one determine in advance how many appliances could be used on one circuit at the same time without relying on a "blown" fuse for the answer? Does each wall outlet represent a separate circuit? Explain.

5. Assuming that adequate circuits were available, which of the following foods could be *cooked* entirely by use of *portable* appliances: hamburgers, French fries, frozen pizza, rotisserized beef roast, baked potatoes, frozen green beans, frozen pastry?

6. Make a list of the portable appliances you hope to own some day soon. Measure the linear shelf space and head-room required to store each of the appliances on your list. Make another list of other types of items ordinarily stored in the kitchen besides portable appliances. Measure the linear shelf space in a small kitchen or in one of the school unit-kitchens.

7. Assuming you knew you would be moving many times in the next few years, what *portable* kitchen appliances might you wish to own and take with you? State the criteria you considered in making your choices.

8. List examples of portable electric kitchen appliances which perform only one task (as opposed to multipurpose use). Under what circumstances would you consider it desirable to own each appliance you have listed?

9. Make a list of portable equipment for which there is a nonelectrical counterpart —for example, a mixer. Indicate the price of both the electric and the nonelectric item. Appraise the worth of the more expensive one, that is, give your reactions as to whether you would consider it money well spent. What factors would enter into your decision to buy the electric type rather than the less expensive, nonelectric one, or vice versa?

10. On the basis of jobs you have held, how many hours of work would be required to pay for any three of the appliances on the list you made in question?

20

Major Kitchen Appliances

THE TERM "major kitchen appliances" includes ranges, refrigerators, freezers, and dishwashers. Also included in this chapter are garbage disposers and incinerators, since they too are nonportable kitchen appliances. All of these appliances are expensive enough to warrant care in selection. They represent a major expenditure for long-term use, since a well-built appliance, properly used, should last ten years or more. This should mean years of satisfaction and enjoyment from one's kitchen appliances. The purpose of this chapter is to provide some information on selection, use, and care of major kitchen appliances.

RANGES

Choice between a gas or an electric range will be largely a matter of personal preference. Such factors as comparative fuel rates, initial cost, amount of electrical equipment in the house, frequency of power failures, and availability of both types of fuel will influence the decision. From the standpoint of cooking performances neither fuel can be said to be superior to the other.

If safety is of primary importance, because of children or very elderly persons in the family, electricity is the better choice, but for average use the new safety devices on gas ranges give more than adequate protection. Older electric ranges were slow to start and limited to high, medium, and low heats. This is no longer true. Speed burners and infinite heat controls have eliminated these drawbacks. Badly adjusted gas burners smudge the bottom of utensils, but modern gas burners are better designed for proper combustion. The electric industry claims "clean, flameless cooking," but in ovens and broilers of gas ranges gas flames incinerate a large part of the greasy vapors which settle on lining and racks in electric ovens.

Common Features

Both gas and electric ranges have certain similarities. These will be discussed first, followed by a discussion of the unique features of each.

Construction. The frame of both gas and electric ranges is of sturdy steel, welded for

In an electric range the elements can be hidden beneath a ceramic material that mounts flush with the counter top. This cooking top has four heating areas.

rigidity. The exterior finish is porcelain or synthetic enamel. The cooking surface should be porcelain enamel, preferably acid-resistant, or stainless steel. The sides and back may be of synthetic enamel, which is less expensive than porcelain enamel, since these parts do not need to be acid-resistant. Synthetic enamel will scratch but not chip. Acid-resistant porcelain will retain its original gloss. One should look for porcelain enamel which is also resistant to thermal damage. Titanium added to the porcelain enamel of appliances standardizes the whiteness. This is of particular interest when one is selecting major kitchen appliances of more than one brand.

Other materials used in the construction of ranges include aluminum, chrome, and stainless steel. Stainless steel may be used in place of acid-resistant porcelain in reflector pans under the unit or burner. Stainless steel is also the material frequently used for oven racks. Anodized aluminum, chromium, or steel are used as trim.

Oven linings may be of chrome, stainless steel, or porcelain enamel. It is desirable for the porcelain to be acid-resistant so that spillovers will not dull the finish. Look for a one-

Surface burners recessed in the counter allow for a small amount of additional under-counter storage. This tilt-out drawer provides a convenient place for spices and herbs.

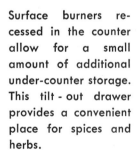

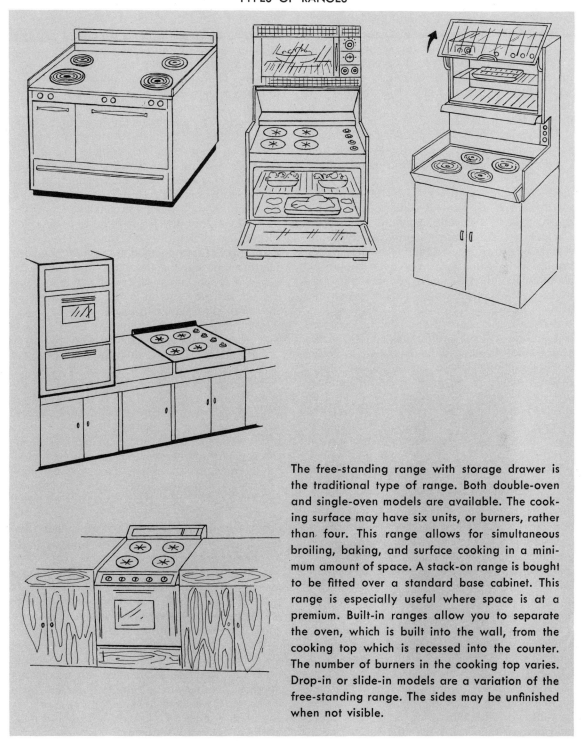

The free-standing range with storage drawer is the traditional type of range. Both double-oven and single-oven models are available. The cooking surface may have six units, or burners, rather than four. This range allows for simultaneous broiling, baking, and surface cooking in a minimum amount of space. A stack-on range is bought to be fitted over a standard base cabinet. This range is especially useful where space is at a premium. Built-in ranges allow you to separate the oven, which is built into the wall, from the cooking top which is recessed into the counter. The number of burners in the cooking top varies. Drop-in or slide-in models are a variation of the free-standing range. The sides may be unfinished when not visible.

piece oven lining which is vapor-tight to prevent escape of steam into insulation.

The fit of the oven door is an important factor in the efficiency of the oven operation. To check this fit, close the door on a piece of paper and then try to withdraw the paper while the door remains closed. If the paper is held tightly, the oven door fits well enough to prevent loss of heat.

Insulation. The walls and sides of the oven are insulated. This decreases the heat loss from the oven, thus increasing its efficiency in operation. Glass wool or spun glass are the two most commonly used materials for insulation. Fiber glass is used in high-quality ranges because it doesn't pick up moisture and is very efficient. It is fireproof, lightweight, vermin-resistant, and does not settle or pack. The insulation on the top of the oven should be about twice the thickness around the sides to keep the work surface cooler when the oven is in use.

Electric ranges are more heavily insulated and tightly enclosed than gas ranges, since they do not require air for combustion. Ovens in both gas and electric ranges require a vent through which steam or products of combustion can escape. The vent may be located on the back splash, in the oven door, or under a surface unit. A vent located on the back of the range is likely to stain or discolor the wall.

Types. Both gas and electric ranges are available in several types. The free-standing model may have the oven below the surface units or at eye level. Some models have ovens both above and below the surface units. The free-standing, low-oven range provides the greatest flexibility when changing models.

Built-ins separate the oven (which is built into the wall) from the surface units, which are recessed into the counter. These typically have storage drawers or cupboards built below them. Since at least 24 inches of wall space is needed in addition to that required for surface units, a wall oven is not suited to a very small kitchen.

The slide-in and drop-in models fit between cabinets. The sides of these models need not be finished, although they may be. These models have the oven below the surface units.

The free-standing model with eye-level oven has been widely advertised with emphasis on the advantages of the oven which can be used without stooping and the generous storage space available in the base cabinet of some models. There are some important drawbacks to these ranges. Although such ranges resemble built-ins, they are not as adaptable to individual needs. The height of the oven in the eye-level model is dictated by design, not by individual preference. Accessibility to the oven creates some problems for anyone who is short, particularly if the oven is high enough to clear the utensils used in surface cooking. Using the oven for such small products as pies creates no problem, but articles as large as a 15-pound turkey are difficult to get into and out of a high oven. In some models, pull-out cooking platforms permit the oven to be set somewhat lower, but one must still reach over the extended surface units or burners, which means the oven is not easier to reach.

Another limitation of the eye-level oven is that food must be removed from the oven for attention, as in basting. In transferring it to a lower surface there is danger of burns.

Before selecting this type range, look at the controls and determine how complicated they will be to operate. Surface-unit controls and oven controls on the same panel may be confusing. The location of the oven controls affects the capacity of the oven. In models with side-mounted controls, the oven may be as much as 4 inches narrower than it is in conventional free-standing ranges. However, side-mounted controls are easier to reach than the over-the-oven controls which are about 60 inches from the floor. Some models have controls both above and to the side of the oven.

Other drawbacks to models with eye-level ovens include the discomfort from the heat of the oven while one is working at the surface units; more difficulty in cleaning than with conventional or built-in ovens; the safety hazard of igniting clothing in reaching over an open flame or of burning oneself in reaching over hot saucepans; damage to protruding overhead cabinets or to cabinet doors left open if the gas oven is vented in top front; higher cost than comparable brands and quality units of the other types of ranges.

Range controls should be placed outside the reach of young children. A range with a specially designed Braille control panel is available for blind housewives.

Sizes. Ranges are available in sizes ranging from approximately 20 inches to 42 inches. Drop-in or fold-up cooking tops may have as few as two units, but free-standing models typically have no fewer than three and may have as many as six. One may select either a single oven or a double oven model. The size one chooses will be influenced by the amount of space into which it is to fit, but the use that will be made of it should also be considered. For a large family or a family that frequently entertains guests at home, the added cooking space contributes to efficiency and adds to the joy of cooking.

Selection features. When selecting a model with eye-level oven, look for one with a cooking platform that has rounded corners and edges to reduce the likelihood of injury from bumps. If the cooking surface pulls out, look for platforms that lock into position, can be unlatched from the front, and which slide easily. One will have a choice between the convenience of counterbalanced glide-up doors, which are difficult to get to for cleaning and swing-out doors, which are more easily cleaned but which expose the user to burns from hot edges.

For any below-counter oven, look for these features: a counterbalanced door to assure a tight fit, easy closing, and a stop to insure constant broiling heat and to allow vapor and moisture to escape from the oven while cooling (a lock stop is not so necessary on a gas oven as on an electric oven); four to eight shelf supports in the oven for varying positions of the racks; sturdy, rust-resistant oven racks that have lock stops to prevent dropping or tipping when rack is pulled forward; and sturdy, rust-resistant hinges on the oven door.

Controls should be easy to read. (Metal dials with raised lettering are difficult to read. Those with large lettering or with transparent sections through which color shows to indicate the cooking speed are easy to read.) The control of a gas range should be so designed that one can see across the room whether the burner is on or off. On a range with the controls on the back panel, the controls should be high enough so that they won't get spattered with frying fat. This also reduces danger of burns from hot utensils.

The placement of the units and burners is also important. They should be located in such a way that all four can be used at once without

Range tops can be easily cleaned when various parts are removable.

large utensils touching each other or the back of the range.

Easy-care design includes: a minimum of seams, creases, and crevices; as many removable parts as possible—for example, a removable drip-tray to catch spillovers from surface units or burners, removable oven bottom and walls, or an oven lining that can be pulled out for more accessibility; burner or unit reflector bowls and oven linings with fluorocarbon finish which make soil removal easier by preventing soil from adhering so tightly; removable oven-rack guides; and lift-off oven doors.

Special features. The following are some of the special features available on top of the line models: two ovens rather than a single oven; oven light and a light on the back panel; push-button controls; automatic timers for turning the oven on and off, or to low heat for keeping food warm, or for turning on appliances plugged into the convenience outlet; timers for timing surface cooking; fast-speed surface units; rotisserie-grill; a meat thermometer which plugs into the side of the oven and is inserted into a roast or fowl and which will set

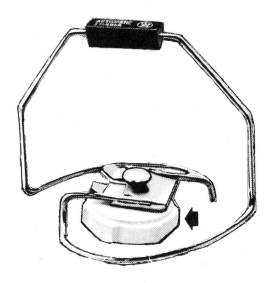

Reprinted from Nov./Dec., 1966, issue of "What's New in Home Economics"

An automatic stirrer agitates the food during the cooking process. This reduces the chances for food to stick.

Some control panels have separate controls for each oven. They may contain a clock which turns the ovens on and off automatically.

A meat thermometer, which plugs into the side of the oven, registers the internal temperature of the meat on the control panel.

Reprinted from Nov./Dec., 1966, issue of "What's New in Home Economics"

In the type of thermostatic burner control shown here, the flame size is automatically controlled by the setting on the dial. An electric range may also have a similar thermostatic control on one surface burner.

off a buzzer or chime when the meat has reached the preset temperature selected on the panel; automatic ignition of gas burners and ovens; thermostatically controlled surface burners or units; self-cleaning ovens; and for electric ranges, an automatic stirrer that can be attached to the front unit for stirring food.

The thermostatic control on ovens is standard equipment, but at present thermostatically controlled surface cooking is found only on top-of-the-line ranges. The thermostatic control is a temperature-sensing device, which, if working properly, will maintain a preset temperature automatically. For proper functioning of such a device, pans must be of materials which are good conductors of heat and must rest solidly against the thermostatic control. Pans which are dented or warped do not work satisfactorily. The desired cooking temperature is "dialed" on a special control just as it is when setting the oven thermostat.

Care of the range. A clogged burner head interferes with combustion and is a fire hazard. Burners on modern gas ranges are of the non-clog type so they require little cleaning. However, if a burner does become clogged, the

ports may be cleaned with a stiff brush or by gently inserting a small wire to remove the obstruction.

If the reflector pans under the surface units or burners are washed each time food boils over before it has had a chance to cook on, they will usually come clean when washed with a dish-cloth or scrubbed with a plastic scrubber. Some reflector pans are coated with a nonstick finish for ease of cleaning. Steel-wool soap pads are especially effective in removing burned-on food from aluminum reflector pans. Although they are also effective for enamel reflector pans or drip trays, these cleaning aids are eventually destructive to the enamel finish. Noncaustic oven cleaners of the cream or paste type are effective and safe to use on enamel reflector bowls or drip trays.

Chromium should never be cleaned with anything abrasive. Clean, soapy water, followed by buffing with a soft paper or cloth will restore its luster. Chromium used as oven lining is likely to present problems in cleaning, since it is easily scratched. Only oven cleaners that are known not to scratch should be used.

Prevention or reduction of soiling helps to minimize the work of cleaning the oven. By not filling a casserole too full, one can reduce the chances that it will boil over. The floor of the oven can also be protected against soiling by placing a piece of aluminum foil slightly larger than the utensil, or a cookie sheet or pizza pan, on the rack below a pie or casserole that is likely to boil over.

Oven cleaners are available in a variety of forms which may be brushed on, sprayed on, or rubbed on. Some are caustic. Their labels warn that one should protect the kitchen floor against possible spills and one's hands by rubber gloves. Few are as easy to use as the commercials and labels claim. The noncaustic types are safest to use. Safety here refers both to the user and to the surface being cleaned. There are some very effective oven cleaners on the market which are noncaustic and can be used without rubber gloves. They not only remove burned-on food from enamel-lined ovens or reflector pans, but they protect the original gloss of the finish.

Also available are oven sprays which claim to protect the oven surface with a film which makes grease and other soil more easily removable. They are of limited value. Also, the dull protective film hides the oven's glossy sheen.

Both gas and electric ranges are available with automatic oven cleaning. There are two systems being used. The *pyrolytic* system cleans by decomposing oven soil at very high temperatures, when the oven is empty and the controls have been set. The *catalytic* system uses a catalytic material which is mixed into the porcelain enamel used on the oven liner panels. Oven soil is oxidized during use of the oven if it is set at 350°-500° F. Each system has certain advantages and drawbacks. Compare before choosing.

Stainless steel, which may be used in the oven racks or in the ring around the surface units, may be cleaned safely and effectively with steel wool soap pads.

Use of the range. Cooking utensils should fit the cooking unit or burner. A small saucepan on a large burner or unit wastes heat. A large pan which overlaps the unit or burner is likely to check or score the enamel as a result of the reflected heat from the bottom of the pan. Pans which are warped on the bottom and do not rest flat on the unit or burner waste heat and require a longer cooking time. Covering utensils speeds cooking, reduces evaporation of liquid from food, permits cooking with a minimum of water, and prevents excess water vapor in the air. The heat should be turned on high only until the food starts to cook. Maintaining too high a cooking temperature wastes fuel, evaporates the cooking liquids, causes food to spatter or boil over, and sometimes spoils the quality of the food.

By rotating the use of a unit or burner—that is, by not always using the same one—the life of a burner or unit will be extended. Don't let the fuel burn with nothing on the unit or burner. A utensil with water or food in it absorbs the heat and saves the grate. Just as the utensil should be placed on the burner or unit before turning on the heat, so the heat should be turned off before removing the utensil when the cooking is finished. In addition to prolonging life of the grate, this practice eliminates fuel waste and is a good safety practice.

Gas ranges should always be located out of open drafts and away from windows and doors.

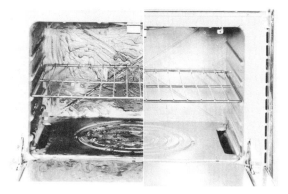

Courtesy Modern Maid, Inc.

One form of self-cleaning oven is cleaned by high-intensity heat, which is produced when the special cleaning control is set.

Courtesy Caloric Corp.

The control for self-cleaning ovens of the pyrolytic type may be a part of the regular oven control or a separate control unit.

Cooking utensils should fit the cooking unit or burner. Some ranges provide for adapting a unit to the size of the utensil.

When a gas oven is first turned on, the oven door should be left ajar briefly so that moisture will not condense on the door and run down to lower parts causing rusting. With both gas and electric ranges, the oven door should be left ajar after use while the oven cools and moisture evaporates.

Ranges equipped for "programmed" baking or "automatic cook and hold" are not designed for the homemaker who is away from home all day. Many foods develop a high bacterial count if kept at room temperature for any length of time. Such foods are not suitable for this type of cooking. Since the oven temperature does not drop immediately and cooking will continue for a short time, foods requiring exact baking times are not suitable for this type of cooking either.

The oven of a range should not be used as a heater. The thermostat could be damaged, since the oven temperature will probably never reach the temperature designated on the control. If it is necessary to use the range for heat, put a pan of water on the unit or burner, as suggested on page 391.

Electric Range

The correct assortment of small electric appliances would make it possible to cook food without the use of a range. With the small appliances or with an electric range, food can be fried, broiled, baked, rotisserized, or boiled. However, small electrical appliances are seldom used to the exclusion of the range. Since a range is more adaptable, and therefore more compact, a kitchen usually has a combination of small electrical appliances and a range.

How does an electric range work? Electric current, controlled by switches, flows through wires which are sealed in a casing of stainless metal to protect them from injury and corrosion. There may be two coils in one casing or two coils, each in a separate casing. The casings are flattened on the top surface for efficient contact with the bottom of utensils.

Wiring. The amount of electric power used is expressed in watts. The higher the wattage the faster the unit will heat if it is turned on high speed. A range needs a special three-wire circuit of 120/240 volt 60 ampere service. A total of 16,500 watts is often needed. The connection between the range and the outlet is called the "pigtail cord."

To obtain information concerning the voltage requirements and the total number of watts used by the range, read the name plate. This is ordinarily visible when the oven door is open. It is located on the outside frame of the oven or below the oven. If the name plate is below the oven, it is visible when the storage drawer is pulled out.

Ovens are available which cook electronically and conventionally. Ranges may contain both a dual-type lower oven and a conventional eye-level oven with rotisserie features.

Courtesy General Electric

Super-speed units. So-called "super-speed" units which get red hot in seconds have wattage ratings of 4,000 to 5,600 during this time. When the control is turned from OFF to any of the heat settings, double the usual voltage is released, producing a surge of electric current for a few seconds. It then automatically resets the unit so that is operates at regular voltage for the remainder of the cooking time.

Ovens. The oven of an electric range has two heating units. The bottom unit is for baking and roasting; the top unit is for broiling. In ovens which require cleaning manually, the lower unit, and in some ranges the upper unit as well, may be removed for easier cleaning of the oven; or the bottom unit tilts up for cleaning. The oven should be cleaned only when the unit and the oven are cool. In replacing the unit after the oven has been cleaned, one must be sure that the terminal points are all the way into the terminal blocks; otherwise the current cannot flow through the heating element, and the oven will not heat. Oven units vary in wattage from about 2,000 for baking to 4,000 for broiling.

Safety. The Underwriters Laboratories symbol (UL) means that the model has been tested and approved for safety if installed and used as recommended. The name plate will include the UL stamp if the range has been approved for listing. It will also give information for proper installation. An "O" means that the range is safely insulated for installation flush to the wall or base cabinet.

Electronic Range

Another quite different variation of the electric range is the electronic range. Cooking is done with high-frequency waves, called microwaves. Electricity which vibrates at 60 cycles per second is converted by means of a magnetron tube to microwave energy which vibrates at 2,450 million cycles per second. A fan distributes the microwaves throughout the oven.

Food absorbs the microwaves; this produces heat and causes the food to cook very rapidly. Containers made of glass, paper, and china do not become hot because the microwaves pass through them. Metal containers reflect the microwaves and thus are not used for cooking food in an electronic range. The cooking time by microwave is cut from $1/8$ to $1/2$ the time required by conventional ranges. For example, one hamburger can be cooked in 20 seconds. Increasing

A portable electronic range is adaptable in many situations because it can be plugged into an ordinary 115-volt outlet.

Courtesy Amana Refrigeration, Inc.

In the electronic range the magnetron (A) converts electric energy to microwave energy. A fan, or stirrer (B), distributes the microwaves throughout the oven. Cooking time is greatly reduced by this cooking method.

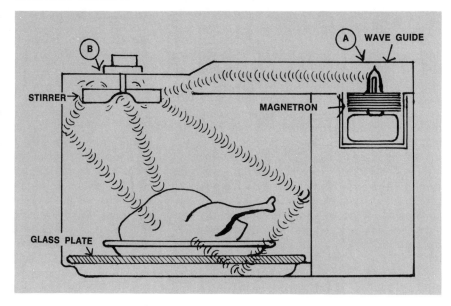

the number of hamburgers increases the cooking time. Cooking time is affected by the type, quantity, size and shape of food being cooked. The larger the mass the longer the time required.

Since the food cooks so rapidly that it does not brown as it would in a conventional range, some electronic ranges have a unit which produces browning in the same way as in a conventional oven. Others have an oven which may be used as either a conventional or an electronic oven, separately or simultaneously.

A timing device, marked in seconds, rings a bell when the cooking time is completed. Care and cleaning of an electronic range are very easy since the range itself remains cool and does not burn fat on the lining. Food which might have a tendency to spatter could be covered with a paper towel unless the browning unit was being used.

Gas Range

The type of gas used will depend upon the locality where one lives. Thus this decision is made automatically when one chooses one's housing. However, it is of interest to know about the types of fuel used in gas ranges.

Fuel types. There are three types of fuel used for gas ranges—natural gas, manufactured gas, and LP gas. Natural and manufactured gas are supplied to homes from underground mains. LP gas is delivered by truck to areas where gas from mains is not available.

Natural gas comes from gas deposits in the earth. It is carried by steel pipes to all parts of the country. Natural gas usually costs less than other commonly used fuels. Manufactured gas is formed by releasing gas from coal and petroleum. It is often manufactured as a by-product of the coke and petroleum-refining industries. Liquefied petroleum gas (LP gas) is also called bottled gas. LP gas can be changed readily from gas to liquid and vice versa.

Heating value of gases varies. Natural gas has approximately 1,000 Btu's (British Thermal Units) per cubic foot; manufactured gas has 500 Btu's per cubic foot; and liquefied petroleum has from 2,500 to 3,200 Btu's per cubic foot. Because of this difference in heating value, appliances need adjustment by trained and competent servicemen when one changes from one kind of gas to another.

Since LP and natural gas are odorless, an odorant is added to make leakage detectable.

Many mobile homes come already equipped with an eye-level range.

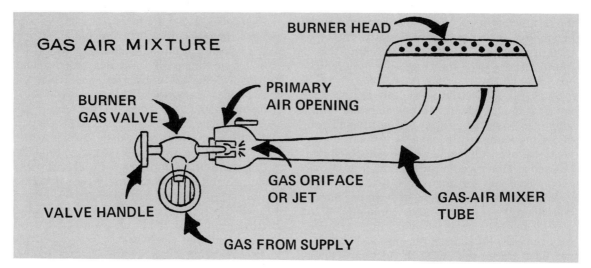

The schematic drawing of a gas burner shows how gas and air are premixed for proper combustion.

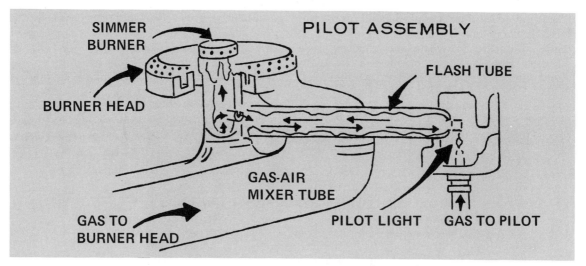

When a gas burner is turned on, some of the air-gas mixture is fed into the flash tube where it is ignited by the pilot light. The burning gas in the flash tube in turn ignites the gas mixture in the burner head.

These "protective odors" are known as mercaptans. The odor of the mercaptan resembles rotten eggs. A leak of less than 1 percent concentration of gas in air can warn of the leak. If a leak occurs, the service company should be called without delay. Gas servicemen carry a device known as an explosimeter for detecting gas leaks.

Operating principle. For a gas burner to operate, gas and air must be premixed before the actual burning takes place. Only the proper mixture of gas and air will burn. As the stream of gas enters the base of the burner tube, it draws air into the tube with it. Gas and air are mixed in the tube. They burn at the top with a blue flame. A desirable flame will be completely blue (not yellow), and the flame will not lift or blow from the top of the burner.

In order for the gas to pass through the burner head and be ignited at the openings in the burner head, the burner must be turned on by a valve handle. For added safety in homes where there are small children, ranges with a control that has to be pushed in might be used to prevent accidents.

A gas burner permits infinite heat control unless there are definite settings on the burners. In this case the "speed" of cooking has been predetermined by the manufacturer of the range, as is commonly done in electric ranges. In top-of-the-line models with thermostatically controlled burners the heat is controlled automatically once the control is set for the type of food being cooked.

If the range has a pilot light, the burners will light automatically when the valve is turned on. Pilot lights may burn continuously in the center of a group of burners. Pilot lights add to the operating cost and give off heat. Some models have individual pilot lights for each burner. They are tiny beadlike flames which burn less gas and give off less heat than does the center pilot light. More expensive models light the burners automatically by electric ignition rather than by continuous-burning pilot lights.

Some models have a grate over the burners to support cooking utensils. Below the burners is a burner bowl, which helps control the amount of air around the burner, reflects heat, and catches any food which may boil over.

If the range has two sizes of burners, one size will be a fast-cook burner with around 12,000 Btus of heat input per hour. The other size will be 9,000 Btus per hour. Simmer settings have a heat capacity of 1,200 Btus per hour.

Ovens. The oven of a gas range may have a pilot light which burns continuously. Some ovens have electric ignition in place of the continuously-burning oven pilot light.

Ordinarily the oven of a gas range is heated by a burner which is located below the bottom

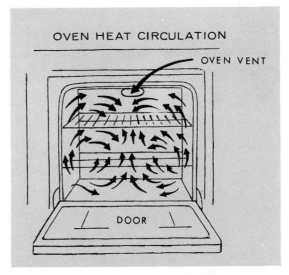

OVEN HEAT CIRCULATION

OVEN VENT

DOOR

Adapted with permission of American Gas Association

This schematic drawing shows the circulation of heat in a gas oven. The small vent in the back wall of the oven permits steam and cooking wastes to escape. In both gas and electric ranges the ovens must have a vent for proper operation.

of the oven. The heated air reaches the oven through small openings at the sides of the oven floor. The same burner provides heat for the broiler in models where the broiler is located below the oven. Some models have a burner above and below the oven.

The broiler may be in a variety of locations. When it is located to one side of the oven, it has a separate burner and control. One type holds food vertically between two burners for broiling on both sides at once. Counter and top-of-range broilers are also available. Additional varieties of broiler locations can be found in eye-level models.

Safety. Look for the Blue Star Seal of Approval of the American Gas Association or the Canadian Gas Association symbol. Ranges must pass hundreds of rigid test before being approved so that they can carry the Blue Star Seal of approval. This seal shows that the range has been tested for quality of construction, performance, and safety from fire and explosion.

Because gas fuel is explosive and poisonous, a gas range is always a potential hazard. Auto-

Courtesy Jenn-Air Corporation

Cooking odors can be removed from the kitchen by means of a built-in ventilation system. Steam, smoke, and grease from both the rotisserie and the surface units are exhausted to the outside through the vents behind the control knobs between the two cooking areas.

Courtesy Berns Air King Corporation

Range hoods are used for the purpose of removing cooking odors, smoke, and heat. Vented and nonvented models are similar in outward appearance. Check carefully to be sure that the type of range hood you select is appropriate to your situation.

matic ignition on all burners can reduce this hazard as well as increase convenience. Pilot lights are subject to being extinguished so one should make sure the burner lights. Burners can be extinguished by food boiling over, so a gas range in use should not be left unattended for long periods of time.

A very important safety feature is an automatic gas cutoff on the pilot. In case the pilot light is accidently extinguished, the gas will automatically cut off. Dangers of asphyxiation and explosion can be avoided by this simple safety feature.

The "burner-on" light is another important safety feature not found on all models. If the flame is so low that one may not know the burner is on, the light will signal this information.

One should find out at the time of purchase whether the model under consideration has automatic ignition. If not, it is important to determine before the purchase has been completed how easily the pilot light can be reached to light.

Range Hoods

Range hoods that are vented out-of-doors are a necessity in homes which are air conditioned or which for other reasons are kept tightly closed. Vented hoods remove cooking heat, moisture, cooking odors, and smoke. Non-vented hoods remove odors and smoke by use of activated charcoal filters or by an electric charge filter.

REFRIGERATORS

The refrigerator is one of the most taken-for-granted household appliances in today's American home. No household appliance contributes more to efficient home management practices than does the refrigerator. It is considered essential to health. In homes without refrigerators, food shopping must be done a day at a time (or even a meal at a time for perishable food) unless some substitute system for keeping food cold has been devised.

With a properly operating refrigerator quantities of food can be bought and held at a 35° to 40° temperature range for several days without souring, molding, or otherwise deteriorating.

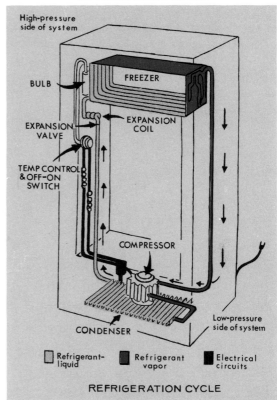

REFRIGERATION CYCLE

Adapted from "A to Zero of Refrigeration" by permission of General Motors

As the refrigerant in the cooling coils (freezer section) (1) absorbs heat from the food-warmed air, the refrigerant vaporizes. The compressor (2) pulls the vapor through a suction line. The vapor changes back to liquid (condenses) in the condenser (3). As the refrigerant leaves the condenser, it passes through the expansion valve (4), and the cycle begins again.

Electric Refrigerator

The most common type of refrigerator in use today is powered by electricity. This type of refrigerator works on the compressor principle.

Operating principles. A compressor-type refrigerator operates on several fundamental principles: (1) Heat passes from a warmer body to a cooler one. (2) Liquid has the ability to absorb heat as it vaporizes. (Vaporization takes place at the boiling point.) (3) The

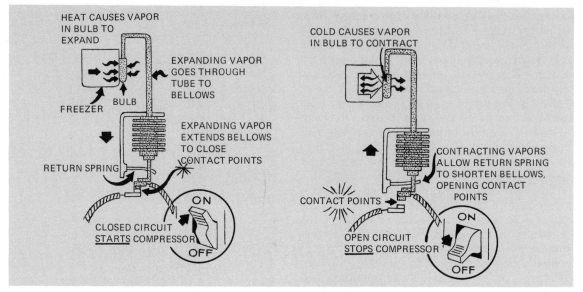

HEAT CAUSES VAPOR IN BULB TO EXPAND

EXPANDING VAPOR GOES THROUGH TUBE TO BELLOWS

FREEZER   BULB

EXPANDING VAPOR EXTENDS BELLOWS TO CLOSE CONTACT POINTS

RETURN SPRING

CLOSED CIRCUIT STARTS COMPRESSOR

ON
OFF

COLD CAUSES VAPOR IN BULB TO CONTRACT

CONTRACTING VAPORS ALLOW RETURN SPRING TO SHORTEN BELLOWS, OPENING CONTACT POINTS

CONTACT POINTS

OPEN CIRCUIT STOPS COMPRESSOR

ON
OFF

Adapted from "A to Zero of Refrigeration" by permission of General Motors

As the temperature inside the refrigerator rises, the gas inside the bulb expands, extends the bellows, and flips a switch to ON to start the compressor motor. As the inside of the refrigerator cools, the operation is reversed.

boiling point can be changed by changing the pressure. (Raising the pressure raises the boiling point; lowering the pressure lowers the boiling point.) (4) When vapor gives off heat, it changes to liquid.

Let's see how these physical laws make a refrigerator work. Look again at the first principle. Heat from food placed in the refrigerator passes into the surrounding air inside the refrigerator. The warmed air moves by convection currents to the cooling unit. The circulation of air may be aided by a fan. Efficient circulation of air is essential to effective refrigeration.

The liquid used for cooling according to the second principle is known as the refrigerant. Water has the characteristics of a refrigerant, but it has an important drawback; its boiling point is too high. So Freon 12, which boils at −21.7 degrees Fahrenheit at atmospheric pressure, is commonly used in compressor-type refrigerators as the refrigerant. Inside the cooling unit, also called an evaporator, Freon 12 absorbs heat from the food-warmed air, which is passing over the evaporator coils, and starts

to boil. It continues to boil and absorb heat as it vaporizes, changing from a cold liquid to a cold gas.

The cold temperature of the gas must be raised enough to give off its accumulated heat at room temperature. A compressor is used to raise the temperature to about 25° above the surrounding air according to principle three. The refrigerant circulates through the condenser (located at the back of some refrigerators and at the bottom of others) and heat is given off.

As the refrigerant gives off heat into the room it changes from a high temperature gas to a liquid, as in principle four. As the refrigerant leaves the condenser, it passes through an expansion valve and expansion coils which reduce the pressure, thereby reducing the temperature. The entire cycle then begins again. The temperature at which the thermostat is set will determine when the motor will start the cycle in operation.

To review, there are four parts in a refrigeration cycle: (1) The evaporator, or cooling coil, where air, passing across it, is cooled by the refrigerant which is absorbing heat as it boils and vaporizes. (2) The compressor, which pulls the vapor or cold gas from the evaporator through a suction line and compresses it, thereby raising the pressure as well as the temperature. (3) The condenser, where the vaporized high-temperature, high-pressure refrigerant is cooled enough to condense. (4) The thermal expansion valve where the liquid is instantly changed to a mixture of cold liquid and cold gas. The pressure has now been reduced. Remember, when pressure is reduced, the temperature is reduced, and now the refrigerant is once more ready to start absorbing heat.

Construction. The refrigerator is essentially a large box or cabinet made of steel which has been covered with either porcelain or baked-on enamel. Baked-on enamel is less expensive than porcelain enamel. It resists chipping and cracking. Acid-resistant porcelain enamel is especially desirable for interiors. Some exterior finishes include brushed chrome or anodized aluminum on the trim.

Between the interior and exterior walls of the refrigerator some type of insulating material, such as fiber glass boards, mineral wool, or plastic foam (polyurethane) is used. The plastic-foam type is especially desirable because in addition to its low heat transfer, it can be tightly fitted into corners while it is applied in its foam state, before it becomes rigid and bonded to adjoining surfaces.

Since heat flows from a warm to a cool area, one function of the insulation is to prevent heat from the room from entering the refrigerator through the walls. Experiments have shown that more heat enters the refrigerator through the walls than from opening the door or from the heat of the food. The quality and thickness of the insulating material are important factors in determining the efficient performance of the refrigerator. Whereas a minimum thickness of 3 inches is considered desirable for conventional insulation, a 1½-inch thickness of the polyurethane insulating material will give equivalent insulation.

The insulation of the door should be of the same thickness as that of the box or cabinet. Unless the door fits tightly, heat or water vapor from the room will enter the refrigerator. A

Courtesy Better Homes and Gardens, © Meredith Corporation, 1967

A portable refrigerator which provides some ice plus space for a limited amount of food is a useful supplement for special entertaining.

gasket of rubber or plastic around the rim of the door contributes to the tightness of the fit. A double gasket, (consisting of two narrow gaskets) or a wider gasket is more effective than a single narrow gasket.

For the safety of children, federal regulations require that it be possible to open the door from the inside as well as the outside. This is accomplished by means of a magnetic element within the plastic door seal. This does not interfere with the tightness of the seal of the door.

Shelves should be sturdy enough to withstand without warping the weight of items normally stored in a refrigerator. Wire racks of stainless steel or aluminum are more durable than plastic racks. Plastic is used primarily for door shelves and door racks.

"NO-FROST" OR "FROST-FREE" REFRIGERATOR-FREEZER

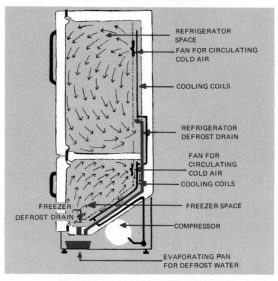

REFRIGERATOR SPACE
FAN FOR CIRCULATING COLD AIR
COOLING COILS
REFRIGERATOR DEFROST DRAIN
FAN FOR CIRCULATING COLD AIR
COOLING COILS
FREEZER DEFROST DRAIN
FREEZER SPACE
COMPRESSOR
EVAPORATING PAN FOR DEFROST WATER

Diagram reprinted from CONSUMER REPORTS with permission

Frost which forms in this model is never seen because it collects on the cooling coils which are located in the space between the storage areas and the outer shell rather than in the storage area walls. When the frost melts from the cooling coils, the melted water is collected in an evaporating pan at the bottom of the refrigerator.

Compressor-type refrigerators depend upon open shelves rather than solid shelves to permit free circulation of air.

Types. Refrigerators are available in three main types: 1) All-refrigerator with only enough freezer space for two to four ice-cube trays. 2) The one-door or conventional refrigerator. 3) The combination refrigerator-freezer. These may be free-standing or built in.

The freezer may be above the refrigerator section, below the refrigerator section, or beside the refrigerator section. In a combination refrigerator-freezer the freezer compartment has its own completely separate opening.

Some models require manual defrosting of both the refrigerator and the freezer compartments; some defrost automatically; some are frost-free in the refrigerator only; some models are completely frost-free in both the refrigerator and the freezer.

Controls. Temperature control is an important factor in refrigerator selection since this affects the quality of the food being refrigerated. Separate temperature controls for the refrigerator and the freezer are more desirable than a single control. Freezer temperature should remain at zero or below to maintain the maximum of original quality of color, flavor, and texture of the food. Temperature in freezer doors has been found by testing laboratories to range from 12° to 17°F., with some going as high as 20° to 25°F., which is satisfactory only for short-term storage. The temperature on refrigerator doors is higher than in the main area of the refrigerator. Therefore the doors should be used only for foods not adversely affected by the higher temperature.

Factors which affect cost. Size and special features are two factors which influence the initial cost within any one brand. The larger the capacity and the more special features, the higher will be the initial cost. The total operating cost is higher for a larger model than for a smaller one, but the cost per cubic foot is less for the larger model. A two-door refrigerator-freezer combination costs more to operate than a conventional model, but it does a more efficient job of holding frozen food. According to an article in the American Society of Heating, Refrigerating, and Air-Conditioning Engineers Journal, November, 1962: "Frost-free models can cost up to twice as much to operate as those in which frost is deposited in the storage cabinet. The additional costs are attributed to fan operation for air circulation in the cabinet and heaters used in defrosting." However, if one is lax about defrosting a manual-defrost freezer, operation costs will increase due to excessive buildup of frost.

Rules of thumb have been devised for helping consumers decide how large a refrigerator is desirable for their specific situation. The recommended minimum is 8 cubic feet for the first two people plus 2 cubic feet for each additional person in the family and 2 additional cubic feet for entertaining. For a family of four a fourteen cubic foot refrigerator would be the minimum. However, advertised capacity is sometimes misleading because it includes the space occupied by evaporator coils, fan housing, and any other small projections, rather than net usable space.

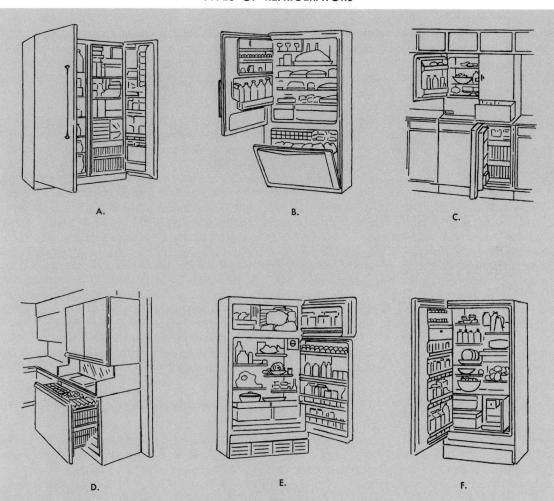

A. B. C.

D. E. F.

An upright refrigerator-freezer may have the freezer compartment to one side of the refrigerator (A) or below the refrigerator compartment (B). A built-in combination refrigerator-freezer may be provided with counterspace. There is a two-door refrigerator above the counter. The center section of the refrigerator has drawers for fresh vegetables or meat. The freezer section with pull-out baskets is below the counter. Another type of combination model has a double-door refrigerator above the counter and a large-capacity freezer drawer below the work surface. A refrigerator-freezer may have the freezer compartment above the refrigerator. The all-refrigerator appeals particularly to those who have a separate freezer. An ice-cube compartment is shown in the lower right-hand corner.

403

Since the most important thing one is buying with the refrigerator is storage space, it is more important to spend extra dollars on larger capacity than some of the added features.

What are some of the special features from which consumers may choose? This is a partial list: Modern art doors for an additional $300 or $400; foot pedal door release; dispenser for non-carbonated beverages; automatic ice-maker that fills, freezes, dispenses and holds ice cubes in a bin or container (note that these have to be connected to a cold water line, which may pose an installation problem); a butter conditioner that holds butter or margarine at soft, medium, or hard consistency; egg racks; meat containers; vegetable crispers; air-glide design which floats the refrigerator off the floor for ease in moving the unit to clean the floor.

At no additional cost one can get a model with either a right- or left-hand door hinge. For convenience in use it is desirable for the door opening to be next to the work counter. Also, for maximum efficiency in use, it is desirable to have movable shelves which provide for more flexibility in use than do fixed positions when storing food in containers of different heights. Ham, watermelon, and gallon jugs of milk require more head space than does a package of bacon, cheese, a dish of salad, or a container of cooked food. Shelves that swing out add convenience for accessibility, but some shelf area is sacrificed for the sake of this convenience.

Both design features and the material from which the refrigerator is made contribute to or detract from the ease of care. Desirable features include rounded corners; absence of crevices where food particles can collect; easily removable racks; and rust- and stain-resistant materials which can be easily washed.

Regular cleaning of the refrigerator is necessary to prevent or reduce undesirable food odors. This is true even for "frost-free" types. Keeping leftovers near the front of the refrigerator so they will be seen and used before they spoil is one way to reduce the amount of unpleasant odor. At least once a week one should check and discard any food which is no longer usable. Wrapping in foil, plastic, or other material which can be made airtight prevents any pronounced food odor such as that of smoked meat, onions, or cantaloupe from being transferred to milk and other food which may absorb it.

It is desirable to wash any removable shelves and storage bins or racks in clean sudsy water at the sink and then rinse thoroughly to remove any trace of fragrance from the detergent. The interior of the refrigerator and freezer area should be sponged out with a solution of two tablespoons of baking soda per quart of water. Soda cleans, sweetens, and leaves no after-odor for food to pick up.

How should the refrigerator be cared for during one's absence from home for an extended period of time? Nothing in particular need be done if the period of absence is a month or less. However, any food which might spoil in the refrigerator within a four-week period should be frozen, if possible, to preserve its quality. If one plans to be away for longer than this period of time, the ice-cube maker should have its water supply shut off and all food should be removed from the refrigerator. In general, the refrigerator should be cleaned well, the power turned off, and the door left open (or follow the directions for long-term disuse recommended by the manufacturer).

Thermoelectric or Nonmechanical Refrigerators

The thermoelectric, or nonmechanical, refrigerators operate on the principle of the thermocouple. Electric current flows through two wires of unlike metal. One will heat and one will cool. There are no refrigerants, no compressors, and no moving parts except for a fan.

These refrigerators were originally introduced on the market as "portable models," usually under 4 cubic feet in capacity. Any wall cabinet area can be used for a thermoelectric refrigerator for storage of any fresh food at various desired locations rather than all in one location as with a mechanical refrigerator. Early models were costly and inefficient.

The thermoelectric principle is used in the kitchens of space ships. The cold portion of the thermocouple keeps the food cold in one compartment and the hot portion warms (but can't cook) the food in another compartment. This makes for compactness in use of space, so essential in space travel.

FOOD FREEZERS

For many families a combination refrigerator-freezer with 6 to 8 cubic feet of storage space will provide adequately for their needs to store small amounts of frozen food. When this is sufficient, it eliminates the added initial cost of a freezer and the additional operating cost (approximately $3 a month). To provide real economy, a home freezer should be used to full capacity, or at least to two-thirds capacity, at all times, and the contents of the freezer turned over two or more times a year. If the freezer is used only occasionally or not at its full capacity, the costs cancel any possible savings. Probably a freezer can't be justified on the basis of economy but rather on convenience.

A food freezer is a time-saver in reducing the number of food shopping trips. Also, food can be prepared in advance at the convenience of the homemaker. This can reduce preparation time just prior to the meal. A food freezer can reduce food waste, especially in families that have a negative attitude toward leftovers. Double or triple portions can be prepared all at once and the amount not needed for one meal

Courtesy Gibson Refrigerator Sales Corp.

A chest-type freezer is more economical to operate than an upright freezer with similar features. Chest-type freezers may be defrosted automatically or manually.

can be frozen for later use. This also adds variety to meals throughout the year, as "out-of-season" foods can be brought from the freezer from time to time.

The recommended temperature for holding frozen food is 0°F or colder. Most meats and vegetables will keep from six months to a year with only slight deterioration in quality at this temperature. Highly perishable seafoods and dairy products will keep satisfactorily for several months.

Types

Food freezers come in two types—chest or upright. The upright type, which resembles a refrigerator in appearance, is more convenient to use, but the chest type is more economical to operate, since less cold air is lost when the freezer is opened.

Upright freezers. The upright freezer takes up less floor space than a chest freezer, but since the weight of an upright freezer is concentrated in a smaller area, one would need to make sure that the floor is strong enough to support the filled weight of the freezer.

Automatic-defrost and frost-free upright freezers cost more to buy and more to operate than manual defrost models, but the task of manual defrosting is eliminated. Frost buildup on food packages and freezer walls is prevented by a fan which circulates air in the freezer.

Chest-type freezer. Chest-type freezers may be frost free or the manual defrost type. The freezer is cooled by several refrigerator coils which are located within the insulated walls surrounding the chest or within the dividing walls.

Desirable features include a counterbalanced lid, a light, audible signals to to indicate when the temperature rises to 15°, and a temperature control in an easily accessible location.

Installation and Location

Convenience of location is one factor to consider. But step-saving is of less importance in placement of a freezer than of a refrigerator, since it is opened less frequently. A dry basement or heated garage may be a desirable location because of the strength of the floor in supporting the weight. Dampness damages the metal parts and the motor, and it causes mois-

The outstanding feature of an upright freezer is that all the food is easy to reach.

ture to condense on the exterior of the freezer. A freezer should not be placed where it is so cold that the motor will not run easily, nor where there is too much heat from direct sunshine or from other heat sources. Excess heat increases the operation cost by causing the motor to run more to maintain the freezer temperature. A freezer should not be placed so close to a wall that air carrying heat from the condenser cannot circulate freely.

Operating Suggestions.

When the freezer is new and then at periodic intervals, check the temperature with an accurate refrigerator-freezer thermometer. This can be done by placing the thermometer in the center of the main space but on a package of food or a block of wood, not on a cooling coil. Locate the thermometer so it can be easily read without touching it, leave it overnight, and check the reading when the freezer is first opened the next morning. Do this for several nights, moving the thermometer around to locate the warm spots. These areas should be used for food stored for a shorter period of time.

If the alarm signal sounds it may indicate that the temperature has risen due to too much warm food being placed in the freezer at one time (the recommended maximum amount is one-tenth the capacity at any one time); that the fuse has blown; that there is power failure on the line; or that the trouble is in the motor. If there is a power failure which will be restored within twenty-four hours, there is no need for alarm, for most freezers can keep food frozen for from twenty-four to forty-eight hours if the freezer is full. For longer periods of power failure, dry ice, broken into small pieces and distributed throughout the food packages, will have to be used. A 50-pound cake will provide thirty-six hours protection.

Cleaning and Defrosting

The ideal time to defrost is when the food supply is low. This is difficult to schedule if one is following the advice of keeping the freezer at capacity all the time. Before defrosting, the temperature control should be set at its lowest setting and left overnight or for several hours in order to get the food as cold as possible. If it is possible, pack the food into cartons and leave it in the freezer until ready to start the defrosting process; this will keep the food colder while it is out of the freezer. The freezer should be disconnected at the time the food is removed. Insulate the cartons with heavy blankets or many layers of newspaper, to help prevent the food from thawing.

Many manufacturers provide a scraper for removing the frost. A good windshield defrosting tool works satisfactorily. One should never use a sharp metal tool. Scraping the frost from the freezer walls and packages when it is in thin layers reduces the frequency of having to do a major defrosting. Frost should never be allowed to accumulate to a depth of more than ½ inch, for such frost causes the freezer temperature to rise.

When all ice and water have been removed, sponge the freezer walls with a solution of baking soda in water as suggested for the care of the refrigerator. Rinse with clear water, and dry with a clean towel.

Connect the freezer and allow it to run at its coldest setting until the temperature has been restored to 0°F. Wipe the frost and moisture from the food and replace it in the cold freezer. Then return the temperature control to the normal setting.

DISHWASHERS

There are several reasons for the popularity of mechanical dishwashers. Dishwashing time, including clearing, scraping, and drying, is cut in half. The dishes are more sanitary because the water used is hotter than one's hands can stand, and dishes are dried by hot air rather than towels. Dish breakage should be less than when dishes are washed by hand. However, in loading the dishwasher, some care must be used to see that dishes do not touch, since the force of the water could thus cause chipping.

There are certain limitations to the dishwasher. Because of the high temperature, the high-alkaline dishwasher detergent, and the strong force of the water during the wash cycle, it is suggested that certain items be washed by hand rather than in the dishwasher. The list includes dinnerware with gold or platinum trim or overglaze decoration, wooden materials, polyethylene (pliable) plas-

A portable dishwasher may slide under the counter and give the appearance of a built-in, front-loading model. This one can be operated from the under-counter position because the faucet connector and power cord are located in the front.

Courtesy The Maytag Company

It is important to check the ease with which the portable dish-washer hose may be connected to the faucet.

tics, rubber, milk glass, lacquered ware, cast iron cookware, silver knives with hollow handles, fine crystal, and anodized aluminum ware. Some dishwasher detergents are stronger and therefore more damaging than others. Advertised capacities may be exaggerated by two to six place settings.

Types

Dishwashers are available in four types: (1) Portable. (2) Convertible. (3) Free-standing built-in, or permanently installed. (4) Sink-dishwasher combination. Convertible dishwashers can be rolled around like a portable, or they can have the wheels removed and be permanently installed. Those who buy a dishwasher knowing that they will soon be moving from rental property to a home of their own will find this type or the portable especially desirable. The portable models are rolled to the sink where a hose is connected to the sink faucet, and the sink drain is used. An electric outlet near the sink will be needed.

Portable models are usually top-loading. Built-in or permanently installed and sink-dishwasher combinations may be either top-loading or front-loading. Front-loading models require additional floor space (because the racks roll out approximately 2 feet), but they free the counter space above.

Operating Principle

A dishwasher requires only two plumbing connections, hot water and a drain. Unlike an automatic clothes washing machine, a dishwasher does not fill completely with water. Only about two gallons are used per cycle. It is important to keep in mind that since the washing will all be done without the aid of hands, the force of the water must be strong, and nothing must block the passage of the water to the soiled areas of the dishes. The water pressure must be high enough to permit the right amount of water to enter the dishwasher in the allotted time. Water at too high a pressure may cause noise in the plumbing. One should make sure that the manufacturer's recommendations regarding water pressure are followed carefully.

In addition to the force of the water which sprays over the dishes, chemical cleaning ac-

Courtesy Kitchenaid by Hobart

In one type of wash action the water is forcefully sprayed over the dishes by a rotating impeller located in the floor of the dishwasher.

tion takes place from the detergent. Only detergents specially designed for use in dishwashers should be used. These are low-sudsing and highly alkaline. Never use high-sudsing soap powders and liquid detergents because they not only reduce the washing action, but cause mounds of suds to pour out of the machine. These suds may damage the motor. Never use dishwasher detergents for washing dishes by hand.

For the dishwasher to give clean, sparkling dishes, the water should be between 140° and 160°F. Some brands have a heating element within the dishwasher for maintaining the temperature or boosting it as high as 180°F. If hard water must be used, try different brands of detergent until you find the one which is best for your situation. A rinse conditioner will help reduce spotting and clouding. Top-of-the-line models have built-in rinse-agent dispensers. Rinse agents are available in small plastic bottles or nylon net containers which can be used in any dishwasher.

Water consumption varies somewhat from one brand to another, ranging from 6 to 15 gallons. Since water is recirculated during parts of the cycle, the water consumption is kept lower than it would otherwise be. In the soak or prerinse cycle, water is sprayed over the dishes and loose food particles removed and drained away. Following the wash cycle, there is a clear rinse, which may be followed by a second, third, or fourth wash-and-rinse cycle. For the dishwasher to give satisfactory results, there must be provision for removing the water and food particles without their being redeposited onto the dishes. This is the purpose

This cut-away view of a top-loading dishwasher shows bed-of-nails (or random-design) racks. The top rack is divided to allow access to the bottom rack.

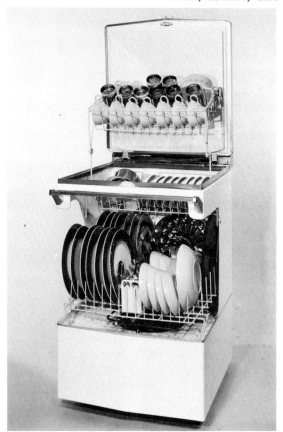

of the filter. Soil is trapped and flushed away. Following the final rinse the dishes dry by evaporation which is speeded by heat. In some models the air is circulated by a fan. These have been found to be no more effective than those without a fan.

An electric dishwasher should have its own 15- or 20-ampere, 60-cycle, 115-volt individual circuit. During the drying cycle a dishwasher uses from 750 to 1,000 watts. Dishwashers must be adequately grounded to eliminate electrical hazards.

Design Features for Efficiency of Operation

All dishwashers have two racks. Front-loading dishwashers are more convenient when the two racks roll out independently. In some top-loading dishwashers a portion of the rack is removable or is attached to the lid and lifts up as the lid is opened to give access to the lower rack. The design of the rack determines its flexibility in use. Those requiring a systematic loading pattern are less flexible in use than a bed-of-nails or random-design or racks with adjustable sections. Baskets with openings that are close-spaced to prevent such small utensils as metal measuring spoons from falling through contribute to efficient use. Look for models with adequate space between racks to accommodate large dinner plates and serving platters. If well designed, the corners will also be usable. Square racks have a larger capacity than round racks.

Heat-resistant, heavy, plastic-coated wire racks or spikes are more desirable than uncoated wire ones. The latter type tends to leave black marks on chinaware. Porcelain enamel or stainless steel is preferable to plastic lining for interior walls.

A single wash arm, when well designed, gives as satisfactory results as the multiple-arm models.

Flexibility of controls might also be considered a design feature. These are typically found on push-button models. Although they contribute to flexibility in use of the dishwasher, they do not add anything to the washing performance. Within any brand, the washing performance should be about the same in the custom model as in the elaborate, top-of-the-line model.

Use and Care

The way in which the dishwasher is loaded is a factor affecting the final results. Unless each surface is exposed to the spray of water, soil will not be removed. One should take care, therefore, to avoid nesting silverware, bowls, or other items. The design of the racks and the location of the source of the water will influence the method of loading. The instruction book will give information on this point. The method of loading also affects drying. Unless the dishes are placed so that the water can drain out, there will be a water mark on the dried dishes or water will spill out when the dishes are removed from the dishwasher. Dripping water from glasses or cups from the top rack will not spot dishes if the bottom rack is unloaded first.

If the dishwasher is going to be turned on right away or if it has a rinse-and-hold cycle, dishes need little or no rinsing before they are placed in the dishwasher, but loose food, bones, scraps and the like should be scraped off.

Modern dishwasher detergents are designed to react with the grease on soiled dishes.

It cuts down on the noise of operation if the dishes are loaded so that they do not bump together from the strong force of the water. This precaution also protects the dishes from chipping.

FOOD WASTE DISPOSERS

Food waste disposers are not generally thought of as major kitchen appliances, but it seems reasonable to discuss them here, following dishwashers.

Although some cities require the use of food waste disposers, other cities prohibit their use so as not to overload the sewers and sewage treatment plants. One should check with the city ordinance before buying a food waste disposer. It may not be feasible to install a disposer for any house that depends on a private cesspool. The added load of food waste may require frequent cleaning of the cesspool. The cost of this extra cleaning may be too high in

TYPES OF ELECTRIC FOOD DISPOSERS

The continuous-feed type disposer operates as soon as the switch is turned on. In order to prevent particles from being ejected, put the cover on when grinding up hard waste such as bones. A batch-feed type disposer will operate only when the cover is locked in place after the disposer is loaded. Batch-feed disposers have a built-in safety advantage; you cannot put your hand into the unit while it is running.

411

comparison to other methods of food waste disposal to justify the purchase of a disposer.

Operating Principle

A food waste disposer is a motor-driven grinder installed below the sink and connected to the plumbing and sink drain. Powerful metal blades grind, shred, and pulverize food waste into small particles which can be flushed down the drain by the force of cold running water.

Most disposers operate on a 15-ampere circuit, but a combination dishwasher-disposer uses a 20-ampere circuit.

Types

Disposers are of two types: (1) Continuous feed. (2) Batch feed. In the continuous-feed type, as soon as the cold water and the switch are turned on, the disposer grinds up the food scraps as fast as they are scraped into the disposer. This type requires a separately installed switch.

With the batch-feed type, the waste food is scraped into the disposer, the cold water is turned on, and a cover, which also serves as the sink drain plug, is placed over the opening. Grinding does not start until the cover is locked in place in the "ON" position. The motor is turned off by turning the cover to the "OFF" position.

Selection Features

See that the cover of the batch-feed type is easy to insert and turn on and that the ON position is easy to identify. Water must flow freely through the drain while the disposer is running. Costly damage could be done if anything should block the water flow causing the disposer to run dry.

The continuous-feed type is more convenient and somewhat less expensive to buy. The saving may be somewhat offset by the cost of the additional electrical switch. Somewhat more caution is required in the use of this type since the disposer operates with the drain open, and dishcloths, silverware, or other items may drop in accidentally. There is also the possibility of danger to one's fingers in this type.

Food waste disposers are usually available in ¼, ⅓, and ½ horsepower. Heavy duty models have a larger horsepower rating (some

also have more revolutions per minute) than do the less sturdy models. Sometimes disposers of smaller capacity have more revolutions per minute than larger models to compensate for this difference in size. Some of the guides to quality in selecting either the continuous-feed or the batch-feed type are: the horsepower, the revolutions per minute, and the quality of the steel in the cutting blades.

Desirable features are a reverse-action to prevent jamming and a splash guard. Top-of-the-line models tend to have thicker insulation for more quiet operation than the lower priced models.

Safety Features

As in selecting any electrical equipment, one should buy only if the Underwriters' Laboratories or CSA seal is present to assure that the disposer is electrically safe. The batch-feed type has the safety feature of not operating until the cover is in place. A thermo-electric control prevents the motor from operating if overloaded; this protects both the disposer and the house wiring.

Use and Care

Safety in use is always important. Obviously, you should never reach into the disposer to retrieve something that fell in by mistake unless the switch is turned off. If an unnatural sound indicates that the blades are striking metal, or a hum is heard that indicates that something may be interfering with the operation, turn the disposer off immediately and investigate. If a jam has occurred, the motor will become overheated and the overload switch will break the circuit. Give the motor time to cool, push the reset switch and try it again. If it is still jammed so it will not start, turn off the switch, break the circuit at the fuse box, and use a hammer handle to dislodge whatever is caught.

The disposer should not be overloaded nor the waste packed in. Best results will be obtained by cutting citrus rind and corn cobs or husks into smaller pieces before placing them in the disposer. Other types of food waste most disposers are built to handle include peelings, coffee grounds, loose tea leaves, plate scraps, a normal amount of cooking fat, and bones of chickens. More durably built disposers can

Courtesy Magic Chef

Some types of gas waste disposer can be installed under a kitchen counter. The pull-out ash drawer is shown at the base. Heat and smoke are vented to the outdoors.

handle small chop bones, paper napkins, cigarettes, and coffee-filter paper from nonelectric coffee makers. None is intended as a disposer for paper cartons, wastepaper, cans, aluminum foil, string, tea bags, filter-tip cigarettes, or glass. Large quantities of cooking fats should be hardened in the refrigerator before being added to other food waste for the disposer. Mixing hard wastes, such as bones, fruit pits, and corn cobs, with other food waste, helps them to go through faster and more quietly. Pulverized bones and pits, which have a scour-

ing action on the plumbing, keep the chamber clean and sharpen the blades.

It is very important that *cold* water, not hot water, be used in large enough force to flush out the ground food waste. Cold water solidifies fats and grease so that they can be ground into small particles that will flush down the drain rather than cling to the walls of the plumbing lines. The disposer should be allowed to run until the chamber is empty. Even after the disposer has been shut off the water should be allowed to continue to flow for 30 to 60

413

seconds in order to flush out the drain. This is even more important when using the disposer just before leaving home for an extended period of time. Failure to adequately flush out the drain may mean that food spoils, causing an unpleasant odor. This standing food may even block the drain, requiring the expense of a service call.

As part of the routine care, close the sink drain, partially fill the sink with water, then remove the stopper to permit a full flow of the water through the disposer while it is running. Lye or a drain cleaner should never be used because they would corrode the metal making the machine inoperable.

By following to the letter the instructions for grinding certain food wastes in the food-waste disposer, the consumer can determine to what extent the instructions must be adapted to his own situation.

Disposers are permanently lubricated so that no oiling is necessary.

UNDER COUNTER INCINERATORS

Another type of waste disposer is the under-counter incinerator. This may be installed on either an inside or outside wall and vented through the wall or through the roof to outdoors. All waste except cans, bottles, and metal foil can be incinerated.

Proper loading of waste is essential for best results. Paper and cartons should be placed in the incinerator first before wet food waste. For complete combustion, air circulation is needed just as it is when burning trash in an outdoor incinerator. An important rule for proper operation is to set the timer properly to provide time for the waste to be completely consumed. Follow carefully the instructions given in the operating manual.

LEARNING EXPERIENCES ————————————————————————

1. Define the meaning of the following words as used in this chapter: abrasive; batch-feed disposer; convertible dishwasher; compressor; condenser; evaporator; counter-balanced door; pigtail cord; refrigerant; thermocouple; thermoelectric.

2. Explain why you would prefer one of the following types of ranges: (a) free-standing, low-oven model; (b) built-in wall oven with separate surface units or burners; (c) free-standing model with eye-level oven. Use pictures or sketches to point out features you consider especially desirable.

3. To determine the heat pattern during broiling in a given range, place five slices of bread on the broiler pan, with one in each corner and one in the center. Find the position for the broiler pan that will place the bread about 2 inches from the flame or electric unit. Turn on the heat. Watch continuously until the center slice is toasted to a golden brown. Leaving the broiler turned on, remove the broiler pan long enough to turn each slice over, being

careful to keep the bread in the same position for toasting the second side. Return the pan of bread to the oven and repeat toasting, using the golden brown color of the center slice of bread as the guide for removing the pan of toast. Leaving the toast on the broiler rack in the same position it was during toasting, compare the slices of toast as to evenness of browning. How can you apply what you have just observed? What made the difference in the degree of browning? Where on the broiler rack would you place toast if you preferred it crisp and dry? If you preferred it less crisp? Where on the broiler pan would you place meat you wanted to be well done? If you preferred it rare, medium rare, or medium well done?

4. Using "spec" sheets for at least five models of either gas or electric ranges, find out the selling price of each model and point out the features which have been added as one moves up the scale from the least expensive to the most expensive model. Tell which model you would buy (or hope

to find in your first home) and why you selected this model. What factors should influence your choice of model?

5. Assume you have rented an apartment which has a 20-inch, bottom-of-the-line model range. Make a list of the ways it can be used to cook. Next make a list of any small portable appliances you might want to own to supplement the range, and tell how they would be useful in this situation.

6. Using magazine advertisements, TV commercials, or visits to appliance stores, make a list of *special* features found on current top-of-the-line models of refrigerator-freezers. Evaluate these features and their costs in terms of their worth, their usefulness, and the family situation for which they would be most appropriate.

7. Describe several family situations, representing different stages in the family life cycle, showing how a home freezer could contribute to effective management of time and energy.

8. What do you predict will be the effect on a cake if the oven thermostat is inaccurate —either above or below the temperature setting? Try the following experiment to see if your predictions are accurate: First, make sure the ovens you are going to use are accurate by using an oven thermometer and comparing its reading with the setting on the oven control. If your classroom has three ovens available for use all at once, using identical cake pans and cake mixes make three one-layer cakes. Set one oven for the temperature recommended on the cake package. Set one oven 25° lower and the third oven 25° hotter than the recommended temperature. Compare the finished products as to brownness, texture, and moisture content. How important is the accuracy of the oven thermostat? What can be done to correct an inaccurate thermostat?

9. Tell what will happen if, when you have a dishwasher, you choose to put into the dishwasher all those items for which hand-washing is recommended. Discuss the values which will enter into your decision if you decide to ignore the recommendations for care of these items.
Explain why dishwasher detergents should *not* be used for handwashing dishes.

10. Discuss the advantages of a continuous-feed type food waste disposer over the batch-feed type. What are the disadvantages?
Point out the advantages of a kitchen incinerator over a drain-installed food waste disposer. Cite disadvantages of incinerators as compared with disposers.

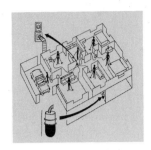

21

General Equipment

The term "general equipment" refers to the following household equipment: (1) room air conditioners, (2) portable humidifiers, (3) hot-water heaters, and (4) equipment for floor care. This equipment is not identified with any specific room but may be used in several locations throughout the house.

ROOM AIR CONDITIONERS

Few today who have experienced the comfort of air conditioning need to be convinced of its advantages. Studies done by the National Warm-Air Heating and Air Conditioning Association show that people in air-conditioned homes are healthier than families in non-air-conditioned homes because they maintain their appetites, eat better, and sleep better during hot, humid weather.

Since an air-conditioning system filters some dust and pollen from the air, people with respiratory allergies find relief from their trouble in addition to comfort. High humidity for extended periods of time causes damage from mildew and mold; air conditioning reduces mildew by lowering humidity.

There are several available forms of air conditioning: (1) a system which heats in winter and cools in summer; (2) an add-on unit for converting the house heating system to year-round air conditioning; or (3) a window unit for summer air conditioning. The first two types are mentioned in Chapters 5 and 7, which deal with basic structural elements and remodeling. The third type, the portable electric window unit for summer air conditioning, will be discussed here.

An understanding of essential body functions is basic to understanding air conditioning. The body always generates more heat than it needs, so in order for the body to maintain its normal temperature of 98.6°F, excess heat must be given off. The body constantly gives off heat in three ways: (1) convection, (2) radiation, and (3) evaporation.

We are probably most aware of the third method, evaporation. Moisture is given off through the pores in the form of perspiration. As the moisture evaporates, it absorbs heat from the body, cooling it. This process of evaporation goes on whether it can be seen or not.

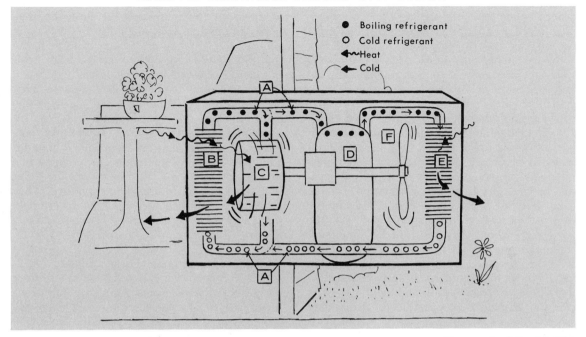

Diagram courtesy Fedders Corporation

A large portion of a room air conditioner is on the outside of the house. Inside the cooling coils (B) the cold refrigerant fluid (A) boils as it absorbs heat from the room air, which is circulated over it by the blower (C) and discharged back into the room as cool air. The compressor (D) raises the temperature of the refrigerant even more before it enters the condenser (E), where the hot vaporized refrigerant changes back to liquid. The refrigerant, once more cold, flows back to the evaporator. Outdoor air is circulated over the condenser by fan (F).

When one sees drops of perspiration, it means that the body is producing more heat than it can reject at the normal rate.

Surrounding conditions affect the body's ability to reject heat. These conditions are temperature, relative humidity, and air motion. Changes in each of these will speed up or slow down convection, radiation, or evaporation.

Everyone has experienced the cooling effect of a fan. Whether of the electric or hand-held variety, a fan cools by setting the air in motion. Moving air enables one's perspiration to evaporate faster.

What does an air conditioner do to contribute to our comfort? It does what a fan does and more: it cools—that is, it refrigerates the air; it removes some of the moisture, thereby lowering the humidity; and it moves the air, or creates air currents.

Operating Principle

How does an air-conditioning system do all this? What makes an air conditioner cold? It is cold because the refrigerant is boiling inside the coil. An air conditioner uses the principles of refrigeration discussed in Chapter 20 (see pages 399–401): (1) a liquid has the ability to absorb large amounts of heat as it vaporizes and (2) the boiling point of a liquid can be changed by changing the pressure. Raising the pressure of the liquid raises the boiling point; lowering the pressure lowers the boiling point.

You will recall from Chapter 20 that inside the cooling coil or evaporator, Freon 12 absorbs heat from the air which is passing over the evaporator coils. It continues to absorb heat and boil until it vaporizes, changing from a cold liquid to a cold gas.

There are four parts in a refrigeration cycle: (1) The evaporator, or cooling coil, where air, passing across it, is cooled by the refrigerant which is absorbing heat as it boils and vaporizes; (2) the compressor, which pulls the vapor or cold gas from the evaporator through a suction line and compresses it, raising the pressure as well as the temperature; (3) the condenser, where the vaporized high-temperature, high-pressure refrigerant is cooled enough to condense; and (4) the thermal expansion valve where the liquid is instantly changed to a mixture of cold liquid and cold gas. The pressure has now been reduced. Remember, when pressure is reduced, the temperature is reduced. Now the refrigerant is once more ready to start absorbing heat.

This is all there is to the refrigeration cycle of the air conditioner: the refrigerant absorbs heat from the air as it boils and turns to vapor in the evaporator. The compressor raises the pressure and temperature so that the refrigerant can be changed back into a liquid as it is forced through the condenser. In the expansion valve the refrigerant expands very rapidly and changes to a mixture of cold liquid and cold gas as it flows into the evaporator, where it starts once more absorbing heat as it boils and vaporizes.

Fans inside the air conditioner keep the air circulating. One fan circulates outside air over the condenser and motor to cool them. Other fans circulate room air through the filters and over the evaporator coils where it is cooled and blown back into the room. Moisture from the room air condenses and drips down into the floor of the air conditioner.

Selection Features

The first decision to be made when buying an air conditioner is the choice of size, or cooling capacity. Many factors influence this decision: for example, the size of the opening into which the unit is to be installed; the area of all the windows in the room and the direction they face; the amount of insulation in the walls and ceiling; the number of persons who will use the room; and the light wattage and heat-producing equipment in the room.

Size is not a decision to be made haphazardly. Careful calculations need to be made. Some dealers may recommend a larger air conditioner than is required so that the customer won't complain to them later about inadequate cooling. Others may recommend one that is too small for the conditions in order that the price will be more competitive. Thus it would seem wise to learn how to estimate for yourself the capacity needed. The National Electric Manufacturing Association, 155 E. 44th Street, New York, N.Y. 10071, has a Cooling Load Estimate Form available for 10 cents. The form may also be obtained from the Association of Home Appliance Manufacturers, 20 North Wacker Drive, Chicago, Ill. 60606. You should ask a reputable dealer in the field of air conditioning to come to the home and acquire the needed information about the factors mentioned above. Then he can calculate the size which is best for the situation.

It is better to err by buying an air conditioner that is too small rather than one that is too large. If an air conditioner is too large, besides the extra cost, it will tend to cool the air before a sufficient amount of moisture has been removed. This creates a cold, clammy feeling. If the air conditioner is too small, it may not cool the room to the desired temperature but the humidity will be lowered, which in turn will make the room more comfortable.

Air-conditioning capacity is expressed in British thermal units (Btu), in tons, or in horsepower. The Btu rating gives the number of units of heat per hour that the air conditioner will remove from the room. It is the most useful of the three ratings in giving information on cooling capacity. The larger the Btu rating, the greater the cooling capacity. For night cooling only, smaller Btu per hour ratings may be used satisfactorily. If house wiring cannot adequately accommodate an air conditioner of high Btu rating, two smaller units may be used *provided* they are not both used on the same circuit.

Installation Requirements

Air conditioners are available on the market that require either a 115-volt or a 230-volt supply of current. The local electric code will be the guide as to the size of circuit the air conditioner in question will require. The local power distributor can provide information regarding code requirements. A general rule of thumb is that a 12,000-Btu air conditioner requires a 230-volt circuit.

When choosing a 115-volt air conditioner, use a fustat or fusetron—time-delay fuses. Do not use any other appliance on the circuit at the same time. The time-delay fuse is needed since the air conditioner draws in excess of its ampere rating when the compressor motor first comes on. An ordinary 15-ampere fuse might "blow" during the initial demand for current.

It is wise to put the air conditioner in a shaded opening since the hot sun shining directly on the air conditioner will lower its cooling capacity. The shade may be provided by an awning if natural shade is not available.

Other Factors to Consider

There are two seals for which to look. One is the UL seal for assurance of its electrical safety. The other is the National Electrical Manufacturers Association (NEMA) seal which certifies the manufacturer's Btu-per-hour claims. One major company that does not submit its room air conditioners to NEMA for certification offers its own guarantee that the rated capacity is as stated.

Many people find air conditioner noise very annoying. Much of the noise comes from the compressor. When the air conditioner is so designed that it can be mounted in the window so that the window can be closed part way and sealed, leaving the compressor outside the closed window, the noise is greatly reduced. Vibration also contributes to the noise. In order to evaluate the amount of noise for a particular air conditioner, be sure that the air conditioner is set for maximum cooling. It will operate more quietly on low speed. Cooling capacity will be lowered at reduced fan speed. Conditioners in larger cabinets operate more quietly than do the smaller models.

Choice of controls will be between models with only an on-off switch and those with push buttons for controlling the fan speed and ventilation. The chief advantage of two fan speeds is that on low speed the conditioner runs more quietly. Highly desirable features include a fresh-air intake and a stale-air exhaust, a thermostat for automatic control (within limits) of the room temperature, and fins or louvers for directional control of the air coming into the room from the conditioner.

The filter should be checked about every two months and either washed or replaced. Therefore, it is important that it be accessible for ease in cleaning or replacement. Cooling capacity is reduced when the filter becomes clogged so that air cannot flow through freely to be circulated past the cooling coils. At least once a season the condenser coils and fins which are on the outdoor side of the conditioner, the cooling coil fins, and the fan blades should be cleaned. Otherwise the cooling capacity will be reduced. With reduced capacity the motor may become overloaded and perhaps a fuse may blow.

If the inside mechanical system slides in and out of the outer cabinet, the air conditioner will be easier to service than if the whole cabinet must be removed from the window.

Cost of operation averages $5 to $7 per month. The cost depends upon the operating efficiency of the conditioner, the location, and the local rates per kilowatthour. To determine the cooling efficiency, divide the cooling capacity by the wattage rating. This will give the Btu of cooling effect provided by each watt hour of electricity consumed. For example, assume that the cooling capacity is 8,000 Btu and the wattage rating is 860. The relative efficiency is found to be 9.3, which is an excellent rating. Eight is ideal; 6 is average. The range is generally between 4 and 10. The higher the number, the lower the operating cost. The cooling capacity and the wattage rating will be stated on the name plate and in a Directory of Certified Room Air Conditioners. Every dealer should have this directory.

PORTABLE HUMIDIFIERS

When temperature and relative humidity are high, the problem is how to remove excess moisture from the air. But in winter the prob-

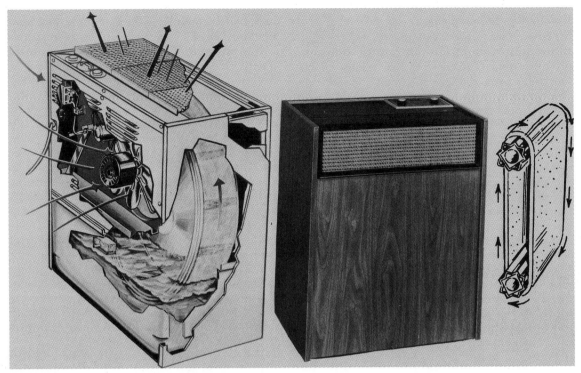

Courtesy The West Bend Co.

Courtesy Sears, Roebuck and Co.

In a revolving drum filter, moist air is directed upward through adjustable grills. In a moving belt filter, a fan directs moist air out into the room. For a humidifier to perform its task, the sponge-like filter has to be saturated with water. This is achieved either by moving the filter through the water or by circulating the water through the filter. Cylindrical or flat filters are not so hard to visualize as those in the form of a moving belt or revolving drum.

lem may be how to add moisture to the air in the house. The most comfortable relative humidity is between 45 and 55 percent.

Excessively dry air is uncomfortable because it makes your nasal passages, throat, and skin feel dry. It also causes wood to warp, houseplants to dry out, and furniture to come unglued.

Humidifiers should be used only in houses or apartments which have vapor barriers inside every outer wall. Otherwise too much moisture will pass through the walls into the insulation space. Moisture from the air condenses inside the wall during cold weather. Excessive moisture can cause wood to swell or even deteriorate, and it can cause paint to peel. Excessive moisture in the insulation makes it less effective. Unless the house has storm windows, increasing the relative humidity in the room will cause the windows to frost over or steam over.

In some houses, humidifiers are a part of the heating system. A humidifier on the furnace is connected to a water line, and the entire house is automatically humidified as moist warm air is circulated throughout the house. These humidifiers may not be very effective because minerals in the water tend to build up or accumulate on parts of the humidifier and cause it to cease to function.

Operating Principle

Since most portable humidifiers are used in rooms having no plumbing connections, they must have a container for water. The larger the reservoir, the less frequently the humidifier must be refilled.

The porous, spongelike filter may be in the form of a stationary hollow cylinder, a flat sheet, or a moving belt or revolving drum that passes through the water. In the first two types, water is pumped from the reservoir up through the tubes over the filter. The latter types have no pump or tubing. A fan blows air through the water-filled filter and out into the room as vapor.

Humidifiers plug into a 115-volt general-purpose circuit. Sometimes there is a heating element for warming the air as it is blown out into the room. This feature is desirable primarily in console models and where the humidifier must be located so that people are in line with the draft which is created when the humidifier fan is running. It is a feature not likely to be found on the canister type where the air flow is directed toward the ceiling.

Selection Features

Although no harm can be done to the humidifier if it runs dry, it is helpful to have a humidistat—a light that signals when the water level is low—and an automatic low-water shutoff for the sake of maintaining the desired relative humidity. The humidistat is a humidity-sensing device for the purpose of automatically controlling the moisture output by cycling the motor on and off. Without the automatic low-water shutoff, a gurgling noise may develop as the water level gets low; this could be distracting.

Most models have a fan with at least two speeds. The chief advantage of the high speed is to raise the relative humidity more quickly. In normal use, the humidifier will be operated on low speed so that it will run more quietly. It is important to evaluate the noise level of the fan before making the purchase.

Louvers for directing the air flow are particularly desirable on console models.

It is very important that the humidifier be easy to fill and that it have filters which are easy to take out and replace. It is important to wash the filters because the efficiency of the humidifier is reduced as the sediment builds up in the filter. The frequency with which the cleaning will need to be done will depend upon the amount of mineral and other sediment in the water. Plastic filters have a longer life expectancy than do those of wood fiber.

It is desirable to avoid models which do not bear the UL seal and those which spray a mist into the air instead of evaporating the moisture.

Operating Cost

The operating cost is low unless the heating element (when available) is used frequently. Otherwise, only enough current is needed to operate a motor of small horsepower.

Care and Maintenance

The filter must be removed and thoroughly cleaned at least once a season. Sometimes this must be done as often as once a month. At the end of the season the humidifier should be emptied and wiped out before storing. A drain in or near the bottom of the reservoir makes this task easier. All solids should be removed from the filter, the reservoir, and all accessible parts. The humidifier should be stored in its original carton if possible. At the very least, keep it covered to keep out dust. No oiling should be necessary unless the manufacturer's instructions require this.

HOT-WATER HEATERS

Hot water, day or night, at the turn of a faucet, is a luxury item in some cultures and an unknown resource in others. But to the vast majority of Americans it is another convenience which is taken for granted.

Aside from the comfort aspect for personal cleanliness, hot water is necessary for laundering and dishwashing. When using an automatic clothes washer or dishwasher, an adequate supply of water of 140 to 160°F is recommended.

When water is heated in an enclosed container, there is potential danger of explosion. Water expands when heated. Steam forms when water boils, which increases the internal pressure. For this reason the storage tank of the water heater should be very durable. Steel is usually used because of its strength. In addition, certain safety features are of utmost importance.

Common Features

Water heaters may use electricity, gas, or oil as fuel. All have certain common requirements regardless of fuel.

Safety. Safety devices include a thermostat, which controls the water temperature by regulating the flow of fuel. If the thermostat should fail, the fuel would continue to flow, the temperature would rise to the boiling point, steam would be formed, and the internal pressure would build up. The water heater should have temperature and pressure relief valves as additional protection against explosion. These relief valves should have been approved by AGA (the American Gas Association) or by the Underwriters Laboratories and should be installed by a licensed plumber who knows and follows the local electrical and plumbing codes. The heater should be checked annually by a competent person to assure that the safety devices are operating correctly. In addition to the thermostat and the relief valves, there should also be a high-limit cutoff device, irrespective of the type of fuel used, to shut off the fuel supply when a certain temperature is reached, in case the thermostat and the mechanical safety controls fail.

The cold-water line is customarily connected to the top of the tank. The cold water is carried to the bottom of the tank through a "dip tube." A dip tube of enameled steel, copper, or other nonsoftening material is safer than one made of plastic. Plastic softens and melts under high temperature, such as that which occurs in cases of thermostat failure. There have been cases where a plastic dip tube melted, plugging the relief valves. An explosion was the result. It is wise to have a plastic dip tube replaced with one made of nonsoftening material.

Construction features. Water heaters are constructed of an inner tank for water storage and an outer shell, with insulation (usually Fiberglas) in-between. The outer shell may be enameled or anodized for attractive appearance.

An easily accessible drain in the bottom of the tank is important. Sediment of lime and rust needs to be flushed from the bottom of the tank. Once a month 2 or more gallons of water should be drawn off into a bucket. This not only protects the tank but provides a cleaner supply of hot water. The entire tank should be flushed out once a year. Turn off the cold water and drain the tank. All but the last 10 gallons or so could be used for showers or laundry.

Lining material. The material with which the storage tank is lined is important. The material should be as corrosion-resistant as possible. The hardness of the water, its chemical composition, and the temperature of the water all affect the amount and rate of corrosion. Rusting occurs rapidly in water above 140°F. Soft water is less corrosive than hard water. Only a few areas of the United States have naturally soft water. In some communities the city water supply is softened by the water company. Some homes have their own water-softening tanks, which are connected to the water line ahead of the water heater so that the water is softened before it enters the heater. This reduces corrosion.

The type of lining selected will depend upon the local water condition. Lining materials used include porcelain enamel (referred to as glass-lining); stone (which is made of a thick coating of cement or used in combination with a seal-coating of porcelain enamel); monel metal (which is an alloy of 65 percent nickel, 30 percent copper, and small amounts of iron, magnesium, or aluminum); copper; or galvanized steel. Galvanized steel is the least expensive while copper and monel metal are the most expensive.

Glass-lined water heaters are probably the most popular. It is important that one select only a high-quality glass-lined heater so that the lining will be less likely to have blisters or cracks which could expose the base metal to corrosion.

Location and installation. The place where the water heater is to be installed may influence the choice between a cylindrical tank or a square, counter-top model. The water heater should be installed as near as possible to the place hot water is used most frequently. Frequency of use is more important than the amount used, although amount too is important. Water left in the pipes cools. The shorter the distance from the storage tank to the point of use, the less water will be wasted in letting it flow until warm. There is a 10- to 20-degree loss of temperature from the tank to the appliance or faucet. Small copper tubing reduces the amount of cooling in the water line. When larger pipes must be used to supply the demand of many faucets, the pipes should be insulated to minimize heat loss.

In some homes, more than one water heater may be needed if there are two widely separated areas of heavy use—for example, in a large ranch-type home where the laundry and

The heating elements of some electric water heaters are immersed in the water. Two electric units are recommended for water heaters where hot water usage is high.

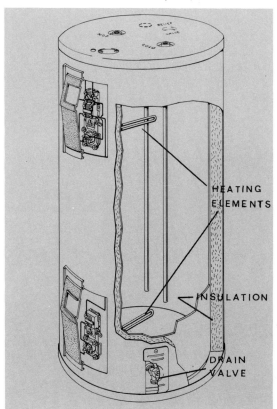

kitchen are widely separated. A temperature booster in the dishwasher does not take the place of an adequate supply of hot water from the heater.

Recovery-rate. The recovery rate refers to the time it takes for a 100° raise in the water temperature of a full tank. In a fast-recovery heater this should take a little more than one hour. A slow-recovery heater requires three to ten hours to raise the water temperature 100 degrees.

Care and maintenance. Have the temperature and pressure relief valves checked by a competent service man at least once a year. Drain the tank as described on page 000. If the house is to be closed for a long time, the cold water and fuel supply should be turned off and the tank drained before the house is closed.

Electric Water Heaters

Electric water heaters have a longer service life than heaters fueled by gas or oil. There are no fumes or odor and they are clean and require no vent or flue.

Some of their disadvantages are: (1) They require a separate 230-volt circuit. This can add to the cost unless the house already has this wiring. (2) The initial cost is ordinarily higher than for gas heaters. (3) They tend to have a slower recovery rate, so that a larger heater may be needed. (4) The operation cost may be higher than for gas or oil, depending upon local rates.

The water is heated by one or two electric units. These units may be either immersed in the water or wrapped around the inner tank under the insulation. Two units are recommended when hot-water usage is high and when rates for electricity are lower during an off-peak period, as during the very early morning. The unit near the bottom of the tank comes on during this period and heats at a lower-cost rate. The top unit operates only as needed to keep the top one-fourth of the water at the desired temperature. Quick-recovery type electric water heaters use the immersion-type units.

Hot water is drawn from the top of the tank. It is replaced by cold water, which is fed to the bottom of the tank by a dip tube.

A baffle above the cold-water inlet will reduce the amount of mixing of cold water with the hot.

Gas Water Heaters

Gas heaters have several advantages over electric heaters: (1) They often cost less. (2) They tend to have a faster recovery rate than some electric heaters. This allows you to use a smaller size, which reduces the initial cost as well as the amount of floor space needed. (3) Operating cost may be lower than for electric heaters, depending upon the local utility rates.

Some of the disadvantages of gas water heaters are: (1) They may have a shorter use life than an electric water heater. (2) A vent or flue is required to carry off fumes. (3) They give off odor, heat, and sometimes soot. (4) There is a chance of fire or explosion in case of a gas leak.

Operating principle. The water is heated by means of a burner located below the water tank. The flame should not touch the bottom of the tank. The heat from the burner flows up the center of the tank through a single flue or through an external flue surrounding the water tank and located between the tank and the insulation. Products of combustion are vented up the flue.

It is possible to buy nonautomatic gas water heaters which are lighted and turned off by hand. However, fully automatic heaters have fewer safety hazards than nonautomatic ones.

Installation. American Gas Association specifications for installation must be followed closely. Gas water heaters should never be installed in a bathroom, bedroom, closet, or any enclosed area where good ventilation is not possible. They should be no closer than 2 inches to the wall. They must be connected to a good flue.

Oil Water Heaters

Oil-fired water heaters are similar in operation to gas models. They should bear the UL seal of approval and be checked annually for safety of operation of their relief valves and cutoff devices. In general, their operation cost is lower and their recovery rate faster than electrical models. They are comparable to gas models on these points. Their appeal will most likely be to those who are already using fuel oil to heat their homes.

EQUIPMENT FOR FLOOR CARE

Floor care involves removal of soil from floor coverings, removal of soil from bare floors, and waxing-polishing some types of bare floors. Nonelectric carpet sweepers, electric vacuum cleaners, and shampoo-polishers have largely replaced brooms and mops for these cleaning jobs.

Vacuum Cleaners

Vacuum cleaners employ one or more of three basic principles of cleaning—suction, agitation, or sweeping. In earlier models the difference between cleaners was that they were of the tank, or horizontal type, which cleaned by suction only, or upright, which cleaned by suction, brushing, and/or agitation.

SCHEMATIC DRAWING OF AN AUTOMATIC GAS WATER HEATER

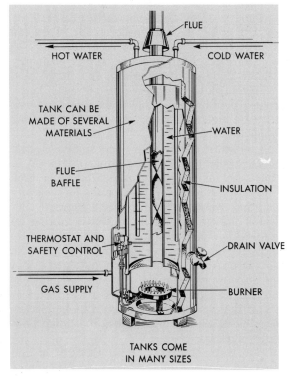

FLUE

HOT WATER   COLD WATER

TANK CAN BE MADE OF SEVERAL MATERIALS

WATER

FLUE BAFFLE

INSULATION

THERMOSTAT AND SAFETY CONTROL

DRAIN VALVE

GAS SUPPLY

BURNER

TANKS COME IN MANY SIZES

Courtesy American Gas Association

424

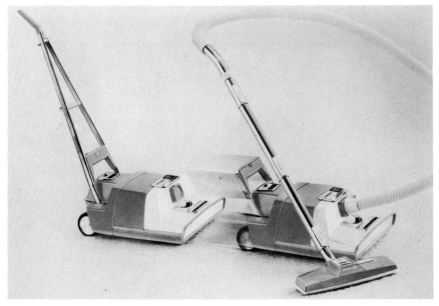

For carpet cleaning, this vacuum cleaner is used with the handle and with the motor switch set on upright. It converts to a canister by changing the motor switch, removing the handle, snapping on the hose, and adding the appropriate cleaning attachment.

Courtesy Westinghouse

Courtesy The Hoover Company

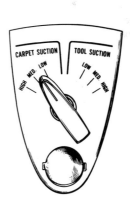

For carpet cleaning, this vacuum cleaner is used without the special attachments. A dial above the hose connection lets you dial the power you need for any cleaning job.

TYPES OF VACUUM CLEANERS

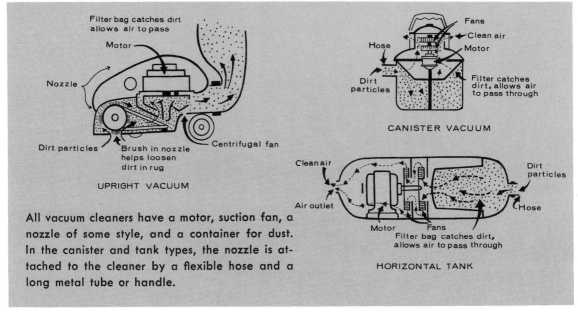

All vacuum cleaners have a motor, suction fan, a nozzle of some style, and a container for dust. In the canister and tank types, the nozzle is attached to the cleaner by a flexible hose and a long metal tube or handle.

Adapted from "How to Take 'Work' Out of Your Housework" by permission of Vacuum Cleaner Manufacturers Association

Considerable change has been going on in the vacuum-cleaner field. Designers have attempted to blend the best features of the earlier models by developing upright cleaners which have more suction in their cleaning attachments and canisters which have more efficient rug-cleaning power.

It has been stated that 85 percent of all dirt in a room is in the carpets and rugs. Removing grit and sand, which becomes deeply imbedded in the carpet pile, requires more care than does the removal of surface soil. According to one manufacturer, the upright model, with a motor-driven brush and agitator, removes three times as much dirt from a carpet as do some earlier canister models which used suction alone. For above-the-floor cleaning and for hooked or looped rugs, straight suction cleaning is preferable.

Operating principle. Vacuum cleaners operate on the principle that air rushes in to fill a vacuum. A decrease in pressure is created by a fan which is motor driven. Air rushes in to fill the partial vacuum thus created. This air carries dust, grit, and litter with it through the nozzle or opening of the cleaner. As the air passes through the filter(s) and dust bag or container, the dirt is deposited.

The dust bag must be porous to allow air to pass through. Many makes of vacuum cleaners use disposable dust bags. When the dust bag is of the throw-away type, it is well to keep in mind that the strength and filtering properties of the paper affect the operation of the cleaner. For this reason it is important that only the dust bags distributed by the maker of the specific brand of vacuum cleaner be used. Although disposable dust bags do involve added expense, throwing the bag away is simpler than emptying it.

All electric cleaners contain fan(s), filter(s), a motor, a dust container, and a nozzle or opening through which the dirt-laden air enters.

Factors affecting efficiency of performance. Motor horsepower ratings are often used as an indicator of overall quality of performance. The implication is that the higher the horsepower the better the cleaner. However, the design and construction of the cleaner as well as the way it is used are the real factors which affect the quality of performance.

The nozzle should form a good "seal" with the rug or floor without pulling the rug up too firmly against the nozzle. It must be possible to keep the entire rim of the nozzle in contact with the surface being cleaned, rather than one side only.

The dust container should not be allowed to become overloaded. If the container is a disposable paper bag, it should be replaced when the accumulated dirt noticeably reduces suction. Some models have an indicator which automatically tells when the dust bag should be changed. Using the bag to its entire capacity cuts the cleaning efficiency of the cleaner and increases the time required for cleaning. It is recommended that the nondisposable dust containers be emptied after each use, thus providing maximum cleaning power each time.

When cleaning carpeting, the American Carpet Institute recommends three individual strokes—forward, back, and forward—for light cleaning with an upright cleaner with a rotating brush and agitator. A thorough cleaning requires up to seven individual strokes (four forward and three back). When using a canister, or tank-type cleaner that cleans by suction alone, the number of strokes should be increased to two or three times this number. Canisters having a nozzle with a rotating brush and agitator would require fewer passes over the carpet than would those which clean by suction alone. A single stroke over a bare surface should be enough.

Long, slow strokes with an upright cleaner remove more soil and use less energy than do short, fast strokes. Going slowly provides more opportunity for the motor to do the job of soil removal. Short, fast strokes and some pressure to ensure a good seal between the nozzle and carpet are required for a canister cleaner.

When the brushes in the nozzle become worn so that they do not touch a piece of cardboard placed across the nozzle, they should be replaced by new ones. Brush replacement is usually a simple operation which can be done at home.

The soil-removing ability of a cleaner, especially of the upright type, is improved if the carpeting is laid over a rug pad. The resilient pad improves the seal between the

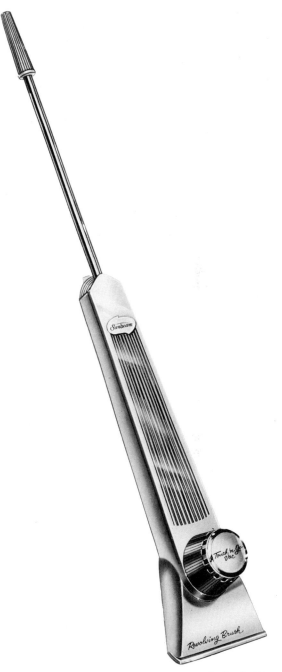

Courtesy Sunbeam

A lightweight cleaner is useful for quick pick-up from carpets and bare floors. This sweeper is also available in larger models with attachments for above-the-floor cleaning.

cleaner nozzle and the rug surface. Also, the wheels can sink into the rug, allowing the revolving brush or brush and agitator to do a better job. Some upright cleaners have an adjustment for depth of carpet pile. This raises or lowers the back wheels to improve the seal between rug and nozzle.

Types. With the canister, or tank-type, cleaner, the nozzle, like all of the attachments, is a separate cleaning tool attached to the canister by a flexible hose and a long metal tube or handle. Nozzles with rollers are easier to push than those without. The rug nozzle may have no brush, it may contain a stationary brush, or it may have a motor-driven or air-driven revolving brush or an agitating mechanism. A revolving-brush nozzle is not recommended for use on hooked rugs.

With the upright cleaner, the rug nozzle is not a separate attachment but an integral part of the cleaner. It contains a motor-driven roller with brushes or a bar and brushes. As the roller turns, dust is vibrated loose. It is swept up as well as sucked into the stream of air flowing up through the nozzle and through the filter bag where it is deposited.

Attachments for bare floor and above-the-floor cleaning are available for both types of cleaner. These attachments are standard equipment with the canister type and included in the sale price. Dusting brushes or an upholstery nozzle are attached by means of a flexible hose and a metal wand or handle. A suction regulator is desirable for dusting lightweight fabric which may be sucked into the nozzle when the suction is too high. This is especially important on a canister model. The suction of the upright cleaner is lower in the attachments than it is in the canister model. Modifications made in some of the new up-

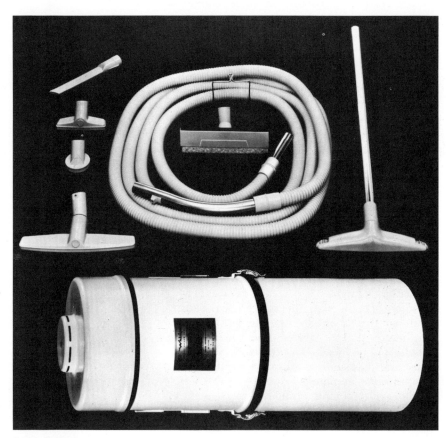

Central vacuum systems are available with a wide variety of cleaning nozzles.

right models have largely eliminated this difference.

Lightweight vacuum cleaners are used to supplement rather than substitute for the heavier models, since they do not have the cleaning power of the heavier models. They are convenient for quick, daily use.

One type of lightweight cleaner is the electric broom, or vacuum broom, which is built in the upright style but cleans by straight suction. It may have either a reusable dust bag or a disposable one. Most models require a 6- to 11-inch clearance when cleaning under low furniture, which is greater than that of the tank-type rug nozzle.

Hand models, some of which have a shoulder strap, are available for furniture and stair-carpet cleaning, and for car, boat, and workbench vacuuming. These put the emphasis on portability rather than power.

Another type of cleaner for the home is the central vacuum system which may be included in the house as it is being built. It costs $500 or more to install such a system in an old house. A large tank, containing a motor, a fan, and dirt receptacle, is permanently installed in a garage or basement. For cleaning, a long flexible hose is inserted into one of the cleaner inlets which are set in the walls throughout the house.

Selection features. Whether buying a canister or upright model, you should check to see that the nozzle can maintain a tight seal between nozzle and surface being cleaned, even when used close to or under heavy furniture.

The cleaner should be easy to handle—that is, it should maneuver and move easily across the floor, door sills, and rug edges. The switch should be easy to reach and turn on, especially if it is a toe switch. The dust bag should be

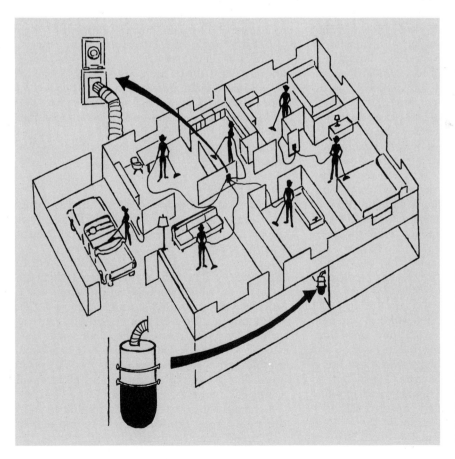

In a central vacuuming system, the long, flexible hose is inserted into an inlet (or opening) in the wall. Dust is sucked up by the powerful motor and deposited into a dirt receptacle located in a remote part of the home.

easy to remove or the dust container easy to empty.

A bumper on the nozzle is desirable to protect furniture. You should observe whether any part of the cleaner could scratch or mar floors or furniture. An upright cleaner which does not require that the belt be removed when attachments are used is handier to use than one where this step is necessary. Not all cleaners are equally adaptable to use on stairs. Compact portable cleaners or lightweight cleaners are easiest for this use.

A consumer should be reasonable in her expectations where noise of the motor is concerned. It is desirable that the cleaner be as quiet as possible, but a powerful motor cannot be completely quiet.

Special features which add appreciably to the cost should be evaluated carefully before making the decision to purchase. Sometimes the wide price range between brands is largely due to the added accessories and the variety of jobs the cleaner can do. Keep in mind that the basic function of a vacuum cleaner is to vacuum clean. Dusting brushes, upholstery nozzle, and a crevice tool are standard equipment with a canister type and desirable accessories for the upright type, especially if there is only one cleaner. Before deciding to buy a cleaner that will perform a wider variety of jobs than those which standard attachments can perform, consider how often the accessory attachment will be used. Will the use be frequent enough to justify the added cost? Consider how this cost compares with the present method being used to perform these jobs and with the degree of satisfaction with the present method. Can the cleaner be bought with only the desired tools or must they all be purchased? Also, how does the cleaner being considered rate as a vacuum cleaner for rugs, bare surfaces, and upholstery?

Use and care. It is desirable to vacuum sweep a carpet lightly every day and thoroughly once a week. Don't bump or drop the cleaner. Empty the dust bag after each use if it is of the nondisposable type. Brush but do not wash the dust bag. Replace a disposable bag when its recommended capacity has been reached. Keep the filters clean by the method recommended in the instruction book. Replace the filters when they are saturated with dust and have lost their ability to filter.

Avoid running over the cord. The beater bar may knick the protective coating and expose the wires. Always turn off the switch before pulling out the plug, otherwise the prongs of the plug may become corroded or burned. Always disconnect the cord by grasping the plug, not by jerking the cord.

In storing the hose, avoid a sharp bend. If storing it over a hook, use two well-spaced hooks.

Avoid picking up sharp objects, such as tacks, hairpins, and the like, since these may cut the belt or become lodged in the hose or nozzle opening, thus blocking the passage and preventing dust from passing through. String and large pieces of paper, too, can clog air passages.

The belt on an upright model should be checked from time to time to see that it is correctly taut and free of cuts which will cause it to snap. When the belt is loose, the roller will turn slowly and perform less effectively.

Brushes should be kept clean. When vacuuming very dusty areas, the brushes should be removed from the extension wand several times during cleaning and vacuumed with the open wand or with the crevice tool. Occasionally they should be washed in a solution of mild detergent, rinsed, and dried before storing.

Floor Polisher

The electric floor polisher can be used to apply floor wax and to buff or polish floors. It is important to read the directions on the can of wax very carefully. Certain types of floor coverings are damaged by the chemical solvent in some waxes. The label will indicate the type of floors on which the wax can be safely used. Solvent-type waxes give a tougher, long-lasting finish and thus may be more desirable, particularly in areas of heavy traffic, than water-base waxes. An electric floor polisher is especially useful for applying solvent-type wax to large areas, but getting into corners and other small areas may be done best by hand.

Before deciding to buy this appliance, rent the type under consideration. Try more than one brand over a period of time. Unless the

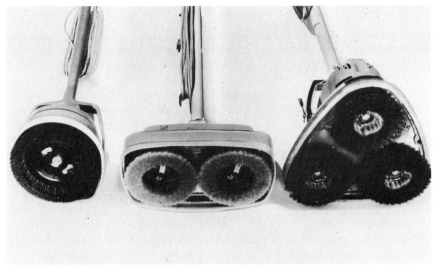

A floor polisher may have one or more motor-powered brushes. The number of brushes is not an important factor since models with one, two, or three brushes all polish well.

rented machine is fairly new and in good condition, it will not serve as a basis for evaluating current models on the market. Factors to observe when using rented models are (1) noise of motor, (2) ease of guiding, (3) whether it can get into corners and near baseboards or a bathtub without splashing wax, and (4) whether it tends to streak or does a uniform job of polishing. This last point is more important on plain wooden floors or floor coverings than on patterned floors such as terrazzo tile or figured linoleum.

Operating principle. A floor polisher has one or more motor-powered brushes which snap into place under the motor housing. There are one, two, and three-brush types, but twin-brush models are somewhat more common. A long cord runs through the handle. The switch may be located in the handle for finger-tip control or on the base for toe operation.

A liquid-wax dispenser may be part of the polisher. This is operated by a separate control on the handle. Such a dispenser may be difficult to clean.

Most models have different brushes for scrubbing or applying wax or for shampooing. The stiffness of the bristles varies, depending upon the type of job to be done. When the polisher is used for scrubbing, the water has to be sponged up or mopped up by hand unless the model has a special suction feature. A removable splash guard for use during scrubbing or waxing is available on some models.

For a higher gloss, disposable cotton pads, wool felt pads, or lambs wool pads can be snapped on over the buffing brushes. Waffle-knit pads are more durable and give better results than nonwoven cotton pads.

Rug shampooing. Although many polishers have rug-shampooing attachments, it is not always desirable to try to clean carpeting yourself. It depends upon the type of carpet and upon the mechanical shampooer used. Some shampoo attachments remove an undue amount of nap. Cleaning should come from foam or suds; no water should be allowed to come in contact with the carpet. Excess water which seeps into the backing may cause a change of color in the carpet which would cause permanent discoloration. In general, there seem to be more disadvantages than advantages in shampooing a rug at home. The exception is where the carpeting is inexpensive, light in color, and where pets and children make frequent rug cleaning a necessity. Be sure to follow closely the instructions given on both the cleaning agent and the rug-shampooing equipment.

1. Define the meaning of these words as used in this chapter: Btu rating, louvers, dip tube, recovery rate, baffle, nozzle, agitator.

2. If you know someone who has a room air conditioner, ask if you may do the following experiment to find out the direction of air circulation and how the room air passes into and out of the air conditioner. Do this: take a sheet of tablet paper or a cleansing tissue and hold it up to the front of the air conditioner. Does the paper blow out toward the room or is it sucked toward the air conditioner? Move the paper to different locations and find out what difference you can observe. Ask the adult in charge to adjust the louvers, or levers, which change the direction of air flow so you can observe the effect.

3. Ask if you may have someone remove the front panel so that you can see the filter and the type of fan(s) which circulates air. *Be sure to remember to unplug the air conditioner before removing the panel.*

4. Read advertisements in local papers or magazines, and compare the amount and type of information given in them with that found in mail order catalogs. How much of the information suggested in this chapter as needed for choosing an air conditioner can be found in ads or catalogs?

5. Find out from advertisements, catalogs, and stores the following information about portable humidifiers: (1) variation in capacity, styles, and price; (2) shape and composition of filter, whether the filter is washable or must be replaced when dirty, and how easy or difficult it is to remove.

6. How will type of floor covering influence your choice of floor care equipment? Under what circumstances might you select an electric broom?

7. Look in *Consumer Bulletin* and *Consumer Reports* for a discussion of vacuum cleaners. After studying the information, do some comparison shopping, making notes on what you find out. From information obtained in these ways tell the type, brand, and model as well as the price of the cleaner you would buy for (a) a three-room apartment; (b) a six-room, one-story house. In each case explain the type of floor covering you would have in the various rooms. Justify your choices of cleaners for situation (a) and situation (b).

8. What factors would influence your decision regarding whether to pay extra to get the dusting and upholstery attachments for a particular brand of upright cleaner?

9. Examine a vacuum cleaner in a home and evaluate its cleaning effectiveness by using it for rug cleaning and for surface cleaning. What can you personally do to improve its performance? What improvements will need to be made by a repairman? If worn parts need to be replaced, which of these could you install? Price the needed parts. Does the anticipated improvement in performance warrant this cost?

10. Where in order of priorities would you rank ownership of a floor polisher? In what situations would it seem especially desirable?

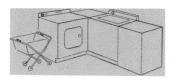

22

Laundry Equipment

OFTEN A FAMILY must decide whether to purchase laundry equipment or to use coin-operated laundry facilities. A family may be living in an apartment where laundry facilities are provided in a central location or the occupants may be expected to use a public coin-operated laundry. The amount of money available for purchasing laundry equipment also affects the choice. There may be more money during the early stage of the family, especially if the wife is working outside the home, than there will be after the family begins to expand and there are many more demands on the income.

In deciding whether to use a laundromat rather than buy laundry equipment, you should consider the factors in Chart 12 on page 435.

One can expect a washer and dryer to last about ten years. Usually, after about ten years they require repairs which can be costly. Also, in a ten-year period the design, performance, and special features may have changed considerably. The family is often ready for a newer model.

Studies show that some brands have better service records than others. The cost of re-pairs over the life of the laundry equipment will probably average about 2 to 5 percent of the purchase price per year.

WASHERS

When selecting a washing machine to buy you have a choice among automatic or nonautomatic; combination washer-dryer or separate units; and top-loading or front-loading automatic washer.

Nonautomatic

The nonautomatic washer does the mechanical work of washing. It usually extracts the water by means of a wringer. A few brands have an attached tub for spin-drying the clothes—that is, extracting the water. Nonautomatic washers require constant attention except during agitation.

The nonautomatic washer is used where there is a limited supply of water or where the water pressure is very low. Water pressure may be low in rural areas where the family has its own water system. It may also be low at or near the end of a water line of a public water system. The available water may

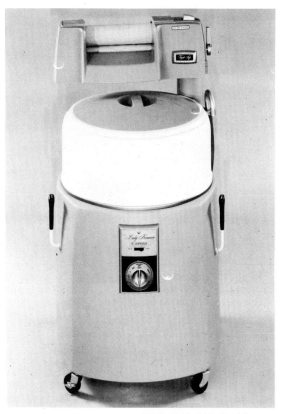

A nonautomatic washer is more economical than an automatic washer and may be used where the water supply is limited or the water pressure is low. Desirable features found on this model are a safety wringer (wringer stops and the wringer rolls release when the push-bar is hit); automatic roll pressure adjustment; automatic drain pump for emptying the tub; and a timer that signals when wash time has elapsed.

be limited in rural water systems. Some farm families have purchased automatic washers only to find that there is not a sufficient water supply for their operation.

A nonautomatic washer is more economical to operate than an automatic washer only because fresh water is not used with each wash-and-rinse load. Research shows that no more than two loads of soiled clothing should be washed in the same water. On the third load, soil begins to be redeposited onto the

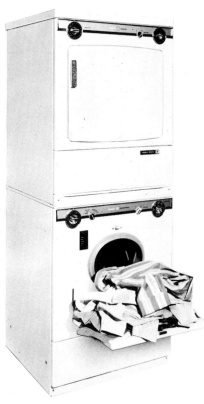

A front-loading washer with a dryer stacked on top is a good arrangement for limited floor space.

clothing as the detergent can no longer hold the soil in suspension.

Automatic

The first automatic washer was introduced in 1937. The modern machine does the entire job of washing, rinsing, and extracting the water without attention after the machine has been started on its cycle.

The automatic washer is available in three price ranges. The bottom-of-the-line washer performs the basic laundering functions well, but it usually does not offer extra convenience features. If the laundry consists primarily of cottons and linens, this machine will be adequate.

The middle-of-the-line washer offers more convenience features. It usually provides a

CHART 12. FACTORS AFFECTING DECISION WHETHER TO BUY LAUNDRY EQUIPMENT OR USE LAUNDROMAT

Factors favoring using a laundromat

If less than five loads per week are washed, it is more economical to use a laundromat than to buy laundry equipment. The fewer loads washed per week, the less expensive it is to use the laundromat and the more expensive it is to own laundry equipment.

No personal investment in equipment is involved.

Several loads can be washed at one time.

Washers and dryers of larger capacity than those used in homes provide an opportunity for washing bulky items.

The water might be conditioned better at the laundromat than at home.

Disadvantages in using a laundromat

Transportation must be provided to and from the laundry.

The user cannot be doing other homemaking activities simultaneously since she is away from home.

It may be difficult to find a time convenient to do the laundry when all family members are considered.

Coin-operated machines do not offer as wide a choice of temperature, speed of agitation, or spin-speed as most middle-of-the-line equipment bought for the home.

More clothes may be needed, since the family is likely to wash only once a week at a coin-operated laundry.

It is cheaper to own laundry equipment than to use the laundromat if five or more loads of laundry are washed each week.

Unless suitable disinfectants are used during laundering, bacteria on the clothes of one family can be transferred to the clothes of another family.

---

choice of laundering cycles for speciality items. The washer often has dispensers for bleaches and fabric softeners. A wide range of fabrics, such as woolens, wash-and-wear cottons, and those from man-made fibers, may be laundered in the middle-priced washers. Most dealers prefer to sell this washer.

The top-of-the-line model offers every feature provided by the manufacturer. This often includes "programmed" cycling. The user merely indicates the type of fabric to be washed. The controls then automatically choose the correct conditions—such as temperature, agitation speed, and time—for washing that particular fabric.

Types. Some manufacturers make a top-loading machine, while others produce a front-loading machine. The top-loading machines provide the action of forcing the water through the clothes by means of agitation. The front-loading machines provide washing action by tumbling the clothes through the water. The soil is removed at least in part by the slapping action of the clothes as they fall against the water. The front-loading machine lends itself to the washing of large articles.

In the top-loading washer the washing action may be provided by a to-and-fro movement of the agitator. The agitator rotates in an arc of approximately 180 degrees. It moves at a speed of about one arc per second. In some models the agitator moves up and down very rapidly. A few manufacturers use a high-frequency action for soil removal. The high-frequency action is obtained by the high-speed water waves which the agitator jets out, thus moving the clothes up, down, and around. A fourth means of providing agitation is the eccentric principle. Here the agitator axis, which is off-center, rotates and provides washing action.

Construction—materials. Most manufacturers use synthetic enamel for the sides and front, with porcelain enamel for the top, lid, and tub. Some use porcelain enamel for the sides and front, in addition to the top, lid, and tub.

Tubs may be made from stainless steel, aluminum, or porcelain enamel. Porcelain enamel is used most frequently because the alkali of soaps will not affect it. It is not particularly subject to abrasion and it is less expensive than stainless steel or aluminum.

Construction—design. Tubs of top-loading machines may be solid or perforated. Both types have advantages and disadvantages. The suds and water are usually spun over the top of the inner tub in a washer which has a solid

Having storage space for laundry supplies and for baskets used in presorting loads makes laundering easier. In this case, folding doors hide the area when not in use and give the room a neat appearance.

Courtesy Better Homes and Gardens, © Meredith Corporation, 1967

tub. The solid tub usually does a more thorough job of removing the detergent during the rinse cycles than does a washer with a perforated tub.

The perforated tub does a more thorough job of removing sand and grit from the clothes. In some perforated tubs the water and suds drain through the clothes and are dispelled at the bottom of the tub.

Selection factors. There are many factors to consider when deciding which washer to buy. One is the amount of water the washer uses. A very limited supply of water may limit one's choice to the nonautomatic type of washer.

Automatic washers use between 30 and 53 gallons of water. They use between 17 and 39 gallons of hot water, preferably at a temperature of 140 to 160°F.

A water-level control. Greater variation in size of loads is possible without a waste of water when the washer has a water-level control. If only a few garments are to be washed, the homemaker may turn the water-level control to low. The tub will fill only about one-third full, yet there will be adequate water for the movement of the small number of garments through the water. Some washers allow one to choose from a low, medium, or

For the apartment dweller with too little space for conventional laundry equipment, the portable automatic washer offers a solution. It can later be installed permanently if the owner moves to larger quarters.

full setting, depending on the size and bulk of the load. Bottom-of-the-line and coin-operated machines have no automatic control for the quantity of water flowing into the tub.

Load size. As stated by the manufacturer, load size is in terms of absolute maximum capacity. Most brands wash 8 pounds of soiled clothing very well. Many will wash 10 pounds well.

Bulk is actually more important than weight. Articles must be able to move about freely. Overloading a washer not only produces poorer washing and rinsing but continuous overloading can shorten the life of the washer by as much as one-half.

Water extraction. Automatic washers remove from 25 to 35 percent of the water during the spin cycle. The greater the amount of water removed, the shorter the drying time. One indication of the amount of water that the spin cycle removes is the number of revolutions per minute. The greater the number of revolutions per minute, the higher the percentage of water removed during the spin cycle. This is especially important when drying clothes in a dryer.

Safety. One should examine the washer carefully in order to judge its electrical and mechanical safety. The machine should carry an Underwriters Laboratory seal which assures the user that the model has been tested and has met specifications set up by Underwriters Laboratories for safety.

Controls which are pushed to stop the action are considered to be safer than those requiring a pulling motion to stop the action. Pushing

When the washer and dryer are not in use, the fold-away counter provides useful work space.

is easier and faster in shutting off power in an emergency. Actually, some part of the body other than the hands could execute a pushing action if it were necessary. Pulling may be impossible in some circumstances.

The tub brake that stops moving parts when the lid or door is opened during the operation is a commendable safety feature. Some manufacturers have the action stop only during the spin. The safest feature is the stopping of any action of the washer when the lid is raised. It is recommended that the spinning action stop in ten seconds.

Other considerations. Before purchasing a washer you should observe the noise accompanying the operation. Noise level is of special importance if the machine is to be located in the kitchen or living areas of the house. Observing a model being demonstrated in a store or in an acquaintance's home can give an indication of the noise produced by the operation of the washer.

Number of rinses varies among makes. Most makes have only one deep rinse. A few front-loading machines have two deep rinses. Spray rinses flush suds and loosened soil from the tub and clothes.

Load-balance indicators are important only in the top-loading type of washers. Top-loading machines may handle an off-balance load in two ways. Some brands have signals in the form of buzzers or bells to let the user know something needs to be done. Some machines stop all action. The operator must redistribute the load and restart the machine. Other washers manage to complete the cycle with an unbalanced load. The tub continues to spin at a reduced speed with correspondingly less water being extracted from the clothes. Some vibration occurs which may cause the washer to "walk."

A lint-filter device is probably one of the most inefficient parts of the automatic washer. It is played up frequently in advertising claims. Tests have shown that most filters will remove strings, threads, and large particles. However, much of the fuzz and small lint is not removed.

Automatic dispensers for bleaches and fabric softeners are found on top-of-the-line models. These washing aids are dispensed automatically in the proper dilution and at the right time during the wash or rinse cycle.

Care and repair. Available repair service should be considered at the time of purchase. There are three arrangements which a dealer may have for the provision of maintenance and repair. The best arrangement for most consumers is for the dealer from whom the washer is purchased to provide repairs, adjustments, and maintenance service through his own repair service department. The dealer is usually more interested in the consumer's satisfaction with the appliance if the dealer also provides maintenance and repair service.

If the dealer contracts for another businessman to maintain and repair the equipment sold by him, the dealer's reputation should be an indication of the quality of service which can be expected from the contracted business establishment.

Often the customer left to his own means for arranging needed service and repair becomes confused and unsure of which local business is most reliable and competent. Sending the appliance back to the company is frequently out of the question for the average consumer.

The price would appear to be an easy thing to determine by simply looking at the price tag. However, you should determine whether the price of the washer includes delivery, installation, and a service-and-parts warranty. You should be aware of what the warranty covers and for what period of time.

Installation. The nonautomatic washer should be connected to an appliance circuit or a 15-ampere circuit which will not be serving other appliances while the washer is in use. The automatic washer should be connected to a 15-ampere individual circuit.

The machines should be grounded by means of a three-pronged power cord. An outlet adapter should not be used to connect the three-pronged plug into an ungrounded circuit. The ground wire may be live and thus be more dangerous than no ground at all. If the entire electrical system of the house is grounded, have a competent electrician install the three-pronged outlet.

Make certain that the automatic washer is connected in such a way that both hot and

A separate laundry room located near the kitchen or a bedroom saves time and steps. Here, a bin for soiled clothes permits presorting; the counter provides a place for folding clean laundry; and the sink is handy when pretreatment is needed for stain-removal.

cold water can be shut off after washing is finished. This relieves pressure on the hose and valves of the washer.

Locate the washer as close as possible to the hot-water source to avoid a loss of heat in a long pipe. If the laundry is located a considerable distance from the water heater, a second water heater may be a solution.

Laundry practices. No one type of washer is superior. Laundry practices regarding loading and type and amount of detergent used have more to do with final results than does the type of washing action.

The suggested maximum length of time for washing clothes is ten minutes. At the end of a ten-minute washing cycle soil tends to become redeposited in the clothes. If the clothes are very soiled, it is preferable to let them soak or have a prewash period rather than a longer wash cycle.

An adequate amount of soap or synthetic detergent will produce a clean, white wash without the addition of bleach every week. In hard-water areas, where the water is not softened, more detergent must be used since some of the detergent is used to soften the water. Synthetic detergents give better results in hard water (unsoftened water) than soap does. When the water has been softened, either soap or a "syndet" may be used.

Either a high-sudsing or a low-sudsing detergent may be used in top-loading machines. However, in some makes where the action is very great a high-sudsing detergent may produce too many suds. The suds almost billow over the top of the machine. The low-sudsing detergent provides a simple solution to the excessive suds problem.

Low-sudsing detergents are recommended for use in front-loading washers because excessive suds interfere with the washing process. These suds may cause the washer to "suds lock." This condition is caused by suds preventing clothes from moving freely about and allowing them to pile up. High suds also cushion the fall and thus interfere with the slapping action of the clothes against the water as they tumble.

If a user plans to add bleach, it should be added only after the brighteners in the detergent have had time to become attached to the clothes. This is usually three to five minutes after washing action has begun. With the automatic dispenser, the bleach is diluted to a recommended washing strength and added at the correct time. U.S. Department of Agriculture researchers found that liquid chlorine bleach, as well as some other sanitizing products, can prevent or reduce the spread of bacterial infections by clothing and household textiles. Follow carefully directions on the label regarding quantity, fabrics for which it is suited, and whether the product should be added to the wash or rinse cycle.

If used, fabric softeners should be added during the deep rinse. Some of the more viscous softeners need to be diluted to prevent spotting of the clothes. To ensure absorbency in terry-cloth articles or diapers, omit the fabric softener after every two or three washes. Fabric softeners cause an ion exchange which actually provides a coating for the fibers. This coating cuts down on the amount of water that the fabric may absorb.

DRYERS

Only a few years ago homemakers had to brave the elements to hang the washing on the line in all kinds of weather or else hang the family wash in the basement. Hanging clothes in the basement to dry produced harsh, wrinkled, and not-so-fragrant clothing.

Today many homemakers look upon the washer and dryer as the best servants in the home. Many hours that were used for doing the laundry before the advent of the automatic washer and dryer may now be spent in other activities.

The advantages of having a dryer are numerous. A dryer is a time-and-work-saving machine. The user of a dryer no longer has to lift pounds and pounds of wet clothes; transport them to the line, often up and down stairs; and spend time handling each item as it is hung on the line. Dryers largely eliminate the need for a clothesline in the yard. In some areas building codes prohibit the placing of clotheslines on the property outside of buildings. The homemaker can do the laundry any day of the week regardless of weather conditions. She can be comfortable while doing the family wash. The feel of the clothes is more

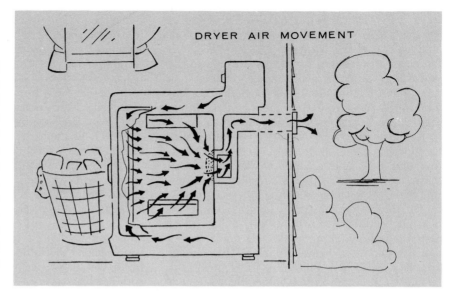

DRYER AIR MOVEMENT

This cut-away view of a clothes dryer shows how moist air is vented to the outside of the house. Air is drawn into the dryer from the room and is heated by a gas or electric source. A rotating drum tumbles the damp laundry so that the warm air can move through and over the fabric to dry it.

pleasant, and ironing becomes a much less difficult task. Towels and other loop-knit fabrics come out of the dryer fluffy and very pleasing to the eye, especially when fabric softener is used and the clothes are not over-dried. A dryer allows the family to have fewer clothes, since the homemaker can wash any time and as often as she wishes.

Gas dryers. The gas dryer has a higher initial cost than an electric dryer, but the operating cost is usually less. The gas dryer uses 18,000 to 20,000 Btu per hour. Depending upon local utility rates, the cost for drying a load of clothes with gas is approximately 3 cents. If a family does twenty-six loads a month, the gas dryer will cost about 78 cents to operate.

A gas dryer may have a continuously burning pilot light, the pilot light may be manually lighted, or an electric ignitor may light the pilot. A continuously burning pilot light will add 15 to 25 cents per month to the cost of operating the gas dryer. The advantage of the pilot light or the electric ignitor is the convenience of only a flick of a switch to start the cycle of the dryer.

Electric dryers. An electric dryer may be connected to a 115- or 230-volt circuit. Those connected to a 115-volt circuit take three or more times as long to dry the clothes as do those connected to a 230-volt supply.

An electric dryer will have a wattage rating of 4,200 to 5,000. It will cost approximately 9 cents a load to dry clothes by electricity, depending upon the utility rates in the area.

Venting. Both gas operated and electrically operated dryers must have some means of disposing of moisture, heat, and lint during the drying process. One common method is through an outside vent. If this method is used, the duct should be as short as possible and have as few turns as is feasible.

Allowing the moisture and heat to be dispelled into the room is a much less desirable method. The interior decoration and comfort level could be affected by the increased moisture and heat in the house. This is especially true if the house is well insulated.

Another method is the routing of moisture and heat through the plumbing system of the house. The steam and lint are routed through a pipe which has a cold-water pipe coiled around it or has access to a spray of cold water. The cold water condenses the steam; then the water and lint are washed down the drain. The condenser dryer is impractical for areas where water is expensive or limited.

Selection features. Most dryers have at least two choices of temperature at which clothes may be dried. A "normal" setting suitable for most fabrics will be available. Most dryers will

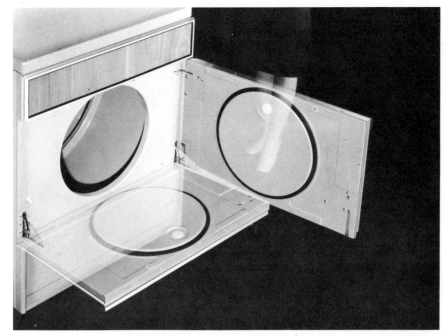

Some dryers feature a two-way door. When pulled down, the door forms a shelf. In this position it prevents wet laundry from accidentally dropping onto the floor. For unloading, the door swings to the side for easy access.

Courtesy Whirlpool

also have a wash-and-wear temperature. Some will have a "no heat" setting for fluffing articles which have been stored or packed away. The "no heat" setting is also good for removing dust from pillows or draperies.

Some manufacturers place an automatic dryness control on their top-of-the-line models. This control senses a predetermined moisture content, depending upon the type of fabrics being dried, and stops the cycle when this point is reached. It has been found that these are more likely to underdry than overdry laundry, especially if the load is made up of a mixture of heavy and light fabrics. In general, dryers require thirty to thirty-five minutes to damp dry a load of laundry and thirty-five to sixty minutes for complete drying.

Some dryers offer stationary heating by disengaging the drum from the motor. The rack placed in the drum allows stuffed toys, nylons, snowsuits, and boots to be dried without tumbling.

Many dryers have a lamp which gives off ozone. Ozone is the source of the fresh smell one is aware of after a rainstorm that is accompanied by lightning. The ozone lamp imparts a fresh, outdoor fragrance to the clothes.

Safety. The drum of the dryer should stop automatically and the source of heat cease to operate when the door is opened in midcycle. It is much safer if the revolving and heating will not reactivate with the closing of the dryer door. The operator should have to start the action by manipulating the control. This would prevent tumbling action and heating if a child were to climb into the dryer and the door were to close after the dryer was stopped before the cycle was completed. The dryer should have an automatic heat cutoff in case there is a mechanical failure and the drum stops revolving.

Location. The dryer should be located as near the washer as possible to save steps for the user. They may be located side-by-side or on adjacent walls.

The door of the dryer should open away from the washer if it is hinged at the side. This eliminates transporting the wet clothes around the door. Some dryers have a hamper door which is hinged at the bottom. These may have settings which allow the door to be used as a chute to direct the laundry into the dryer, thus eliminating any dropping of laundry onto the floor.

443

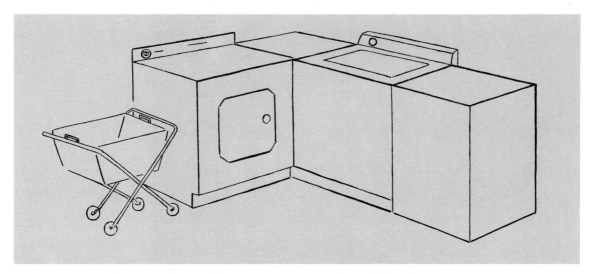

The normal work-flow sequence for a right-handed person is from right to left. Thus the dryer is located to the left of the washer whether they are side by side or on adjacent walls. In such an arrangement, the door of the dryer should be hinged to the left.

When a front-loading washer is used, the washer and dryer should be arranged so that both doors swing outward for efficient transfer of clothes. (Or both washer and dryer doors may be hinged at the bottom.)

Use. Fabrics have a natural moisture content ranging from 0.5 to 15 percent water by weight. Laundry should not be allowed to become "bone" dry. This is extremely hard on the fabric. Wrinkles will be much harder to remove in fabrics which are overdried.

Most dryers allow the drum to continue to revolve for five to ten minutes after the heat is automatically shut off. This allows the clothing to cool and reduces wrinkling. For best results, articles of clothing should be removed immediately after the cycle is completed. This will help reduce the formation of wrinkles.

The accumulated lint in the filter should be removed frequently. Some authorities suggest that the filter be cleaned after every third load. A special check should be made after drying an especially lint-laden load or even during the drying cycle in special cases. If the lint filter is allowed to become too full, drying

An arrangement in which the door of the dryer swings away from the washer makes for efficient transfer of wet clothes from washer to dryer.

A combination washer-dryer requires no attention from the user between the automatic washing and the automatic drying. The combination model is a great space-saver.

time will be prolonged. There is some likelihood too that a short in the wiring may occur because of overheating. When this occurs, the dryer will not operate until repaired.

There are a few items that should not be dried in a dryer. In general, foam rubber items and any article which contains even a trace of flammable cleaning agent should not be exposed to extreme heat or an open source of heat. For example, cloths used in polishing silver or other metals should not be dried in the dryer unless the cloths have been thoroughly washed so that all trace of the cleaning agent is removed.

Care. Occasionally a vacuum cleaner or a long, narrow brush should be used to remove lint from the inner crevices of the dryer, particularly in the corners and crevices around the lint trap. Be sure to first disconnect the dryer from the source of the electricity.

The only other care is the use of a damp cloth to wipe the drum occasionally. Using appliance wax on the exterior of the dryer helps keep it shiny and new looking.

COMBINATION WASHER-DRYER

The combination washer-dryer adds automatic drying to automatic washing with no attention from the user between the two processes.

Only a front-loading, tumble-type washer may be combined with a dryer to produce a combination machine. The tumbling action that is necessary for the dryer is already employed by front-loading washers.

There are some disadvantages to this machine. The machine can do only one load from start to finish at any one time. With a separate washer and dryer, one load can be drying while a second load is washing. If either the washer or dryer is not functioning properly and must be serviced, usually the other one does not operate properly. Neither is available for the homemaker's use if the machine must be removed from the home for repair. Frequently the capacity is limited to 4 to 6 pounds of soiled clothing as compared with 8 to 10 pounds which a separate washer can handle. In spite of the smaller capacity, a combination washer-dryer usually requires more floor space than either a washer or a dryer. However, if space for both a washer and a dryer is not available, the combination washer-dryer may be the solution.

IRONS

Advances in the field of textiles have modified greatly today's fabric-care practices. Less ironing is required today because of "durable press," "drip-dry," and "minimum-care" fabrics. Irons still have their place, however, among household equipment for the American home.

Irons are available as dry irons, combination steam-and-dry irons, and travel irons. Travel and steam irons have certain unique features which will be discussed later. But first, let us consider some of the features which all irons have in common.

Dry Irons

A hand iron which uses dry heat only and has no water reservoir for producing steam is referred to as a "dry iron."

Operating principle. Electric irons are usually thermostatically controlled so that the user

This iron has an interchangeable cord for right- or left-hand ironing. The instruction book explains how to switch the cord. The push button on the top of the handle sprays a fine mist where more dampness is needed. The fabric-guide heat selector is located on the handle at the front.

has only to set the temperature dial at the desired location and the temperature will be automatically maintained. In nonautomatic irons the user must control the temperature herself by unplugging and replugging the iron. Should a nonautomatic iron be accidentally left plugged in for an extended period of time, the iron would reach such a high temperature that the element would burn out and a fire might result. Of course any iron should be unplugged as well as turned off when not in use.

The soleplate (usually made of aluminum, stainless steel, or chromium-plated cast iron or steel) is heated by the electric element which is located either in, or just above, the soleplate. Irons with thermostatic controls have a wattage rating of 1,000 to 1,150 watts and may be used on a 115- to 120-volt circuit. They should be plugged into a wall or small appliance outlet, not into a drop cord. An extension cord may be used where it is a part of a special iron-cord attachment (see page 449). The wire should be of heavy-duty weight, and of course it should show that it has been UL approved.

Selection factors. The soleplate should be smooth so that threads will not be pulled during ironing. The iron will be easier to use if the edges of the soleplate are tapered, the point narrow, and if it has slots in the sides of the point for ironing around buttons. Many manufacturers are coating the soleplate with a nonstick finish to make it glide more smoothly. This feature is of particular importance when ironing starched fabric.

The weight of the iron is somewhat a matter of personal preference, but a lightweight iron—that is, one weighing 3½ pounds or less—is not so tiresome to use as a heavier iron. However, balance may be even more important than weight.

How comfortable the iron is to use will depend largely upon the design of the handle. Since size and shape of the handle vary from iron to iron, just as do the sizes of peoples' hands, it is desirable to try the iron in the store to determine how comfortable it is for you. A thumb rest is a useful feature only if it is located for the maximum convenience of the user. The handle should be of heat-resistant material. If the top of the iron is well insulated, if there is a heat-resistant shield, and if there is ample space between the handle and the top of the iron, there will be less chance of burned knuckles.

Most irons are designed with a heel rest. The stability of the iron when it is in the resting position is an important feature to check. If unstable, the iron may fall if the board is even slightly bumped. This may cause injury to the user as well as to the iron. If the heel rest is metal, it may be necessary to protect the ironing-board cover to prevent scorching.

The cord is usually permanently attached to the iron. Most irons with the cord to the side allow one to change the cord from the right to the left or the left to the right with little trouble. You may have the dealer do this before taking the iron home. If you iron only with the right hand, then having the cord come from the right side at the rear of the iron is desirable. If you are left-handed you will find it more convenient to have the cord attached at the left and rear of the iron. But a cord which is attached at the center rear of the iron permits you to iron with either hand, which is a recommended practice for reducing waste motions when ironing.

A worn cord can be replaced by anyone trained in minor wiring repairs. A wire attachment which clips to the end or side of the ironing board will protect the cord from wear as a result of rubbing against the board. A coil at the base of the holder provides for flexible movement of the holder and cord as the iron is moved from one end of the board to the other.

Temperature controls (sometimes referred to as "fabric guides") may be located at the base of the handle at the rear of the iron, below the handle on the top of the iron, or on the handle at the front. The most desirable location is on the front of the handle because in this location the temperature dial cannot be accidentally moved, it is convenient to see and operate, and it will not become uncomfortably hot to touch.

Since many of the man-made fibers are very heat-sensitive, it is important that the iron have a wide range of temperatures, including a very low setting for man-made fibers.

Some irons have a built-in light for the purpose of reducing eyestrain while ironing.

Use and care. To protect the wires in the end of the cord against damage, always disconnect the iron by gripping the plug, never by jerking the cord. If the iron has a detachable cord, it should be connected to the iron before being plugged into the convenience outlet, and disconnected in reverse order.

To protect fabric against snagging, the soleplate must be kept smooth by avoiding any practice which will scratch the metal, such as ironing over metal fasteners. If starch builds up on the soleplate, it may be removed without damage to the soleplate by wiping off while still slightly warm with one of the following: (1) soapy water, (2) baking soda on a damp cloth, or (3) a soap-impregnated steel-wool pad. Notice that you should always start with the most gentle cleaning agent and work up the scale in terms of degrees of harshness. Ironing several times over wax paper will help restore the smooth finish. With the nonstick finishes now so widely used, starch buildup is largely eliminated.

After the iron is cool, it should be stored upright on the heel rest with the cord wrapped loosely around the handle.

Combination Steam-and-dry Irons

Some combination models also have a spray feature, which is an opening at the front end of the handle operated by a button on top of the handle. The spray feature is more useful for dampening very lightweight fabric and for redampening areas that have dried out during the ironing process than as a substitute for regular sprinkling, especially of heavy fabric. The spray mist should hit the fabric while the iron is kept flat in ironing position; the iron should not need to be tipped or lifted.

Types. The unique aspect of a steam iron, which sets it apart from a dry iron, is the water reservoir it contains. The water is heated by the heating element in the soleplate. There are two types of steam irons. In the boiler or kettle type, all of the water in the reservoir is heated. When the water reaches a high enough temperature, steam forms. When pressure builds up, it forces the steam to escape through the openings in the soleplate. There are very few brands which use this means of providing steam.

More frequently manufacturers use the flash-boiler or drip-type iron which heats only a small amount of water at a time to the vapor point, although all of the water in the reservoir heats. Steam is available for pressing sooner with the drip type than in the kettle type, since one need not wait until all the water is heated to vaporization.

Selection factors. Models vary as to the number and distribution of steam vents in the soleplate. Look for a pattern of steam vents which can produce ample, well-distributed steam. The higher the steam production the more frequently the iron will need to be refilled. Ease of filling and emptying are important factors but hard to evaluate accurately by any method other than actual use. Some combination irons have a water-level gauge which takes the guesswork out of determining how much water is in the reservoir.

Use and care. The iron should be unplugged while it is being filled with water. Distilled water or demineralized water will prolong the service life of the iron. Distilled water is available from filling stations, drugstores, and supermarkets. There are inexpensive devices for demineralizing tap water. However, they lose their demineralizing effect after a time and must be replaced. To check how effectively they have done the job, boil some of the demineralized water and see if any residue is left in the pan.

Some manufacturers claim that their irons can be used with plain tap water. Although the irons will work for a while, mineral deposits may eventually plug the steam vents and corrode the water reservoir. Mineral deposits build up rapidly at high temperature. Thus only distilled or demineralized water is recommended for steam irons. Water softened by home tank-type softeners, which use the transfer of sodium ions for calcium ions, should not be used in steam irons. This water still contains minerals.

If you will do the steam pressing before the dry ironing, any water left in the reservoir will be evaporated during dry ironing. Water should not be allowed to stand in the iron. To empty the iron, take it to the sink and turn it with the point down so that the water can flow from the opening in the handle.

At the first indication of slightly clogged steam vents, use equal parts of distilled vinegar and water, fill the water chamber, set the fabric selector on rayon for half an hour, let cool, empty, and rinse with clear water. A commercial steam-iron cleaner may also be used to clean the steam vents. At least one make of iron is so designed that it can be taken apart for cleaning.

For steam pressing, the temperature control must be set at moderate temperature, within the recommended temperature range. If the temperature is too hot, the water is forced out before it has time to become steam. Therefore droplets of water will be blown out through the steam vents. If the temperature is too low, there will not be enough heat to make the water form steam. Again droplets of water are allowed to escape. An overfull iron can also contribute to spurting water. The usual reservoir holds from one-half to three-fourths cup of water.

Travel Irons

As with other electrical appliances, travel irons should be UL-approved. Travel irons may be of the dry or combination steam-dry type. In most combination models, steam comes from a bulb-shaped pliable plastic reservoir which is attached to the outside of the iron for steam pressing and removed for dry pressing. Some models also have the spray feature.

Travel irons do not all have as dependable thermostats as standard irons do and may require the user to control the temperature by turning the iron on and off. When becoming accustomed to a new iron, test the temperature frequently to determine whether the thermostat is exceeding its setting.

Special features. If you plan to use a travel iron outside the continental United States, you will want an iron which is designed to operate on direct current (dc) as well as on alternating current (ac). The manufacturer's literature will indicate whether the iron has this conversion feature. Some irons are designed to work on either a 115-volt or 230-volt circuit. For other irons, a transformer must be used to lower the voltage from 230 to 115 volts. Other-

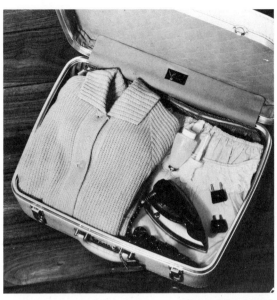

The travel iron pictured has both a steam and a spray attachment. Adapter plugs with different prongs are also shown.

This ironing board adjusts to a comfortable height for sitting or standing to iron. A knob on the front foot makes wobble-free adjustment possible. Wheels make the board easier to move. The size and shape of the ironing surface is also adjustable. A built-in cord holder prevents wear on the cord and wrinkling of clothes during ironing.

wise the iron may overheat. This may damage the iron or cause the fabric to become scorched. An adapter may be needed in order to use rectangular plug prongs in outlets designed for round prongs.

Travel irons have a foldaway handle for compactness. It is important that there be a handle lock to prevent burned fingers during use of the iron. Where regular-size irons typically have a permanently attached cord, travel irons typically have a detachable cord.

IRONING BOARDS AND TABLES

Although a built-in ironing board has the advantage of being easy to get out and put away, it may lack the flexibility of adjustable height. This is important when people of different heights are going to be ironing or when the user wishes to iron sitting down.

Since good light contributes to reduction of fatigue, it is important to consider provision for good lighting, especially when deciding upon the location of a built-in ironing board. Whether it is natural light or artificial light, there should be no glare and no shadow. It is desirable to make provision for a 115-volt small

appliance circuit within the area generally used for ironing.

An ironing board is a purchase which will very likely be made the least often of any household purchase. Some homemakers use the same ironing board for their whole lifetime.

Portable or folding types. Stability and adjustability are two very important factors to weigh when shopping for a folding ironing board. Both factors can be easily evaluated in the store if the board is set up. Or better yet, ask to be permitted to open it up yourself and then fold it up for storing. This provides an opportunity for you to judge how easy the board is to unfold and to put away. And while it is set up, you can easily determine whether it is stable or wobbly.

Adjustable ironing boards offer maximum flexibility in use. Whether you are ironing from a sitting or standing position, the amount of fatigue you feel after an extended period of time will depend largely upon the extent to which good body mechanics have been maintained. If the board is too low, you will have to stoop, which puts strain on back and shoulder muscles. If the board is too high, you will have to raise the shoulders. Both practices cause unnecessary muscle strain. Before buying, check to see if the mechanism for adjusting the height is easy to operate and if the board is held secure and stable at all heights.

Sitting to iron does not in and of itself reduce fatigue. You must be able to sit comfortably, feet flat on the floor, shoulders level. Sitting to iron may be more fatiguing than standing to iron if good body mechanics are not maintained or if you must get up frequently, as can happen when ironing while supervising a child's play.

In order to maintain good body mechanics while sitting to iron, you should choose an ironing table with legs which do not get in the way of your knees and feet. This point too can be determined by trying out the ironing board in the store.

The type of floor covering the ironing board will ordinarily stand on will influence your choice as to leg design. Boards supported by two legs with T-bar feet tend to rock on carpeted floors. An ironing board with 4 feet or an arched T-bar foot design will be stable and will stand securely on carpeted floor. Boards with foot levers for toe-touch adjustment are especially desirable in homes where the floor is uneven.

Some boards are built with tops of open mesh, which allows steam to pass through. It should be cooler to iron on these boards than on boards with a solid surface, provided the cover does not have a metal finish which reflects heat upward.

If you plan to iron sheets and large tablecloths, it will be especially desirable to select an ironing board with the "wing" feature. By adjusting a lever, a triangular-shaped piece lifts up and locks to form a straight line for the full width of the board. In other words, the tapered end of the board becomes square. Some models are easier to operate than others, so this feature, too, should be tried out when shopping.

Pads and covers. For good ironing results and for ease in use, the ironing board should be well padded. All-in-one pad and cover sets are available. The cover may be treated for scorch and stain resistance. Some have a coating which provides traction and holds the item to be ironed in place.

LEARNING EXPERIENCES

1. Define these terms as used in this chapter; agitator (washer); perforated; soleplate; T-bar (on ironing board).

2. Assuming that a homemaker has decided to buy laundry equipment, what questions should she ask herself before making a final choice? Include information on features and costs of bottom-of-line, medium, and top-of-line models. Compare notes in class discussion to arrive at a composite list.

3. Tom and Sally have recently married and moved into a three-room apartment. They are both employed and would have the money to buy a washer and dryer if they chose bottom-of-the-line models. Before making the purchase, what factors should they consider? Give reasons why, in view of these factors, they probably should or should not buy this equipment now.

4. The Masons live in a six-room home. Their children are six months, two years, and four years of age. Mr. Mason is the only wage earner. A good coin-operated laundry is four blocks away. Mr. Mason drives the car to work five days a week. In view of these factors, give reasons why the Masons should or should not buy a washer and dryer at this time. Indicate Mr. Mason's take-home pay and make other assumptions which could influence the decision.

5. Find out the cost of using an installment-payment plan for the purchase of a washer

and dryer. Use local prices and credit terms. Find total dollar cost and true interest rate for both twenty-four-month and thirty-six-month payment periods. Discuss the wisdom of the use of credit on these terms. What alternatives to installment buying are available to most people.

6. The Jarmons have floor space adequate to accommodate only a washer or a dryer but not both. What are several alternatives? Consider the limitations and advantages to each alternative. In view of these considerations, what are your recommendations for the Jarmons?

7. If a homemaker were required to do her housework from a wheel chair, would she more likely select a separate washer and dryer or a combination washer-dryer? Explain your reasoning.

8. Some manufacturers offer a choice of irons with or without the nonstick finish. When would a steam-dry iron with nonstick finish be most desirable? When would the iron give equally good ironing results without the special finish on the soleplate?

9. What are some of the reasons why some people do not sit to iron, even though they own an adjustable ironing board? What circumstances might prompt them to change their habits and start sitting to iron? What additional equipment would contribute to efficiency when sitting to iron?

10. Look for an example of a situation in which the hot water supply in a single-family dwelling is inadequate. See if you can determine which of the following are the causes: (a) Too small tank for family size and water-use habits; (b) the water heater's heating efficiency (i.e. too slow recovery rate); (c) number of appliances which use hot water.

Bibliography

Part I: Housing

Aul, Henry B., *How to Beautify and Improve Your Home Grounds,* Hart Publishing Company, New York, 1967.

Beasley, M. Robert, *Fell's Guide to Buying, Building, and Financing Your Home,* Frederick Fell, Inc., New York, 1963.

Beyer, Glenn H., *Housing and Society,* The Macmillan Company, New York, 1965.

Brett, William S. and Kay Grant, *Small City Gardens,* Abelard-Schuman, Limited, New York, 1967.

Conrads, Ulrich and Hans G. Sperlich, *The Architecture of Fantasy,* Frederick A. Praeger, Inc., New York, 1963.

Consumers All, 1965 Yearbook of Agriculture, Government Printing Office, Washington, D.C.

Craig, Hazel Thompson and Ola Day Rush, *Homes with Character,* D. C. Heath and Company, Boston, 1966.

Day, Richard, *Remodeling Rooms,* Arco Publishing Company, Inc., New York, 1968.

De Benedictis, Daniel J., *Laws Every Homeowner and Tenant Should Know,* Simon and Schuster, New York, 1968.

Doxiadis, C. A., *Urban Renewal and the Future of the American City,* Public Administration Service, Chicago, 1966.

Ewald, William R. Jr., *Environment for Man: The Next Fifty Years,* Indiana University Press, Bloomington, 1967.

Harmon, A. J., *The Guide to Home Remodeling,* Holt, Rinehart and Winston, Inc., New York, 1967.

Hoover, Norman K., *Approved Practices in Beautifying the Home Grounds,* The Interstate Printers & Publishers, Inc., Danville, Ill., 1966.

Kneeland, Paul, *How to Find the Apartment You Really Need,* Simon and Schuster, New York, 1968.

Murray, R., *How to Buy the Right House at the Right Price,* The Macmillan Company, New York, 1968.

New Horizons in Construction Materials, Hudson Publishing Co., Los Altos, California, 1962.

Nulsen, Robert H., *All About Parks for Mobile Homes and Trailers,* Trail-R-Club of America, Beverly Hills, Calif., 1960.

Nulsen, Robert H., *Mobile Home Manual,* Vol. I, Vol. II, Trail-R-Club of America, Beverly Hills, Calif., 1961.

A Place to Live, 1963 Yearbook of Agriculture, Government Printing Office, Washington, D.C.

Rodale, Jerome and staff, *How to Landscape Your Own Home,* Rodale Books, Inc., Emmaus, Pa., 1963.

Rogers, Tyler Stewart, *The Complete Guide to House Hunting,* Charles Scribner's Sons, New York, 1963.

Rose, Jerome G., *The Legal Adviser on Home Ownership,* Little, Brown and Company, Boston, 1967.

Salm, Walter G., *Remodeling Your Kitchen or Bathroom,* Arco Publishing Company, Inc., New York, 1968.

Saylor, Henry H., *Dictionary of Architecture,* John Wiley & Sons, Inc., New York, 1963.

Schwartz, Robert and Hubbard H. Cobb, *The Complete Homeowner,* The Macmillan Company, New York, 1965.

Scott, John S., *A Dictionary of Building,* Penguin Books, Inc., Baltimore, 1964.

Seymour, Robert G., Editor, *Decisions Before the House,* Guideways, Inc., Champaign, Ill., 1961.

Sunset Magazine, *Children's Rooms and Play Yards,* Lane Magazine and Book Co., Menlo Park, Calif., 1960.

Warmington, Carl, *The Family Guide to Suc-*

cessful Moving, Association Press, New York, 1968.

Watkins, Arthur M., *Complete Book of Home Remodeling, Improvement, and Repair*, Doubleday & Company, Garden City, N. Y., 1963.

Watkins, Arthur M., *How to Avoid the Ten Biggest Home-Buying Traps*, Meredith Press, New York, 1967.

Weaver, Robert C., *The Urban Complex: Human Values in Urban Life*, Doubleday & Company, Garden City, N.Y., 1964.

Part II: Furniture and Furnishings

Aronson, Joseph, *The New Encyclopedia of Furniture*, Crown Publishers, Inc., New York, 1967.

Ball, Victoria Kloss, *The Art of Interior Design*, The Macmillan Company, New York, 1960.

Boger, Louise Ade, *Furniture Past and Present*, Doubleday & Company, Inc., Garden City, N.Y., 1966.

Craig, Hazel Thompson and Ola Day Rush, *Homes with Character*, D. C. Heath and Company, Boston, 1966.

Davidson, Marshall B. and American Heritage Editors, *American Heritage of Colonial Antiques*, American Heritage, New York, 1967.

deVan, Dorothy S. and D. Stepat, *Introduction to Home Furnishings*, The Macmillan Company, New York, 1964.

Draper, Dorothy, *365 Shortcuts to Home Decorating*, Dodd Mead & Company, Inc., New York, 1968.

Francis, JoAnn and Editors of Maco Magazine Corporation, *World of Budget Decorating*, Simon and Schuster, New York, 1967.

Goldstein, Harriet I. and Veta, *Art in Everyday Life*, The Macmillan Company, New York, 1954.

Greer, Michael, *Your Future in Interior Design*, Richards Rosen Press, Inc., New York, 1963.

Hayward, Helena, *World Furniture: A Pictorial History*, McGraw-Hill Book Company, New York, 1965.

Hicks, David, *David Hicks on Decoration*, The Macmillan Company, New York, 1967.

Lewis, Dora S., Jean O. Burns, and Esther F. Segner, *Housing and Home Management*, The Macmillan Company, New York, 1961.

Obst, Frances M., *Art and Design for Home Living*, The Macmillan Company, New York, 1963.

Pahlman, William, *Pahlman Book of Interior Design*, The Viking Press, Inc., New York, 1968.

Pegler, Martin, *The Dictionary of Interior Design*, Crown Publishers, Inc., New York, 1966.

Pepis, Betty, *Interior Decoration A to Z*, Doubleday & Company, Inc., Garden City, N. Y., 1966.

Reist, Janet, *Elegant Decorating on a Limited Budget*, The Macmillan Company, New York, 1965.

Rogers, Kate E., *The Modern House U.S.A.*, Harper & Row, Publishers, Incorporated, New York, 1962.

Trilling, Mabel B. and Florence W. Nicholas, *Design Your Home for Living*, J. B. Lippincott Company, Philadelphia, 1953.

Van Dommelen, David B., *Walls: Enrichment and Ornamentation*, Funk & Wagnalls Company, New York, 1965.

Varney, Carleton, *You and Your Apartment*, The Bobbs-Merrill Company, Inc., Indianapolis, 1968.

Whiton, Sherrill, *Elements of Interior Design and Decoration*, J. B. Lippincott Company, Philadelphia, 1963.

Wingate, I. B., K. R. Gillespie, and B. G. Addison, *Know Your Merchandise*, Gregg Division, McGraw-Hill Book Company, New York, 1964.

Zahle, Erik, *A Treasury of Scandinavian Design*, Golden Press, New York, 1961.

Part III: Household Equipment

Books

Fargis, Paul, Editor, *The Consumer's Handbook*, Hawthorn Books, Inc., New York, 1967.

Fitzsimmons, Cleo, *Consumer Buying*, John Wiley & Sons, Inc., New York, 1961.

Fitzsimmons, Cleo, and Nell White, *Management for You*, J. B. Lippincott Company, Philadelphia, 1964.

Fleck, Henrietta, Louise Fernandez, and Elizabeth Munves, *Living with Your Family*, Prentice-Hall, Inc., Englewood Cliffs, N.J., 1965. Chapter 25.

Garrett, Pauline G. and Edward J. Metzen, *You Are a Consumer of Clothing*, Ginn and Company, Boston, 1967.

Gordon, Leland J. and Stewart M. Lee, *Economics for Consumers*, American Book Company, New York, 1967.

Logan, William B. and Helen M. Moon, *Facts About Merchandise*, Prentice-Hall, Inc., Englewood Cliffs, N.J., 1967. Chapters 23 and 27.

Peet, Louise, *Young Homemakers' Equipment Guide*, The Iowa State University Press, Ames, 1967.

Shank, Dorothy E., Natalie K. Fitch, Pauline A. Chapman, and Mary Suzanne Sickler, *Guide to Modern Meals*, McGraw-Hill Book Company, New York, 1970.

Starr, Mary Catharine, *Management for Better Living*, D. C. Heath and Company, Boston, 1963. Chapters 6, 7, 8, and 9.

Wilhelms, Fred T., Raymond P. Heimerl, and Herbert M. Jelley, *Consumer Economics*, McGraw-Hill Book Company, New York, 1966.

Booklets, Magazines, Pamphlets

Better Washdays, Ruth Legg Galbraith, Circular 836, University of Illinois Agricultural Experiment Station and Extension Service in Agriculture and Home Economics, Urbana, Ill. 1965.

Changing Times, Washington, D. C., current and past issues.

Consumer Bulletin, Consumers' Research Inc., Washington, N.J., current and past issues.

Consumer Reports, Consumers' Union of the U.S., Inc., Mount Vernon, N.Y., current and past issues.

Consumers Beware, AFL-CIO Pamphlet Division, Washington, D.C., 1968.

The Maytag Encyclopedia of Home Laundry, Popular Library, Inc., New York, 1965.

Planning Ahead for the Buying of Major Equipment, Jean L. Pennock, Agriculture Research Service, U.S. Department of Agriculture, Washington, D.C.

Removing Stains from Fabrics, Home Methods, Home and Garden Bulletin 62, U.S. Department of Agriculture, Washington, D.C., 1959.

Room Air Conditioners, National Better Business Bureau, New York, 1963.

Sanitation in Home Laundering, Home and Garden Bulletin 97, U.S. Department of Agriculture, Washington, D.C., 1967.

Soaps and Detergents for Home Laundering, Home and Garden Bulletin 139, U.S. Department of Agriculture, Washington, D.C.

Tips and Topics in Home Economics, Vol. IX, No. 2, No. 3, 1969, School of Home Economics, Texas Technological College, Lubbock, Texas.

Your Equipment Dollar, Leone Ann Heuer, Money Management Series, Household Finance Corporation, Chicago.

Your Shopping Dollar, Leone Ann Heuer, Money Management Series, Household Finance Corporation, Chicago.

Index

A

F

G

W